p. 11 call in question
neat dichotomies

D1570598

Converting Women

Converting Women

Gender and Protestant Christianity in Colonial South India

ELIZA F. KENT

OXFORD
UNIVERSITY PRESS
2004

OXFORD
UNIVERSITY PRESS

Oxford   New York
Auckland   Bangkok   Buenos Aires   Cape Town   Chennai
Dar es Salaam   Delhi   Hong Kong   Istanbul   Karachi   Kolkata
Kuala Lumpur   Madrid   Melbourne   Mexico City   Mumbai   Nairobi
São Paulo   Shanghai   Taipei   Tokyo   Toronto

Copyright © 2004 by Oxford University Press, Inc.

Published by Oxford University Press, Inc.
198 Madison Avenue, New York, New York 10016

www.oup.com

Oxford is a registered trademark of Oxford University Press

All rights reserved. No part of this publication may be reproduced,
stored in a retrieval system, or transmitted, in any form or by any means,
electronic, mechanical, photocopying, recording, or otherwise,
without the prior permission of Oxford University Press.

Library of Congress Cataloging-in-Publication Data
Kent, Eliza F., 1966–
Converting women: gender and Protestant Christianity in colonial South India / Eliza F. Kent.
p. cm.
Includes bibliographical references and index.
ISBN 0-19-516507-1
1. Christian converts from Hinduism—India, South—History.   2. Women,
Tamil—Religious life—India, South—History.   3. Protestant converts—India, South—History.
4. Protestant women—India, South—History.   I. Title.
BV3280.T3K46 2004
305.48'6204'09548—dc21   2003049854

9 8 7 6 5 4 3 2 1

Printed in the United States of America
on acid-free paper

Dedicated to the memory of
Norman Cutler (1949–2002)
and
Alice Cooke Kent (1910–1992)

Acknowledgments

I would like first of all to offer heartfelt thanks to my friends, colleagues, research assistants, and gracious hosts in Tamil Nadu who facilitated the research for this project at every step of the way, illuminating for me the meanings of south Indian Christianity and Hinduism through their thoughts as well as through the example of their lives. They are too numerous to mention, but for their extraordinary and timely assistance, I want to express my gratitude especially to Dr. S. Bharati and Krishnaswami of the American Institute for Indian Studies in Madurai, S. Anandaraman and A. Padma of Madurai, Rev. David of Christ Church in Madurai, J. Arun Selva in Madurai, Rodney and Crystal Easdon of Chennai, Vincent Kumaradoss of Madras Christian College, Dr. S. Manickam of Madurai Kamaraj University, Dr. P. R. Subramaniam of the Mozhi Institute, Dr. Gnana Robinson, Dr. George Oommen, and Dr. Sathianathan Clarke of the United Theological College, Lieut. Col. Nandan Nilakantha of the Theosophical Society, P. Raji of Chennai, A. Sivasubramaniyam of Tuticorin, K. Uma Devi of Tirunelveli, D. Kavitha Ranjini of Madurai, and V. Visalakshmi of Madurai. I owe a special debt of gratitude to the Devadawson family in Madurai for warmly welcoming me into their home and for introducing me to Christians all over south India.

Many institutions opened their doors to me during my thirteen months in Tamil Nadu. They impressed me enormously by their willingness and ability to share a wealth of material. The study of Indian Christianity is presently undergoing a profound sea change, in large part due to the dedication and organization of these institutions: Tamil Nadu Theological Seminary in Madurai, United Theological College in Bangalore, Folklore Resources and Research Center at St. Xavier College in Palayamkottai, and the Bishop Neill Archives at St. John's College in Palayamkottai. I also want to thank the staff of the Tamil Nadu State Archives for their invaluable assistance during the period of my research in Chennai.

Generous financial support from the American Institute for Indian Studies and the Fulbright Foundation enabled me to travel to India and England to conduct the research for this book. Grants from the Woodrow Wilson Foundation, the Gender Studies Program of the University of Chicago, and the Committee on South Asian Studies made it possible for me to devote my energy to writing for valuable stretches of time.

Conversations with many people have shaped this book over the years. I owe thanks to those who patiently helped me to untangle the knotted skein of forces at work in religious conversion and the social organization of gender in colonial India: Carol Breckenridge, Dipesh Chakravarty, Virginia Chang, Matthew Condon, Sarah Gualtieri, Anne Hardgrove, Eugene Irschick, Laura Jenkins, Helen Koh, Caitrin Lynch, Theresa Mah, Maria Elena Martinez, Paula Richman, Katherine Ulrich, Kumkum Sangari, Zooey Sherinian, and Hugh Urban. Corinne Dempsey, Selva Raj, and others associated with the Hindu-Christian Studies Society deserve special thanks for their hard work opening up south Indian Christianity, both organizationally and intellectually, as a field of study for anthropology and the history of religions. I am very grateful to the editors at Oxford University Press, especially Cynthia Read and Rebecca Johns-Danes for their patience, hard work, and editorial savvy. Comments from several anonymous readers were also instrumental in improving this book at a crucial stage. Frank Reynolds's incisive criticisms and Norman Cutler's keen appreciation for Tamil culture helped steer this project through its earliest stages. Norman's recent death, which came so suddenly in the autumn of 2002, leaves a great void in the lives of the many people who loved and respected him. This book is dedicated to his memory.

I have been fortunate to benefit from Wendy Doniger's enormous generosity as a mentor and her boundless, irrepressible curiosity about the complex motivations that animate human life and find their way into texts, in sometimes strange and wonderfully distorted ways. Her influence on this project and on my training as a historian of religion has been immense, but I am also grateful for her patience and unwavering support when I willfully strode off in my own directions, in spite of her best efforts to advise me against it. That combination of straight forward direction and capacity to let go continues to inspire me in my own work as a teacher.

From the beginning, my mother and father have supported my adventures in India and academia with their enthusiasm and love. My childhood home was filled with treasures they brought back from their own travels in Asia from before I was born. The hours I spent as a child gazing at these objects and listening to their stories planted the seeds of my interest in Indic religion and culture; their interest in the stories and objects I brought back from India has sustained it. My beloved grandmother, Alice Cooke Kent, granddaughter of missionaries, one-time theosophist, confirmed Episcopalian, and passionate, broad-minded scholar of religion in her own right, has been another influence in my life, the extent of which is impossible to measure. This book is dedicated also to her memory.

Finally, these acknowledgments would not be complete without mention of the immeasurable joy that Mari Shopsis has brought to my life. Living with a writer entails living with someone who gazes into the distance at unpredictable moments and responds to perfectly ordinary questions with odd non sequiturs. I am deeply grateful for her love, playfulness, curiosity about the world, and tolerance for my periodic departures, to India and to regions of space within my own mind.

Contents

Abbreviations

ABCFM	American Board of Commissioners for Foreign Missions
AMM	American Madurai Mission
CEZMS	Church of England Zenana Missionary Society
CMS	Church Missionary Society
LMS	London Missionary Society
LPNIW	Lucy Perry Noble Institute for Women
MCC	Madurai Church Council
SPCK	Society for Promoting Christian Knowledge
SPFEE	Society for the Promotion of Female Education in the East
SPG	Society for the Propagation of the Gospel
TELC	Tamil Evangelical Lutheran Church
TNSA	Tamil Nadu State Archives
UTC	United Theological College
WBM	Women's Board of Missions
WBFM	Women's Board of Foreign Missions
WMMS	Wesleyan Methodist Missionary Society

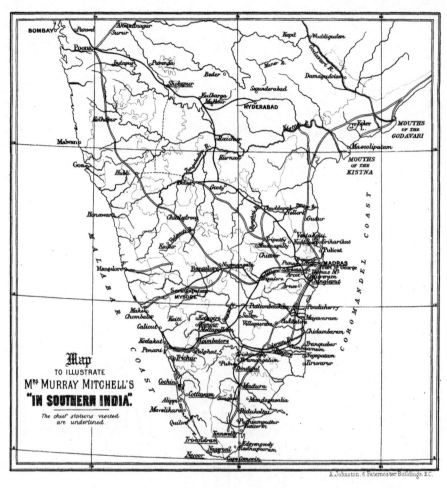

Map of South India in the late nineteenth century, from Mrs. Murray Mitchell,
In Southern India (London Religious Tract Society, 1888).

PART I

Caste, Christianity, and Conversion

Introduction
Gender and Conversion in Colonial India

Colonial rule brought about enormous changes in Indian society. British intervention into all matters of governance, from the collection of revenue to the maintenance of law and order, made it difficult for traditionally dominant groups to police the boundaries of the social order as they once had. The development of print media, increased communication by railroad and trunk roads, and the incorporation of India into new global networks of trade created the conditions for novel ways of imagining communities and selves. In the gaps and fissures thus created in Indian society, many aspiring communities sought to reinvent themselves, constructing new or radically modified identities more suited for social mobility under the conditions of the British Raj. At the southern tip of the Madras Presidency, Indian converts to Christianity were foremost among the groups who made dramatic and far-reaching changes in the signs and practices that constituted their lifeworlds. Drawn for the most part from the lower echelons of the Indian social hierarchy—landless agricultural laborers and artisans who were generally members of ritually polluting castes—Christian converts deployed a wide variety of strategies to improve their social and economic condition.[1] They won many new advantages through their association with foreign missionaries, including right of access to public roads, exemption from extracted unpaid labor (*ūḻiyam*), a regular day off from work to observe the Christian Sabbath, the advocacy of missionaries in disputes with rivals both inside and outside the courts, and access to Western-style education in mission schools, which sometimes led to clerical jobs in the colonial government.[2]

In addition to these important developments, a dramatic reconfiguration of gender roles and expectations accompanied conversion.

As groups of converts and potential converts began to engage in experiments of identity production through the mediation of Protestant Christian missions, a rising tide of concern among foreign missionaries, British administrators, and Indian Christians brought the issue of women's modesty into public discourse. Articulated in moral statements about space, mobility, self-restraint, and sexuality, this concern for decorum created a discourse that had wide-reaching implications for the roles that women would play in the family and society and tended to narrow the already restricted range of behaviors and choices deemed appropriate for women. And yet, the reconfiguration of gender among Indian Christians did not consist only of lifestyle changes in and of themselves. In addition, Christians and non-Christians, Indians and non-Indians all attributed variant meanings to these changes in such a way that the social organization of gender became a crucial measure of a community's relations of power and status with respect to other groups. In other words, the changing status of the groups undergoing conversion to Christianity was frequently understood and expressed in terms of how women were treated and conducted themselves. Although the behavior and appearance of Indian Christian men was carefully scrutinized by people in colonial south India, women's behavior and appearance received a great deal more attention and became a widely recognized index of the general transformations, inner and outer, spiritual and social, that Indian Christians were undergoing.

How did this emphasis on women as a measure of Indian Christian status come to prominence? I argue that the late nineteenth and early twentieth centuries saw the emergence of a "discourse of respectability" among Christian communities in the south of the Madras Presidency during the British Raj that radically transformed the style of femininity to which Indian Christian women were expected to conform. Constituted by a melding of indigenous and imported discourses that linked gender and status, the discourse of respectability was a thoroughly dialogical formation. This is not to say that both parties in the dialogue had an equal say in its outcome, but Indian Christian converts were not passive recipients of the complex of beliefs, values, practices, and habits that accompanied Christianity as it was transmitted by missionaries from continental Europe, Britain, and the United States. Indigenous gender ideologies prevailing in nineteenth-century south India also had a large impact on the emerging discourse of respectability among Indian Christians.

Low-caste Indian women had long been discouraged or prohibited from adopting the practices that connoted modesty and femininity in the hegemonic gender discourse of the region. Upwardly mobile Indian Christian communities tended to appropriate practices from both elite Indian and Western sources related to marriage, labor, clothing, child rearing, and so forth that privileged women's enclosure over mobility, self-restraint over spontaneity, and self-denial over self-indulgence, producing a form of femininity that, from a present-day feminist outlook, appears more restrictive than liberating. However, it is crucial to bear in mind the specific historical context in which the discourse of respectability arose in the nineteenth-century Madras Presidency. Tamil Christian men and women actively participated in the creation of a respectable, if more restrictive community identity, based on new conceptions of femininity and masculinity because they hoped thereby to counter the cultural justifications of their economic, social, and even sexual exploitation at the hands of high-caste landowners and village elite.

My analysis of this process of transformation begins with the two most important key terms of my study: conversion and gender.

Decoding Conversion

Some of the most exciting recent scholarship on conversion examines the centrality of *belief* in modern constructions of religion.[3] Scholars who are interested in conversion to Christianity primarily for the ways it reveals the connections between colonialism and the emergence of "modernity" in Europe tend to argue that the hallmark of religion in modern states is the construction of religious belief as something intensely private and personal. They rightly locate the roots of this construction in the history of religious conflict in seventeenth-century Western Europe. As Peter van der Veer writes in his introduction to the edited volume *Conversion to Modernities*, "With the rise of Protestantism, the universality of the Truth of the Church and of Christendom as the sacred plurality of believers gave way to a plurality of religious truths and communities."[4] The disintegration of religious consensus in Europe resulted in bloody battles that raged through Germany, England, and France. These seventeenth-century wars over religion were succeeded by a (mostly bloodless) legacy of schism within the churches of Protestantism, a tendency to fragment over theological questions. This history of bloody and bloodless religious conflict underlies the observed retreat, as it were, of religion into the inner mind of the practitioner—the modern tendency to consider conscience and the individual's private experience to be the true locus of religion. Yet, the rise of belief itself produced a new problematic. In their contributions to van der Veer's volume, Talal Asad and Gauri Viswanathan argue that in the late eighteenth and nineteenth centuries, doubt and conflict over the sincerity of belief arose alongside the growing significance attached to inner conscience. The problem became, How can one *verify* claims to religious belief if they are located deep within the person and accessible only through verbal belief statements, notoriously subject to mendacity and equivocation?[5]

The understanding of the inner location of conversion in the mind or the conscience, with its attendant doubts about authenticity, was not unique to the modern era. Augustine's *Confessions* served as a crucial precursor to the Christian emphasis on conscience, but it gained new life in William James's psychological account of religious conversion, *The Varieties of Religious Experience* (1902), a study that many scholars take as the paradigmatic nineteenth-century understanding of conversion. For James, conversion was the ultimate private experience, an intense, one-on-one encounter between the self and God that resulted in an enhanced sense of integration. He wrote, "To be converted, to be regenerated, to receive grace, to experience religion, to gain an assurance are so many phrases which denote the process, gradual or sudden, by which a self hitherto divided, and consciously wrong, inferior and unhappy, becomes unified and consciously right, superior and happy, in consequence of its firmer hold upon religious realities."[6] This "interiorist" model of conversion was extremely important to Christians active in the global missionary movement.[7] As the form of conversion most valued by missionaries, by virtue of being "pure" and uncontaminated by historical contingencies, it recurs frequently in the biographical and autobiographical conversion narratives of several elite Indian Christians. But James's model of conversion, in which the inner self is the site of a turning (or returning) toward a new source of salvific power, was not the only model of conversion available in the nineteenth century. Coexisting with the notion of conversion as an inner transformation, a flash of world-changing insight similar to the Apostle Paul's experience on the road to Damascus, was the concept of conversion as a series of stages, a gradual, continual process of change that was both revealed in and aided by changes in external behavior.

One can take too far the assumption that modern religious discourse is primarily preoccupied with conscience. The abiding importance to nineteenth- and twentieth-century individuals of practice and the inextricable relationship between practice and belief is vividly apparent in the history of conversion to Christianity in colonial societies. In the context of the colonization and attempted Christianization of Asia, Africa, America, and the Pacific, doubts about authenticity that were raised by the location of conversion in the inner self grew ever louder. Yet, this was as much a result of the inequities of colonial rule as it was a legacy of the emphasis on belief in modern religious thought. Under the unequal conditions of power in the colonies, the missionaries often met converts' claims to have embraced Christianity with skepticism and disbelief. Missionaries and other Western Christians deemed Indian Christians (or African Christians, or Native American Christians, or Chinese Christians) worthy of the name "Christian" only when converts demonstrated through far-reaching changes in their daily lives and everyday practices that they had *really* undergone the radical transformations associated with genuine religious conversion.

The two schemes of conversion, one instantaneous and internal and one gradual and external, may be regarded as ways of understanding two dimensions of the same process, the personal and the public. Yet, it is striking how, in the Indian context, written representations of conversion reproduce existing class distinctions by stressing the interior dimension for elite converts and the exterior dimension for low-caste converts. The direct personal testimony of elite Indian converts often drew on the interiorist model of conversion. But the model of conversion generally applied to the low-caste converts, who formed the bulk of the Indian Christian church, was the graduated model of conversion. Missionaries frequently denied low-caste converts the capacity for interiority that is a necessary condition for an inner, private experience of conversion because, unlike members of the Indian elite, members of low castes tended to convert in groups—by family, caste, village, and so forth.[8] Critics of what came to be called the "mass movements" feared that because the impoverished and socially marginalized low-caste Indians entering the church were impelled by "impure" material motives they would resist the changes that marked genuine conversion. But, in fact, for reasons not anticipated by missionaries, it was very difficult for low-caste converts to remain merely "nominal" Christians. Indian Christians could not, or not for long, manifest their new allegiances by a simple profession of belief in Christian teaching. The public adherence to Christianity inevitably entailed practical consequences. This was partly because of the missionaries' insistence on seeing evidence of genuine spiritual change in altered styles of self-presentation and partly because converts themselves had reasons of their own for wanting to change their customs and ways of life.

Missionaries generally attributed the reconfiguration of Indian Christian lifestyles to the mysterious workings of God's grace and the civilizing effects of the gospel. Yet, human effort played a big part in cultivating those changes. Indeed, in the gap between belief and the signs of belief manifested in practice lay the opportunity for massive intervention into the lives of Indian converts. The idea that the experience of conversion would be completed and perfected by changes in lifestyle led to the view that recent converts needed a great deal of guidance before that initial, transformative experience could drive the changes necessary for new Christians' genuine conversion in behavior, habit, custom, speech, and so forth. From the other side of the transaction, the eagerness of evangelicals to attract followers created maneuvering room for Indian converts to appropriate selectively those aspects of Christianity that accommodated their social ambitions.

In this study, then, I focus primarily on the public, social aspect of conversion. Whatever may be happening on the inside of a person, conversion is also a gradual, contested, uneven process that involves changes, however subtle or obvious, in dress, diet, lifestyle, speech, and comportment that are undertaken by people as they organize their lives according to the authoritative claims of new religious leaders, guides, or texts. The public aspect of conversion consists, to a significant degree, of the diverse claims that people make about the processes said to occur on the inside on the basis of visible, external changes. Competing claims about their meaning animate the play of tension between the external gesture and the internal psychological, spiritual, or moral transformations it is supposed to reflect. The public changes that an individual or a community undergoes in the process of religious conversion often signify different things to different people, and this makes them the object of a great deal of contention and debate. Indeed, when one examines the process of conversion from the point of view of the group rather than the individual, conversion appears to be less about integration and wholeness (as in James's model) and more about conflict, the sundering of old relationships, and alienation from the shared universe of values and practices of one's old community. It appears to be less a matter of belief and more about disputes over the meanings of practices, old and new. Rather than try to determine what these changes "really" meant according to some extracontextual measure or by divining the intentions of the actors, this study examines the clash of different meanings attributed to these changes by actors positioned in a variety of ways in colonial Indian society.

It may be useful here to describe the theoretical sources I have drawn on in arriving at this methodology. In an effort to modify the interiorist, individualist, and intellectualist view of conversion predominant in scholarship on Christian conversion prior to the 1980s, the anthropologist Robert Hefner argues against the assumption that new adherents to a religion necessarily internalize religious doctrines: "The most necessary feature of religious conversion, it turns out, is not a deeply systematic reorganization of personal meanings but an adjustment in self-identification through the at least nominal acceptance of religious actions or beliefs deemed more fitting, useful or true. . . . conversion implies the acceptance of a new locus of self-definition, a new, though not necessarily exclusive, reference point for one's identity."[9] Indeed, at some level, conversion always entails the declaration "I (or we) have changed." But, as I mentioned before, given the deeply social nature of conversion, even "nominal converts" generally manifest their new self-definition in one way or another, whether verbally in written or spoken statements testifying to their new belief or nonverbally through manifold changes in lifestyle, speech, diet, clothing, and comportment. The recognition that the acceptance of a new "locus of self-definition" rarely takes place without a struggle requires us to push Hefner's identification of the *social* dimensions of conversion still further.

Following social theorists who give importance to the routines and rituals of "everyday life," such as Michel de Certeau, Michel Foucault, Pierre Bourdieu, and Jean and John Comaroff, I do not regard contests over the quotidian expressions of changed identity as trivial but as the terrain on which much larger battles about the very nature of the social order and the cosmos take place. They involve the "values given body" capable, as Bourdieu writes, "of instilling a whole cosmology, an ethic, a metaphysic, a political philosophy, through injunctions as insignificant as 'stand up straight' or 'don't hold your knife in your left hand.' " Bourdieu has been taken to task by some for his pessimistic assessment of the scope of human agency, as in his view that these embodied values are "beyond the grasp of consciousness" and thus reproduced unthinkingly by individuals caught fast within "structured and structuring structures," the import of which they persistently misrecognize. The dim prospects his social theory presents for those wishing to highlight the possibilities for human autonomy and agency are also reinforced in his suggestion that subordinated groups are inevitably complicit in the dominant social structure that oppresses them, that they strengthen and legitimize the symbolic order even, or perhaps especially, when they try to use it to further their own interests.[10] It is notoriously difficult to assess the degree of agency wielded by social actors in any historical era, especially those whose fields of action are systematically constrained by poverty, exploitation, ill health, violence, and degradation. I side with those who argue that, in even the most oppressive social situation, some kind of resistance is evident, whether in small-scale recalcitrance or large-scale rebellion. It is, after all, in the nature of power, understood according to the circulatory model advanced by Foucault, to elicit and provoke resistance in its very application. Michel de Certeau and James Scott have drawn our attention to the low-level resistance offered by subordinate groups in the "tactics" or "weapons of the weak" they use to siphon off resources (whether material resources or symbolic ones such as prestige) for their own benefit.[11] Scott and de Certeau share much in common with Gramscian views of the relationship between consent and hegemony, where any social order is seen as a dialogic product of negotiation among the parties, even the most marginalized. That the oppressed have not completely internalized the values of the majority, even when they have been intimidated into silence, is especially evident in times of rapid social change. When the unspoken limits of the old order that defined what was possible for which members of society are called into question, those who benefit the least from tradition are often attracted to alternatives.

Though this study is greatly influenced by theories of resistance proposed by de Certeau, Scott, and Gramsci and worked out in great detail by the Comaroffs in their monumental study of conversion to Christianity in colonial South Africa, I recognize the value of Bourdieu's insight into the limitations to agency and the ways human beings become entangled in social systems that work against their interests. When disenfranchised groups cast their lot with an alternative social system, whether produced out of a political revolution or a religious revival, the alternative itself eventually comes to rest on "structured and structuring structures" that exact their own sacrifices—taxes, if you will, levied, more often than not, on women more than men, young people more than old, and the poor more than the propertied. The history of Christian missions provides a rich area of research in which to explore these dynamics.

Gender and the Discourse of Respectability

Although the lifestyles of Indians changed in multiple ways over the course of their conversion to Christianity, I am most interested in those changes that had to do with gender because they reveal a pattern that has not been well explored in the literature on conversion to Christianity, in India or elsewhere. Much scholarship on Christianity in a global context asserts that women's status in society improves over the course of Christianization; although that may be true in India in a qualified way, I have observed as well a tendency toward a restrictive form of femininity. The social ambitions that were such a large part of the drive to convert among low-caste Indians entailed, in the Indian context, a radical reformation in gender roles. I define the discourse of respectability as a system of intentions, desires, practices, and beliefs that organize gender and status differences in such a way that behaviors are valued positively to the extent that they exemplify restraint, containment, and orderliness, whereas behaviors are valued negatively that exemplify lack of self-control, spontaneity, and chaos. Though men as well as women could appear chaotic and out of control, these traits were most often associated with women. As a result, the second key term that I deploy is gender.

The historian Joan Scott has developed a dual definition of gender, the components of which are "interrelated but must be analytically distinct." She writes, "Gender is a constitutive element of social relationships based on perceived differences between the sexes and gender is a primary way of signifying relationships of power." The first part of the definition affirms the socially constructed nature of gender. Primary and secondary sexual characteristics may be a given aspect of human bodies, but our perceptions of differences between the sexes are socially constituted and may have more influence on social relationships than any biologically shaped component of sex. Moreover, these perceptions and the social relationships they give rise to are thoroughly imbricated with other social forces. Although much research has focused on how gender is constituted through kinship, that is not the only area of social life that gives meaning to sexual difference. Gender is also constituted through the labor market and state policy and in relation to other significant discourses such as race, religion, and class.[12] In the second part of the definition, Scott highlights the importance of gender in providing a language for talking about other things. Gender serves as a set of metaphors that can be applied to relationships of power in such a way that these relationships seem natural and inevitable by virtue of the apparent "naturalness" of gender. In colonial India, the gendering of the relations of power between colonized and colonizers was a critical component of the ideological apparatus of colonial rule and took many forms, for example, the stereotype of the "weak," and therefore "effeminate," Bengali.[13]

Scholars of nineteenth-century Protestant missions have noted that the mistreatment of women was one of the many "ills" of native society diagnosed by missionaries around the world. The representations of indigenous society that filled missionary journals reveal that the dominant view of the relationship among gender, religion, and civilization was one in which "barbaric" lands were those where women labored in dirty, difficult, or physically demanding occupations and where brides were bought or married off at a young age.[14] As Lata Mani has shown, representation of gender relations in India as degrading to women thus served as an alibi for colonial intervention, conjuring up vividly the image of India as a suffering woman who needed to be saved by the heroic, hypermasculine British.[15] Missionary representations of Indian home life gave an added inflection to this image in seeing Indian women as both glaring symptoms of general Indian degradation and obstacles to the conversion of Indian men (by virtue of their dedication to practices considered "idolatrous" or "superstitious" by Christians). In the eyes of missionaries, Indian women thus needed to be converted for two reasons: to raise the Indian population in general to a new level of "civilization" and to facilitate the large-scale conversion of Indian men.

Both of the components of Scott's definition of gender are important as I examine the changes in constructions of femininity and masculinity over the course of conversion as well as the significance of these changes in the eyes of Protestant missionaries, Hindu Indians, and Indian Christians. Taking Scott's reminder that gender is shaped not only within the family but also within other social domains, I focus on three arenas in which new forms of masculinity and femininity were shaped: ideas of motherhood and the home (Indian Christian domesticity), ideas of conjugality and the conditions for juridically sanctioned sexuality (Indian Christian marriage), and ideas of proper dress and adornment (Indian Christian sartorial style). In each arena one can see that the alleged treatment or status of women in different groups in Indian society is deployed as an index of the level of that group's achieved "civilization," or rather, in the eyes of colonists, lack of civilization.

It is important to bear in mind that the transformation of gender relations that took place over the course of Christianization did not involve the simple imposition of Western gender roles and expectations onto the docile bodies of colonial subjects. To argue this, I maintain, is to reinscribe the presuppositions of the Protestant mission in our own scholarship. Nineteenth-century missionaries frequently anticipated that "heathen" customs, practices, and beliefs, by virtue of not being as substantial as the Christian "truth," would give way before the arrival of the evolutionarily subsequent and culturally superior form of religion. They were almost always disappointed. Increasingly, scholarship on colonialism and imperialism has shown that indigenous societies were not blank slates, nor were indigenous values, practices, and beliefs easily or simply displaced by those held by foreigners.[16] It is equally important to stress that the colonized were not, for their part, always noble rebels defying the imposition of foreign rule at every opportunity. In fact, a much more complicated negotiation of meanings took place between missionaries and converts in the process of conversion in India and the associated transformation of gender norms. This study has been deeply informed by that stream of postcolonial studies that recognizes the culture of colonialism as a dialogical formation born out of a complex dynamic of coercion and collusion, imposition and appropriation, resistance and cooperation.[17]

But rather than stop at the recognition that the relations between colonizer and colonized, missionary and convert were complex formations that call into question neat dualities between oppressor and oppressed, foreign and indigenous, dominator and dominated, this study seeks to discern and describe the concrete patterns that shaped the outcome of those relations. Like Tolstoy's unhappy families, every colonial encounter is messy and complicated, but each is messy in its own way. As a dialogical formation based on the encounter between British, German, and American missionaries and south Indian Hindus (who were themselves internally differentiated on the basis of class, gender, education, and caste), south Indian Protestant Christian culture is distinguished by patterns that arose out of the preexisting cultures and history of the societies that clashed in the colonial encounter. Where did this dialogic formation begin? In the first place, Christianity had to be translated, articulated in idioms that were at least intelligible to local people.[18] In their efforts to communicate the Christian gospel, missionaries inevitably mapped the meanings of Christian beliefs and practices onto preexisting cultural forms, for example, by utilizing words that already had distinctive meanings to convey Christian ideas and employing people who already had a certain location within the Indian social structure to teach and preach those ideas. In addition, the missionaries' notions of appropriate behavior and correct belief were transformed by indigenous discourses as local people appropriated Christianity and made its forms, practices, rituals, and laws meaningful to themselves. One advantage of taking gender as a focus is that gender was one of the most significant and highly contested arenas of conflict between Indians and Westerners. The historical record thus contains a great deal of material for analysis. Another advantage is that by examining changes having to do with the social organization of gender, we can discern with particular clarity at least one of the principal structuring patterns that shaped the formation of south Indian Protestant Christianity, namely, that local elites, upwardly mobile Indian Christians, and foreign missionaries all associated the careful constraint of women's sexuality and public comportment with high levels of status and cultural refinement, albeit in different ways and for different reasons.

The notion that women should be guarded so that access to their sexual and reproductive capacities could be carefully managed was one of the chief organizing principles of gender relations among those groups closest to the ordering centers of political, social, and religious power in south India. British and American settlers in India, for their part, brought with them a preoccupation with women's modest and chaste conduct born of the ideology of middle-class respectability, itself a product of changing gender roles in the wake of the Industrial Revolution. As the discourse of respectability took shape, low-caste Tamil Christians adopted elite Indian ideologies that enjoined women's sexual modesty and regulated contact between the sexes along with Western concepts of feminine propriety. The resulting hybrid form of femininity reflects both the intense pressure that foreign missionaries, with their access to global networks of wealth and power, placed on converts and the creativity and persistence of Indian Christians as they struggled to engage with missionaries (and the forces of modernity that missionaries represented) on their own terms.

Chapter Outline

This study is divided into two parts. The first treats the social, religious, ideological, and historical backgrounds of south Indian, Tamil-speaking converts and the British and American missionaries who endeavored to convert them to Christianity; the second examines the formation of and negotiation over ideals of femininity and masculinity in Indian Christian culture in the areas of marriage, domesticity, and sartorial style. The first chapter provides a description and analysis of the early history of Christianity in south India. In this history, conversion to Christianity appears as the movement of traditionally marginalized social groups toward new centers of power and influence in a manner consistent with local understandings of the interrelatedness of secular and spiritual power. In the second chapter, I undertake a critical examination of the main sources that provide information about the lives of low-caste Indians in the colonial period: the accounts of colonial administrators and eighteenth- and nineteenth-century Protestant missionaries. Nineteenth-century colonial representations of south Indian society increasingly viewed the religious beliefs and practices of low-caste Hindus as a variety of demon-olatry, sharply distinguishable from Brahmanical Hinduism. I show how representatives of low-caste groups, especially Nadars (many of whom were either Christians or Hindus educated in missionary schools), sought to discredit this representation by producing a counterrepresentation of themselves as a formerly noble people, now fallen on hard times, who were the legitimate descendents of an ancient lineage of kings. One significant consequence of this new narrative of Nadar identity was the ideological backing it gave to renovated gender roles, in which Nadar women were to be protected and their sexuality guarded by Nadar men, now conceived of as proud warriors. The third chapter focuses on the social, ideological, and institutional contexts of the nineteenth-century women's missionary movement in the United States and Britain by examining how and to what extent evangelical Christianity empowered women missionaries and permitted them to challenge the patriarchal norms of missionary culture in India.

The second part of the book begins by examining how Tamil Christian women engaged with nineteenth-century U.S. and European gender categories, particularly the notion of separate spheres for men and women, and introduced Christian ideas about motherhood and domesticity to their fellow Indian women through Tamil literary idioms and cultural practices. In this way, Tamil Christian women cooperated with their women missionary employers in the production of an ideal of reformed, respectable Indian Christian femininity. The fifth chapter argues that in nineteenth-century India, marriage became a lightning rod for arguments about the degrees of "civilization," and therefore respectability, that varying groups in colonial society were supposed to have achieved. The debates on Indian Christian marriage were particularly charged because of the apparently ambiguous position of Indian subjects who professed the religion of the colonizers: Indian Christians were close to the colonizer in terms of religion but distant from them in terms of custom and history. A comparison of the writings of Indian Christians who embraced companionate marriage and the nuclear family with Indian Christians who firmly rejected these models of family life in favor of a martial form of marriage drawn from conservative elements of the Indian tradition shows that both viewed marriage as an outward sign of the quality of their inner transformation, a signifier of who Indian Christians were in a cultural, religious, and moral sense. The sixth chapter examines the sartorial styles that Indian Christians adopted in the nineteenth and early twentieth centuries to create new or reformed social identities. As in my examination of changes in the arenas of domesticity and conjugality, here I argue that although American and English missionaries were in some cases the instigators for new fashions, Indian Christians' desires for self- and community improvement were clearly at work in their selective appropriation of Western Christian cultural forms according to criteria based on indigenous concepts of social worth. In the arena of dress we can see with special clarity that the conflict-laden process of creating respect-able social identities hinged on the production of new ideals of femininity and masculinity. Disputes, sometimes violent ones, over the sartorial innovations of Indian Christians reveal with startling clarity just how high the stakes could be when low-caste groups asserted themselves as people worthy of dignity and respect.

I

Into the Fold: Protestant Christian Communities in South India

This chapter lays the groundwork for understanding the gendered effects of religious conversion in the arenas of domestic, marital, and sartorial practices (the foci of chapters 4, 5, and 6). I offer here a history of Protestant Christianity in south India that pays particular, though not exclusive attention to the consequences of Christianization for women. I do not intend to provide a comprehensive history of Christianity in south India or even of women in south Indian Christianity. Rather, I examine here the process of conversion through local categories to establish a framework for understanding the far-reaching transformations of custom and habit that took place over the course of Christianization. After discussing the history of Protestantism in south India, I provide an analysis of the so-called mass movements, large-scale conversions of groups of people that brought the majority of converts into the Christian Church and also contributed to the division of the Church along caste lines. South Indian religious culture in its various modalities is a crucial backdrop to the Christian conversion movements of colonial Tamil Nadu. For, when viewed through the concepts and categories of Tamil religiosity, which positively affirm the potency and efficacy of the divine in this world, conversions appear as the movement of people marginalized from the centers of power and influence in south Indian colonial society toward new centers of power that emerged in the social landscape because of the transformations wrought by the presence of new political figures. As I argue in the following analysis, this move toward a new center could also involve a move "up" in the sense of having expanded opportunities to exercise economic, political, and social power over others, or, more important, being less subject to having power exercised over oneself.

In 1938, a committee of scholars from American College in Madurai took a survey of the social and economic development of Indian Christian communities in the districts of Madurai (Maturai), Ramnad (Rāmnāṭu), and Tirunelveli (Tirunelveḷi) in preparation for an international meeting of missions and churches. The resulting report provides a representation of what the Protestant Christian communities in south India would become in the decades just prior to Independence, the chronological terminus of this study. When the study was released, it confirmed what most people already assumed about the Christian population of south India: They were for the most part heavily indebted, illiterate, and employed in wage labor just at or below the level of subsistence.[1] Also, the surveyors found that Tamil Christians were drawn primarily from three caste groups, the Nadars (Nāṭār), Paraiyars (Paraiyār,) and Pallars (Paḷḷār), and that the churches in these districts were very often composed of a majority from a single caste group.

As Table 1.1 shows, the Tirunelveli churches established in the early nineteenth century by the three main English missionary societies—the Society for the Propagation of the Gospel, the London Missionary Society, and the Church Missionary Society—were by 1938 more than two-thirds Nadar. Though the social status of this caste changed enormously over the course of the nineteenth and twentieth centuries, in the early nineteenth century the Nadars (then generally called Shanars [Cāṇār], a name that came to be used as a term of contempt) were considered a ritually polluting caste the highest of the low castes, yet not among the ritually clean caste Hindus. The traditional occupation of this large group involved collecting the sap of the palmyra tree, which was boiled down into jaggery or allowed to ferment into country liquor, or toddy. The Nadars were most heavily concentrated in the southern districts of Travancore and Tirunelveli, where the palmyra trees that formed the basis of their livelihood flourished, although prosperous traders had extended the community into north Tirunelveli and Madurai.[2]

The churches connected with the American Board of Commissioners for Foreign Missions, bound together as the Madurai Church Council (MCC), were almost half Paraiyar. This large "untouchable" caste was geographically dispersed around the Tamil-speaking regions of the Madras Presidency and was internally differentiated into several hundred exogamous subcastes.[3] Most Paraiyars were landless agricultural workers and artisans. The membership of churches of the Tamil Evangelical Lutheran Church (TELC, sponsored by German and Scandinavian missionaries), though somewhat more diverse than the other denominational bodies, was nevertheless well over half untouchable. One-third of the members were Paraiyars, one-sixth Pallars (untouchable agricultural workers), and one-tenth Chakkiliyars (untouchable leather workers). The TELC also had the highest percentage of Vellalars (Veḷḷālār) among the Christian churches. The early Protestant missionaries called them "Sudras," but the caste name Vellalar could denote any of a number of generally well-to-do and Sanskritized castes (Piḷḷais, Mutaliyārs, etc.) who constituted the dominant, literate, property-owning class in the many Tamil-speaking regions where the Brahman population was quite small.

TABLE I.I. Breakdown by Caste of the Protestant Congregations in Madurai, Ramnad, and Tirunelveli, 1938*

Caste	Tirunelveli Diocese (SPG and CMS)	MCC	TELC	Total
Nadars	77,441—68.7%	7,200—19%	800—8.9%	85,441
Paraiyars	10,474—9.3%	18,000—47%	3,000—33.3%	31,474
Pallars	14,096—12.5%	3,500—9%	1,500—16.7%	19,096
Chakkiliyars		3,500—10%	1,000—11.1%	4,500
Maravars (Kallars, Agamudiars, included)	2,436—2.2%	1,700—2.8%	800—8.86%	4,936
Vellalars	911—.8%	700—1.8%	600—6.7%	2,211
Other castes	7,391—6.6%	3,500—10.4%	1,300—14.44%	12,191
Total	112,749	38,100	9,000	159,849

*Based on J. S. Ponniah, et al., *An Enquiry into the Economic and Social Problems of the Christian Community of Madura, Ramnad and Tinnevelly Districts: Research Studies in the Economic and Social Environment of the Indian Church* (Madura: American College, 1938), 28–35.

One feature of the Christian communities of south India that the American College survey renders clearly is their small size, especially in relation to other religious communities. According to the 1931 census, Christian Indians constituted a mere 3.8 percent of the population of the Madras Presidency.[4] Thus, the significance of the Christian community in India is not to be found in its numerical strength. Rather, the interest of Protestantism in India, for this researcher, in any case, lies in its value as an exemplum of a particular category in the history of religions: conversion. Under the unequal power relations of colonial rule in India, conversion is quintessentially a selective process. What is retained of the previous religion and culture, and what is rejected? Similarly, what is neglected in the newly embraced religion, and what is highlighted? Perhaps another way to pose the question is to ask, How are the boundary lines between "religion" and "culture" drawn in the first place as the condition of the possibility of selection? What arguments are offered for identifying *this* as culture and hence insignificant to the new religion, and *that* as religion and therefore anathema to the new faith? What is entailed by such arguments?

As the American College survey clearly indicates, one of the aspects of the old way of life that was retained by Christian converts was their caste identity. The caste-specific composition of churches is an aspect of Christianity in India that invariably comes as a surprise to outside observers. Frequently it has been interpreted as an effect of the strength of the caste system in India, against which an "imported religious belief," such as Christianity, is largely "impotent."[5] According to this view, articulated most forcefully by Louis Dumont, caste is the central ordering principle of Indian society, with greater authority to organize social relations than any other institution, including the state or any other forms of religion. There is no question that the affiliations and identities that shaped the lives of Indian Christians before their conversion continued to be significant long after their entrance into a new moral community.

Yet, the caste identities that low-caste Christians (and other upwardly mobile groups) rallied around were profoundly reconstituted by the process of conversion and Christianization. They were not, in a sense, the *same* caste identities they had been decades before (a topic I take up in chapter 2).

One needn't assume Dumont's position that the vigor, explanatory power, or seductive elegance of caste ideology was what caused Indian Christians to retain their caste affiliations after conversion. In fact, the continued importance of caste was a result of the way Christianity was appropriated by Indians. In many ways, Christianization was similar to (but not identical with) Sanskritization.[6] For many converts, Christianization represented, among other things, a strategy for moving up within the ranked order of castes, rather than an effort to destroy or escape from the Hindu social order altogether. One compelling pattern in Christianization that I investigate more closely throughout this study was that the lifestyle changes that accompanied Christianization frequently bore a resemblance to changes characteristic of Sanskritization (e.g., in diet, dress, and the treatment of women). Such a pattern necessitates a hermeneutic method that attends to at least three different sets of interpretive possibilities: the interpretations generated by Indian Christians, by Western Christians, and by non-Christians, that is, the Hindu (and Muslim) neighbors who witnessed and reacted to changes in the converts' lifestyle. For Indian Christians did not undertake the transformation of their customs and practices in social isolation: They were responding to cultural pressures and expectations emanating from both Indians and Westerners. In addition, a fourth interpretive possibility occasionally becomes significant: the views of European and American Christians in the metropole who took an at times profound interest in the actions and treatment of Indian converts.

The American College census reveals a third notable feature of the Protestant Christian community of south India: Nearly all converts came from economically depressed and socially marginalized sectors of Indian society. Based on this fact, we may reasonably assume that material concerns were a factor in the decision to embrace Christianity. This is not to say that questions of power, influence, or material well-being were the *only* motivating factors for converts. Such a reductionist interpretation of the Christian conversion movements would involve not only an unwarranted denial of the capacity of Indian converts to describe their experiences as spiritual but also a distortion of the cultural system within which Indian Christians moved. As Duncan Forrester and Dick Kooiman have forcefully argued, the conversion movements of southern India had social, psychological, material, *and* spiritual components. Forrester writes, "A conversion movement is like a group identity crisis, in which the group passes through a negative rejection of their place in Hindu society to a positive affirmation of a new social and religious identity."[7] That a shift in identity, which simultaneously entailed a bid for increased material and social status, was achieved under the aegis of religion in nineteenth-century south India is above all a reflection of the extent to which what we would now call religion was then mixed up with every other aspect of life.

To assume that the material and spiritual dimensions of religion were fundamentally conceived of as distinct in eighteenth- and nineteenth-century south India is to impose on Indian material a metaphysical dualism inherited from the Western Christian tradition. Unfortunately, this dualism has deeply influenced the conceptual understanding of religion as a sacred realm separate from the profane, which has long bedeviled the academic study of religion. As we will see, many Protestant missionaries were also inclined to apply this dualistic model of human nature to Indians when they examined the motives of those who sought alliances with the Protestant Church and sought to winnow the crass material chaff of poverty, illiteracy, and need for protection from the grain of purely spiritual intentions. However, as mentioned before, Tamil Hindu religiosity positively affirms the potency and efficacy of the divine in this world. When examined from within local religious categories, Christian conversions appear as the movement of people marginalized from the traditional centers of power and influence in south Indian society toward the new centers of power emerging in the social landscape under colonialism.

The intensive research on south Indian temples conducted in the 1970s by anthropologists and historians casts some light on this argument by revealing the complicated ways in which material and symbolic goods were exchanged, transformed, and intertwined in Hindu temple ritual practice. According to the reconceptualizations of the Hindu temple proposed by Arjun Appadurai, Carol Breckenridge, and Burton Stein in the 1970s, the Hindu temple is less significant as a place than as a process, specifically a redistributive process, which is not marked off as a sacred site distinct from the profane world.[8] Stein succinctly states the implications of this thesis: "Nor, in the Puranic Hinduism of medieval South India, is there an institution like the church in Christianity or *vihāra* in Buddhism in the sense of a bounded domain of action and meaning which separates it from other domains, such as the church from the state, the clergy from the laity." In the worship of gods through Hindu temple ritual, devotees contributed material goods and services as a form of service (*seva*) to the deity. Offerings varied from those provided for everyday worship, such as coconuts, ghee, bananas, betel nuts, and milk, to elaborate silk garments for dressing the deity on special days and jeweled palanquins for carrying the deity in annual processions. As an expression of the deity's royal largesse, these offerings were only "tasted" by the deity, who returned them to his or her followers as *prasādam* (the divine "grace" or "favor" that imbues the food or other offerings given to and received back from the deity in worship). It was an essential component of the deity's sovereign nature to direct the redistribution of these offerings, bestowing special privileges on devotees according to rank and merit. For a devotee to participate materially in the ritual events that constituted temple-based worship and service to the deity was to have a share (*paṅku*) in this redistributive process. Conceived from within, according to the concepts and categories meaningful to medieval south India, "a temple was wherever a group of devotees founded a deity and were co-sharers in its generosity, whether this was a great shrine like that of Venkatesvara at Tirupati or the tree shrine of a tutelary goddess. Generically, a temple is a nexus of sharers consisting of a deity and its worshippers: its purpose is to protect and to transform the community of worshippers by the boons of the god; and its means are the transvaluing of substances—human and non-human—offered to the god and returned to its devotees."[9]

Those who participated as sharers in a temple through these transactions (which constituted the ritual of *pūjā*) were not, however, all on the same footing. Significantly, the receipt of prasadam was known as *mariyātai*, conventionally translated as "honor" or "honors" but derived from a Sanskrit word meaning "boundary" or "limit." For example, the receipt of the silk cloth draped over the deity during puja by the principal devotee was called *koyilmariyātai*, or "temple honors." Because the redistributive process at the heart of temple worship took place under the inherently limited conditions of time and space, the order in which items of worship were returned to the devotees was crucial to the generation of value. The greatest prestige accrued to the individual who received first honors. Thus, ideally, the king was first in rank among mortals, a status that was enacted by his being first to receive temple honors. In a temple on a smaller scale, in place of the king but acting in the role of sovereign would have been a caste headman, a village chieftain, or other local leader.[10]

At a symbolic level, the king and the deity were even more closely identified. As Appadurai and Breckenridge note, the deity was preeminently conceptualized as a sovereign, and thus the sovereignty of the king participated in the sacred quality of gods. Both human kings and gods "share a rich pool of ritual paraphernalia (i.e., stylus, drum, sceptre, flywisk, umbrella, elephant, etc.) which accompany them during their processional rounds through the kingdom that supports them."[11] The temple-palace itself was a linguistic and architectural reminder of the relationship between king and deity: Both lived in a place designated the *koyil* (from the ancient Tamil word for "king," *ko*, and the ancient Tamil word for "house," or "home," *il*).

Put simply, the Hindu temple was a powerful force for creating order and distinction among the individual elements in Hindu society. It was the center of Hindu society on a material, moral, and religious level. The order of worship represented and instantiated the approximation of human beings to the divine ideal. If the king, chieftain, or other royal figure was first in rank and embodied the divine ideal most closely, who was last in rank? The answer, not surprisingly, is low-caste groups.

Stein argues that who could worship and in what capacity was a matter of geographic and social denotations, as reflected in the etymology of the term mariyātai. Because they did not live within the village boundaries and because they were considered ritually polluting (the justification for their exclusion from the village), low castes were marginalized in the ritual worship of Hindu gods or included in ways that reinforced their low status in the community. For example, low castes such as Paraiyars participated in festivals honoring village goddesses by playing drums that were made from the polluting skins of animals. They were expected to heighten the intensity of the ritual with their enthusiastic, nearly out-of-control, sometimes drunken performances, in stark contrast to the dignity and self-restraint of the principal devotees and the detached, business-like manner of the Brahman priests. Henry Whitehead observed that a Telegu untouchable caste, the Malas, played demeaning roles in the worship of village goddesses. In the processions that punctuated the annual festival to the goddess, a Mala was designated to carry on his head the bloody entrails of a sacrificial animal or to toss blood-soaked rice into the air. The latter was a decoy offering to the hungry ghosts who invariably loitered around the sacrifice, figures with whom the low castes were symbolically identified.[12]

One could argue that the whole system of redistribution and exchange organized around the Hindu temple was based on the exclusion of the low castes. Though Appadurai and Breckenridge do not address the situation of untouchability or bans on temple entry by low castes in their 1977 essay, one must note that members of low-caste groups were *categorically* excluded from the value-laden interior spaces of the temple, where the deity resided in its most powerful form, the stone mula-vigraha.[13] Moreover, the privilege of serving the god by endowing different aspects of the puja was zealously guarded. Even when low castes became wealthy they were not admitted into the presence of the deity; they had to employ a ritually clean broker who would deliver their contributions to the puja.[14] It was not until 1939 that low castes in the Madras Presidency won the right to gain entry to all temples, when the Temple Entry Indemnity and Authorization Bill was passed after a decades-long legal and social struggle.[15]

In a later essay, Breckenridge discusses one of the ways in which upwardly mobile low-caste groups sought to work around these prohibitions. In her revealing analysis of a conflict that erupted in 1898 between the Raja of Ramnad and the Nadars of Kamudi, she analyzes the central role of the Raja as *Setupati*, or protector of the great Saiva temple at Kamudi dedicated to Sri Minakshi and Sundaresvarar (forms of Parvati and Shiva). When Nadars forcibly tried to enter the temple and honor the presiding deities with their offerings directly, contrary to prior usage at the temple, the Raja filed a legal case against them. Though at first he prohibited the Nadars from entering the areas of the temple from which they had previously been excluded, Breckenridge argues that the Raja was prepared to grant the Nadars more direct access to the ritual process. This would have been consistent with the role of the king as redefiner of the various statuses of different groups of loyal followers. However, the colonial state intervened with its own rigid definitions of caste and status. Having arrogated from the Setupati the role of adjudicator of temple disputes, the colonial state ruled against the Nadars, freezing the previously more fluid criteria for determining who could and could not offer worship to the deity.[16]

When temple-based worship is viewed at the level of the individual, the Hindu devotee receives prasadam in return for service to the deity, prasadam being a sign of the intimate relationship between the devotee and the deity, of the promise of boons and the transformation of the self. When it is viewed at the level of the group, as a performance of the relationships among humans bound together through their common worship of a deity, the devotee receives mariyatai, which represents prestige, the positive regard of the community, a "substance" whose quality and quantity varied considerably. As Pamela Price argues in her study of the political symbolism of the "little kingdoms" of Ramanathapuram and Sivagangai in the Tamil country, the existence of multiple arenas for the ritual "display and constitution of honour in a kingdom" meant that social status was not a fixed entity, but "shifted from arena to arena."[17]

Given their marginalization from or degradation within temple-based Hindu worship and Hindu society, it is not surprising that when opportunities emerged in the eighteenth and nineteenth centuries to participate in alternative arenas for the display and constitution of honor by creating alliances with new representatives of religious and secular power, some members of low-caste groups seized them, in spite of the high risks of antagonizing their former patrons and masters. It is also not surprising that Tamil converts to Christianity would apply some of their old cosmological-soteriological assumptions to their interactions with the bearers of a new religious teaching, the Christian missionaries, for example, viewing the church as a space within which distinctions between members of the community are reinforced and displayed or sponsoring Christian building projects or the maintenance of religious specialists with the expectation of a corresponding measure of prestige and respect—in other words, mariyātai.

A History of Protestant Christianity in South India

Contrary to the popular perception that Christianity is a very recent newcomer to the Indian religious scene, it has a long history on the subcontinent. Syrian Christians have constituted an influential sector of society on the southwest coast of India from perhaps as early as the first century c.e.[18] The first Roman Catholic envoys to India, Portuguese merchants, soldiers, and sailors, arrived on the southwest coast following the explorations of Vasco de Gama. The Portuguese expanded their commercial operations in India from their headquarters in Goa as many Portuguese men settled for long stretches of time and began families in their new home. Indeed, the first record of large numbers of Christian converts is a list compiled by the captain of the fort at Cochin in 1514 of more than a hundred Indian women, the wives and mistresses of Portuguese men.[19]

The Protestant evangelical enterprise in India began in 1706 with the Lutheran mission to Tranquebar (Tarangambādi), a Danish port town on the southeastern coast. At this time, the political climate of south India was decentralized and extremely unstable in the wake of the disintegration of the Vijayanagara Empire. Members of the Lutheran mission had to cooperate with and mediate among numerous competing powers, both local and foreign. The Lutheran missionaries came with the grudging support and protection of Danish authorities. Like the English, the Danes arrived in India with no overt intention to conquer local rulers by force; rather, they came as merchants and entrepreneurs with the Danish East India Company. Danish merchants tolerated missionaries in their settlements and surroundings, unlike the British, who explicitly forbade missionaries from preaching in the regions where the

East India Company did business out of fear that they would destabilize the region. However, it would be a gross exaggeration to say that the worldly, high-living Danish merchants in India warmly welcomed these representatives of sober German Lutheran piety.[20] English royal supporters of Protestant expansion managed to circumvent the parliamentary ban on English missionaries by sponsoring the German Lutherans in India. So, though the Lutherans' activities in Tranquebar were initially sponsored by the Danish King Frederick IV, they also received support from King George of England through the newly founded Society for Promoting Christian Knowledge (SPCK). In addition, the Lutherans had connections with the mercantile rulers of the Danish East India Company in Tranquebar, the English East India Company in Madras (Chennai), and the Hindu Maratha rulers of Tanjore (Tañcāvūr), who were their landlords in Tranquebar.[21]

Under the leadership of Bartholomaeus Ziegenbalg, Heinrich Pluetschau, Johann Fabricus, and Christian Fredrich Schwartz, the Tranquebar mission established the groundwork for all further Protestant evangelism in the region. The Lutheran ministers of the Tranquebar mission had been trained by German Lutheran pietists at the University of Halle. Inheritors of Martin Luther's doctrine of *sola scriptura*, they strongly believed in vernacular education and advocated a style of devotional Christianity that encouraged each believer to strive for a personal, direct apprehension of Christ. They translated the Bible into Tamil, created hymnodies in Tamil based on Lutheran hymns, and published both a Tamil lexicon and a Tamil-English dictionary.[22] Yet, given the treacherous nature of translation, these evangelical German Lutherans invariably had to adjust the Christian message and the vehicles for conveying it (in their translations, architecture, and church organization) to the moral and social expectations of their Indian audience.

As with the Roman Catholic Portuguese, the first Protestant congregations in south India were composed for the most part of European soldiers, sailors, and entrepreneurs and their Indian wives, mistresses, and children.[23] Hence, a good deal of the ministry initially centered on the European and Eurasian community. The Lutherans attracted new converts by establishing schools for boys (1707) and girls (1710), which Ziegenbalg called *dharma-p-paḷḷikūṭam* or *dharmapatacalai* (school for religious instruction).[24] According to Dennis Hudson, the first students at these schools were either slaves purchased by the mission as an "investment" in its future growth or the sons of families made destitute by being cut off from their relations after they converted to Christianity.[25] Slaves were not in short supply at this time. Due to the periodic famines and wars in the region, hundreds of impoverished people migrated from the hinterlands to the coastal towns to sell themselves or their children into slavery. The missionaries also urged the Europeans associated with the Danish company to send their slaves to study at the school for one or two hours a day. Given the humble backgrounds of the students, Ziegenbalg's choice of name for the schools is interesting. *Dharma* is a multivalent Sanskrit word meaning, in various contexts, "law," "order," "justice," "practice," "right," and "religious teaching." In describing these schools, Stephen Neill, Dennis Hudson, and

Daniel Jeyaraj retain the name that, presumably, Ziegenbalg's eighteenth-century English translator gave to them: Charity School. Like the eighteenth-century schools for the poor sponsored by the SPCK and the Halle Mission (which served as the model for Ziegenbalg), the Lutherans charged nothing for tuition and often offered free meals or small amounts of money as incentives to attract students, a strategy that missionary educators would rely on for the next 150 years. In this sense, they were "charity schools." But by translating dharma into English, I believe one misses the effect that Ziegenbalg's word choice has of assimilating Christianity to local forms of highly valued religious knowledge. Lutherans mapped many Christian concepts and institutions onto Hindu ones by appropriating Tamil and Sanskrit religious terminology: The Indian word used to refer to Christian Scripture was *Veda*, a term that drew directly on the prestige of the most sacred texts of the Brahmanical Hindu tradition; church pastors were called *Aiya*, a Brahman caste name denoting "learned" or "priest"; and churches were called koyils, the Tamil word for temple.

Adaptation to local practices did not take place at the level of semantics alone. To help spread the gospel more widely, the Lutherans ordained the first Indian pastors. Fourteen Indians gained ordination during the eighteenth century, all of them Vellalars, a caste (*jāti*) of non-Brahman Sudras who, along with Brahmans, constituted the literate, landowning elite of Tamil-speaking society in south India.[26] The Tranquebar missionaries extended this privilege exclusively to higher-caste Christians with the belief that Vellalars and other high castes would not be impeded in their evangelism by caste prejudice against them and could therefore reach more people than low-caste Indian ministers. But the pattern of ordaining strictly Vellalar pastors suggests that the missionaries were also accommodating themselves, consciously or unconsciously, to the sociological order, by ordaining only people who were qualified to disseminate "the Christian dharma" according to prevailing Hindu criteria.

The extent to which the Lutheran missionaries were drawn into the power dynamics of local Indian life can also be seen in the controversies surrounding Ziegenbalg's first big building project, the New Jerusalem Church. When the huge cruciform structure was built in 1718, it seemed a fitting symbol of the new religious power on the scene, but it almost immediately aroused the criticism of Danish supporters of the mission back home. Christopher Wendt, the secretary of the mission council in Copenhagen, objected to its grandeur, taking it as a symbol of the luxurious and self-indulgent habits to which he thought the Lutherans were becoming accustomed. Such habits, he felt, did not correspond to the ascetic, sober lifestyle befitting a missionary. More important, for our purposes, the architectural form of the church itself permitted the organization of social relations within the congregations along local patterns. Early observers noted that during Mass, the Sudras (by which term the Lutherans meant Vellalars, who constituted the majority of the converts of the Tranquebar mission) sat in the central part of the church, on mats, while the lower castes sat in the transepts, on the bare floor, with women and men sitting on opposite sides.[27] The historical sources do not indicate whether Indian or German church leaders intentionally directed people to arrange themselves in this way, or whether the congregation "spontaneously" conformed to the distance taboos that regulated contact between different castes. But whether the seating arrangements were intentional or not, we can assume that the fact of the physical separation of Sudras and lower castes in the new church, and the relegation of the lower castes to the fringes of the church seating area, at some level derived from the same ideas about purity and prestige that led the Lutherans to prefer Vellalars over low castes as candidates for ordination.

The seating arrangements at the New Jerusalem Church have perplexed historians of Christianity in South India for a long time. From the point of view of most forms of contemporary Christianity, in which an egalitarian theology is an unquestioned component of their religion, the frank instantiation of social distinctions in this way seems hypocritical. Dennis Hudson's recent book on the Tranquebar missionaries and their Indian disciples provides the most sensitive discussion yet of what he calls the evangelical "pattern of sitting together separately." By this phrase, Hudson conveys the idea that the mixed-caste congregations sitting in the same room together and sharing the same food was in itself transgressive from the perspective of Hindus and Muslims watching from the margins. That they did so in a manner that allowed for the explicit ranking of individuals by virtue of their physical distance from both each other and the discomfort of the floor is something that Hudson acknowledges but doesn't dwell on. In this way, his work is a refreshing departure from previous studies that have judged the Tranquebar missionaries rather harshly against what one could argue is a historically anachronistic standard of egalitarianism. Nonetheless, the eighteenth-century Lutherans left a legacy of caste-based distinctions that the Vellalar pastors and laymen who led the church after their deaths for one hundred years carried on with great vigor. In the conclusion to his study, Hudson provides an eloquent summary of the arguments that Vellalar Christians gave in defense of preserving caste distinctions.[28] It seems obvious, but necessary, to point out that these arguments, though elegant and beautiful in their rendering of human nature, represent the point of view of those who benefit the most from caste ideologies, not those who suffer the most. The symbolic gestures of who sat where and who drank from the chalice first certainly reinforced and substantiated other significant questions, such as who did what kind of work, for how long, and for what kind of compensation, who got to make what decisions and who had to live with them. Another question raised by the New Jerusalem Church that has not been investigated by contemporary scholars is, Why were gender differences so visibly marked in the physical organization of space?

Like any of the lifestyle changes made by Indian Christians, the separation of women and men in church may be interpreted in at least two ways. First, it may be viewed as a response to the moral laws of Christianity, whether based on the authority of scriptural texts or church tradition, in which case, one would seek the scriptural text or historical precedent that authorizes it. Second, gender segregation in the context of ritual worship may be viewed in terms of its "reception history" among the Indian Christians' Hindu neighbors, people who (in addition to foreign missionaries and fellow Christians) provided a crucial audience to the changes that affected Indian Christians. As I show throughout this study, the alterations in behavior, custom, and lifestyle made by Indian Christian converts did not take place in a vacuum; indeed, the interdependent nature of Indian society made such changes the object of considerable contention and controversy.

As for the first line of interpretation, the Christian scriptural or traditional basis for a practice, historical studies on European Christians indicate that at this time, men and women in Danish and German Lutheran congregations did sit separately, following the biblical tradition that women were not to address men in church. The second line of interpretation, the reception history of the practice among Hindus, is also significant in this case. The Tranquebar missionaries reported that "the Hindus again and again took offense that women, even pariah women, were allowed to come into the church and sit with the others, and that the same thing was permitted in the school with the children."[29] It is not easy to interpret this response of Indian Hindus because men and women are not necessarily spatially segregated in present-day Hindu ritual. Moreover, the nature and degree of women's participation in temple-based forms of Hindu worship in the eighteenth century is not well-known. Women were most prominent as temple dancers (devadāsis), who entertained the gods with their skill in music and dance and thus maintained the auspicious state of the gods' residence, the temple, or kōyil.[30] However, women were limited in their involvement in other aspects of temple ritual, as they were forbidden to learn Sanskrit, the liturgical language of Brahmanical Hinduism, or hear the recitation of the Vedas. Some form of gender segregation most likely shaped women's participation in Hindus' ritual practice, as is indicated by their negative reaction to gender desegregation in Christian churches and schools. If Hindus were shocked at Indian Christian women's simply sitting inside the church, they must have been appalled by the fact that women could listen to the recitation of the Christian Vedam (the Bible) and presumably participate in divine services. Viewed from the perspective of local values, the physical separation of men and women inside the church may then be seen as a concession made to the scruples of high-caste non-Christian neighbors (and those Indian Christians who shared or wished to share such scruples). To offer this interpretation is not to deny that gender-segregated seating in church may also have been an extension of European practice. My contention is that both interpretations were simultaneously available in that specific historical context and could be drawn on by actors situated differently within the social order.

For nearly a hundred years, the German Lutherans were the principal proponents of Protestantism in India. Over the course of the eighteenth century, they spread out from Tranquebar, establishing churches, chapels, and schools in the Maratha strongholds of Tanjore and Trichonopoly (Tiruccirāp-palḷi), in the British political center of Madras, and in Palayamkottai (Pālayaṅkoṭṭai), the site of a British garrison in Tirunelveli district. Two very important conversion movements took place during this period, which I here examine in closer detail because they illustrate some of the gendered effects of group conversion in which a significant motive is upward mobility.

Mass Conversions in the Late Eighteenth Century

As mentioned previously, many low-caste Indian converts to Christianity entered the Church by virtue of bonds constructed on the basis of kinship and caste. In a later section, I discuss the social implications of the so-called mass movements in which whole families or kin groups converted to Christianity at one time. Here I want to sketch out the historical background of two early instances of group conversion in south India and draw attention to two significant patterns that contributed to the transformation of gender relations in convert communities. First, group conversions among socially marginalized and economically weak sections of south Indian colonial society were often initiated by a slightly more socially secure fraction of their peers.[31] Second, they were often led by people one might characterize (perhaps anachronistically) as religious seekers, that is, men and women who had been involved with one or more other religious movements prior to their conversion to Christianity.[32] Both of these factors reflect the influence of the social aspirations that, in part, fueled the movement toward a new religion and contributed to the pressure to reform gender practices to serve those aspirations.

The first movement was begun by Sundarānandam, a young man from Kālaṅkuṭi, near Sāttāṅkuḷam in Travancore, from the (then named) Shanar caste. In 1795 Sundarānandam ran away from home and traveled to Tanjore, where he became acquainted with a small community of Indian Christians associated with the English SPCK. He was baptized in 1797 and christened "David." When he returned to the Tranvancore region as an assistant catechist, many of David's relatives became interested in the new teaching he brought with him. Setting the pattern for many of the conversion movements to follow in the nineteenth century, in which interest in Christianity spread through familial and caste-based networks of association, David's circle of relatives became the center of a large Shanar conversion movement over the course of the next five years. Notable among the followers was one of David's uncles, who had been a leader of a local Shakta (Śakta) group.[33]

Shakta, an antinomian variety of Hinduism, also known as Tantra, was popular in eighteenth-century south India, where it was spread by wandering healers, musicians, and poets known as Siddhas. In Shakta forms of worship, the primary object of devotion is Shakti, the power of the divine feminine that is thought to pervade and animate the universe, driving its original quiescence into the dynamic multiplicity of forms that now characterizes creation. One of the central features of Shakta ritual practice is the deliberate consumption of substances or participation in activities that are considered polluting or taboo according to the purity beliefs of orthodox Brahmanical Hinduism.[34] In south India, low-caste men and women were recruited into groups dedicated to Shakti worship, in part because their very impurity in the eyes of orthodox

Hinduism made them attractive and powerful according to the logic of Tantra. Members of low-caste groups, in turn, were drawn by the antiestablishment rhetoric of the Siddhas, who criticized conventional forms of religion that explicitly denigrated and excluded low castes.[35] Through his participation in Shakti puja, David's uncle would have already been acquainted with a variety of intercaste religious worship that was based on concepts of religious equality similar to the egalitarian ideas in Christian ideology. In many conversion movements one sees that prior to their contact with Christian representatives, key leaders had been exposed to theological ideas similar to the teachings of Christianity, such as the unity of the divine and the spiritual equality of all people. As with the Tantric ideas of the Siddhas, the anticaste message of Christianity as it was articulated by David and his followers quickly found a large audience among the Tirunelveli Shanars.

The leaders of this new movement soon persuaded the SPCK to send a missionary to baptize the hundreds of people who had embraced Christianity. Between April 1802 and January 1803, more than five thousand people were baptized through the coordinated efforts of David Catecist, Rev. Satyanāthan (an Indian pastor ordained by the SPCK), and two Germans (Rev. Gericke and Rev. Jaenicke). From the beginning, the Shanar converts encountered resistance from their landlords and neighbors, as the latter perceived the large-scale conversions as a defection from the social economy of village Hinduism. Women were harassed, chapels burned or torn down, and gardens ruined.[36] To escape from such abuse, many of these Christians founded new villages of their own. Seven of David's close relatives established Mudalur (Mutulūr, "first town") in 1799 on waste land they managed to procure in Tirunelveli district with the help of an Englishman.[37] Soon after, the Shanar Christians founded half a dozen towns. These settlements reflected the new ideas of Christian order that the converts were to embody: The streets were arranged in a grid and lined with trees, the whitewashed houses were equipped with small gardens, and an Anglican church with towering steeple presided over the town. The Christian settlements took their names from important biblical places, such as Jerusalem (1802), Bethlehem (1802), and Nazareth (1804), or Tamil Christian neologisms such as Suviseshapuram (Suvisēśapuram, lit. "town of good news") or the names of European missionaries or lay patrons (e.g., Sawyerpuram, Dennispuram, and Dohnavur).[38]

The second conversion movement that took place during this time was also initiated by a low-caste religious seeker. Mahārāsan was born in a village in south Travancore called Mayiladi (Mayilāṭi) into a family of relatively well-to-do and literate Śaivite Sambavars (Sāmpavars). The Sambavars were a sub-caste of the ritually polluting Paraiyars who resided mostly in south Travancore (in Nanjinad) and were particularly renowned, along with other Paraiyars in this region, for their skill in astrology and soothsaying.[39] Maharasan's family was richer and more Sanskritized than most. They marshaled sufficient social and material capital to endow a temple dedicated to their family deity, Elankamanyan, whose worship included many Sanskritic elements including vegetarianism, abstention from alcohol, and commensal exclusiveness.[40]

According to the legend, though very pious in his youth, Maharasan at some point grew tired of his ancestral religion. His first excursion outside the faith of his forebears came when he read a palm-leaf book extolling the worship of Murugan, a Tamil god regarded in the south as one of the sons of Shiva (also known as Skandha). Like south Indian shakta groups, the cult of Murugan was an important site of intercaste religious worship. In particular, the mythology surrounding Murugan's marriage to Valli (Vaḷḷi), a tribal girl from the hills, attracted many followers with the promise that Murugan was more tolerant of low-caste devotees than were other Sanskritic Hindu deities.[41] Maharasan became a great devotee of Murugan, going so far as to build a *choultry*, or pilgrim rest house, on the road leading from Travancore to Tiruchendur (Tirucenūr), a seaside temple and pilgrimage site dedicated to the god. In the course of his frequent pilgrimages to Tiruchendur, Maharasan learned from a party of Siddhas about meditation on the divine conceived of entirely without qualities. He also learned of an even more inclusive form of worship than that found at Tiruchendur, namely, a special method of worshipping God without images that was practiced in Chidambaram (Citamparam). After hearing about this refined and wonderfully abstract worship of Shiva, however, he was sorely disappointed by the rich, sensual, image-based worship he actually encountered at the temple. C. M. Agur, one of the earliest historians of the Christian Church in Travancore writes, "Upon entering within the precincts of the temple, he [Maharasan] found its 'Sacred' courts full of wickedness and impiety. After sunset dancing commenced, attended with heathenish practices and abominations of all kinds." As the despondent Maharasan made his way home, he stopped in Tanjore to visit his younger sister and brother-in-law, who were Christians, where he chanced to hear the preaching of a missionary of the SPCK. This was in about 1800. After just eight days of religious instruction he was baptized, changing his name to Vedamanickam (Vētamāṇikkam, "jewel of the Veda/Bible").[42]

Vedamanickam, like David, became the center of a large conversion movement among his relatives and caste people. Instead of selling his land and moving to Tanjore, as he had been instructed by his SPCK mentors, he preached among his own people and attracted hundreds of followers to this new teaching. In 1805, he journeyed to Tranquebar to invite a newly arrived German missionary, Rev. William Tobias Ringeltaube of the London Missionary Society, to come to Travancore, where he could supply Ringeltaube with land to build a chapel and a parsonage.[43] Ringeltaube was an eccentric individual whose voluntary poverty and humble dress made him a figure of fun in the European community.[44] Although he proved to be an important bridge between the converts and the British representatives who virtually ruled Travancore from 1810, he was physically absent for much of the time, leaving Vedamanickam as the de facto leader of this community of two hundred to eight hundred adherents. Vedamanickam thus had to contend with numerous difficulties arising from the challenges of founding a new religious community with very little support from the foreign bearers of the Christian teaching.

Vedamanickam marked the separation of the Christians from their former way of life by replacing their old "heathen" names with Christian ones. Whereas the names traditionally given to children of the Sambavar caste were often derived from the epithets of the sometimes fierce local deities (e.g Mātan and Ratacāmanti Mallan), or from words designed to avert the envious attention of others (Piccai, "beggar"; Tūci, "dust"), many of the Christian names were Indian Christian neologisms with connotations of refinement and distinction. For example, the name of Vedamanickam's grandson, Masillamaṇi, literally means "uncrushed gem." Vedamanickam also created new rituals to replace old "heathenish" customs with Christian ones. Where the community used to perform dramas for the entertainment and honor of local deities, he encouraged the production of Christian dramas. Similarly, where young men of the community used to play music and dance at the funerals and weddings of high-caste individuals, now they sang Christian songs "inculcating nobler doctrines" in the crowds that gathered at such occasions.[45]

Of all the elements of their former system of worship, however, new Sambavar Christians were least willing to relinquish astrology. Vedamanickam reported that in times of sickness, many families resorted to their old horoscopes and consulted astrologers to diagnose and treat illnesses. Women were particularly skilled astrologers. Agur notes that when the women of the community were not at work in the fields, they used to travel among the neighboring villages singing and reading horoscopes. Vedamanickam was opposed to this apparent apostasy and suppressed their activities with verbal and physical punishment.[46] It is important to note that Sambavar women had been granted some expertise in an area of religious knowledge that was thoroughly discredited after conversion. Agur's rendering of women as the source of superstitious practices in the Sambavar Christian community needs to be viewed in the context of a more general tendency in nineteenth-century religious discourse in India to associate women with superstition (examined in detail in chapter 4). Nevertheless, when viewed in conjunction with the following changes in gender roles that accompanied Christianization, Vedamanickam's disciplining of women astrologers appears to be part of a larger project.

Like Ziegenbalg's New Jerusalem Church in Tranquebar, the physical structure of the church of the Sambavar Christians facilitated the reorganization of gender differences by the new community. In the small chapels the community built for themselves women sat separately from men and covered their heads for worship.[47] Agur did not specify how or with what kind of garment the women concealed their heads. The adherence of the new Christians to the Pauline injunction against women attending church with uncovered heads (1 Cor. 11:1–15) bears a resemblance to local purdah practices. It is possible that this form of veiling allowed Christians to imitate the practices of local Hindu elites while justifying such innovations with references to Christian authoritative texts. For the efforts to conceal women's bodies, silence them, and keep them from moving around outside the home were all integral to the strategies used to maintain social distance between the sexes in elite Hindu and Muslim communities. One possible reason the behavior of female astrologers who roamed beyond the physical boundaries of the community in the course of their work was punished so severely is that their suppression was part of a general program to institute a more rigid set of gender practices. In the reorganization of gender relations to correspond more closely to that of elite Hindu and Muslim groups, Christian women were to cultivate "modesty" by maintaining a discreet physical distance from men, concealing parts of their body culturally constructed as provocative, and staying close to home.

My conclusions here are necessarily tentative as the evidence from this period is too scanty to provide a reliable basis for comparing the conditions of Sambavar women before and after their conversion to Christianity. In general, one can say that Christianity as it was presented by missionaries was more inclusive of women (and low castes) than was orthodox Brahmanical Hindu-ism. There is much in biblical scriptures that specifically addresses women and thus provides a basis for such inclusiveness. But, whether because of the patriarchal background of German Lutherans or pressure felt from Hindu neighbors, or some combination of the two, women were segregated from men even in church and, in some instances, saw the scope for their active partici-pation in ritual activities (and gaining money or prestige thereby) rapidly di-minish after conversion to Christianity. On the other hand, the biography of one Indian Christian woman provides a powerful example of the resources offered by Christianity for the exercise of influence by women, both moral and social.

Conversion and the Sexual Politics of Imperialism: The Royal Clarinda

For this study of gender in the Tamil Christian community, it is significant to note that the foundation stone of the Christian Church in Tirunelveli (destined to become the largest and most influential population of Christians in India) was the tiny yet diverse congregation presided over by a Brahman widow, the famous Clarinda, born Kohila, to a Maratha Brahman family influential at the court in Tanjore. Clarinda has become a legendary figure in the Tirunelveli church.[48] A widow, a concubine, and a high-born woman who "lost caste" to become a Christian, she occupied many of the most negatively valued subject positions available in colonial south Indian society, yet she became a powerful patron through a series of alliances with influential men. The trajectory of her life exemplifies how an increasing concern to project a respectable image in colonial society caused the male Christian leadership to disparage and some-times actively to thwart the attempts of Christian women to assume leadership positions in the Church and to relegate women to supporting roles. Here I examine Clarinda's capacity to exercise leadership in the early growth of the Christian community in the light of Ann Stoler's analysis of the dynamics that characterized relationships between Indian women and European men in the colonial period, a subject I have carefully deferred until now.[49]

Kohila was born into an elite family of Tanjore Brahmans. She married a Maratha Brahman officer who served in the court of the Raja of Tanjore and, some years after her husband's death, became the mistress of an English army officer, Henry Lyttleton. Between 1765 and 1775 she lived with Lyttleton in Tanjore and Palayamkottai, a town adjacent to Tirunelveli where the British army kept a garrison. It is said that Lyttleton promised to marry Kohila and prepared her for this by teaching her about Christianity. Though they never did actually marry, one could say that he made good on his intentions: Lyttleton was disabled by gout for much of his later life, and in return for her faithful service to him he left her his entire estate.[50]

In February 1778, a few years after Lyttleton's death, Rev. Christian Friedrich Schwartz, one of the Tranquebar Lutheran missionaries stationed in Tanjore and a significant mediator between the British and Indian rulers, arrived in Palayamkottai to perform a marriage and a number of baptisms. Kohila had received some Christian teaching from her English consort and asked at that time to be baptized herself. Schwartz reported in his journal:

> Just as I was about to baptize some children, a young Brahmin woman came forward with her adopted son, and asked for baptism herself, since the child had already received emergency baptism at his birth. I must observe that this Brahmin woman had previously been the mistress of an English Officer. Soon after she had begun to live with him, she sent word to me that she was willing to embrace Christianity. My answer [then] had been that so long as she lived in that sinful state, I could not with good conscience baptize her. . . .
> She came forward and said, "Some years ago I requested you to teach and baptize me, but the mode of life I then lived made you refuse me. The former reason of your refusal does not hold now, though I have not been without temptations." Since all bore witness to her respectable life I could no longer withhold teaching from her. I therefore gave her teaching as long as I was in Palayamkottai. Many Brahmins came to her, whom she openly exhorted to give up heathenism. She received baptism with much emotion, and she desired that she should be given the name Clarinda, which was done.

Readily apparent in this quote is Schwartz's opposition to the riotous life that many Europeans living in India indulged in and his initial perception of Clarinda as a woman of questionable virtue who enabled such decadence.[51] Though he did eventually give credence to Clarinda's transformation from concubine to respectable widow—enough to baptize her—Schwartz shared with many churchmen of the day a profound disapproval of unsanctified sexual relationships between Indian women and European men. For decades, such criticism went almost entirely unheeded.

In the eighteenth century a large proportion of English men in India had sexual relationships with Indian women through prostitution, concubinage, or, more rarely, marriage. In general, historians have accounted for this by noting the disproportionately small number of English women in the colonies at this time and the financial considerations that inhibited colonial men from establishing families and households with European women. It was far beyond the means of most British men in the employ of the East India Company to maintain a genteel household suitable for a British woman; indeed, just the passage to India for wives or would-be wives was a very expensive endeavor, an expense the Company never took as its responsibility to pay. After a short-lived experiment to encourage local marriage between its employees and local women, the Company ultimately took an ambivalent stance toward concubinage, furtively allowing the practice while publicly condemning it.

Thomas Williamson, the author of the widely read *East India Vade Mecum* (1810), an advice manual for British servants of the East India Company newly arrived in India, wrote extensively on the subject of maintaining an Indian mistress, echoing the tacit encouragement given to the practice of concubinage by the East India Company. "Marriage is not so practicable in India as in Europe," he wrote. "[Except for] those platonic few whose passions are unnaturally obedient, it is impossible for the generality of European inhabitants to act in exact conformity with those excellent doctrines, which teach us to avoid 'fornication and all other deadly sins.' "[52] Though considered by present-day historians "the best authority on the subject,"[53] in many places Williamson's two-volume tome reads like titillating cheap literature designed to excite the fantasies of colonial men by giving a libidinal charge to the mission of imperial expansion. The *Vade Mecum* is a classic example of sexuality used as a trope for colonial dominance, of the representation of sexual relations between colonizers and colonized to illustrate in graphic fashion the asymmetries of rule. But, as Ann Stoler notes perceptively, sex in colonial society functioned as more than just a metaphor of what was going on in the realm of economy and politics; it was materially implicated in the constitution of the social categories on which domination was based.[54]

According to a pattern that obtained in European colonies around the world, the East India Company formulated policies regarding sexual relations between company servants and local women. As Stoler puts it succinctly, "Who bedded and wedded with whom in the colonies of France, England, Holland, and Iberia was never left to chance." Indeed, the regulation of sexuality by colonial administration was based on the need to define a coherent "white" population of rulers who could be clearly distinguished from colonial subjects. In establishing the boundaries between ruler and ruled the crucial factor was "who counted as 'European' and by what measure." As Stoler writes, "Skin shade was too ambiguous; bank accounts were mercurial; religious belief and education were crucial but never completely sufficient. Social and legal standing derived from the cultural prism through which color was viewed, from the silences, acknowledgments, and denials of the social circumstances in which one's parents had sex."[55]

The regulation of sexuality in the colonies began by assigning different values to sexual unions based on prostitution, concubinage, and religiously sanctioned marriage, and culminated in a colonial society in which hierarchical relations between natives and Europeans, soldiers and officers, and men and women were ordered through the complex conjunction of racial, sexual, and class-based ideologies. It was not only hierarchical relations between European men and Indian men that were expressed through interracial relations; hierarchy among European men in the colonies was also shaped by the kind of Indian women different sorts of men had sexual access to and the kind of relationships they could form with them. The rank-and-file British personnel in India could afford to keep neither a British lady nor a high-born Muslim or Hindu woman in the style to which she was accustomed. Therefore, British men who were lowest on the social scale of the European community, soldiers in the army, were for the most part restricted to having sexual relations with the prostitutes who worked in the cantonments and temporary camps. Company servants and army officers of Henry Lyttleton's status, on the other hand, often lived with Indian women in long-term relationships that had every appearance of marriage. Some men at least partly recognized the children born to them by Indian mothers by ensuring that they were baptized Protestants and providing for their education. Many others, like Lyttleton, passed on all or part of their estate to their companion in their last will and testament.

The hierarchy thus instituted in colonial society, however, was constructed on the unstable basis of sexuality and reproduction. The relations of intimacy and attachment that resulted (e.g., between masters and mistresses, and children and fathers) did as much to confuse and complicate the boundaries between the different interest groups in Indian colonial society as it did to confirm them. The situation of Indian mistresses in these relationships was particularly complex. Although Indian mistresses often began their acquaintance with their British lovers as domestic servants or bought concubines, they apparently could enjoy a certain degree of autonomy by maintaining their own way of life while cohabiting with British men.

It is important to note that most mistresses were tied to the British men with whom they lived by bonds of profound economic and social dependency. Frequently referred to euphemistically as "housekeepers to single gentlemen," they provided not only sexual services but domestic ones as well.[56] The wills written by colonial men who left some or all of their property to their Indian paramours almost never refer to the latter as wives, but rather as housekeepers, servants, or nurses, for example, "to Commaul, a girl formerly in my service"; "to Betsy, she having proved herself a faithful servant for many years." Other wills indicate that some British men purchased their companions. For example, Robert Grant (the brother of Charles Grant, director and chairman of the East India Company and active advocate of Christian missions) "bought his devoted Zeenut in 1778 from her uncle who sold her to pay off his gambling debts."[57] Moreover, a woman who took up residence with a European man paid a high price for her financial security by being excluded from the community into which she had been born. An Indian woman's European consort likely would have been considered a ritually polluting mleccha (foreigner) from the point of view of orthodox Hindus and a kafir (unbeliever) by orthodox Muslims.

An intriguing aspect of these relationships is that Indian mistresses' economic dependency and isolation from their natal communities did not necessarily entail a lack of liberty in choosing their own cultural and religious path. Historical accounts of cohabitation between Indian women and British men suggest that, in general, the men respected the traditional way of life of their mistresses. The Resident of Hyderabad, James Kirkpatrick, for example, set up a zenana (separate women's quarters) for his companion, Khair un Nissa, within the residency compound so that she could live in purdah protected from the gaze of unknown men, in a space "adorned by paintings and made cool by fountains."[58] One of the most significant realms in which Indian mistresses exercised their autonomy was religion: The vast majority of Indian mistresses never accepted the religion of their paramour. In fact, one of the reasons given for the infrequency of church marriage among Indian-British couples was that the women resisted converting to Christianity, a requirement for formalizing the relationship in a church-sanctioned ceremony.[59]

British men's willingness to tolerate their mistresses' religious observances was in part shaped by the general ethos of the colonial community at the time, which took a hands-off approach to Indian custom and religion. Like the men themselves, the Company, especially in its early years in India, preferred to take a pragmatic approach to the project of imperialism and enjoyed whatever could be gained by creating comfortable alliances with those Indians who cooperated with them. Thomas Williamson remarked jocularly that Muslim mistresses continued their regime of ablutions even with a European lover. He observed that to purify herself after intercourse a Muslim woman must get up to bathe in the middle of the night sometimes multiple times, indicating by metonymy the frequency of sex. Yet, the salacious manner in which Williamson noted the "exotic" customs of an Indian mistress should not cause us to overlook the significance for the women of the fact that they did not give up their religious practices.

Does the fact that these Indian women did not convert from their religion or alter their lifestyle suggest that they had some negotiating power in these relationships? Stoler notes that individual colonized women were sometimes able to "parlay their positions into personal profit and small rewards," but she stresses that these were "individual negotiations with no social, legal or cumulative gains."[60] Although Stoler's sharp focus on the economic and political aspects of these relationships has certainly cut through the nostalgic fog that obscures their basis in exploitation, her concentration on these matters causes her to overlook the importance of religion as a discursive space within which women could potentially garner some measure of independence and social influence. Perhaps Indian women's ability to choose their own religion (whether by observing their own religious practices or taking on the religion of their consorts) was part of the trade-off they received in exchange for their domestic and sexual labor.[61] Religion thus could function as a space of autonomy in these complicated relationships. It could create subject positions that allowed women more scope for decision making and exercising personal influence beyond their own lives, as the case of Clarinda suggests.

After her baptism, Clarinda became the leader of a very diverse congregation. According to the first Palayamkottai parish register, in 1780 the congregation boasted forty members from at least thirteen different castes.[62] Clarinda's position as leader of the community is made apparent by the fact that her name is at the top of the membership list, and the first five names are individual members of her household (including her adopted son, Henry Lyttleton, a servant named John, and his wife, Mariammal, whom Clarinda considered her foster daughter).[63] Clarinda supported the growing Christian community in the area around Palayamkottai in numerous and diverse ways. She encouraged the conversion to Christianity of several families in Tērivilai, one of several villages in the region that had been mortgaged to her.[64] Caldwell wrote that nothing came of the movement to Christianity in this village, and that it was totally unconnected with the large-scale conversions among Shanars that would become so important to the history of the Church.[65] This may be so, but it is belied by the report that Clarinda also paid two visits to the Shanar Christians in Mudulur to offer them "comfort and support" when their church was burned down.[66]

In addition to attracting and supporting new followers, Clarinda was instrumental in gaining legitimacy for the small community of Indian Christians by employing qualified religious teachers and building permanent institutions for the growth of the Church. In 1783 she journeyed with her adopted son to Tanjore to entrust little Henry into Schwartz's custody and request a catechist for Palayamkottai. She was made to wait fruitlessly for one month and then given a catechist named Visuvasi, a Paraiyar whom Caldwell characterizes as the "least considerable and reliable" of those working for the Tranquebar mission. Given the nature of caste politics in the Christian community at the time, such a gesture may well have been interpreted as a slight. Indeed, Schwartz's biographer, Wilhelm Germann, attributed her ill-treatment to "various rumours" about her that had reached the Lutherans in Tranquebar before her arrival. Eventually, due to Schwartz's intervention, she received a catechist trained by Schwartz himself, Gnanaprakasam, for whom Clarinda provided a salary, a house, and a small chapel in which to conduct services. Also in 1783, Clarinda sponsored the construction of a stone church in the Palayamkottai fort for the use of both Indian and European Christians. Schwartz dedicated the building in August 1785 and spent three weeks in Palayamkottai preaching, sometimes three times a day, explaining the doctrines of Christianity, and giving Communion.[67] The structure, known as Clarinda's Church, is still in use today.

While Clarinda exercised her role as founder and patron of the small Christian community in Palayamkottai, Schwartz retained his prerogative to discipline her as her spiritual teacher. In one of his letters, written at the time of his consecration of the church in Palayamkottai, Schwartz wrote, "I have earnestly exhorted the Brahmin woman, as she is called, to be on guard against her frivolity, and have faithfully admonished her."[68] What did Schwartz mean here by "frivolity" and "foolishness"? Did Clarinda take pleasure in the sartorial finery that signified power in the Tamil socioreligious universe of signs, or enjoy unsanctified relationships with other men besides Lyttleton (the "temptations" to which she referred in her request for baptism), or simply revel in the exercise of leadership over her group of fellow Christians? It is impossible to know. What seems clear is that in many of her projects Clarinda sought to transform her economic capital into social capital in a manner that was consistent with the Indian relationship between material and religious power.

In spite of her resourcefulness, Clarinda's personal clout could never fully compensate for the social disabilities with which she was burdened by virtue of being a woman, a widow, and an ex-concubine. Gossip or criticism could always undermine her authority (as it did when Schwartz's fellow missionaries denied her a suitable catechist because of "various rumours"). In any case, Schwartz revealed in his letters the extent of the power struggle between himself and Raja Clarinda (the Royal Clarinda, as she was known in her community), a struggle in which money, prestige, and virtue were the foci of contention. Schwartz wrote that after he lectured her about her pride and frivolity, Clarinda offered him 100 rupees (an enormous sum in those days) to defray the cost of his journey. He wrote, "I didn't take it, but told her that though I regard in itself right and reasonable, that she should, as a well to do person, bear part of the cost, I could not and would not accept it, lest evil disposed persons would calumniate her as having set everything right by paying. She promised that she would bahave Christianity [sic]. She has up to now maintained the schoolmaster there, and also given large help to the poor."[69] Clarinda may have promised to behave in a Christian manner, but she was also behaving in a Tamil manner, endowing a religious institution with the fruit of her wealth with the frank expectation that she would receive back the honors that centers of religious power alone could provide.

After her death, Clarinda continued to be the object of considerable suspicion. She was largely written out of the earliest accounts of the Tirunelveli churches because, as Robert Caldwell explained, "her antecedents were not well fitted to produce a good impression in favour of Christianity in the minds of a people among whom it had but recently been introduced."[70] In other words, the Indian Christian community's early nineteenth-century historians were deeply embarrassed by the fact that the first Indian convert and the founder of the first Christian church in this significant region had been the mistress of a British soldier.

Indeed, according to the logic of local gender ideologies, Clarinda would not have been considered a respectable woman. A good reputation for a woman of her community depended on a very tightly controlled sexuality, whereas Clarinda had had two sexual partners and was perhaps tempted by the prospect of more. Widows like Clarinda were considered threats to community order because they were not protected (from sexual contact with men outside the community) or contained (by an appropriate male, a husband, who could satisfy the woman's own supposedly voracious sexual appetite). The fear of widows found expression in the custom of *sati* (immolation of widows) and the ascetic rigors of a widow's lifestyle, which sought to extinguish her own sexual impulses and dissuade those of others. Widows were to shave their head, wear only white, coarse garments without any ornamentation, consume only one meal a day, and sleep on a bare mat at night. Yet Clarinda chose neither suicide by immolation nor a life of celibate self-deprivation. That she refused these options in favor of the companionship of a mleccha foreign man would almost certainly have been a scandal to the moral sensibilities of her natal community.

Disapproval of Clarinda's independent nature also emanated from the scruples of the British community in India. As we have seen, the Company turned a blind eye for many years to the numerous unsanctified sexual relationships between Indian women and British men that took place during the early years of Company rule, even though they condemned the practice in public policy statements. In the later years of the eighteenth century this public disapproval became increasingly strident. When the overriding purpose of the British imperial project shifted in the first decades of the nineteenth century from a largely amoral commercial and revenue-generating enterprise to an overt mission to regenerate the decadent East, these unsanctified interracial, interreligious relationships fell into extreme disfavor.[71] Concubinage could no longer stand even as a furtive symbol of colonial domination that invited colonial men to augment the project of conquest and rule with libidinal pleasure. Instead, the need to define the boundaries between colonizer and colonized was met by constructing a moralistic regime in which the supposed sexual restraint of the West was contrasted with "Oriental" sensuality and decadence.

Caldwell articulated very well the shift in morality that took place when he appended to his own history of the Tirunelveli church this excoriation of Lyttleton, written in 1881: "The officer's inconsistency in instructing this woman in the principles of the religion whose precepts he was openly violating and teaching her to violate, appears more anomalous and extraordinary to us than it would have been considered at that time, the inexcusableness of such connections not being so distinctly and generally recognised in India then as it is now."[72] What made the "inexcusableness" of unsanctified interracial sexual relationships so apparent when Caldwell wrote, compared to the 1780s, when Clarinda and Lyttleton lived together? The change in perspective can be traced to the fact that after 1813, as we shall see in the next section, the Protestant missions in India took a more active role in exhorting colonial men to adhere to the behavioral standards of a reformed English Christianity.

Opening the Flood Gates: English Evangelicals and the "Pious Clause" of 1813

A shift in the policy of the East India Company toward evangelism in 1813 marked the beginning of a new era of Protestant expansion in India. For many decades the Company had actively discouraged missionary activity in the Indian colonies. Supporters of mission within the Company had succeeded in hiring a few Anglican evangelicals as chaplains who engaged in a certain amount of evangelizing, such as James Hough in the south and Claudius Buchanan in Calcutta. But even these men were regarded by some with suspicion. The Company feared that active efforts to spread Christianity would upset the religious sensibilities of the locals, stir civil unrest, and thus threaten its tenuous status as accepted ruler in the territories over which it exercised political control. Crucial to the maintenance of its power was the Company's role as patron of established elite religion in the region. When the East India Company became the principal political force in the Tamil-speaking regions of the south, it went to great efforts to control all existing power structures. One strategy was co-optation. The government took over the responsibility for guarding, supervising, and participating in pujas and melas in those Hindu temples whose management was entrusted to their care (which included the collection of a hefty temple tax).[73] District collectors appeared at temple festivals in the role of chief devotee (like a Hindu raja in former days), to the mortification of Christians in India and abroad.[74] But in 1813, under enormous pressure from English evangelical activists, the Company reversed its policy with the inclusion of a clause in its charter that not only permitted missionaries to enter the country and supported the appointment of an Anglican bishop for India, but also set aside £10,000 for Indian education.[75] The history of this change illustrates a great deal about the conflicting (and often conflicted) philosophies of rule that competed for prominence during the consolidation of British imperialism at the turn of the eighteenth century.

During the late 1700s and early 1800s a series of evangelical revivals in England and Europe generated support for a more activist style of Protestantism that sought to apply Christian ethical standards to public life.[76] Key figures in this movement in England were a group of politically well-placed evangelicals in the Church of England known as the Clapham Sect, among whom was Charles Grant, an influential director and sometime chairman of the East India Company and, ironically, "brother-in-law" to Zeenut, the Indian concubine mentioned earlier.[77] Insofar as they focused their attention on India, proponents of this civic-minded form of religiosity condemned the Company's tactical support of Hinduism and rallied opinion in favor of actively promoting Christianity in India as a means of improving the moral conditions of England's "Asiatic territories."

With the help of William Wilberforce, a member of Parliament, Charles Grant initially launched his campaign to elicit the Company's support for missions in 1793, on the occasion of Parliament's renewal of the Company's charter. His famous tract, *Observations of the State of Society among the Asiatic Subjects of Great Britain*, was written to support a measure that would add a paragraph pledging the Company's financial support for both Christian missions and public educational establishments.[78] Grant's tract was a crucial element in the contest between "British Indomania" and "British Indophobia" to construct an authoritative representation of Indian society that would undergird the specific policies and practices of British imperialism.[79] In explicit opposition to the political philosophy of administrators like William Hastings who felt that British rule should adapt itself to Indian customs and religious traditions, which he viewed with "warm tolerance," Grant felt that the British had a duty, as bearers of a higher civilization, to reform India along the lines of its own customs and religion. As Ainslie Embree puts it, "What made Grant's tract significant was that it was a serious attempt to find a sanction for permanent British rule in India through a comparative evaluation of the intrinsic merits of the two civilizations that were confronting each other."[80]

Observations begins with a lengthy assessment of British moral influence during Britain's thirty-five-year tenure as political ruler of its Indian territories. In this time, Grant argued, the Company did little or nothing to improve the moral conditions of its "Asiatic subjects." But, were the British to withdraw, Grant feared that Indian rulers or other European rulers would be even more rapacious and unscrupulous than the British had been. What India needed, he argued, was for Britain to take a firmer hand in its administration, and such a shift in political engagement should begin with a thorough assessment of the moral conditions of the Company's Indian territories.

Grant culled the most damning statements from reports and travelogues written by Europeans and drew on his own twenty-two years of experience in Bengal to conclude that Indians were "a people exceedingly depraved . . . [who] exhibit human nature in a very degraded, humiliating state, and are at once, objects of disesteem and commiseration." As many British missionaries, administrators, and legislators would do in the years to come, Grant traced the root cause of India's moral degradation to its political system (despotism) and its religion. In India, opined Grant, "every man is a slave to those above him, and a despot to those below him; the more he is oppressed, the more he oppresses; and thus is diffused a temper of universal enmity, acting secretly or openly according to opportunities." The reason was the pervasive influence of the caste system endorsed by Hindu priests and enshrined in Brahmanical law texts such as the *Manusmriti*.[81]

According to Grant, any effort to reform Indian society through the British administration of justice was futile as long as Hinduism prevailed, and the reform of Hinduism was hopeless. But, he felt, considerable hope lay in reforming Indians. Opposing those who argued that Indians were *inherently* backward, Grant argued, "The history of many nations who have advanced from rudeness to refinement contradicts this hypothesis; according to which, the Britons ought still to be going naked, to be feeding on acorns, and sacrificing human victims in the Druidical groves." The best remedy for the social ills that he felt degraded Indian society—mendacity, ignorance, cruelty, and blind faith in tradition—was the introduction of "light and knowledge" onto what he took to be the "benighted" Indian scene. Toward this end he proposed that the state empower the Company's Court of Directors to send missionaries to British territories in India and provide for their maintenance, along with establishing "at modest expense . . . places of gratuitous instruction in reading and writing English."[82]

The political rhetoric that Grant marshaled in this tract to provide moral legitimation for the continuation, indeed, the expansion and intensification of British rule in India came to be shared by many in the decades to come. Grant's strong sense of Britain's moral and civilizational superiority and its moral obligation to improve the conditions of inferior societies under its rule would become, in time, "almost unquestioned assumptions" among civil servants in India.[83] In short, he provided a logically coherent and emotionally satisfying justification for imperialism. But it is worth considering the perspectives of those against whom he and his supporters had to contend. As Stanley Wolpert observed, "Britons were no more united on how to handle and rule their Indian empire than Indians were in their responses to the consolidation of British rule."[84] First of all, there were many who objected that Grant's representations of Indian moral character were grossly exaggerated and unfair.[85] Furthermore, at least three schools of thought argued in favor of the Company's established policy of noninterference with regard to India's customs and religious practices: those who felt that Indians couldn't or wouldn't change, those who felt that they shouldn't have to, and those who felt that if Indians did change it would not serve British interests. Many Company servants and directors shared a very pragmatic interest in India, and their primary concern was to maintain public order so that trade and the regular collection of revenue could continue undisturbed. They may well have agreed with Grant as to the moral condition of Britain's "Asiatic subjects," but they felt that little could be done to change them.[86] In support of their position that Indians were incapable of changing in the manner envisioned by evangelicals and reformers, such men frequently resorted to popular racial and climatological theories to account for everything from the Indians' supposed "indolence" and "feebleness" to their easily offended religious sentiments. The second point of view that argued for the maintenance of the status quo came from those who felt that India had a perfectly good civilization and therefore didn't need the improving efforts of missionaries. This school of thought had and would continue to have considerable support among Company officers. Influenced by the work of British Orientalists, notably William Jones, Rev. William Robertson, and contributors to the journal *Asiatic Researches*, they saw in Indian culture evidence of a civilization of great antiquity and depth, with a literature in Sanskrit and Persian that rivaled that of the West in its poetic beauty and philosophic depth.[87]

Interestingly, the most vocal opposition to the evangelicals' proposed "Pious Clause" in 1793 centered on yet another objection: that if Indians were exposed to Christianity and Western learning, they would change, but in such a way that would spell the end of British imperialism. With both the American and the French Revolutions in the background, some British leaders feared that if Indians got a taste of English education and "English" religion, they would start to desire "English liberty." Grant anticipated this objection in his *Observations* and met it with a tortured explanation of how Christianity did not *necessarily* inspire the desire for liberty, but could indeed create more obedient subjects, and that, in any case, the Indians (unlike the colonists in America) were too "feeble" to fight for their independence.[88] Nevertheless, at this time, the Pious Clause met with so much opposition that it was withdrawn.

Twenty years later, on the occasion of the next renewal of the Company's charter in 1813, Wilberforce and Grant made their bid again and prevailed. Key to their success was their removal of language that stipulated the government's material support of missionaries; instead, they settled for legal permission for missionaries to enter the country and a bishop, reserving their plea for financial support for education. Still, there remained some resistance to the clause in Parliament, many of whose members felt that interfering with Indian customs would arouse opposition to British rule. Memories of the Vellore Mutiny of

1806 were still fresh, and the concept of Indians as extremely sensitive to violations of their national honor or tradition was gaining widespread support. The Clapham Sect wore down this resistance through a concerted public relations campaign, which mobilized dozens, perhaps hundreds of different groups that met in taverns and lodges to sign petitions in support of the clause. According to one account, fifteen hundred different groups sent petitions to Parliament.[89]

As a result of this energetic lobbying, the East India Company charter renewed in 1813 included a paragraph that permitted missionaries to be sent to the colonies. The crucial Pious Clause ran: "Whereas it is the duty of this Country to promote the Interest and Happiness of the Native Inhabitants of the British Dominions in India and such measures ought to be adopted as may tend to the Introduction among them of useful Knowledge and of religious Improvement . . . it is expedient to make provision for granting Permission to Persons desirous of going to or remaining in India for the above Purpose."[90] In spite of the opposition its supporters met, the language of the new clause clearly reflects a change in the British government's understanding of the imperial mission. Although over the years the explicitly religious model of improvement advocated by evangelicals would shift to a secularized version of progress touted by utilitarians, with the signing of the new charter the civilizing mission of British colonialism was made official.

This is not to say that elements opposed to Christian evangelism disappeared altogether at the start of the nineteenth century. On the contrary, even after they were granted permission to enter the country, missionaries in India had to contend with administrators who might be more or less supportive of their aims. In addition, there certainly were also individual missionaries and even missionary societies that had a less salutary view of the relationship between the British Empire and the Church and who did not subscribe to the ideology of British superiority. And yet the legitimating discourse behind British imperialism that was articulated in Grant's *Observations* and made official in the Pious Clause of the Company's 1813 charter opened the doors to missionary societies, unleashing a flow of persons and ideas and critiques that could not be reversed. Proponents of the ideology of British racial superiority urged on British residents in India the "public observance of Christian morality as an affirmation of British racial superiority over the character, religious beliefs and customs of India's peoples."[91] The British, it was felt, had a higher calling in India. As Thomas Middleton, the first bishop of Calcutta, put it before a gathering of Company agents in 1814, "God had not conferred empires on nations merely to gratify their avarice or ambition."[92] This renovated imperialist regime intensified racial divisions between Europeans and Indians, condemning as immoral, among other things, the unsanctified liaisons between Indian women and European men. In addition, the controversy over the introduction of the Pious Clause made the nature and purpose of the British presence in India a subject of national debate.[93]

Missionary societies of the early nineteenth century sought to channel this interest in Britain's overseas ventures into material and social backing for their projects. In response to hundreds of sermons and pamphlets decrying the "state of moral darkness" that hung over Britain's territories in India, congregations and voluntary societies in India and Britain over the years raised thousands of pounds to send a small but steady stream of missionary personnel to the colonies. In 1814, the Church Missionary Society (CMS), closely associated with the Church of England, established a corresponding committee in Madras. In 1816 the Wesleyan Methodist Missionary Society (WMMS), a nonconformist British group, started a chapel in Madras. Around this time, the nonconformist London Missionary Society (LMS) also expanded its efforts, which at the time were focused mainly on Travancore. For fifteen years Rev. William Tobias Ringletaube had been the only European missionary in the far south, but between 1816 and 1819 four other men arrived to bolster the ranks, and in 1838, five more arrived at once.[94] British Christians were by no means alone in these efforts to send and support missionaries in India; Germans and Americans also took an active part. Thanks to international networks of evangelical activists that emerged out of the eighteenth-century Protestant revivals in Europe, many of the men who actually staffed the missionary stations of the British Church Missionary Society were German-speaking Lutherans trained at the pietist mission center in Basel, Switzerland.[95] These networks extended across the Atlantic as well. The American Board of Commissioners for Foreign Missions (ABCFM), an interdenominational but predominately Congregationalist American missionary society with its base in New England, established a mission in Ceylon in 1816 and founded a mission in Madurai in 1835.[96]

Motives and Mass Movements: Individual versus Group Conversions in the Nineteenth Century

The Protestant missionaries who arrived after 1813 used a variety of techniques to attract followers and disseminate Christian teachings. They published and broadcast tracts in English and in the local vernacular, preached in bazaars, held divine services in the open air, visited homes, attended religious festivals and fairs, and itinerated through villages with attention-grabbing novelties such as pianos and magic lantern shows. One of the most important methods of evangelism of this period was the establishment of Christian schools. The Protestant educational project was always a two-tiered system: English medium schools for the elites and vernacular medium schools for the masses. Although the vernacular schools were extremely important in terms of providing basic literacy skills to many thousands of students, English medium education arguably had greater influence on colonial Indian society at large.[97] The strategy of proselytizing to the elite through the establishment of English medium Christian schools was a classic top-down strategy of social change inspired by missionary educators who were deeply influenced by the eighteenth-century Scottish Enlightenment. Particularly influential were Alexander Duff in Calcutta and John Anderson and William Miller in Madras, all of whom worked under the rubric of the Scottish Free Church Mission. This strategy depended for its success on the demand for English education by an increasingly influential stratum of Indian society, those sophisticated, wealthy translators, scribes, clerks, and brokers known in Bengal as the *bhadralok*, a group of people "in the middle" of the old landed aristocracy and the new mercantile rich, the English-speaking colonial rulers and their heavily taxed Indian subjects.

Although Indian elite families actively lobbied for missionary schools, there were significant trade-offs for the benefit of English education. The sons of Indian elite families found themselves separated from their home environment and subjected to a forceful, unrelenting critique of Indian religion, history, and society and a corresponding exaltation of Christian scripture and doctrine. As many scholars have noted, the critique of Hinduism launched in these schools motivated a number of Hindu social reformers to reevaluate and reformulate the Hindu tradition by applying the principles of rationalism and historical criticism to the Brahmanical textual corpus.[98] Other Indian intellectuals educated in mission schools channeled their opposition to the onslaught of the evangelicals into political resistance, in some cases taking courage from defenses of Hinduism and Indian culture proposed by the Hindu reformers. Another effect of English education was that some students were attracted by the systematic, rational, and empathetic presentation of Christianity in mission schools, and a few of them converted.

Missionaries made much of the high-caste converts they attracted through their schools. To this day, literate high-caste converts such as the Veḷḷāla brothers from Tirunelveli, Krishna and Muttaiya Piḷḷai, the Bengali Brahman converts Lal Behari Dey and Krishna Mohan Banerjea, and the Maharastrian Brahman Pandita Ramabai continue to receive a great deal of attention in scholarship on Christianity in India.[99] Such converts were the pride and joy of missionary educators, who longed to believe that the inherent superiority of their religion would be proven when rational, educated, "well-bred" men and women embraced Christianity on the sole basis of its "objective" comparison with any other religious system. Nineteenth-century missionaries were deeply committed to millennialist ideas that promised that the Second Coming of Christ would take place only after the whole world had been informed about the saving power of Jesus Christ. Antony Copley argues persuasively that much of the hubris of English and American missionaries can be explained by their expectation that Hinduism (and other "heathen" religions) would collapse like "the walls of Jericho" once the trumpet of the Christian gospel was sounded.[100] High-caste and well-to-do converts were highly valued because they confirmed such beliefs and demonstrated that someone could be persuaded to embrace Christianity on its spiritual merits alone, without any material inducements.

High-caste converts suffered enormously as a result of publicly committing themselves to Christianity. Because of their contact with *mleccha* foreign missionaries and low-caste converts, high-caste converts were considered polluted by their caste fellows and ostracized from Hindu civil society. Perversely, it was this very suffering, this ordeal by fire, that made high-caste converts "pure" in the eyes of missionaries, as they did not gain anything materially by converting. On the other hand, because of the taboo restrictions placed on them, members of high-caste groups who embraced Christianity did not precipitate conversion movements among their families and caste fellows as members of low-caste groups did. As Geoffrey Oddie writes, "Generally speaking, high-caste converts were effectively isolated, and Hindu society, having ejected the affected member, sealed itself against the possibility of further contamination."[101]

Many of the best-known Indian converts embraced Christianity on the basis of an individual experience of conversion, brought about by their formal exposure to the teachings of the Protestant Church through mission schools, but most accessions to the Christian community came through the simultaneous conversion of a family or caste section. These so-called mass movements occurred mostly among rural members of the lower castes, and in many cases took place during or just after a period of famine or epidemic disease.[102] Because these massive group conversions took place at moments of acute social and environmental crisis, many critics dismissed them as inauthentic. Indeed, the specter of inauthenticity hung over the subject of conversion in colonial India for a long time, generating anxiety about the motives that brought thousands of impoverished, socially marginalized Indians into the Christian fold.[103]

To a great extent, the concern about authenticity had to do with the fear that converts were only pretending to be interested in Christianity in order to receive material benefits from the mission. Yet, as we saw in the case of the Shanar converts in Tirunelveli in 1800–1803, persecution, not prosperity, often followed close on the heels of conversion. Abuse similar to that experienced by Tirunelveli Shanars (such as physical attacks, looting, boycotts, and exclusion from use of village wells) continued to afflict low-caste converts throughout the nineteenth and twentieth centuries. As the census supervisor of 1911 testified, for many low castes the benefits of conversion scarcely outweighed the costs: "The Panchama ['fifth' caste, untouchable] convert is reminded sharply of the debts that he or his ancestors have contracted to the village magnates; he finds it difficult if not impossible to obtain land on *darkhast* [an application, petition, or contract to rent land]; water difficulties crop up; occasionally the fine old Indian war-horse, the false case, snorting takes the field."[104] In spite of these obvious material disincentives, critics of the Protestant missions worried that converts came to their decision to embrace Christianity because of the promise of material goods and protection from exploitation by secular or religious authorities. The presence of such inducements, whether actual or perceived, was said to eliminate the possibility that converts could be acting out of free conscience. This argument effectively denied the agency of all converts except for a very few financially independent ones, and thus coincided with racist stereotypes about the weak will and passivity of the Indian population.

Despite their reservations about the validity of group conversions, supporters of Christian missions had to arrive at some justification to permit the acceptance of these large accessions of new converts. Given the missions' near obsession with statistical measures of success, any countable increase in new members could not be dismissed. In the late nineteenth century missionaries sometimes sought to deflect attention from the novelty of these large accessions, or their coincidence with the distribution of famine relief, by assimilating them to outpourings of faith from biblical times.[105] Many recognized that Indians who became Christians in large groups did so for "unspiritual" reasons but argued that it would be indefensible to deny them access to religious education and the guidance of the Church on this basis.[106] If members of the first generation were less than model Christians, they argued, with education and training subsequent generations would be.[107]

By the 1930s, most supporters of Christian missions came to grant the mass movements a certain validity. Instrumental in bringing about the change in opinion was the publication of J. Waskom Pickett's *Christian Mass Movements in India* (1933). Using a systematic study of the social and economic conditions of villagers in ten areas that had experienced mass conversions, along with survey data on motives culled from converts themselves, Pickett articulated in the cool language of sociology the unsurprising conclusion that poor and low-caste converts indeed had both spiritual and materialistic motives for seeking alliances with Christian missions. He also recorded the various lifestyle changes observed by both the surveyors and the converts' non-Christian neighbors, testifying to the ability of "mass movement Christians" to improve their living conditions when efficiently organized and aided by Christian institutions. Pickett argued, in conclusion, that given the social organization of Indian society, where collective identities through family or caste membership were primary, group conversion was the mode most "natural" to India, and should be encouraged rather than discouraged.[108]

Although the focus of my study is on the period between 1850 and 1920, it should be noted that changes in the nature of the colonial state in the twentieth century gave mass conversion movements new meaning, which people tend to project backward onto the conversion movements of the nineteenth century and earlier. New modes of governance introduced by the British, particularly the practice of classifying and counting individuals in the census, transformed the relationship between religion and the state. Census operations gave rise to an awareness of the rates of population increase or decrease, investing religious conversion movements, in which large numbers of people appeared to exit one category and enter another, with new emotional resonance, whether of hopeful expansiveness or a dread of extinction.[109] Even more significant, these census categories, especially those having to do with religion, became the basis for political mobilization when the constitutional reforms of the Indian Councils Act (1909) and the Montagu-Chelmsford Reforms (1918) transferred more political power to Indian subjects through elections.[110] Finally, another modern form of governance that radically transformed the meaning of religious identity (and thus of large groups of people changing their religious identity) was the development of a system of personal law, where every colonial subject (and eventually, every Indian citizen) had the right to be governed in matters related to the family according to the "traditional" laws of his or her community. As religious identity became more deeply imbricated with notions of citizenship both in electoral politics and in the emergence of personal law, conversion, but especially mass conversion, came to be seen as a profoundly disruptive political act, in which people's claims to be motivated by spiritual feelings were regarded as hollow at best. Many present-day opponents of religious conversion in India would no doubt look back on the nineteenth-century conversions and see them in the same light. But such a view, depends on two unsubstantiated assumptions: first, that religion as such is a realm of human action completely or largely separate from material or social concerns, such that if materialistic motives enter into religious matters these matters are no longer really religious; second, that the religion one is born into is the natural, default form of religion, adherence to which has a "halo of disinterestedness," whereas conversion needs to be explained.[111]

Within the religious worlds of nineteenth-century Tamil Hindus, secular and spiritual power were by no means differentiated. From the temple ritual examined earlier to the trance-based rites of prophesying and exorcism that I will examine in the next chapter, Tamils looked to deities for *both* protection in the world and salvation beyond it. This is particularly evident during ecological, social, and *religious* crises brought about by natural disasters such as famine, floods, and epidemics. During times of terrible natural disasters, when repeated sacrifices, vows, and festivals were unable to induce the gods to restore their protective shield over the communities, some people began to doubt the effectiveness of traditional worship and abandoned their koyils and *deyvams* (deities). Missionaries reported (with considerable satisfaction) that during the crises brought about by famine, recent converts frequently destroyed their old temples and images and erected Christian churches or schoolhouses on their ruined remains. But disappointment and disillusionment with the capacity of protectors, whether human or divine, to shield the follower from harm could go both ways. Through careful examination of the membership lists of Christian churches connected with the LMS in Travancore and their fluctuations during the famine years, the historical anthropologist Dick Kooiman found that people could lose faith in either Christian or Indian gods (or presumably both) when confronted directly by disease and starvation.[112] The records of the LMS indicate that during the famine of 1870, the missions reported substantial losses rather than gains in adherence. Ten years previously, during the 1860 famine, when the Protestant mission sponsored a variety of food-for-work programs, many hundreds of new converts entered the Church. Kooiman notes that the difference in the direction of adherence can be explained by the presence in 1870 of large-scale employment offered by the Public Works Department and the coffee plantations in the Western Ghats. In other words, by 1870 (as opposed to 1860) famine victims had alternative ways to obtain relief and survive the calamity besides turning to the charitable outlets of the Christian missions. The unpublished letters and reports of missionaries in the field indicate that many Christians at this time abandoned the Church and returned to their ancestral faith.[113]

The movement of Indians back and forth between Christianity and the worship of their traditional deities suggests that there was, as Kooiman puts it, a "continual border crossing between Hinduism and Christianity." He writes, "Famines and epidemics merely created a kind of rush hour in an already existing religious boundary traffic." On the other hand, he argues, one should not attribute to the Indians the assumption that people could have only one religious identity at a time. What missionaries decried as "backsliding" could have been a function of the fact that "people could easily combine their old religion with Christianity, and change of religion often amounted to a change in emphasis from one trend to another within a larger religious complex."[114] The changes back and forth may also be read as a result of the fact that converts sought out the same things from the Christian god as they did from their traditional deities: relief from present difficulties and protection against their return.

Just as Indian Christians occasionally resorted to the protection of traditional deities by engaging in sacrifices, so did they carry over into their new faith some of the old assumptions about the nature of the divine. A strong belief that the protective function of the divine was vital to the well-being of the community is apparent in the modes of worship that Indian Christians directed to the Christian deity. Tamil Christian lyrics from nineteenth-century hymnbooks abound in references to God's "blessing," his *asirvātam*, which extended over the Christian flock, maintaining health and ensuring the fertility of both crops and women.[115] Songs praising God's ability to ward off drought and the famine and disease epidemics that almost invariably swept through in its wake testify to beliefs in the effectiveness of the divine in the world: "The cruelty of the mounting plague has overflowed the banks./Change it, oh compassionate God, by your assistance and unbounded generosity./Oh Lord of all why don't you look with a loving glance!/Why don't you look with a loving glance!"[116] That these lyrics employ the metaphor of God's powerful, transformative "glance" or "gaze" (*kaṭaikkaṇ*), so prominent in Hindu ritual and myth, may be yet another indication of the ways Christian religious ideas were mapped onto old ones.

The imbrication of worldly and otherworldly power is also seen in the correspondences between the relationships established in temple ritual among deities, the principal sponsors of Hindu temples, priests, and the rank-and-file worshippers and the relations of patronage and protection, service and exchange that bound together the social community outside the temple. As converts transferred their allegiance to new centers of power in Indian society, they sought to gain protection and assistance from the missionaries and other foreign authorities, just as they would have from high-caste patrons.

Summary

In the next chapter I provide more detailed descriptions of the lives of those groups of low-caste Hindus who converted to Christianity in great numbers. For now, it is important to stress that even though the socially marginalized castes who converted in large numbers to Christianity were oppressed and economically exploited, they had social institutions, values, and religious practices that ordered and gave meaning to their lives. The large-scale conversion to Christianity of members of low castes was integrally related to processes by which groups that had been marginalized in precolonial and early colonial social formations were able to forge new identities better suited to their aspirations of social mobility. When considered in the light of the concepts and categories of Tamil religiosity, which positively affirm the potency and efficacy of the divine in this world, conversion movements to Christianity appear as the movement of marginalized people toward new centers of power and influence emerging in the social landscape. For this reason, mass movements to Christianity need to be viewed in relation to alternative strategies used by socially and economically marginalized groups for gaining autonomy in precolonial and colonial India.

2

Colonial Knowledge and the Creation of Respectable Castes

One of the good qualities of Sir Thomas Munro, formerly Governor of Madras, was that, like Rama and Rob Roy, his arms reached to his knees, or, in other words, he possessed the kingly quality of an *Ajānubāhu*, which is the heritage of kings, or those who have blue blood in them. This particular anatomical character I have met with myself only once, in a Shānān, whose height was 173 cm. and span of the arms 194 cm. (+21cm.). Rob Roy, it will be remembered, could, without stooping, tie his garters, which were placed two inches below the knee.

—Thurston and Rangachari, *Castes and Tribes of Southern India*

How do we know anything about the low-caste groups that converted in large numbers to Christianity? They were not the kind of people usually included in the annals of written history. Economically dependent, excluded from the primary channels of gaining prestige and status as well as from the literate domains of Indian society, who would have written anything about them? Descriptions of the social lives and customs of low castes in the nineteenth century come mainly from two sets of colonial sources: missionary reportage and administrative records. In the first two sections of this chapter, I deal with each of these in turn, attempting to identify the preoccupations that missionaries and colonial administrators brought to their representations of Indian culture, religion, physiognomy, economics, and so forth, particularly their representations of low-caste groups. As is widely acknowledged, far from merely reflecting the nature of Indian society, the categories and concepts that missionaries and colonial administrators generated out of their studies were instrumental in shaping it.[1] Yet, it is important to emphasize that Indians did not submit passively to the epistemological machinations of the colonizers. Indian Christian converts were in the forefront of efforts to contest the representations produced by colonizers. After examining the production of colonial understandings of caste, gender, and religion, I investigate how Shanar converts appropriated these and deployed them in the creation of a new, respectable identity as Nadar Kshatriyas. The controversies surrounding Rev. Robert Caldwell's infamous tract, *The Tinnevelly Shanars*, illustrate how Shanar/Nadar Christians, in cooperation with their non-Christian caste fellows, countered colonial representations of their group and gained support for their own self-descriptions.

The British developed several key ideas about India in their effort to govern a large and culturally diverse region. The conception of India that grew out of these ideas was based partly (perhaps mostly) on the drive to *know* India in such a way that it could be *ruled*. Several scholars, notably Ronald Inden and Bernard S. Cohn, have reexamined Indian history and colonial historiography in the light of Edward Said's insights into the relationship between power and knowledge under colonial rule, and have identified caste and religion as key concepts used for knowing and subordinating India.[2] Following Ashis Nandy and Mrinalini Sinha, I would add that gender is another key category that contributed to the ideological formation that constituted colonial knowledge about India.[3] In his psychologically nuanced studies of British colonialism in India, Nandy persuasively reveals how deeply relations of domination at the heart of the colonial project were gendered so that British rule was naturalized by conceiving of the British as hypermasculine and the Indians as hyperfeminine. I want to add that relations of power among indigenous groups in India were gendered as well. It was not simply that the salient differences between castes were identified as those having to do with gender and sexuality (e.g., marriage customs, puberty ceremonies, behavior of women); different castes themselves were subtly represented by the British as being more masculine or more feminine in relation to one another.

Colonial Knowledge about India

North American and English debates over the abolition of the slave trade, stimulated in large part by the Clapham Sect, brought about an increasing sense of social responsibility among Protestant Christians around the world.[4] Protestant missionaries in India took the lead in documenting and publicizing the abuses perpetrated on the marginalized groups from among whom they drew the largest numbers of converts. As we saw in the previous chapter, missionaries agitated for the reform of abuses perpetrated by both British and Indian officials and nonofficials. But missionary activism did not stem from social altruism alone. From the point of view of Protestant theology, the low castes' depths of degradation made their material and spiritual uplift a persuasive index of the power of the Christian faith. As the words of Methodist hymns attest, God's greatness was affirmed by his ability to lift up wretches from their lowly and benighted state. The low castes' conversion to Christianity, moreover, helped to justify the imperial presence of the British in India, lending a humanitarian hue to colonial rule. Imperial and evangelical aims converged when missionaries sought to learn about Indians to evangelize to them more effectively so that Christianity would prevail throughout the British Empire.

What Missionaries Knew

Missionaries recorded their observations and analyses of Indian society in a wide range of books and periodicals, from those intended for a mass audience to more learned studies. European readers were not always entirely receptive to such studies. Rev. Bartholomaeus Ziegenbalg's study of south Indian religion, *Genealogy of the South-Indian Gods* (1719), languished on a shelf for 150 years due to the resistance of Ziegenbalg's former teacher, A. H. Francke. As Francke, a renowned pietist theologian at the University of Halle, asserted, "Missionaries were sent out to extirpate heathenism, not to spread heathenish non-sense in Europe."[5] But as the foreign missionary enterprise grew throughout the nineteenth and early twentieth centuries, British and American churchgoers acquired an enormous appetite for accounts of the "heathen" in foreign lands. Books written by missionaries for consumption in the metropole drew on the conventions of social uplift literature, travel literature, and colonial ethnology to induce what might be called the *rasa* (lit. "flavor, taste") of lurid fascination. These conventions located the low-caste converts and the village communities in which they resided in a recognizable history: the Western Protestant narrative of global conquest/rescue. Missionary authors created elaborate word pictures to evoke the filthy and disease-ridden low-caste hamlets lying outside the boundaries of the village proper and lingered on those "exotic" practices involving blood sacrifice, prostitution, and spirit possession by means of which the villagers worshipped a panoply of fierce "demons and fiends." As popular literature such narratives required a happy conclusion, which was supplied by the arrival of the intrepid, dedicated missionary who delivered his low-caste followers from persecution, filth, and satanic practices. These texts share a great deal with another nineteenth-century genre, Christian literature set in the urban slums of London, Paris, New York, and other industrialized cities. Like social uplift literature, tales of missionary work in India were used to inspire Christians to support the missions with prayer and money and, in exceptional circumstances, to become missionary evangelists themselves.

The other branch of missionary literature was made up of scholarly studies of south Indian history, culture, and religion produced by nineteenth-century missionaries such as Robert Caldwell, Gustav Oppert, Henry Whitehead, and Samuel Mateer.[6] These books were also written mainly for Christian audiences in the metropole, but they were widely read by scholars and administrators in the colonies. Though missionary authors such as Caldwell and Whitehead openly interpreted Hindu religion and society through the lens of their exclusivist theology and millenarian expectations, their studies were received with great seriousness by colonial administrators (some of whom shared their evangelical assumptions).[7] Works such as Caldwell's *Tinnevelly Shanars* and Mateer's *Land of Charity* were widely quoted in official documents ranging from government orders and legal proceedings to the decennial censuses, district gazetteers, and encyclopedic studies of regional castes. However, to create a hard and fast distinction between "high" and "low" missionary literature would be mistaken. Sometimes—notoriously, in the case of Caldwell's tract, *The Tinnevelly Shanars*—a text produced for a European Christian audience was circulated and received as authoritative by officials in the colonies. As the example of *The Tinnevelly Shanars* attests, knowledge produced by missionaries and disseminated by the colonial government had decisive effects on the "objects" of knowledge.

The efforts of missionary activists brought low-caste groups into the spotlight as no other movement had before, generating knowledge about their customs and practices and the large-scale social forms in which they were enmeshed (such as the *jajmāni* system of village economic and social organization). In several notable instances, missionaries won rights for their charges, overturning centuries of oppressive custom. In Travancore, the London Missionary Society was involved in gaining relief for its Shanar (later called Nadar) converts from the hated poll tax, or head tax (which was levied on all members of the lowest castes, dead as well as living!), and *ūḻium* service, corvée labor required by the king of all his subjects. Shanars, for example, were required to provide jaggery for the mortar used in royal building projects, fresh leaves for the temple elephant, and dried palmyra leaves (*cadjans*), which the royal scribes and accountants used for writing materials.[8] Col. John Munro, resident of Travancore from 1810–1819, exempted Christian Shanars from the obligation to perform this service to the king on Sundays (so that they could observe the Christian Sabbath) and Hindu religious festivals (when they would be compelled to participate in events that offended Christian conscience).[9] As I investigate more thoroughly in chapter 6, the LMS missionaries were also instrumental in a movement among Shanar women to defy the traditional taboo against members of the low castes wearing garments above the waist or below the knees.

One of the Christians' victories that had the widest-ranging impact on the social condition of the low castes had to do with gaining access to roads. In districts throughout south India, foreign missionaries intervened on behalf of their low-caste followers to obtain the right of entry onto "public" roads. As historian Robert Frykenberg has shown, in south India roads were deeply bound up with the honor that accrued to royalty by means of their ritual perambulations through their territory (*kṣatra*). These processions mirrored the ritual treatment of gods when they were taken out of the temple to survey their territories and feted by their devotees as kings. As part of the general tendency in south Indian Hindu culture to restrict access to centers of ritual prestige to a select few, members of very low castes were forbidden from using proper roads, even when these had been built by the British. To the missionaries' repeated disappointment, colonial jurists, police, and administrators often did not endorse the Church's efforts to secure the use of public roads by low castes. For, in order to keep the support of the conservative elements in Indian society the colonial administration frequently adopted a stance of non-interference toward local customs, even when such customs were highly prejudiced against low castes.[10] In response, missionaries documented and publicized the abuse of low castes through newspapers and missionary society reports and derided the colonial state for supporting "irrational custom." This was consistent with their criticism of Hindu society as based on superstition as opposed to what they took to be the rational truth of Christianity. In addition, the missionaries' support of the low-caste cause conformed with the tendency on the part of many of them (who in many cases were themselves upwardly mobile members of artisan classes) to bridle at social prejudices that bore a resemblance to class-based prejudices in Western societies. Through this strategy of shaming the colonial state into upholding more egalitarian values missionaries and low-caste Christians prevailed in many places and won the right of access to British roads.

Notwithstanding the significance of the missionaries' concern for the social conditions of low-caste converts, foreign evangelists were still very much a part of the material and ideological enterprise of colonialism. To be sure, the number and variety of missionary societies working in nineteenth- and early twentieth-century India cautions against sweeping generalizations. Along with the social activism of the LMS missionaries, the unorthodox behavior of missionaries belonging to more progressive societies brought them into conflict with colonial authorities. The Officers of the Salvation Army, for example, radically transgressed the norms of the foreign settler community in south India by dressing as mendicants, complete with shaved heads and forehead marks, begging for alms among the Indian community, and ordaining women to serve as pastors and preachers.[11] Missionary societies connected to the official Church of England, on the other hand, like the Society for the Propagation of the Gospel (SPG), were less likely to challenge the concessions that colonial rulers made to the prejudices of local elites. As non-British citizens, U.S. and German missionaries had their own distinct and complex relationship to colonial rule. However, to overstate the benevolent influence of Protestant missionaries in colonial India would be to ignore the cultural bigotry that erupts in the writings of even the most progressive missionaries and the paternalism that often characterized missionary interventions into Indian society. More important, in my view, is that to present the assault on caste prejudices as initiated solely by foreign missionaries threatens to convey the wrong impression that low-caste groups were altogether helpless before the arrival of their would-be saviors from the Christian West. The oppression and exploitation of low castes and women in precolonial south Indian society was intense. But the representation of low castes as thoroughly downtrodden and dependent beings elides the many fine distinctions and complex relationships of patronage, dependence, and exchange that constituted the south Indian social order and tends to minimize the multiple ways in which members of the so-called low castes fought for dignity on their own behalf.

In their writings, Christian missionaries naturally paid particular attention to the religious lives of Indians and generated many models for making sense of the diversity of Indian gods, practices, beliefs, rituals, and myths. Like the Orientalists in Bengal and Madras—for example, Sir William Jones, Charles Wilkins, Nathaniel Brassey Halhed, and Francis W. Ellis—missionaries dedicated a great deal of energy to learning the indigenous languages of India. Together with the Orientalists, Christian missionaries made the religious beliefs and practices of the Indians into a discrete object of study. But whereas the Orientalists had a more empathetic approach to Indian religion and culture, nineteenth-century missionaries were almost entirely denigrating and derisive toward it. Their aim in scholarship was to identify the errors of the religion of those they wanted to transform.

One of the most important missionary scholars, whose influence on south Indian society, both Christian and non-Christian, can hardly be overstated was the Rev. Robert Caldwell of the SPG (1814–1894). His investigations led to the groundbreaking discovery of the linguistic distinctiveness of the Dravidian languages (Tamil, Telegu, Malayalam, and Kannada) from Indo-European languages such as Hindi and Gujarati.[12] Caldwell took to the intellectual debates that animated Orientalist and missionary circles with alacrity. A Scotsman of apparently nonillustrious heritage, Caldwell did not have a formal literary education until he enlisted with the LMS at age 20.[13] The later stages of his missionary training took place during a time of extraordinary revivalist ferment in Glasgow, but Caldwell described himself as a solitary reader, who took pains to keep himself out of theological controversy. He became fascinated with comparative philology through courses he took with a teacher well-acquainted with the work of German linguists, who were the acknowledged leaders in the field at the time. Caldwell left for Madras in 1837 (at the age of 23), where he spent three years learning Tamil and ministering to a congregation of Paraiyar domestic servants. He soon grew tired of the "rationalism" that was then in vogue among educated Indians, both Christian and non-Christian, and sought a new placement among a simpler, more tractable kind of people, who he felt would be more open to Christianity. His own theological inclinations led him eventually to embrace the teachings of the Church of England and transfer his loyalties from the nonconformist LMS to the theologically and socially more conservative Anglican SPG in 1840. One year later, after traveling by foot all the way from Madras to Tirunelveli, he established his home among the Shanars of Edeyengoody (*Itaiyankuṭi*, or "abode of shepherds"). Caldwell's description of his first meeting with the Shanars is typical of colonial representations of India in its fixation on their unfamiliar physical features, but it also represented his belief that among the Shanars he had found willing, malleable subjects for his reformist ambitions: "I could not but be struck first by their long ears, long pendent earrings, long hair tied in a knot behind the head like the women, their presents of sugar-candy, and their graceful salaam with folded hands. I was struck also by their mild, subdued expression, so different from the rough forwardness I had been accustomed to further north. All I saw seemed to me to augur that they belonged to an impressionable and improvable race—an augury which, generally speaking, has been amply fulfilled."[14]

Caldwell did not publish his *Comparative Grammar of the Dravidian Languages* until 1856, but it is clear from his earlier writings that he was investigating the cultural and linguistic differences between Dravidians and Brahmans as early as 1849. In his account of the religion of the Shanars, *The Tinnevelly Shanars*, whose reception history I examine in greater detail below, he argued that the Shanars were the original inhabitants of the Tamil region and a separate race from the colonizing, sacerdotal Brahmans. Apparent throughout the book are the traces of his favored intellectual method, comparative philology. This new science, the precursor to historical linguistics, analyzed languages into their purest, oldest forms by sifting out borrowed words and undoing the phonological transformations that words underwent over time and space as they migrated along with their human bearers from one region to another. In Caldwell's short treatise on the Shanars he applied this same method to religion, seeing through the current practices of the Shanars to their "original faith" and subtracting from Dravidian practices what had been borrowed or transformed through contact with the practices of Brahmans. According to the Anglican savant, such critical discernment was necessary to perceive the different influences and transformations in Shanar religious beliefs and practice. He asserted that over the centuries since the "Aryan invasion," many Shanars, along with other "Dravidian tribes," had come under the influence of the Brahman priests. The more well-to-do among the Shanars, particularly the elite class known as Nadans, or "lords of the soil," had consciously adopted some practices such as wearing the *kuṭumi* (or topknot, associated with Brahmans, as I examine in chapter 6) and Brahmanical funeral ceremonies. The rest of the Shanars manifested more subtle evidence of cultural colonization in such things as liturgical language and iconography. However, Caldwell insisted that a solid core of untouched original beliefs and practices remained the most important component of the Shanars' religious lives. In this, he followed the practices of his contemporaries in minimizing the fluidity and dynamism of identity production that today's scholars emphasize and stipulating an unchanging Dravidian core at the heart of the Shanars' religion that he grounded ultimately in a quasi-biological category: race.

Caldwell initiated his analysis of Shanar religion by identifying which of their deities were Brahmanical and which were Dravidian. His assumption that the common run of Shanars were only superfically affected by the "Brahmanization" of south India is evident in his statement that "such of the Brahmanical deities as have obtained a place in their esteem are honored merely with an annual festival and the compliment of a passing bow. But their own devils, being spirits of a very different temper, jealous, watchful, and vindictive, are worshipped with the earnestness and assidulty of a real belief." Caldwell considered the Amman goddesses and deities such as Murugan and Aiyannar to have derived from Brahmanical deities. The village Amman goddesses were "corrupt" forms of Parvati, he claimed, and Murugan and Aiyannar were really Brahmanical deities by virtue of their relationships to Shiva and Vishnu.[15] Caldwell here differed from later missionary scholars like Whitehead and W. T. Elmore, who considered the Amman goddesses totally autochtonous and therefore the paradigmatic Dravidian deities.[16]

Although Caldwell acknowledged the importance of the Amman goddesses to the Shanars, he identified "demonolatry," or demon worship, as the center of the Shanar religion. By "demons" Caldwell referred to the class of supernatural beings called *pēykaḷ*. He derived the figure of the Tamil pēy from the "popular superstition" that when a person dies a sudden, premature, or violent death, his ghost haunts the place where his body lies. But the pēy was not to be understood simply as the spirit of a deceased person. "The Shanar spirit," Caldwell wrote, "is . . . an aerification and amplification of the bad features of the deceased person's character, a goblin which, with the acquisition of super-human power has acquired a super-human malignity" (10). Any man or woman, of whatever class, caste, or race, could potentially be transmogrified after death into a pēy, but usually they were persons who had died a strikingly violent or sudden death. There was even an English officer, Capt. Pole, who died of battle wounds in Travancore in 1809 and was subsequently worshipped with offerings of alcohol and cigars (27). As this example indicates, different pēy preferred different kinds of food offerings: Some demanded that a goat be sacrificed, others desired a hog, and still others a cock (13). Though ultimately less powerful than the Amman goddesses and guardian deities of the village, pēys could be extraordinarily potent agents of disorder.

According to Caldwell, these creatures would on occasion "take a fancy to dispossess the soul and inhabit the body" of a Shanar, causing a variety of maladies that could be alleviated only by performing a ceremony in which the will of the pēy was inquired after and a sacrifice offered to induce it to leave (14). Such offerings were presented to pēy in special buildings called *pēy kōyil*, which varied considerably from the ornate style of Brahmanical temples:

> A heap of earth raised into a pyrimidical shape and adorned with
> streaks of white-wash, sometimes alternating with red ochre consti-
> tutes in the majority of cases, both the temple and the demon's im-
> age; and a smaller heap in front of the temple with a flat surface
> forms the altar. In such cases a large conspicuous tree—a tamarind,
> an umbrella tree, or even a palmrya whose leaves have never been
> cut or trimmed—will generally be observed in the vicinity. The tree
> is supposed to be the devil's ordinary dwelling place. . . . This py-
> ramidal obelisk is a distinguishing characteristic of devil worship,
> and appears to have no counterpart in Brahmanism or any other-
> ism in India. (17–18)

Caldwell read the aniconic form of worship as a sign of the primitiveness of the Shanars, indicating that, like words, architectural styles and iconography were also to be taken as clues to racial origin.

Caldwell described in great detail the ceremonies that Shanars undertook

BELL MUSIC USED IN DEMON WORSHIP.

FIGURE 2.1   "Bell Music Used in Demon Worship," from Samuel Mateer, *Native Life in Travancore* (London: W.H. Allen, 1883).

to identify and rid a person of the afflicting pēy, rituals he termed "devil dances." Such ceremonies did not require the mediation of a special priest-hood, Caldwell claimed, but rather anyone, male or female, could step forward to be the "devil dancer" (*sāmiyāṭi*).[17] He acknowledged that the dancer was usually, but not necessarily, a male village leader or official. After dressing the appointed dancer in the "vestments and ornaments appropriate to the partic-ular devil worshipped" (19), the worshippers assembled a band of musicians. The instruments used at such ceremonies included drums, horns, and an instrument Caldwell identified as "the bow," a gigantic strung bow adorned with bells, one end of which rested on a large empty pot (see figure 2.1).[18]

Caldwell's description of the beginning of the dance, during which the musicians induced trance in the devil dancer, is worth quoting at length as an example of his tendency to emphasize those elements of Shanar society that seemed most "primitive" and "barbaric:"

> When the preparations are completed and the devil-dance is about to commence, the music is at first comparatively slow, and the dancer seems impassive and sullen, and either he stands still, or moves about in gloomy silence. Gradually, as the music becomes quicker and louder, his excitement begins to rise. Sometimes to help him to work himself up into a frenzy he uses medicated draughts, cuts and lacerates his flesh till the blood flows, lashes himself with a huge whip, presses a burning torch to his chest, drinks the blood which flows from his own wounds, or drinks the blood of the sacri-fice, putting the throat of the decapitated goat to his mouth. Then, as if he had acquired new life, he begins to brandish the staff of bells and dance with a quick but wild, unsteady step. Suddenly the

afflatus descends. There is no mistaking that glare, or those frantic leaps. He snorts, he stares, he gyrates. The demon has now taken bodily possession of him; and though he retains the power of utterance and motion, both are under the demon's control, and his separate consciousness is in abeyance. The by-standers signalize the event by raising a long shout attended with a peculiar vibratory noise, caused by the motion of the hand and the tongue, or the tongue alone. The devil-dancer is now worshipped as a present deity, and every by-stander consults him respecting his disease, his wants, the welfare of his absent relatives, the offerings to be made for the accomplishment of his wishes, and, in short, every thing for which superhuman knowledge is supposed to be available. (19–20)

Despite the "I was there" authoritativeness of this visually intense, vivid account, Caldwell confessed at the end of the section that he himself never personally witnessed a devil dance except from a distance; this description thus was based on second-hand reports (20). The melodramatic tone that he adopted here reinforced the depiction of Shanars as irrational and primitive. His lingering descriptions of the types of self-mortification used to induce trance progress from the relatively mild draughts of medicine to more and more gruesome measures. Based on present-day ethnography on south Indian popular Hinduism, it seem unlikely that in a single ritual all of these methods would be used at once. Moreover, his emphasis on the visual leads him to ignore the distinction between malevolent possession by ghosts (pēy) and benevolent possession by gods (sāmi) so evident in linguistic usage. Whereas pēy are said to "catch" (piṭikka) the person whose body and voice become their vehicle, a god (sāmi or deyvam) is said to come to (vara) him or her. Caldwell's rendering of both pēy and sāmi as devil vitiated the essential distinction between possession that is sought after and welcomed and that which is feared and avoided, between pēy who spread disorder and bring affliction and gods who restore order and heal.[19]

Educated Shanars who read *The Tinnevelly Shanars* many years after its original publication vociferously objected to Caldwell's portrait, much to the author's chagrin. They did not deny that belief in pēy and the practices surrounding them were important parts of their religion, but they were angered by Caldwell's condescending tone and his relegation of Shanar religiosity and, by extension, the Shanars themselves to a place outside the fold of Hinduism. One particularly articulate Tamil spokesperson, Y. Gnanamutthoo Nadar, wrote, "Familiarity breeds contempt; and because a part of the unfortunate Shanars have placed themselves, unmasked, before the Europeans they being easily accessible to Christianity, their life was closely studied, which appeared to the Europeans as something semi-civilized and unique." Gnanamutthoo contested the missionary's claim that the beliefs and rituals centered on *sā-miyāṭutal* were exotic forms peculiar to the supposedly primitive, "Dravidian" Shanars. "Let them also study the lives of the other so called high castes," he wrote, "they will in every respect find that they are in no way superior to the average Shanar level." Gnanamutthoo referred to English-language newspaper reports in the *Madras Mail* to prove that Kammalars (goldsmiths) and Maravars (hereditary watchmen) also participated in these kinds of rituals. He also advocated a kind of scientific survey of the 266 small temples found in the town of Tinnevelly to prove that many castes shared the religious beliefs and practices that Caldwell attributed uniquely to the Shanars.[20] As I will discuss further, the way Caldwell's Shanar critics deployed the forms of colonial knowledge production illustrates the way colonized groups seized the instruments of knowledge that the British used to objectify Indians and turned them to their own purposes.

Economic and Social Conditions of Low Castes

Before presenting my analysis of the representation of low-caste groups produced by the colonial administrators, it seems appropriate to offer a sketch of their social and economic conditions as these have been distilled from colonial archives by present-day scholars. One feature shared by those caste groups who converted to Christianity in large numbers was their putatively "polluting" nature. The low castes' purported state of pollution was associated with their traditional occupations, which put them into frequent contact with substances considered ritually impure in Hindu culture: blood, human and animal corpses, excrement, and dirt of all sorts. The leather-worker caste of Chakkiliyars and subsections within the predominately agricultural Pallar and Paraiyar castes who served as scavengers, sweepers, grave diggers, barbers, midwives, and leather workers all worked with such substances. While carrying out their so-called traditional occupations, these groups transported impurities outside the village boundaries. In this way they provided essential services to the community while fulfilling an important ritual function, that of preserving the village from its own pollution. The permanent state of impurity that was thought to adhere to them as a result, however, also served as justification for their expulsion beyond the very village boundaries they maintained.[21]

Because of the systematic enforcement of taboos based on their putative impurity, low castes were excluded from nearly all the established channels for gaining prestige in Tamil society. In Tamil-speaking areas of the Madras Presidency, a physical boundary, marked by a road, lane, or fields, separated the residences of the polluting castes (the *cēri*) from those of the nonpolluting castes (the *Kirāmam*).[22] In addition to being excluded from the spatial center of the Hindu village community, low castes were also prohibited from approaching its religious center, the Brahmanical Hindu temple. Members of low-caste groups could not, therefore, participate in the primary system of distribution of widely recognized social goods.

In spite of their shared status as polluting members of society marginalized from centers of ritual power, the low castes of south India were not one undifferentiated mass who were equally subject everywhere to the domination of other castes. The different caste groups that were classified as outside the fourfold *varṇa* system had distinctive traditions, practices, occupations, and modes of life. They were sometimes bitter rivals with one another, as were, for example, the Malas and Madigas of Andhra Pradesh and the Chakkiliyars and Paraiyars of Tamil Nadu. And frequently, there were distinct status divisions within low-caste groups. The elite sector among Pallars and Paraiyars, for example, were the caste headmen, who were responsible for raising labor gangs to work on the fields of their masters. These leaders had their own ritual perquisites and a generally higher status and standard of living than the rank and file.[23] Shanars also had their elite class, called Nadans, or "lords of the soil." In the palmyra-growing regions of Travancore and Tirunelveli, the Nadans controlled large tracts of land and exploited the labor of Shanar climbers, who did the difficult work of collecting the sap while the Nadans reaped the profits.[24]

Even members of the same caste who resided in different ecological regions enjoyed different degrees of status and independence. As indicated by David Ludden's painstaking analysis of the different ecologies and economies of the wet and dry regions of the Tirunelveli district, the social situation of Pallar and Paraiyar cultivators depended in great measure on the availability of water and the method of agriculture used as a result. Very low-caste laborers in wetland areas along the banks of rivers like the Tambraparni in Tirunelveli district were locked into tight relations of dependency with landlords, whereas members of the same castes in dry-zone areas were more independent. In the wet zone, complex techniques for artificially irrigating land were developed which allowed small amounts of land to produce large yields. These conditions also gave rise to a two-tiered social order consisting of a landowning elite that controlled the technology of irrigation and did not work the land and a degraded class of impoverished laborers who did. It is relevant to note that the caste name *Veḷḷāḷar* comes from the Tamil compound *veḷḷam* ("water," "flood," and, by extension, "abundance") + *āṇmai* ("lordship," "management"). Thus, *Veḷḷāḷar* literally means "those who manage water" or "irrigators." Ludden concedes that it is not altogether clear how landowning Brahmans and Vellalars induced others to work for them. Perhaps the laborers were willing to exchange a precarious existence as independent cultivators in the dry "sky-looking" regions (the *vāṇampārttu pūmi*, which depended on rain for its fertility) for subsistence and clienthood in wet areas. Such an option would naturally have been more attractive in times of drought or famine.[25]

But security in such cases came at a high price. As Ludden writes, "Laboring client cultivators, of course, entered the caste system at the very lowest stratum. They traded subsistence for untouchability in each generation. Their lowliness found expression in public behavior directed towards them—in temples, fields, housing locations, and on roads." In addition, their own bodily hexis connoted lowness relative to higher castes. Members of very low-caste groups had to shrink in the presence of higher castes by lowering their body or moving to a place of lower elevation, such as the side of the road. Once again, the etymology of caste names is relevant. *Paḷḷar* is derived from the Tamil word for "lowness," *paḷḷam*, as of a ditch, a furrow, or the artificially lowered rice paddy fields in which the Pallars toiled.[26] Ludden's analysis of the social consequences of wet-zone agriculture in Tirunelveli could be extended to the other water-rich climates in south India: Travancore on the western side of the Western Ghats and the river valleys of the Vaigai and the Kaveri, which spawned the rich urban culture of Madurai, Trichonopoly, and Tanjore. Here too, labor-intensive rice paddy cultivation on irrigated lands facilitated the emergence of similarly hierarchical and interdependent social orders.

In the dry-zone areas, ecological conditions permitted very different modes of social life. Ludden writes: "Very low-caste families, such as untouchable Pallas and Pariahs, could in the dry zone set themselves up as relatively independent peasant households, giving their very low status in the regional caste system much less degraded social content here than in the wet zone."[27] An abundance of land that required only the coordinated labor of a well-integrated family allowed virtually anyone to set up cultivation in his own domain. The Christian villages of Nazareth, Jerusalem, and Dohnavur were established in such dry-zone areas. The relative autonomy that Christians enjoyed in these settlements was directly related to the absence of competition from other castes. In such villages, Shanars, Pallars, or Paraiyars were the dominant and often the majority caste.

Consequently, the self-concept of the very low castes who resided in dry-zone areas differed from that of low castes in other, wetter ecological regions. Though it is difficult to ascertain this precisely, some evidence suggests that low-caste residents of dry-zone areas did not internalize a servant mentality to the same degree that their counterparts in wet-zone areas did. Ludden writes that the British discovered that they could not induce the "laboring castes" of the dry-zone areas to do road work in exchange for coolie wages, for they "did not consider themselves mere laborers at others' command." Moreover, "because they would not volunteer, and because they were not under the command of village high-caste families, [East India] Company officers had to use force to put them into road gangs, under the justification that all untouchable castes were of the same status, whatever their local circumstance."[28] This is just one, somewhat anecdotal piece of evidence, but it clearly suggests that the British themselves were in part responsible for promulgating the notion that untouchable groups were uniformly servile, slave-like castes who lacked the material or ideological resources necessary for self-assertion. They derived this notion from their encounters with slavery in other parts of the world as well as from their observations of the treatment of very low-caste, untouchable groups in the wet-zone regions of south India.

Among the very low castes, there were numerous forms of agricultural bondage (*aṭimai, paṇṇaiyāl, paṭiyāl*), which foreign observers tended to group under the term "slavery," though the conditions of bondage in south India did not correspond with the slavery of ancient Rome or Egypt or the African slave trade. When the English East India Company assumed the role of regional ruler, responsible for the collection of revenue, it put a great deal of energy into understanding the property relations of the area. The notion of shares was fundamental to the economic systems of the region (just as it was central to the religious systems). Ownership, in the sense of having exclusive rights to property, was relatively unknown in the region; rather, dominant groups had greater rights (*kāṇi*) to the shares (*paṅku*) in any given property or enterprise, whether it was the produce of a palmyra tree or the yield of a rice paddy or cotton field. Economically vulnerable individuals, like the laborers in the wetland areas, received small amounts of shares that were disproportionate to the large amount of labor they expended. Indeed, in the form of Tamil bondage relations that was closest to forms of slavery familiar to Westerners, the economically and socially powerful held shares in a Pallar or Paraiyar individual's own productive labor. The British inserted themselves into this indigenous system of labor relations quite neatly, appropriating for themselves as the *sirkar*, or "government," the largest share of all.

According to eighteenth- and nineteenth-century British sources, there were two main kinds of agricultural laborers: *paṇṇaiyāls* and *paṭiyāls*. Paṇṇaiyāls, whose Tamil name comes from the word for farm (*paṇṇai*), were known to the British as "agrestic slaves." They were permanently tied to the land they worked or to specific *mirasidars* (individuals who held hereditary rights to the largest share of the harvest of a particular plot of land).[29] Though very much exploited by their landlords, Pannaiyals could call on widely recognized moral claims that ensured a certain amount of protection and support from dominant castes (e.g., cash advances to cover the costs of life-cycle rituals such as weddings and birth and puberty ceremonies). Paṭiyāls were basically tenant farmers who were hired from either within the village (*uḷkuṭi*) or outside the village (*parakkuṭi*) to do agricultural work for a specified wage. Paṭiyāl comes from the Tamil word *paṭi*, a measurement of about 100 cubic inches, which corresponded to the measure of rice or other grain given to them in exchange for their labor.[30] Both Patiyals and Pannaiyals were subject to the violence of higher castes.[31] They could be beaten at will, and women from the laboring castes were extremely vulnerable to sexual exploitation at the hands of locally dominant groups.

The most potent weapon against mistreatment that Patiyals and Pannaiyals had at their disposal was unannounced flight.[32] In areas or times where land was abundant or labor scarce, low castes could abscond from the fields of their mirasidars, or threaten to do so and thus garner better conditions for themselves, such as a higher proportion of the harvest or more ritual benefits.[33] For example, the Paraiyars of Nanjinad, the Sambavar caste to which the Christian convert Vedamanickam belonged, were thought to have migrated from the Tanjore area to the Travancore area to gain greater freedom and safety.[34] However, except in rare cases, low-caste agricultural laborers could do no more than run away from one master to another, a circumstance that limits the effectiveness of striking workers, runaway slaves, and other dependent laborers the world over.[35] As late as the 1830s, as part of their policy of supporting indigenous elites, British collectors actually helped to capture runaway "slaves" and return them to their masters, reflecting one among the many changes set in place when the British gained the role of prime revenue collector of the region by virtue of their military successes. Indeed, changes in the collection of revenue under British rule altered this system dramatically.

The *ryotwari* settlement instituted by the British in the Madras Presidency in 1820 (and firmly established by 1855) deprived landless laborers of much of their traditional negotiating power. It was largely the brainchild of then governor, Thomas Munro, the long-armed gentleman mentioned in the epigraph to this chapter. Whereas formerly, under the *zamindari* settlement, whole villages would be taxed corporately, now land was assigned as private property to those who worked it. Thus, ideally, the peasants (*ryots*) who worked the land would be both its main beneficiaries and those held responsible for supplying the government with its portion of the harvest. Contrary to British expectations, however, the ryotwari settlement created more social instability than the previous forms of taxation. Under the new settlement, members of very low castes were prevented from obtaining land by the widespread prejudice and corruption of local officials. Thousands of small farmers of the higher castes had to alienate the land to pay off the increased tax rate, either mortgaging it to unscrupulous lenders at high rates or selling it altogether to pay their tax debt. In this way, land tended to accumulate in the hands of a few. Also, general indebtedness increased due to the monetization of society, as the government tax could no longer be paid in kind but had to be remitted in cash. Some scholars have gone so far as to assert that laborers who were not tied to the land through traditional bonds of patronage were actually more insecure under the new form of revenue collection because they could be driven off the land without recourse to traditional codes of loyalty.[36]

What British Administrators Knew

As demonstrated by the British desire to understand the share-based system of the Tamil agricultural economy and their treatment of very low castes as they thought such groups were uniformly treated by Indians, one of the distinctive features of British colonialism was the aspiration to rule India through indigenous institutions. This aspiration was part of a historical narrative the British generated about India (reinforced by ideas of history found in some Hindu texts) in which a prior "golden age" of rationality, peace, and social justice had progressively deteriorated due to the actions of variously identified regressive elements in society: the ignorant folk, rapacious and fanatical Muslims, and greedy local power brokers such as Brahmans, chieftains, and kings. As Lata Mani has argued, "The regenerating mission of colonization was conceptualized . . . not as the imposition of a new Christian moral order but as the recuperation and enforcement of the truths of indigenous tradition."[37] In areas of social life as diverse as property rights and the rights of certain groups to enter Hindu temples, the British profoundly transformed the very institutions they sought to learn about and "restore" to their former glory.

The desire to rule according to indigenous institutions immediately ran up against the need to find uniform categories by means of which the colonists could govern an extremely diverse population. From the earliest days of British rule, caste and religion came to serve this function. As colonial rulers sought to understand and define religion and caste, they tended to prioritize textually based Brahmanical values and to de-emphasize values embedded in local cultural systems that derived their authority from diverse sources, including custom, kingship, caste councils, and nontextual religious systems.[38] The organizers of the first imperial census in 1871–1872, for example, initially tried to list the many thousands of castes (jātis) according to one of the four varṇas as described in Sanskrit texts. This strategy to fit complex and highly congeries of jatis onto the procrustean bed of varna was a failure, but it demonstrates how confident colonial rulers were that they could find or develop an "all-India system of classification of castes."[39]

Colonial knowledge about low castes in south India was significantly shaped by research conducted by both colonial ethnographers and scholarly minded missionaries that sought to distinguish the original inhabitants of the region from migrants who had entered the Tamil country over the course of the preceding five hundred years. On the basis of scanty textual, archaeological, and oral evidence, colonial experts constructed possible genealogies for each of the different caste groups. This urge to trace the earliest beginnings of each group was bound up with a nineteenth-century predilection to explain phenomena by their origins, a tendency especially prominent in discussions of "race." The character of a people could be deduced, it was thought, from their history—their traditional occupations, migration history, and relationship to the land in which they resided. Were they the "original inhabitants" of a region, whose customs retained traces of the oldest layer of its distinctive culture and ethos, like the quintessential Dravidians, the Paraiyars? Or were they interlopers from distant parts who insinuated themselves into positions of power through conquest or cultural or mercantile colonialism, like the "Aryan" Brahmans or the Marwari merchants originally from Rajasthan? Colonial knowledge producers projected many of their own concerns onto their constructions of caste, particularly the urge to distinguish between the original "folk" of an area and foreigners (like themselves).

Administrators at all levels of the colonial government undertook large-scale efforts to identify and characterize the different significant groups in Indian society through such means as the imperial district gazetteers, the censuses, and the compendiums of castes and their "manners and customs." One of the most significant studies of caste differences in the Madras Presidency was the encyclopedic Castes and Tribes of Southern India (1909), produced by the official colonial ethnographer for the Madras Presidency, Edgar Thurston. For all these projects of collecting and compiling, British administrators consulted Western-educated Indian informants (such as Thurston's assistant K. Rangachari) and Europeans of long residence such as planters and missionaries and directed teams of investigators to collect information from Indian subjects on the practices and beliefs of different groups of people.[40] Colonial ethnology also relied on other racial sciences of the day: linguistics and anthropometry. Thurston in particular was impressed by the findings of anthropometry, the science of deducing racial identity by measuring bodies, as suggested in his cautious endorsement of the Nadars' claims to be the descendents of an ancient lineage of kings (given as the epigraph to this chapter).

As we saw earlier, the new science of linguistics was another tool favored by colonial knowledge producers, employed skillfully by the SPG missionary Rev. Robert Caldwell. Caldwell brought into being a whole new discourse through the publication of his most influential work, *A Comparative Grammar of the Dravidian or South-Indian Family of Languages* (1856), which documented the fundamental linguistic differences between Indo-European (Sanskrit, Hindi, etc.) and Dravidian (Telegu, Tamil, Malayalam, Kannada, and Tulu) languages. Not content to draw attention to differences in the construction of verbal and nominal forms, he correlated linguistic differences with racial differences in accordance with the regime of racial discourse that was prevalent at the time. As many scholars have noted, Caldwell's *Comparative Grammar* ushered into being one hundred years (and counting) of steady efforts to establish the distinctiveness of a "Dravidian race."[41]

But ultimately, caste and religion came to be seen as the primary structuring institutions of Indian society over such institutions as either race or kingship. As caste and religion were increasingly understood in this way, they became privileged arenas within which many aspiring groups sought to stage bids for higher social status. The institution of the census was particularly significant in constructing caste and religion as the source of the socially significant boundaries that marked off one group of people from another. The grand project of enumerating the entire population of India, and classifying its inhabitants into neat categories, was the ambition of the All-India censuses from 1870 to 1931. It is true that census categories were not invented out of whole cloth, but were based on pre-existing forms of collective identity. And yet, the census helped to objectify and invest these identities with new meaning. It provided a new arena within which old identities could be contested and new identities shaped.[42] By persuading census administrators that the caste name or social status traditionally ascribed to one's community was wrong, one could rewrite history and settle ancient intercaste grudges anew. Arjun Appadurai notes well the paradoxical effect of the census, in that, though it "was intended to quantify previously set classifications . . . [it] had just the reverse effect, which was to stimulate the self-mobilization of these groups into a variety of translocal forms."[43] One extraordinary example of this is provided by the Shanars, who sought to escape their categorization as one of the lowest castes of the Indian social hierarchy by, among other things, insisting that they be known collectively as Nadars, "lords of the soil." The remarkable thing about their efforts to challenge their customary ranking in the social order is that they so persistently and directly engaged with the colonial state. Where many other Indians ran from Thurston and the census takers when they arrived with their calipers and rulers, terrified by rumors that he intended to cart them off to be slaves in Mauritius, the newly mobilized Shanars/Nadars actively sought him out, along with other representatives of the colonial state.[44]

Nadars and the Appropriation of Colonial Knowledge

Robert Hardgrave's now classic history, *The Nadars of Tamilnad* (1969), offers an astute, wonderfully detailed analysis of the various strategies used by Nadars (then called Shanars) to improve their social status over the course of the nineteenth and early twentieth centuries by claiming that they were *not* untouchables but Kshatriyas, warriors descended from the royal Pandyas whose true identity had long been wrongfully obscured. However, one category that Hardgrave does not treat with the same care that he gives to caste, politics, and economics is gender. In this section, I follow Hardgrave in demonstrating that the claims to Kshatriya status that animated the Nadar social movements of the nineteenth century were as important to Christians as to Hindus. Through an investigation of the arguments and proofs given by Nadars to substantiate their assertion that they were Kshatriyas and not untouchables, I go on to show that this strategy was based on a profoundly gendered theory of caste differences and thus consequently entailed dramatic changes in gender relations within the Nadar community.

By virtue of his close association with Shanars/Nadars in Tirunelveli, many of whom converted to Christianity in the early nineteenth century, Rev. Robert Caldwell became the acknowledged expert on the caste. In 1849, after eight years of residence in Tirunelveli (twelve altogether in India), he wrote of them, "They may in general be described as belonging to the highest division of the lower classes, or the lowest of the middle classes: poor, but not paupers; rude and unlettered, but by many degrees removed from a savage state" (4). Though other, earlier experts had made similar observations, Caldwell's formulation of the Shanars' status became the established opinion of the time.[45] In his book *The Tinnevelly Shanars* (1849), he described in very unflattering terms the community from among whom the vast majority of his converts were taken, intending to impress on his audience back home how urgently the SPG missions needed their support. We had a glimpse earlier of the style and tone of Caldwell's account: In his eyes, the Shanars were dim-witted, litigious, and addicted to demonolatry, the term he used consistently to refer to the possession rituals and worship of deified dead that were the foci of religious life for Shanars (along with many other groups in Hindu society). Most controversially, he argued that the Shanars were members of an aboriginal Indian race conquered by the technologically and morally superior Aryans, seen as the bearers of a more sophisticated Brahmanical civilization. The Shanars, Caldwell argued, could be considered Hindus only to the extent that "Hindu" was a geographical category that included "any class in India." He wrote, "Their connection with the Brahmanical systems of dogmas and observances, commonly described in the mass as Hinduism, is so small that they may be considered as votaries of a different religion" (7).

Caldwell's writings frequently adopted a tone midway between theology and ethnology, as he attempted to classify the distinctive way the Shanars expressed their fallen human nature. In the introduction to *The Tinnevelly Shan-*

ars, he wrote, "In describing the religions, beliefs and moral condition of the Shanars and other inferior castes in Tinnevelly connected with them or influenced by them, it is not my intention to refer to those prejudices, passions, and practices which characterize Shanars and Pariars in common with all unregenerate men" (5). In their propensity for sin and corruption, their "love of evil and dislike of good," the lower castes of south India are the same as any group, argued Caldwell. Indeed, that the taint of Original Sin is shared by all humans is a fundamental component of Christian doctrine. What fascinated missionary ethnographers like Caldwell was how this innate impulse manifested itself in practice in culturally distinct ways. " 'All like sheep have gone astray,' " writes Caldwell, "but 'everyone . . . hath turned to his own way,' and some advantage and interest may be found in considering the characteristics of the very peculiar phase of error which obtains in this province" (6). Caldwell's popularity as a writer was due at least in part to his ability to synthesize social evolutionary thought, the popular science of the times, with the ancient Christian tradition of apologetics, in which one carefully describes, classifies, and exposes the limitations of various forms of heresy. He wrote with such authority that his work was received with acclaim and taken as authoritative in both England and India.

However, when educated Nadars got hold of Caldwell's study several years after its initial publication they were furious. In retaliation, they produced a series of arguments to substantiate a counterrepresentation. These took the form of street corner oratory, pamphlets by the dozen, and, in the early 1880s, a move to officially petition the government to censure Robert Caldwell and remove *The Tinnevelly Shanars* from publication. Hardgrave hypothesizes that a disgruntled catechist of the SPG, Rev. Arumai Nayakam Sattampillai (whom I discuss at length in chapter 5), provided the impetus for this movement. Dismissed from his post as catechist in Nazareth, Tirunelveli district for his alleged insubordination, Sattampillai was supposed to have journeyed to Madras in 1850 to plead for his reinstatement with the SPG Corresponding Committee. There he somehow discovered Caldwell's pamphlet, and its disdainful statements about the low nature of his caste threw oil on the fire of his resentment against the European missionaries. If Hardgrave is correct, which I think he is, Sattampillai's reaction to *The Tinnevelly Shanars* fueled a massive counterpropaganda campaign. Between the years 1857 and 1927, historians of the Nadar caste produced no fewer than thirty-six caste histories.[46]

In these histories, Shanars claimed that far from being mere Dravidians, the uncivilized aborigines of the region, they were in fact the region's original Kshatriyas, a once powerful ruling community who had been displaced when the Pandyan Empire was conquered many centuries earlier. The most prominent of the arguments put forward in support of this claim was based on an etymology of the word "Shanar." According to Shanar activists, *Cāṉrār*, one variation on their caste designation, was derived from the ancient Tamil word *Cāṉrōr*, which means "learned" or "noble."[47] *Cāṉrōr* was first used in Tamil Sangam poetry to describe literate and socially refined people (such as warriors, or the Sangam poets themselves) and was also found in the Tamil dictionary, the *Tolkappiyam*. Although British lexicographers and philologists denied that the word was anything more than an honorific applied to men from a variety of different jatis, nineteenth-century Shanar scholars seized on the term as a reference to a single, specific group, the Sandror, their own glorious predecessors.

Nadar leaders, many of them educated Indian Christians, argued that the Sandror's historical degradation had been accompanied by widespread neglect of the community's original moral code. Another Indian Christian leader who lobbied for the Nadar cause was the first Indian pastor in the American Madurai Mission (AMM), S. Winfred. Winfred wrote a pamphlet in 1874 entitled *Sāṉror kula marapu kāttal* (To safeguard the customs of the Shandrors). Having gone to great lengths to establish the royal ancestry of the Nadars, he "exhorted all Nadars to assume the customs of the Kshatriya," including keeping their wives in purdah: "Ladies of Shandrors must not go outside, and if they leave to go out, they can do so in a covered vehicle so that nobody can see them."[48] This kind of acute awareness of the past and sensitivity to the demands it made on proper caste etiquette to distinguish themselves from other castes in the present was evidently shared by large numbers of Nadars, perhaps especially the Christian Nadars, who were lumped together by others with low castes like Pallars and Paraiyars.

In their reports to the missionary societies, Indian evangelists frequently complained that Christianity was perceived as a low-caste sect, a "Paraya Vedam." As Rev. Jesudasan John of the CMS reported in 1853, one respondent reviled him with the words, "You do not know how to speak anything but this Paraya Vedam. You have deceived the unlearned Shanars to a great extent. We will not be deceived as Shanars."[49] According to Hardgrave, the first organized attempt by Shanars to resist their classification with the low castes was initiated by Christians in 1856. A congregation of Shanars in the Tirunelveli district (Sawyerpuram) angrily petitioned their missionary to censure or remove the Pallar catechist assigned to them, on the grounds that he had referred to the Shanars with a term of abuse, calling them an *ilappajati* (*iḷappajāti*, "uncouth, contemptible caste"). Even after the catechist formally apologized, the Shanar congregation rejected his services, stating, "We refuse in future to have catechists of any caste not equal [to] or higher than our own."[50]

The controversy over *The Tinnevelly Shanars* initiated by Sattampillai in 1850 was resuscitated in the early 1880s when Y. Gnanamuthoo Nadar, a Tamil Christian clerk in the Tirunelveli courts, began sending petitions far and wide to various representatives of the British government and the missionary ecclesiastical structure demanding that the British censure Caldwell (who had by then become a bishop) and remove his offending book from circulation.[51] Gnanamuthoo, who referred to himself as "Antiquarian and Representative of the Shanar Race," was the son of one of the first Indian catechists hired by the SPG in the Nazareth area. He was a graduate of Sullivan Garden's College in Madras, a former catechist of the CMS, and had worked as a clerk for fourteen years in the district court at Tirunelveli. In a printed book entitled *Cāṉār Cattiriyar* (Shanars are Kshatriyas), a collection of correspondence between himself and various opponents from missionaries to representatives of other castes, he documents the long battle over Caldwell's tract that took place between 1880 and 1885. According to Gnanamuthoo, crowds of angry Shanars twice disrupted the provincial meeting of the SPG demanding that the committee consider a petition asking the bishop to retract his slanderous statements about the caste.[52] Harassing crowds followed the bishop when he traveled to villages to baptize and confirm congregants. Ultimately, according to Gnanamuthoo, out of anger at Caldwell's statements about the caste, many hundreds of Nadar Christians either reverted to Hinduism or joined an independent Tamil Christian church founded by Rev. Sattampillai in 1858 (see chapter 5).

In a letter asking Caldwell himself to retract the odious publication, Gnanamuthoo stated plainly that the problem was that Caldwell's works, the *Comparative Grammar* and *The Tinnevelly Shanars*, had become canonical, serving as the authoritative basis in all government reports having to do with caste.[53] It is indeed a testament to Caldwell's rhetorical power as a writer that Gnanamuthoo could complain that "every writer having read Bishop Caldwell's work writes as if he were quite sure of the non-Aryan, and aboriginal origin of the Shanars, and their degraded condition."[54] What they blamed Caldwell and his fellow missionaries for most bitterly was the way the foreign missionaries' obsession with caste led them "thus to depreciate [the Nadars] in the eyes of their fellow countrymen instead of bringing them forward and to reinstate them in the position formerly occupied by their ancestors." Such treatment was especially galling insofar as it seemed to fly in the face of the missionaries' professed egalitarian ethos. As Gnanamuthoo wrote, "This is the way the European Missionaries deal with their converts and fellow Christians, whom they pretend to acknowledge to have equal claims to sense, and honor, and to the kingdom of Heaven."[55]

The arguments made by Shanar spokesmen in their printed diatribes against Rev. Caldwell in the late nineteenth century illustrate vividly the tug of war over words and representation that animated relations between Indian Christians and foreign missionaries. Such contests were all the more heated when they had to do with changes in the lives of Indian Christians that were judged not only by missionaries and other Christians, but by non-Christian Indians as well. Clearly the judgments of the latter mattered deeply to Indian Christians. As one Nadar spokesman wrote, "We thought Bishop Caldwell would be our supporter, not our abuser, but we find he is the cause of our being abused by our fellow Hindu caste-men, as well as by other Hindus, who look upon us with a sneer and say 'Lo the men that have embraced the religion of the whites.' "[56] Sometimes the opinions of fellow Indians mattered more to Nadar Christians than did the opinions of foreign missionaries. At times, as in this letter, the opinions of foreigners appeared to be only secondarily important, that is, to the extent that these opinions could sway the minds of the converts' countrymen.

Caldwell did partly retract his statements, specifically his evaluation that Shanars were "not Hindus," in a letter that was reprinted in the *CMS Record* of February 1880: "This expression had better be avoided for the future, as the use of it is erroneous and misleading, the Shanars being not only Hindus by domicile, but also (in the original heathen condition) Hindus by the profession of the ordinary Hindu religion, though it be a low type of that religion, and Hindus in virtue of their being members of a recognized Hindu caste."[57] In Gnanamuthoo's reading of Caldwell's published modification of his earlier claims, he laid great stress on the phrase "members of a recognized Hindu caste," construing this phrase to refer to one of the three Hindu varnas classified as "twice-born" (i.e., Brahmans, Kshatriyas, and Vaishyas). On the basis of this understanding, Gnanamuthoo argued that Caldwell's modified opinion of the caste supported his own contention that the Nadars were in fact Kshatriyas, a noble, nonpolluting, martial caste.

The flood of petitions produced by Nadar Christians urging colonial and missionary authorities to validate their claim to be Kshatriyas represents one of the challenges to the paternalism of European missionaries that were launched periodically by disgruntled converts. On many occasions Christian Nadar spokesmen used the same kinds of arguments that colonial "experts" on caste used to classify the different groups: linguistics, history, and numismatics. But some of the most interesting arguments frankly contested European assumptions about the caste system and European methods of scholarship. For instance, in a letter addressed to one Rev. Alexander, who made the mistake of publishing in the *Church Missionary Record* observations he made during a two-week tour of Tirunelveli, Gnanamuthoo ridiculed him for writing that Shanars were non-Aryans: "Here is a gentleman who visited the paltry mission stations only for a fortnight expressing his opinion to the effect that they do not belong to the Hindus!! To form an idea of a nation merely by their appearance without referring to the Sastras of the Hindus is ridiculous." Interestingly, in exemplary Vaidika fashion, Gnanamuthoo here privileged textual knowledge over empirical knowledge such as that gained by the European "science" of anthropometry. He continued, "It is not by their appearance, that you have found them to be non-Aryans (for you cannot distinguish one caste from another by their general features), but by some misinformation, which has misled you as to this fact."[58] This misinformation, he makes plain, came from nowhere but Caldwell's notorious *Tinnevelly Shanars*.

Another Nadar Christian who contested Caldwell's representations of his caste was Samuel Sarguner, a subregistrar employed in the Chingleput district and the author of a tract entitled *Bishop Caldwell and the Tinnevelly Shanars*. In this tract, Sarguner attempted to undermine Caldwell's authority on a number of grounds: his inadequate Tamil, the limited nature of his experience of the region given that he had only lived extensively in one town, Edeyengudi, and his inadequate application of the rules of historical hermeneutics. In one section relating to Caldwell's statements about the relative status of Shanars and Pallars or Paraiyars, Sarguner fumed, "The whole of this discussion by the Bishop is nothing but a mass of unadulterated falsehood, which appears to have originated with the Bishop's unsound and superficial knowledge of Tamil, which took it too readily for granted that what it found to exist now had existed always just as it believed . . . [and] that what was true of a few Shanars, or about

Edeyengudi must be true of each of the Shanars all over the Tinnevelly district."
In addition to criticizing Caldwell's language skills, Sarguner denounced him
for his ignorance of the regional and temporal variability of caste, a criticism
that may have been justified if one considers the British misunderstanding of
the status of Paraiyars in dry-zone areas examined earlier. He wrote of Caldwell's acclaimed scholarly skills, "His forte is to compare a dozen Grammars
and Dictionaries of as many languages and boil down bundles of papers, be
they Government records, Missionaries' letters, or copies of inscriptions, into
the forms of narratives."[59] Although an entirely unmediated apprehension of
pure data is surely a fiction in any era, Sarguner's critique lays bare the short-
comings of much colonial knowledge production.

Contrary to the arguments of the supporters of the Nadar-Kshatriya cause,
most of the high castes in the region were uniformly opposed to Nadars' aspirations. Indeed, it was to avoid conflict with the Nadars' rivals that the colonial state did not list them as Kshatriyas. Throughout the nineteenth and
early twentieth centuries, Hindu Nadars in Travancore, Tirunelveli, Ramnad,
and Madurai districts were still considered a polluting caste and, for that reason
were prohibited from entering Brahmanical temples (a prohibition they challenged by petition, bribery, force and, finally, appeal to courts of the British).[60]
Such evidence suggests that many people outside of the community did not
believe the Nadars' claims to be a twice-born caste but continued to see them
as a caste distinct from the untouchable Paraiyars and Pallars, but nonetheless
closer to the out-castes than to the twice-born castes.

Gender and the New Kshatriya Identity

In their battles with the missionaries and the colonial state over words and
representations, what the Nadars were primarily reacting to, I have argued,
was their classification with other low castes. Essentially, educated Nadar Christians were concerned that they were being wrongly grouped with the other low-
caste groups that had converted to Christianity. By the late nineteenth century,
and even more so with the large-scale mass movements of the early twentieth
century, the prevailing perception was that all Indian Christians were from
low-caste groups, a perception the Nadars tried mightily to refute. For those
who did not take the insults they received as an occasion to revert to Hinduism,
the problem became how to remain Christian and still garner the respect they
believed was their due. Insofar as the most widely accepted indigenous criteria
for ranking castes were occupation and gender norms, one would expect to
see the most concerted efforts at reform directed to these areas. Here I briefly
discuss how Nadar Christian converts moved out of traditionally polluting occupations, such as toddy tapping, into "cleaner" ones such as trade, and then
turn to an analysis of how gender norms were changed to accommodate the
desire for higher social status.

As the 1856 incident with the Pallar catechist suggests, Nadars saw themselves as being very different from and superior to the other castes classified
as low. On what basis did they distinguish themselves from the latter? The

traditional occupation of Shanars/Nadars, the toddy-tapper caste, put them into daily contact with a substance not obviously polluting: the sugary sap of a palm tree. One of the principal uses of this sap was as a mildly alcoholic beverage. Many Sanskrit legal texts, including the Laws of Manu, consider the consumption of intoxicating liquors a very grave sin, equal in virulence to cow killing and stealing. Much as in Christian arguments in favor of temperance, Manu opposes intoxicating liquors because they could lead a man to commit other sins, such as eating polluting foods (see Manu 11.96—98). At first, Nadars tried to valorize what was detested by the hegemonic Brahmanical tradition: They argued that *kaḷ* was actually the Tamil *amṛtam*, the nectar of the gods.[61] But they had few takers. The more successful tactic was avoidance.

Nadars who were able to assert their claims to high status most successfully were the ones who had given up the traditional occupation of toddy tapping for more lucrative, "cleaner" ventures such as trade along the trunk roads built by the British and the management of coffee plantations established in the hills of Ceylon (Sri Lanka) and the Western Ghats. Many Nadars benefited directly from these new sources of income as workers, supervisors, labor contractors, and even owners. Also, as Nadars in Travancore and the neighboring district of Tirunelveli left the palmyra fields to work in the plantations, those who stayed behind were able to increase their income considerably by immigrating from one region to another in concert with the alternating months of the tapping season. In Tirunelveli the trees exhuded sap during the months of March and August, and in Travancore between September and February. In addition, Nadars in Travancore and neighboring Tirunelveli district to the north became involved in trade. They dealt in commodities such as jaggery, tamarind, and cotton, plying their wares along the trunk roads built down the center of the Madras Presidency by the British.[62] In southern Travancore and in the northern parts of Tirunelveli (around Sivakasi) some wealthy Nadars were able to obtain the services of Brahman priests, palanquin carriers, and other kinds of servants who cooperated in making their claims to higher status meaningful.

Besides occupation, the other main criterion for classifying castes high or low in the Hindu social order was gender. Castes considered "high" guarded the chastity of their womenfolk, whereas castes who were considered "low" tended to have fewer restrictions with respect to the behavior of women. One Tamil proverb sums up the contempt felt toward the low castes on account of their purportedly lax sexual morality: "The palmyra tree casts no shadow, and a Paraiyan has no sexual morality [(*paṇaimarattirku niḷal illai, paṟaiyaṉukku muṟaiyillai*)]."[63] *Muṟai*, which has the general meaning of "manners, propriety," also refers more specifically to the kinship relationships that determine who is or is not a proper, nonincestuous marriage partner. The ability to carefully regulate the sexuality of members of one's caste group by arranging marriages strictly according to the caste *muṟai* was regarded as a prized indicator of corporate discipline and the power of the community. In this way, it is related to the concept of *kaṭṭupāḍu*, the customary laws that prescribe particular behaviors so as to form a kind of caste code of conduct, along with the use of sanctions to enforce them. As Nicholas Dirks argues for the Kallars of Pudukottai, the tight regulation of women's sexual behavior was essential to social mobility, as an index of the caste's corporate unity and the power of leaders to command and control subordinates within the group.[64] The converse was also true: Elite and upwardly mobile Tamils regarded a caste's inability or unwillingness to regulate sexuality as indicative of lack of power, low morality, or both. It bears mentioning that the capacity to control women's sexuality was not always a matter of willpower or morality, but frequently depended on social power. The wives and daughters of tenant farmers, landless agriculturalists, and other socially marginalized groups were vulnerable to sexual assault and exploitation in a way that the women of powerful groups were not. And yet, the indigenous stereotype of the sexually "loose" low-caste man or woman whose low morality led to his or her deserved low status was taken up by the British in India and reformulated in their own guides to the caste system.[65]

In Edgar Thurston and K. Rangachari's encyclopedic collection of information on the customs, practices, and histories of *The Castes and Tribes of Southern India*, the sequential ordering of castes in the seven-volume study was determined not by their rank according to Brahmanical Hindu models, nor by more local ranking systems, nor even by a British version of one of the latter. Rather, it was organized by a seemingly value-free mode of order: the alphabet. Nevertheless, in the entries themselves one still sees a subtle ranking as a set of criteria are applied, not always in the same order and not always exhaustively, to distinguish castes from one another. The distinguishing features identified most frequently are sexual customs, marriage customs, diet, dress, and "religion." The entry for the Chakkiliyars, considered the most debased of all the Tamil-speaking castes, deploys the criteria based on gender and sexuality most overtly:

> In social position the Chakkiliyans occupy the lowest rank, though there is much dispute on this point between them and the Parai-
> yans. . . . Girls are not usually married before puberty. The bride-
> groom may be younger than the bride. Their widows may remarry.
> Divorce can be obtained at the pleasure of either party on payment
> of Rs. 12-12-0 to the other in the presence of the local head of the
> caste. Their women are considered to be very beautiful, and it is a
> woman of this caste who is generally selected for the coarser form
> of Shakti worship. They indulge very freely in intoxicating liquors,
> and will eat any flesh, including beef, pork, etc.[66]

In this text, one can see how many features associated with very low-caste groups have to do with sexuality, especially restrictions on women's sexuality or the lack thereof: Women are not married as children to men much older than themselves, they may remarry after being widowed, and they may obtain divorce through a simple exchange of money; the women also work as prostitutes, albeit religious ones. Official, written records of caste customs such as these became especially important as rival castes increasingly brought their disputes over precedence to the British courts for resolution. Gender relations and customs having to do with marriage (especially widow remarriage, a highly regarded index of the purity of women) were frequently offered as evidence of a caste's or subcaste's superior status vis-à-vis another, as Uma Chakravarti describes for the Deccan.[67]

In light of the emphasis placed on gender relations in colonial accounts of caste, perhaps one of the reasons the Shanars were considered by colonial observers as the highest of the low castes is that their codes of gender relations tended toward lifelong monogamy and patriliny. Even in Travancore, where they were in close contact with the matrilineal dominant castes (Nairs) who did not practice monogamy, the Shanars were known for their relatively strong marriage ties and their patrilineal form of descent. Samuel Mateer wrote that they were "usually faithful in the observance of the marriage bond, and somewhat more chaste and truthful . . . than many other classes of the Hindus."[68] As wealthier Travancore Shanars adopted more of the customs of the dominant castes of the region, they did not tend toward the matrilineal Nairs, but rather toward the patrilineal Nambudiri Brahmans. The wealthy Nadans of Travancore, the dominant fraction of the community, kept their women in *purdah*, a custom that Rev. S. Winfred, as we saw earlier, wanted to extend to the whole community.

It was precisely this issue of the chastity, the controlled sexuality of the community that most incensed the Nadar–Shanar activists. Samuel Sarguner, in particular, took issue with the characterization of the sexual relations of his community as loose. In response to the assertions of Dr. W. R. Cornish, commissioner of the 1871 census, Sarguner wrote:

> The Doctor cannot be sufficiently condemned for his wild assertions about the relations of the sexes among them. Comparisons are odious, or I can here tell the reader which class in Southern India, or which sub-divisions of which class in Southern India is the most notorious in this respect. I shall therefore for the present content myself with the counter assertion that the Shanars—I mean the Shanars proper, not the Doctor's Shanars—as a whole, are one of the chastest classes, if not *the* chastest class, in all of South India. Any person who has a personal knowledge of the Shanars will find himself constrained to admit that the relations of the sexes among them are as rigid as among any class or race on the face of the world.[69]

If advocates of the Nadar cause such as Sarguner and Winfred are correct, the strict observance of chastity by this caste had been a feature of their gender relations from time immemorial. However, I think it is more likely that the attempt to become recognized as Kshatriyas involved a transformation of gender roles as the women in the community went from being freely involved in the public sphere to being "guarded" women whose sexuality was closely managed in the interest of maintaining discipline and the "purity" of their caste.

This represents a large shift from earlier modes of gender. For much of the nineteenth century, and presumably long before, the majority of Shanar women worked alongside their menfolk outside the symbolic shelter of the home, as did the women of other castes regarded as low. While men of his jāti climbed the trees and collected the sweet sap in pots, women boiled the sap down into coarse sugar kept burning in temporary sheds erected in the palmyra forests and molded the thick syrup in the hulls of coconut shells.[70] As Caldwell observed, "Unquestionably it is a more exhausting and stupefying species of labor than any other performed within the tropics."[71] After pouring the syrup into coconut shell molds, Shanar women were responsible for marketing the end product, jaggery (or rather, what was left of it after giving half to the owners of the trees), in local bazaars or to local traders. The mutual dependency between husband and wife was such that, as Dick Kooiman writes, "a Shanar toddy-tapper would climb the tree in vain, if he had no wife to boil the *pataneer* and make the jaggery."[72] With the move of the community's menfolk to trade and salary-earning professions, community activists urged newly "respectable" Nadar women to withdraw from the public sphere of productivity. For example, the *Tirunelveli District Gazetteer* stated that in 1902 in Ovari, a town in south Nanguneri taluk, "The Shanars decided that their women should no longer carry headloads and wear beads or leaden bracelets and should not go to market."[73]

Male as well as female gender roles were radically changed by the increasing "respectability" of the community. Thurston wrote that in the course of his ethnological research into the Shanar caste the caste leaders in Nazareth came to him in palanquins "bearing weapons of old device." There he witnessed "a programme of sports, which was organised in my honour." This event included many physical feats displaying strength and courage:

> Fencing and figure exercises with long sticks of iron-wood (Mesua ferrea).
> Figure exercises with sticks bearing flaming rags at each end.
> Various acrobatic tricks.
> Feats with heavy weights, rice-pounders, and pounding stones.
> Long jump.
> Breaking cocoanuts with the thrust of a knife or the closed fist.
> Crunching whisky-bottle glass with the teeth.
> Running up, and butting against the chest, back and shoulders.
> Swallowing a long silver chain.
> Cutting a cucumber balanced on a man's neck in two with a sword.
> Falconry.[74]

This display of manly courage was part of an organized effort by many members of this community to persuade the superintendent of the ethnological survey that the Shanars were descended from kings, that they were, in fact, local Kshatriyas. Thus, the transformation of gender also constructed new images of Nadar men as courageous, physically strong, and impervious to pain. Just as Nadar women had to conform to a model of Kshatriya femininity, so did Nadar men adapt to an ideal of Kshatriya masculinity.

It is important to note that it was not Thurston who called for this demonstration. Rather, the two sons of Rev. A. N. Sattampillai took credit for persuading Thurston to come. They also took responsibility for organizing and financing the program of physical feats.[75] What is significant is that they at-tempted to enlist Thurston in their own project, urging him in print and in person to overturn the classification of Nadars with the low castes, which had been reinforced solidly by Rev. Caldwell, and accept their self-definition as the original Kshatriyas of the region.

This campaign to get British officials and census administrators to rec-ognize the status claims of Nadars was, in the end, partially successful. In 1921, after petitioning the government for ten years to change the way they were entered in the census registers, the government agreed to list them as Nadars, and not Shanars (which by then, had become a term of reproach) and to omit the caste's traditional occupation of toddy tapping in the census tables. The government stopped short, however, of conceding to their earlier requests to be listed as "Kshatriya," or Kshatriya-Sandrores or Nadar Kshatriya. The government order that made the name change official stated that "the proce-dure followed at the recent census was to leave everyone to return his caste name as he chose."[76] Although this statement was consistent with the govern-ment's overt position of neutrality, the fact that the state withheld its endorse-ment of the more controversial claim that the Nadars were Kshatriyas is indic-ative of the subtle ways the colonial state continued to locate itself as the ultimate arbiter of status and station.

Summary

Many Christian Nadar leaders educated in the schools of the various U.S. and English missionary societies, like Sattampillai, Gnanamuthoo, Winfred, and Sarguner, were in the forefront of the effort to prove that Shanars/Nadars were Kshatriyas. They were persistent and resourceful, deploying a variety of current ethnological and linguistic conventions of evidence to support their claims. It remains to be seen in this study whether, by appropriating the categories or the language of colonial discourse to pursue their own project of upward mo-bility, Nadars (along with other Christianized groups) fell prey to the hidden forms of power and subjection embedded in these categories. In particular, I am interested in discovering whether the urge to create and inhabit more re-spectable identities, whether Indian or European in origin, entailed more op-pressive forms of gender relations.

One result of the tendency toward cross-regional uniformity in colonial sociology was that the status of those who were viewed on the basis of Brah-manical values as ritually polluting and morally degraded was congealed into a newly rigid form at this time. In conjunction with these epistemological tendencies, widespread structural changes having to do with property law, monetization, and revenue collection further destabilized those who were al-ready economically dependent within the land systems of southern India. In this way, the "outcaste" or the "untouchable" was reconstructed by colonial knowledge and the economic transformations of the nineteenth century. I am not arguing that the groups characterized as untouchable or outcaste were not exploited, abused, or categorically excluded from many of the centers of power, privilege, and prestige in precolonial society. Rather, I stress how a multiplicity of practices, customs, knowledges, and rules having to do with those groups at the very bottom of Indian society was obscured in the attempt to define the untouchable and legislate means for his or her improvement. Out of older systems of degradation, new ones were built in their place, offering new footholds from which liberatory strategies could be construed and eliminating old footholds that previously had provided some purchase in a dynamic, shifting, but extremely hierarchical social field.

In this context, we can begin to discern the horizon of possibilities within which conversion to Christianity makes sense. Both the history of the Church and the history of the engagement of Indians with the categories of colonial knowledge show that some Indians, especially Indian Christians, sought to ameliorate their position in the social order by approaching new centers of power emerging in the local landscape. However, even as they sought to make relationships with representatives of Western religious and secular power, they tried to bring those representatives into the fold of their own understandings of patronage and obligation. In the next chapter, I investigate how and why English and American colonizers, particularly women missionaries, wanted to incorporate Indians into their own notions of relationship and dependence.

3

Women's Missionary Societies

Let us in our Master's name lay our hand on the hand that rocks the cradle, and tune the lips that sing the lullabies. Let us win the mothers of India for Christ, and the day will not be long deferred when India's sons also shall be brought to the Redeemer's feet.
—Miss Greenfield, "Paper on Zenana Education"

In the last three decades of the nineteenth century, British and American women founded diverse institutional centers aimed specifically at converting women: zenana missions (for women secluded in their homes), medical missions, orphanages, and schools. In these manifold institutions, united by a common commitment to the reform and uplift of *women*, the paternalistic justification of colonial rule found a counterpart in the maternalistic ideology of the women's foreign missionary movement. Like the rhetoric of colonialism, the rhetoric of the women's foreign missions contrived an alibi for intervention out of the supposedly infantile condition of Indian subjects. In an ironic twist that has been well noted by scholars of British and American nineteenth-century women's movements, the same ideology that justified the disempowerment of colonial subjects empowered white women to extend themselves beyond the domestic household and contribute their talents to the public project of imperial reform.[1] Yet, it is important to emphasize that white women were not alone in their endeavors to Christianize Indian women. Indian Christian women themselves were crucially involved in the missionary project, a subject I take up extensively in the next chapter. In this chapter, I concentrate on the social, ideological, and institutional context of the women's missionary movement in the United States and Britain to examine how and to what extent evan-

gelical Christianity empowered women missionaries and enabled them to challenge the patriarchal norms of missionary culture in India.

Long ago, Max Weber drew attention to the social consequences of one
interpretation of Protestant Christian teaching, namely, that the devout Christian is but an instrument of God's will.[2] Such a move of voluntary self-
subjection to a higher power can be fantastically empowering. By effacing his
own self and obscuring his own interests so that he appeared as the mere
instrument of God's will, an individual could ask for complete obedience in
turn. Could women in nineteenth- and early twentieth-century colonial India
tap into this charismatic potential of Christianity? In particular, to what extent
did the charismatic potential of Christianity allow Western women missionaries to overcome the gendered constraints of colonial society? Nineteenth-
century religious women lived in a social and intellectual milieu in which the
very nature of a woman's will was a cause for perplexity (Was she rational or
irrational? independent or in need of a stronger will to direct her own?). I argue
that, in spite of these cultural constraints, some women missionaries in India
managed to achieve remarkable success in the missionary field by submitting
their own will to God and claiming to act according to his will. Although the
strategy of voluntary self-subjection gave women the confidence to defy the
gender norms of the culture of missionary stations, which tended to see
women as helpmeets who supported the work of men but should not lead, it
had serious limitations. Combined with a conviction in the civilizational superiority of European culture, the notion that devout individuals were simply
empty vessels carrying out the will of God led to a singularly unself-critical
approach to missionary work and gave carte blanche to a generally dismissive
attitude toward Indian agency and leadership capacity.

I begin this chapter with a discussion of previous scholarship on white
women in India in order to situate Western women missionaries more precisely in the context of colonial gender relations. Next I analyze the social
conditions in England and North America that gave rise to the women's missionary project and describe the theological dispositions that women missionaries shared with male missionaries of the time. These dispositions included
an emotional, pietist orientation to Christianity, strong millennial expectations,
and a conviction of the reality of heaven and hell. In the final section of the
chapter, as a way to address whether and how Christianity empowered Western
women missionaries, I compare the styles of two women missionaries who
were motivated by two very different varieties of Protestant Christianity: Amy
Carmichael, the Keswick missionary initially attached to the Church of England
Zenana Missionary Society in Tirunelveli, and Eva Swift, a missionary sent by
the American Board of Commissioners for Foreign Missions to the American
Madurai Mission.

Previous Scholarship on Women in India

In the aftermath of the 1857 rebellion, in which thousands of Indian troops, mostly in north India, mutinied against their British officers, the rulership of India passed from the English East India Company to the British Parliament. One consequence of the increased political stability that resulted was that the cost of the sea passage between India and England decreased. This made it easier for white women to come to India and facilitated the emergence of segregated communities of Westerners in which living conditions that were considered suitable for white women could be maintained. As many historians of colonial India have noted, with the arrival of large numbers of women the lifestyles of the European residents of British India changed significantly. Because more men were able to establish homes with their European wives it became easier and more desirable to reproduce the English way of life in India. A new era of luxury came into being, marked by complex social rituals that enacted a commanding and regal style of government. The height of British colonialism in India, the Raj years from roughly 1870 to 1910, continues to be romanticized in contemporary popular culture as an era of "sumptuous imperial balls in the Himalayan summer capital of Simla; of cricket matches on the manicured lawns of Calcutta's Bengal Club; of polo games on the sunburnt plains of Rajputana; of tiger hunts in Assam; of young men sitting down to dinner in black ties in a tent in the middle of the jungle, solemnly proposing their toast in port to the King-Emperor while jackals howled in the darkness around them."[3]

In the past fifteen years, a great deal of unusually good scholarship has uncovered, explored, and analyzed the involvement of European women in colonial rule during the "heyday of the Raj."[4] Influenced by the self-critical turn in women's studies that took place in the 1980s, when the ethnocentricity of white feminism's claim to speak for all women came under sharp critique, much of this scholarship undertakes a rigorous examination of the interconnected workings of race, class, and gender in imperial politics and culture. It is also attuned to the connections between metropolitan politics, in Western Europe and North America (such as the movements for women's suffrage), and the politics of empire. Situated firmly in the midst of postcolonial reconceptualizations of the place of authorized knowledge in the constitution and maintenance of colonial power, it is self-conscious of its own historicity, its own location in a context of academic, first world privilege. Virtually all of these studies recognize the influence of evangelism on Victorian ideology and acknowledge the religious commitments to Christianity affirmed by individual women involved in the colonial project; however, they tend not to explore the role of religion in the lives of these women in a sustained way. Excellent historical studies of American women missionaries in Hawaii and China have set a high standard of scholarship in this area, but the wave of feminist scholarship on women in colonial India has produced only a single book-length study of women missionaries.[5]

Many of the first efforts to consider women's involvement in colonialism addressed an older, negative version of Western women in the colonies. In the histories of colonial India written in past decades, when white women were written about at all they were held responsible for the intensification of racial divisions that took place in the post-1858 period. What Margaret Strobel has called the "myth of the destructive female" is pervasive in male-centered histories of colonialism. This myth assigned blame to white women for destroying an imagined Arcadia of harmonious relations between colonizer and colonized by their racism, sexual jealousy, and petty preoccupation with the rituals of bourgeois society.[6]

Some historians have sought to counter the notion that white women's "insular whims and prejudices widened the racial gulf" by investigating the social reform projects that white women undertook to ameliorate the most deleterious effects of colonialism.[7] Indeed, one could argue that some Western women did help to soften the impact of colonialism or actively militated against it. In addition to the many missionaries who would have placed themselves in this category, there were also secular reformers who criticized the excesses of colonial exploitation and wanted to give India back something in return. Consider the example of Mary Carpenter, an educationist who campaigned in both India and England for Indian women's education and promoted India in the 1860s and 1870s as a potential field for the labors of women trained in Britain to be teachers; or two Irishwomen, Margaret Cousins, who founded the All-India Women's Conference in 1927, and the theosophist Annie Besant, first president of the Congress Party. Yet, women-centered histories that attempt to counter the negative image of white women prevalent in masculinist histories risk performing a whitewash job of their own by eliding or diminishing white women's contributions to a racist, exploitative colonial project. The current challenge of the historiography of white women's involvement in colonial rule (in India as elsewhere, of missionaries as of secular reformers) is to describe and understand their contribution in ways that recognize both their complicity with and resistance to the exploitative, racist dimensions of colonization. This is the ambition of recent feminist historiography such as that collected in Nupur Chaudhuri and Margaret Strobel's edited volume, entitled, appropriately, *Western Women and Imperialism: Complicity and Resistance.*[8]

To meet this challenge, a crucial first step is to dismantle our assumptions of a unified concept of "woman." One of the most important intellectual developments of recent years—across the disciplines—has been the examination of the way gender, race, class, and other constituents of identity (such as sexuality, age, marital status, and religion) are mutually imbricated. In the area of gender studies, the theoretical work of Denise Riley, Joan Scott, and Judith Butler has been instrumental in shaping an understanding of gender that does not assume that women across time and space necessarily share a singular experience as women or possess the same political interests. In terms of the historiography of women in colonialism, such insights have allowed scholars to relinquish the comforting feminist fiction that nineteenth-century white women would have "naturally" promoted the interests of other women.

Granted that one can neither absolve white women of their participation in what appears in retrospect a morally reprehensible and tragic episode in the history of the world, nor assign them sole responsibility for its racist, classist, exploitative nature, how does one deal with the participation of women in the colonial rule of India? In two serious, well-researched, and theoretically sophisticated essays, Jane Haggis shows how one might take into consideration the agency and intention of individual western women missionaries in colonial India. In one particularly self-reflexive essay, she heeds the cautions of post-colonial criticism that one cannot privilege one's own interpretation of events in a world where all historical narratives are equally fictional. Haggis presents her own analysis of missionary women's complicity with racial discourses of colonialism alongside the women's own understanding of their endeavors in India. In the writings of these women, their presence in India was nothing less than an appropriate response to the call of God.[9] In the sections that follow I extend Haggis's investigation of the religious dimension the women gave to their own work so as to perceive the hermeneutical horizon within which their efforts to convert and reform Indian women gained meaning. Before I discuss the theological and historical context of the women's missionary movement, however, I address the relevance for missionaries of one of the most important insights raised by recent scholarship on colonial women, namely, that although the colonies offered multiple opportunities for professional women, including teachers, doctors, and social workers, their independence was severely restricted by a generalized paranoia about racial miscegenation.[10]

If the arrival of large numbers of white women in India hastened the "embourgeoisment of colonial communities," it also generated a host of anxieties about white women's sexuality. These anxieties turned on the figure of the lustful Indian male whose supposedly intense sexual desire for white women threatened the honor of those men entrusted with her protection: white husbands, fathers, and father figures. The presence of white women justified the construction of a multitude of social practices and procedures that tried to ensure women's protection, practices that in turn entailed an intensification of racial divisions and the vigilant policing of the behavior of both white women and Indian men.[11] The discourse of protection that took shape around stereotypes of the lustful Indian male and the desirable European woman constituted probably the most significant limit that white women of all kinds—missionaries, wives, widows, and reformers—had to negotiate to carry out their projects.

The articulation of male honor with female chastity was even more exaggerated in the colonies than in the metropole by virtue of being triangulated with the domination of colonial subjects.[12] Here, threats to male control by colonial subjects or underlings almost always resulted in an increase in accusations of sexual impropriety and the harshly punitive acts of retribution it was thought such crimes justified.[13] Such a pattern is visible in the reportage surrounding the Rebellion of 1857 in which colonial accounts of the uprising contain numerous references to the sexual assault and mutilation of British women by Indian men. The ruthlessness with which the revolt was suppressed can be seen as fueled in part by jealous rage and the desire to avenge the outraged virtue of English women.[14] Women were constructed as passive signifiers of British male honor, conjuring up by their very vulnerability the brutish violence that smoldered beneath the sullen, resentful compliance of the Indian subject. White women also came to stand for all that was pure and good in British culture itself, what was worth defending at all costs if threatened by the unruly forces of the colonized. In the furious debates, newspaper editorials, and town hall meetings about the Ilbert Bill in 1883 (which would give Indian magistrates jurisdiction to try cases involving white people), white women themselves became particularly agitated over the threat of sexual assaults by Indian men. Their awareness of being a small minority surrounded by millions of Indians only intensified their anxieties.[15]

At the same time, life in the colonies presented women, especially professional women such as doctors, teachers, and social workers, with opportunities that were foreclosed to them in the metropole. Many Western women embarking for India were well aware of this. One secular reformer, Mary Carpenter, spent the last decade of her life promoting organizations that trained English women to go to India as teachers. Before setting out to India for the first time, she wrote in her journal of her "strong and settled conviction" that India was "a new field . . . about to open to me . . . in which my natural powers will have free scope."[16] Although it is true that Western women did have more scope in the colonies than at home for exercising skills and talents, colonial women were hedged about by conventions and expectations of proper conduct, which, if transgressed, could result in a hasty and humiliating loss of reputation. That women missionaries were not immune from the dynamics of sexual jealousy is vividly illustrated in the trial of Miss Pigot, a single lady missionary with the United Scottish Mission.[17] Her case illustrates the multiple social forces with which "unprotected" European women had to contend.

Sexual Scandal and the Unprotected Woman

Miss Pigot, an unmarried middle-aged Anglo-Indian woman, ran the Church of Scotland's orphanage and zenana mission in Calcutta from 1870 to 1883.[18] From newspaper accounts from the period, it seems that she did a tolerable job of managing these institutions and was well liked by both foreign missionaries and Christian and non-Christian Indians. However, starting in 1879 a clergyman newly arrived in Calcutta, Rev. William Hastie, circulated reports that she was both incompetent in her professional capacity and, more important, indiscreet and immodest in her dealings with men. Hastie, the head of a college run under the auspices of the Church of Scotland, insinuated in reports that he sent to the Home Committee that she had had improper relationships with both an Indian Christian teacher at her school, Babu Kali Charan Banerjee, and Prof. Wilson, a lay teacher at the college managed by Rev. Hastie. In 1883, after a trip to Scotland to try to reclaim her good name with the principal men of the church, Miss Pigot returned to Calcutta and charged Hastie with libel. The timing of the case was particularly significant in that it took place in the midst of racial tension provoked by the Ilbert Bill. After rushing through the proceedings, the judge gave an almost completely inconclusive verdict, maintaining that Hastie's accusations were groundless, yet finding Pigot's friendship with Banerjee not of "a proper character."[19] Justice Norris awarded Pigot nominal damages of one anna, with both parties paying their own legal costs. In the end, Pigot did achieve a partial victory. In an appeal raised in 1884 before the Appellate Bench of the High Court, the judge ruled that Hastie's libelous accusations were totally groundless and influenced by "malicious motives." Pigot was awarded 3,000 rupees in damages, which Hastie avoided paying by claiming insolvency.[20]

In his analysis of the case, Kenneth Ballhatchet makes the astute observation that Hastie's accusations stemmed from "a classic occasion for the sexual jealousy to which men of a dominant group are peculiarly liable."[21] Hastie suspected Banerjee, the Indian Christian whom he alleged was on intimate terms with Pigot, of writing articles in the *Indian Christian Herald* that were critical of Hastie's theological positions. Banerjee thus represented a galling challenge to Hastie's intellectual authority. His friendship with Pigot only exacerbated Hastie's ill will, as it compounded Hastie's sense of intellectual rivalry with sexual rivalry. In this episode one sees a replication in miniature of the dynamics that drove patriarchal colonialists to perceive sexual transgression whenever Indians challenged British authority.

Both Mrinalini Sinha and Ballhatchet note that the secular Indian and the English press condemned Hastie and the judgment arrived at by Justice Norris and gave its support to Miss Pigot. The missionary community in India, however, was not so generous. In a departure from the rest of public opinion, Pigot's coreligionists held up her morals to public scrutiny and found them lacking. In the *Harvest Field* of October 1883, an editorial appeared reviewing the case. The author, Rev. J. Hudson, concluded that even though there was not enough evidence to convict her of immorality, the trial had brought to the surface several unflattering facts about her conduct. Surprisingly, the fact that she was a confirmed spinster tended to help her case, for in Hudson's opinion, her habitual freedom with men was paradoxically evidence of her actual chastity. He wrote, "No doubt below a certain level vice is openly shameless, but when outward appearances have to be maintained it puts on the cloak of excessive prudery." In evaluating Pigot's moral and sexual propriety, Hudson factored in not only her commitment to lifelong chastity, but also her age: "Much weight should likewise be allowed to the fact that Miss Pigot was past middle life and in almost independent charge of the Scotch female mission. Her age and office might appear to her to offer of themselves a sufficient guarantee and thus help to put her off her guard." In spite of these concessions, however, Hudson considered her behavior to be out of line with normative feminine propriety: "There was ample proof that Miss Pigot was most indiscreet and unlady-like and that her manner was altogether wanting in female delicacy."[22] Although Victorian gender ideology generally permitted women a certain measure of authority as they aged, the case of Miss Pigot indicates that seniority was no defense against the charge of immodesty, a charge that was deeply corrosive of a woman's authority. Although Hudson absolved her of the charge of immorality (if not immodesty), the libel trial and the publicity surrounding it led to an investigation of Pigot's professional competence, and in that analysis she again came up short. Hudson filled his letter with veiled references to the misuse of funds and the need for careful oversight of accounts to avoid misappropriation.

Scandals such as this were deeply embarrassing to the Church leadership. The impulse of patriarchal males to close ranks on supposedly recalcitrant women is apparent in Hudson's editorial when he lays the blame for the problem on the notion that Hastie did not have sufficient "control" over "the female department" in the first place. "The constitution of the Church of Scotland Mission, at any rate of the Female Department," he concluded, "seems altogether unsatisfactory."[23] The judgments made about Pigot are similar to those made about Clarinda, the leader of the Tirunelveli church (see chapter 1). As in Clarinda's case, the leadership capacities of a woman were called into question by being tied to her sexual conduct. Though the missions offered women the opportunity to exercise leadership and develop as individuals through the project of "soul-making" rather than through motherhood and marriage, the threat of sexual scandal hovered constantly in the background, limiting what women could do and acting as a break on their activities.[24]

Historical Background of the Women's Missionary Movement

The women's missionary movement was organized around Victorian ideas about gender that glorified women's role as the moral guardian of the home. According to the prevailing (though not uncontested) "doctrine of separate spheres," men and women were by nature suited for work in distinct arenas of life. Women's social responsibility was to create a home where weary husbands could retreat from the morally unsavory, profit-driven world of the marketplace and where women could exercise a benevolent moral influence over their children.

The Doctrine of Separate Spheres

The ideology of separate spheres, a complex set of beliefs, practices, and assumptions about gender, profoundly influenced relations between the sexes in both Western Europe and North America from the late eighteenth to the early twentieth century.[25] This ideology had its material basis in the separation of the activities of production from those of reproduction in the organization of labor that was ushered into being by the Industrial Revolution and the accompanying accumulation of capital.[26]

Like its causes, the effects of this discourse were manifold. Among other things, the idea of separate spheres lent force to the idea that women's moral influence through their nurturing activities could be extended beyond the literal home to a world felt to be badly in need of such influence.[27] The women's foreign missionary movement was a particularly assertive interpretation of the ideology of separate spheres insofar as it involved the conceptualization of women's involvement in foreign missions as a "natural" extension of women's role as moral guardian of the home to encompass the whole world, leaping over, as it were, the world of men in Western Europe and North America.[28] In addition, the women's missionary movement provided an outlet for women's professional aspirations at a time when gender discrimination excluded women from many fields (notably medicine) and from the higher reaches of fields in which they had been active for many years (such as education).

Inspired by the belief that converting mothers and wives was essential to bringing about the spiritual regeneration of society, the women's foreign missionary societies had many links, ideological and institutional, with other kinds of social reform movements in England and the United States. Like the women who started Sunday schools for female mill workers in industrial London or established settlement houses for immigrant women in urban Chicago, supporters of the women's foreign missionary movement believed that women held the moral fate of society in their hands. The proverbial phrase "The hand that rocks the cradle rocks the world" was the rallying cry of these organizations, in which women were targeted as the most effective agents of social improvement by virtue of being the primary socializers of young children.

With the frank essentialism that marks many successful social movements, women were understood as a single class whose common sentiments, responsibilities, and interests cut across all racial, class, religious, or national boundaries.[29] But in the estimation of the middle-class Protestant women who supported these different movements, not all women were living up to their maternal responsibilities. Whether poor, uneducated, non-English-speaking or non–Protestant Christian, the various women who received charity from women's benevolent societies were judged deficient in their execution of their womanly duties. Their apparent inability to manage an orderly home (as defined by the ideal of the middle-class home) was taken as evidence of their essentially immature and uncivilized nature, for, according to the evolutionist idiom of the times, nonconformity to middle-class, Protestant Anglo culture was considered tantamount to childishness. Their childish incompetence in turn was seen as requiring the forceful management of more mature middle-class women. This kind of "maternalism" was starkly evident in the discourse of female reformers in the British colonies, including India, as in the "depraved" slums of Western European and North American cities.[30] Even though she was not a missionary, but a secular activist for women's education in India, Mary Carpenter was representative in seeing a direct connection between Hinduism and bad mothering. "Extreme ignorance, and the vices connected with idolatry," she wrote, "render women in India very unfit to perform the duty nature intended for her—the care of children; for even if she can take proper care of their little bodies (which is doubtful) she infuses into their opening minds a degree of deception and willfulness which years may not be able to eradicate."[31] That Carpenter cannot specify exactly *how* "idolatry" was supposed to lead to deception and willfulness suggests that for her, "Hinduism" stood for an entire way of life, which she contrasted unfavorably with the Christian way of life.

The importance of Christianity in nineteenth-century women's social movements centered on the belief that it had done more to improve the condition of women materially, socially, and spiritually than any other religion. Even more radical wings of the women's movement drew on the moral authority and prestige of Christianity to legitimate their causes. Consider, for example, the intense, if heterodox, religiosity of American suffragists like Elizabeth Cady Stanton, who published her own commentary on the Bible.[32] Advocates of the foreign missionary society were as triumphalist as their counterparts who focused on reform in the metropole. The New Testament provided them with ample evidence of the favor that Jesus had shown to women. Mrs. Pitman, an English promoter of women's foreign missions, wrote, "By being born of a woman Christ Jesus set eternal honour upon womanhood; and through all His life He manifested His kindliness to woman. . . . As she was first in the transgression, it seemed as if He were determined that she should be foremost in blessing."[33] Women like Pitman repeatedly contrasted the esteem Christianity gave to women with the degradation to which they felt women were subject in other religious traditions.

Consistent with the Christian principle that those who had been specially blessed had a special responsibility to share their good fortune, the women's foreign missionary movement exhorted white women to spread among the "heathen" the benefits of Christian womanhood. Their keen sense of responsibility toward those they considered less fortunate cannot be underestimated, nor can their unflappable sense of superiority. An American Methodist advocate of the women's foreign missionary movement, Annie Wittenmeyer, wrote, "We stand here at the radiating centre of Christian civilization, exalted and crowned by a religion of purity and love. But just over there, our sisters are crushed to the very earth by the barbarism of false religion—a religion that knows no purity, no love, no mercy, that tramples down every holy instinct, and degrades women to the level of brute beasts."[34] As Wittenmeyer's words suggest, the moral valuations placed on different religions and cultures could easily slide into racial valuations.

Comparisons between English-speaking, fair-skinned Christian women and their swarthy, non-Christian sisters helped form the crucible out of which a coherent sense of identity among "white women" was forged. In one quasi-mythological anecdote based on a pun, Wittenmeyer offered a historically dubious but apparently persuasive account of the moral leadership of whites. When Julius Caesar first encountered the indigenous inhabitants of the British isles, Wittenmeyer reported, he judged them unfit even for slavery. A more perspicacious observer who happened to be Christian responded that if the flaxen-haired "Anglo" savages were given Christianity, they would be like "Angels." "Today the fair-faced women who speak the English language are, more than any others," wrote Wittenmeyer, "the angels of man's spiritual destiny, and the hope of the women of heathen lands."[35] Via two sets of exclusions, racial and linguistic, Wittenmeyer identified the class of women who represented the pinnacle of civilization, the kind of beings farthest from beasts and closest to angels: They were fair-faced (not Asian, African, or Native American) and English speakers (not German, French, Italian, Polish, or other continental types, likely to be Roman Catholic or Jewish). To fulfill their duty to their "heathen sisters," white women had to harness their maternal qualities—patience, compassion, piety, self-sacrifice—to the engine of progress and exert themselves untiringly in philanthropic and proselytizing endeavors.

Social Context of the Women's Foreign Missionary Movement

Though Western women were involved with the missionary endeavor in India from the eighteenth century, their independent agency in the mission field did not really begin until the 1860s. Before this time, the primary way for a woman with a strong sense of evangelical duty to enter the overseas missionary field was to marry a seminary graduate bound for foreign lands. Other women accompanied their male relatives overseas as the daughters or sisters of missionaries, later finding husbands among the ranks of the missionaries.[36] The wives of missionaries were, generally speaking, as committed to the evangelical project as their husbands. In their capacity as wives, they were to exhibit to the surrounding population—Christian, non-Christian, and inquiring—the virtues of companionate marriage and an open, well-ordered Christian home.[37] In addition, missionary wives frequently established schools for girls and "visited," where possible, with the women of socially respectable classes, an extension of the visiting that pastors' wives did in England and New England. But such projects often floundered in the wake of domestic crises—sick children, sick husbands, or the sudden flight of servants—as these women discovered that the demands of family life took precedence over evangelism.[38] Among the most important factors in the expansion of women's missions was the active recruitment of unmarried women not burdened by the responsibilities of housekeeping and raising a family. Beginning in the early nineteenth century, overextended missionary wives themselves urged the denominational missionary boards to recruit single women as teachers to support the girls schools and newly formed zenana missionary societies. In one of the many ironies of the women's missions, the bearers of Western ideals of feminine propriety in the arenas of motherhood, conjugality, and domesticity increasingly came to be single women traveling far beyond the confines of their own homes and natal families, unattached to husband or children.

One of the first institutions that articulated an awareness of the importance of recruiting unmarried women as missionaries was the London-based Society for the Promotion of Female Education in the East, whose formation in 1834 was inspired by an American missionary, Mr. Abeel, recently returned from China.[39] The SPFEE was representative of women's missionary societies in several significant ways. First, the primary focus of its mission was education. The goal of the organization was to train women to be missionary teachers, because local customs in much of Asia prevented male missionaries from reaching women. The curriculum envisioned by the SPFEE, like that of the women's missionary societies that followed, was designed not to equip Indian women to enter professions, but to make them better wives and mothers to Christian men.[40] Second, the SPFEE reflected the trend toward international cooperation evident in the nineteenth-century foreign missionary movement, in which British and American church people frequently worked side by side in spite of the fact that the United States had won its independence from England only a generation before. To identify this kind of solidarity at the ideological level is not to assume that in the mission field missionaries cooperated without conflict. The records of the different missionary societies reveal considerable competition across the lines of denomination and nationality. But at least as far as the rhetoric of the Anglo-American vanguard was concerned, denominational or even national affiliations were less significant than a shared commitment to bring Christianity to the non-Christian world. Wittenmeyer reflected the us-against-them mentality that galvanized missionaries of different nationalities when she wrote, "The people of every kindred, nation and tongue under the skies, are coming to be one with us, in all things. And we are to lift them up to our Christian civilization, or they are to drag us down towards their barbarisms. . . . We must oppose with our whole force the world and overcome it, or the enemy will come in like a flood and overcome us."[41] This shared sense of imperial purpose created a remarkable degree of solidarity among Protestants of diverse denominations in spite of considerable theological and ecclesiastical differences.

The founding of the SPFEE in 1834 anticipated the major period of growth in women's missions by about thirty years. The full flowering of women's missions in India in the years between 1860 and 1890 depended on a number of social and ideological conditions: the availability of educated single women as workers, reliable funding sources, and the organization of vast networks of supporters who could couch the moral and social worth of such work in terms persuasive to the people of the time.

Women's missions drew their personnel mostly from the unmarried graduates of newly established women's seminaries and normal schools. Faced with a shortage of suitable employment opportunities in the United States and Britain, many women graduates looked to the missions for positions consistent with the ambitions cultivated in these schools, to bring women's nurturing and edifying talents to the world.[42] In the United States, the experiences of female nurses on the battlefields of the Civil War made many people aware of the untapped resource of women's "great executive ability and amount of energy."[43] The example of women like Clara Barton, a nurse during the Civil War who founded the American Red Cross, made it possible for women to contemplate lives of professional service that channeled their nurturing capacities outside the home and into the world at large.

In England, by a fortuitous coincidence, the perceived excess of single women in the mid–nineteenth century helped to supply the womanpower necessary to realize middle-class women's interest in philanthropy.[44] The recruitment of single women missionaries capitalized on a widespread fear that Britain was overrun by "redundant females," a fear fueled by misreadings of the

1851 census report. Erroneous interpretations of the report, published in 1862, argued that from 350,000 to 1,100,000 women of marriageable age were unable to marry because of a shortage of men. Several commentators tried early on to counter this impression by noting that the "excess" of women consisted primarily of older widows and was due to the greater longevity of women, but the mistaken belief persisted throughout the nineteenth century, fueling, among other things, the enthusiastic support of emigration for young women engaged in philanthropic endeavors.[45] Whether or not they had the opportunity to marry in England, many single women missionaries discovered opportunities to do so in the colonies. One of the earliest Tamil historians of the Protestant Church, Paul Appasamy, noted in his description of women's work connected with the Church Missionary Society that the "lady missionaries who came over from England were all married sooner or later and all thus lost to this special department of mission work."[46]

Notwithstanding such sardonic comments, it is important to note that missionary work constituted an important alternative for women outside of marriage and the heterosexual household. The importance of this vision of an alternative feminine vocation is apparent in the frequency with which the heroic female missionary appears as a figure in women's and girls' fiction of the time.[47] As much as the "romance of missions" served to obscure the highly organized, bureaucratic aspect of missions, missionary societies were the launching ground of serious professional careers for many women as well as men. As Jeffrey Cox has written, "It is a serious and common error to think of missionaries as evangelists in pith helmets rather than professional institution builders."[48] Many of the missionaries who stayed in India the longest and had the most impact on the communities in which they worked were "spinsters," unmarried women dedicated to the institutions they helped to found, fund, and manage.

The rise in women's auxiliary organizations was another important factor in the success of women's missions. These organizations created fund-raising channels for women's projects that ran separately from those of the male-dominated denominational missionary boards and allowed women missionaries to pursue their own philanthropic ventures.[49] In the United States, for example, two "women's boards" were founded by Congregationalists: the Women's Board of Missions (WBM), in January 1868, and the Women's Board of Mission of the Interior in October 1868. In 1881, the women's work committee of the Anglican Church Missionary Society branched off to become a more independent subsidiary society, the Church of England Zenana Missionary Society (CEZMS), and by the 1890s almost every Protestant missionary society in India had a branch devoted to what became known generically as "women's work."[50]

Through these bodies, women missionaries were able to promote their own projects to an unprecedented degree, backed by networks of personal and monetary support that ran parallel to yet separate from the general missionary sources. Using methods well-established by the church-run charities of England and the United States, the WBM, for example, set up networks for the collection of funds—"mite-boxes for pennies, and envelopes for weekly pledges"—and by this means raised $5,000 in its first year and nearly $200,000 over the course of its first six years of operation. The very act of giving money was urged on women as a beneficial spiritual practice, as women were asked to "clothe" each dollar "with the faith, prayers, and self-denials that gathered it" and thereby increase its value.[51]

Theological Context of the Foreign Mission

The evangelical leanings of most Protestant missionaries in colonial India have been well-noted but less often defined explicitly. Certainly, missionaries were evangelical first of all in the sense of being evangelists, people who believed they were carrying out the commission given by Jesus after his resurrection to go among the nations of the world preaching the Christian gospel (Matthew 28:19; Mark 16:15). Their theological leanings, that is, how they actualized the "Great Commission" and for what reasons, varied considerably. Here I highlight the beliefs that most affected the tone and tenor of missionary work. I begin with a discussion of the beliefs that Methodists had about practice, a somewhat neglected aspect of Protestantism insofar as it is considered a religion more oriented toward belief than praxis.

Evangelicals are understood as (and generally understood themselves to be) Christians "who believed that the essential part of the Gospel consisted in salvation by faith through the atoning death of Christ and who denied that either good works or the sacraments had any saving efficacy."[52] But if, in their view, charitable works, communion wafers, and consecrated wine had no supernatural efficacy, this did not mean that they were indifferent to the significance of action for salvation. Whether High Church Anglican or dissenting Congregationalist, evangelicals placed great importance on an intense, personal experience of conversion. Understood as a one-on-one encounter with God, conversion in the evangelical tradition could be a powerfully emotional and visceral experience, as described in the tearful witnessing of revivalists, or it could be a simple renewal of confidence, as in Rev. Robert Caldwell's conversion experience. Caldwell wrote that after months of tarrying,

> a day arrived when "thoughts above my thoughts," destined not to
> pass away but to take shape and live, took possession of my mind.
> Various difficulties had appeared to lie in the way of my acting on
> my convictions, but one day, when altogether alone and considering
> again what course I should take, all my difficulties seemed to have
> suddenly ceased. The way seemed invitingly open. If I was ever to
> give myself to God a voice within me said, why not now? The will
> was given me then and there to realise this "now" and together with
> the "will" the power to "do." I rose up and went out into the open
> air virtually a new being, with a new governing idea, a new object in

life, and what seemed to be "new heavens and a new earth" to live in.[53]

As Caldwell's reminiscences suggest, the evangelical experience of conversion ideally awakened in the convert a desire to grow toward a greater realization of Christian virtue by the application of this "new governing idea" to life. This new idea was to shape the Christian individual's responses to all the choices in life, from the grand question of his or her proper vocation to the very particular dilemmas raised by the need to act in a world full of conventions and customs.

The exercise of strict discipline in regulating manners and morals so as to live a holy life was common to both Calvinism and Methodism, and arguably less significant in Lutheranism. For Calvinists, discipline's ostensible purpose was not only the "safeguarding of the sacrament" (so that the holy body of the elect who communed together would not be sullied by the participation of any corrupt individual) but also the collective creation of a holy "city" that would serve as an exemplar to the whole world, as in Calvin's reformed Geneva, or the "City on a Hill" envisioned by American Puritans. Calvinists in Geneva and Zurich instituted boards of moral discipline to ensure that this holy society was realized in actual practice. These boards, along with the Consistory (a regulatory institution composed of ministers and laymen), were entrusted with the responsibility of punishing transgressors through sanctions that ranged from monetary fines to excommunication and even execution.[54] In India, the Scottish Presbyterians and the American Congregationalists could be said to have been inheritors of this understanding of discipline, without, obviously, nearly the same degree of state cooperation to enforce it.

Methodists too had their spiritual police and codes of conduct to distinguish themselves from less disciplined, unsaved folk. As a dissident movement that grew out of the established Church of England, Methodism was more staunchly opposed to the mixing of state and church authority. It encouraged a more personal, experiential, and emotionally charged concept of the sanctified life. Nevertheless, the concept of discipline was very important to them. As E. P. Thompson writes: "Wesley wished the Methodists to be a 'peculiar people'; to abstain from marriage outside the societies; to be distinguished by their dress and by the gravity of their speech and manners; to avoid the company even of relatives who were still in 'Satan's kingdom.' Members were expelled for levity, for profanity and swearing, for lax attendance at class meetings. The societies, with their confessional band-meetings, classes, watch nights and visiting, made up a lay order within which, as Southey noted, there was a 'spiritual police' constantly alert for any signs of relapse."[55] In India, the inheritors of Wesley's Methodism were manifold: the LMS, the Wesleyan Methodist Missionary Society, and the more evangelical elements within the Church of England's CMS tended in this direction. In the Methodist evangelical context, personal habits were frequently taken to be measures of a person's spiritual state. As the American Methodist Annie Wittenmeyer declared with perfect confidence, "The outward life is the index to the heart."[56] This attitude toward religion manifests itself again and again, as we shall we, in debates about what it meant to be a Christian in India, when behaviors related to marriage, domesticity, and clothing changed or did not change over the course of Christianization.

The complex relationship in Protestant thought between outward practices and their internal meanings took a new twist in the tumultuous ecclesiastical history of early modern England. By discounting the significance of the sacraments as salvific in and of themselves, evangelicals both within the Church of England and among the dissenters were no doubt reacting against a perceived excessive ritualism in both High Church Anglicanism and Catholicism. But they were also responding to a creeping worry about the spread of equivocation, that is, people falsely testifying to things they did not believe in under the pressure of the state. Until the mid–nineteenth century, as the Established, that is, state-sanctioned, church of the nation, the Church of England had a monopoly on all the functions of civil religion. In this capacity, for example, it reserved for itself alone the authority to sanctify marriages and burials. In a conjunction of religious and political loyalty that may appear strange from the perspective of a modern secular state, the Church of England (and Scotland) cooperated with the government in ensuring that every potential or actual state representative publicly attested to his belief in the truth of Anglican doctrine. Members of religious minorities, including Jews, Roman Catholics, and dissenters (Baptists, Methodists, Unitarians, and all other Protestant groups that did not subscribe to the theological or ecclesiastical positions of the Church of England) could not sit in Parliament, gain admission to Oxford or Cambridge, or enjoy full voting rights without swearing by the Thirty-Nine Articles of the Anglican creed.[57] Given this state of affairs, individuals were regularly compelled by the state to go against their conscience and take vows or participate in rituals that had no meaning for them.

The evangelicals' insistence on *vital* Christianity, in which the forms of religion were deemed useless and empty unless filled by intense emotional and psychological energy, must be seen in this context. To protect against false religion and the temptation of equivocation, evangelicals insisted that true believers engage fervently with Christian symbols; it was not enough simply to go through the motions. William Wilberforce, one of the leaders of the Clapham Sect, defined Christianity as "a state into which we are not born, but into which we must be translated; a nature which we do not inherit, but into which we are to be created anew. . . . This is a matter of labour and difficulty, requiring continual watchfulness, unceasing effort, and unwearied patience."[58] Although the Clapham Sect is probably best known for their promotion of sweeping reforms at the level of state politics (notably the British antislavery movement), their ideal of transforming society according to Christian principles had a significant local dimension as well.

Taken to their logical limit, the broad claims of evangelical spokespeople implied that no aspect of social life could be considered too trivial to be significant in one's ultimate salvation: style of adornment, table manners, per-

sonal habits, diction, and comportment were all potentially laden with significance as to the present and future state of one's soul. As the famous American
missionary Henry Judson wrote in a pamphlet on jewelry, "Be not deterred by
the suggestion, that in such discussions, you are conversant about *small* things.
Great things depend on small. . . . Satan is well aware that if he can secure the
minute units, the sum total will be his own."[59] Women's jewelry, in particular,
came to stand for a woman's commitment to Christianity, a subject I take up
in greater detail in chapter 6. As Judson's comment suggests, in activist evangelical rhetoric the minute practices that gave shape and texture to everyday
life were considered to be as intimately connected with cosmic consequences
as was the history of the nation. Now, having duly noted that, contrary to
popular perception, evangelical Christians did give considerable importance to
practice, we should turn to what was, to them, often a more compelling concern: the infinite variety of sectarian positions on doctrine that were possible
within the general framework of Protestant Christian theology.

One of the most significant features of nineteenth-century evangelical
thought was its thoroughly historical outlook. Evangelicals, including missionaries, saw themselves and the objects of their evangelistic endeavors as part of
God's plan for the universe, which had begun with the creation of the world
and was methodically approaching completion with the birth, death, resurrection, and eventual return of Jesus, humanity's savior from sin. The part of this
cosmic unfolding that was most significant to missionaries was the millennium, a thousand-year period of peace and worldwide human unity presided
over by Jesus Christ. In the early years of the nineteenth century, and again
toward the end, widespread belief that the Christian millennium was imminent
(or already upon them) led many missionaries to expect the rapid conversion
of all the nations of the world.[60] At their most ambitious, advocates of foreign
missions claimed that the times were so ripe for evangelical activity that the
population of the entire world could be proselytized in one generation. Premillennialists believed that no improvement in the moral, economic, or social
state of the world was possible until Jesus' return, and the world's complete
deterioration would speed his arrival; postmillennialists argued that to hasten
his return, people had to work to create the ideal Christian Kingdom in the
here and now. Though they disagreed about the extent to which social justice
should accompany Christian evangelism, both pre- and postmillennialists
agreed that all the world's population had to hear about the Christian God and
get a chance to be saved in order for the savior to return.[61]

Like the evangelical conception of salvific practice, the millenarian orientation toward history had a local as well as a global focus. Many evangelical
Christians read fluctuations in society, politics, the natural environment, and
economics as the effects of divine intervention. Just as imperial successes were
read as signs of God's favor, of his election of the British (or the Americans)
to be the people chosen to act as moral guides for the rest of the world, so
were setbacks interpreted as indications of God's disfavor. For example, many
Christians viewed the violent disturbances of 1857 as a catastrophe sent by God
to punish the British for laxity in Christian values; they interpreted the "mu-

tiny" as a sign that God wanted the British government to place the conversion of India at the center of its imperial agenda.[62]

In addition to this historical orientation toward the millennium, the core theology of most missionaries, male and female, included a realistic conception of heaven and hell. Heaven and hell were not metaphors to describe a state of being close to God or alienated from God, but were conceived of as actual places that were described by God in the Bible in language suitable for human visualization.[63] The doctrine of predestination associated with Calvin's teachings intensified the socially conservative implications of this emphasis on hell, whereas Methodist Arminian ideas tended to mitigate them. Arminianism constituted a radical break from strict Calvinism in maintaining that salvation was potentially available to everyone, not only the preselected few. Liberal Christians who elaborated on the Arminian view of universal salvation reasoned that even though "the heathen" would most likely be condemned because of their idolatry, they might still be redeemed by good conduct arrived at by the exercise of their own inherent moral reasoning.[64] The liberal notion that people who had never heard of Christ could still attain salvation by inadvertently acting like Christians, however, remained a very controversial doctrine and did not gain widespread acceptance among missionaries. Rather, missionary writers used the language of hell to inspire pity, as in the stock scene in missionary literature of "heathens" dropping into hell by the thousands, or righteous indignation, as when descriptions of Hindu religious practices or noncompliant individuals were juxtaposed with references to smoking sulfur and brimstone. One should keep in mind that this metaphoric language gained special force when accompanied by the conviction that ultimately, hell referred to an actual place, where sinners spent eternity.

One of the features of evangelical Christianity that allowed for the rapid diffusion of its ideas was revivalism. The eighteenth-century revivals in England, such as those generated by the preaching of John Wesley, the founder of Methodism, accounted for much of the energy behind British missionary movements. In the United States, several waves of intensified religious feeling swept through particular regions, from the Great Awakening (circa 1720–1776) that rocked the colonies of New England to the slickly orchestrated revivalism of traveling preachers like Dwight Moody (1837–1899) and Billy Sunday (1862–1935), who brought camp meetings to small towns and cities from Boston to Birmingham. Far from being locally contained events, these revivals were notable for their tendency to spread, often across the Atlantic and back.[65] During these periods of heightened religious feeling, the ideas and particular flavor of evangelical Christianity were circulated rapidly among a large population. Prayer meetings were held several times a week, sometimes several times a day, and various techniques were used to persuade the ambivalent or the uncertain of the need to revitalize their religious commitments. Although the emotional outbursts that invariably attended these episodes of collective effervescence were the object of considerable debate among religious and civic leaders, they reinforced a tendency stemming from pietism to characterize conversion as a deeply emotional experience.

The vividness of heaven and hell, the biblical temporal frame provided by predictions of the Second Coming, and an emotional, pietistic affective tone all contributed to the distinctive style of nineteenth-century evangelicalism. Yet one would not want to overstate the homogeneity of evangelical doctrine or religious style. Certainly, some evangelical Protestants rejected the reality of hell, denied that they were on the brink of the Christian millennium, or scorned the emotionalism of revival-based religion. Whatever doctrinal agreement there was among evangelicals tended to converge on the concept of the Atonement. This is the teaching that Jesus Christ's suffering and death brought about the reconciliation—the "at-one-ment"—of humanity and God by overcoming the alienation of sinful humans from God. Several theories, based on different images found in the New Testament, offered technical explanations of the atonement; for example, Christ was killed as a ransom that paid for the lives of all sinners, or, through his perfect, sinless life Christ accumulated enough superfluous merit to act as an appropriate sacrifice to satisfy God and quell his righteous wrath at the sinfulness of humans.[66] But to ordinary nineteenth-century Christians the technical aspects of the atonement remained a mystery, and the important part of the doctrine was its simplicity: Christ's crucifixion and resurrection made universal salvation possible; one only had to believe and let oneself be transformed by God's grace. The *universal* nature of salvation was something that missionaries particularly emphasized. In a departure from Calvinism's elitist emphasis on predestination, Methodist-leaning missionaries stressed the equal worth of all souls in the eyes of God.[67]

Though it has been far less recognized as an element of nineteenth-century missionary theology than the doctrine of the Atonement, the personal holiness movements of the late 1800s were also critical in shaping missionary thought and practice. Teachers of this school of Christianity sometimes positioned themselves as critics of the liberal interpretation of Atonement theology. Though advocates of "higher Christian life" agreed that faith in the atoning death of Christ was the most essential part of the gospel, they abhorred its being transformed into an excessively generous doctrine that excused sin rather than pushing for a more intense and complete realization of Christian ideals. As one missionary in India wrote, "There is a strong tendency to look upon the Atonement of Christ as possessing some quality by virtue of which God can excuse and overlook sin in the Christian, a readiness to look upon sinning as the inevitable accompaniment of human nature, 'until death do us part,' and to look upon Christianity as a substitute for rather than a cause of personal holiness of life."[68] John Wesley's position on sanctification provided the theological foundation of the personal holiness movement. His belief that a sort of continual peak experience was available to Christians who fully and completely gave themselves over to God was encapsulated for nineteenth-century followers in his statement, "Entire sanctification or Christian perfection is neither more or less than pure love; love expelling sin, and governing both the heart and life of a child of God. The Refiner's fire purges out all that is contrary to love."[69] Late nineteenth-century advocates of personal holiness understood this passage to mean that true sanctification laid waste to the impulse to conscious sin and instilled in believers an expansive outlook on life that flowed from their absolute trust in the power of God to lead them where he willed. One of the most prominent outlets for people who had experienced this kind of "spiritual deepening" was the Christian foreign mission.[70]

The nineteenth-century reinterpretation of sanctification gained a great many adherents through the annual Keswick Convention, a conference of British evangelicals that was inaugurated in July 1875 in the wake of Dwight Moody and Ira Sankey's widely popular revival meetings in Britain. Inspired by a charismatic if doctrinally unconventional American husband-and-wife team of evangelists, Robert Pearson Smith and Hannah Whitall Smith, the Keswick Convention grew into a major interdenominational event, bringing together men and women from among virtually all the different sects of English Protestant Christianity.[71] The speakers at Keswick taught that a higher plateau of Christian experience was available to those willing to undergo a full and complete surrender to Christ. Mr. Smith's experience of being "perfected" at a camp meeting, as described by his wife, is paradigmatic: "Suddenly from head to foot he had been shaken by what seemed like a magnetic thrill of heavenly delight, and floods of glory seemed to pour through him, soul and body, with the inward assurance that this was the longed-for Baptism of the Holy Spirit. The whole world seemed transformed to him, every leaf and blade of grass quivered with exquisite color, and heaven seemed to open out before him as a present blissful possession."[72]

The holiness movement is usually associated with American Pentecostal churches like the Assembly of God and the Church of the Nazarenes, but in England this particular conceptualization of genuine Christian experience led not to mystical quietism or anarchic emotionalism, but to a commitment to action. According to one of the English clergyman who "regularized" the theological basis of the Keswick Convention, Bishop Handley Moule, sanctification was meaningful only insofar as it was translated into action. For Moule, sanctity meant "to displace self from the inner throne, and to enthrone Him; to make not the slightest compromise with the smallest sin. We aim at nothing less than to walk with God all day long, to abide every hour in Christ and He and His words in us. . . . It is possible to cast every care on Him daily, and to be at peace amidst pressure, to see the will of God in everything, to put away *all* bitterness and clamor and evil speaking, daily and hourly. It is possible by unreserved resort to divine power under divine conditions to become strongest through and through at our weakest point."[73] Such an empowering interpretation of obedience to God had enormous appeal to foreign missionaries, who frequently lived in almost complete isolation from the comforting and confidence-boosting presence of like-minded people and who bore a weighty sense of responsibility under circumstances that frequently were far beyond their control. Indeed, the Keswick Conventions exercised an extraordinary influence on several major missionary leaders stationed throughout the world: J. Hudson Taylor, founder of the China Inland Mission; Eugene Stock, historian of the CMS; and Handley Moule, missionary to Japan and later bishop of Durham. These leaders revived the early evangelical commitment to practical religion and amplified it. Extending the early evangelical emphasis on self-scrutiny and self-discipline, the theology of sanctification taught individual Christians to rely on prayer, earnest and frequent, to learn of God's will for them in their everyday life. As we will see, its theology was to be very influential in the development of Amy Carmichael.

One more theological movement of the late nineteenth and early twentieth centuries that bears mentioning in a discussion of foreign missions is the rise of liberal Christianity. This "movement" was much less self-contained than, for example, the Keswick movement or the evangelical movement spearheaded by the Clapham Sect. Because it was actually a move away from specific doctrine it is difficult even to assign it a distinctive name, but it has generally been described as "liberal Christianity." Broadly speaking, as articulated by spokespeople such as Horace Bushnell and William Newton Clarke, Protestant liberalism affirmed God's immanence in nature and humanity, downplayed immediate millennial expectations, took a more tolerant stance toward non-Christian religions, and held that "salvation was a gradual process in which environmental influences played a major role."[74] Christian duty thus involved taking seriously the immanence of God in this world by committing oneself to the building of the Kingdom in the here and now, creating social conditions of justice and peace that would be conducive to salvation. The most theologically distinct and radical brand of liberal Christianity, which took these general tendencies to their logical limit, was the Social Gospel. This movement sought to "Christianize society by applying the Biblical principles of love and justice to such institutions as the family, the state and the economy."[75]

The liberalization of evangelical Christianity also involved an increased tolerance for non-Christian religions. Such events as the World's Parliament of Religions of 1893, sponsored and attended largely by liberal Christians in the United States, represented a departure from the exclusivist claims of a generation before. A new attitude of tolerance toward different religions opened the door for a reconceptualization of Christian duty as social service. Liberal Christians conceived of the central Christian virtue of obedience to God less as a command to "conquer" people of other faiths for Christ than as an exhortation to manifest the virtues of Christianity in one's own life so that others would be drawn to follow one's example.[76]

Nineteenth-century missionaries thus brought with them to the mission field several versions of salvation and the ideal Christian life that coexisted, sometimes uneasily, sometimes cooperatively. The simplest version maintained that all that was necessary to gain salvation was to believe in Jesus Christ as the savior. This represented the theology of missionaries insofar as it was centered on the doctrine of the Atonement. For proponents of the personal holiness or sanctification movement, on the other hand, conversion was, in a return to the theology of Wilberforce and other early evangelicals, a continual process of perfecting oneself by conforming one's will more and more closely to that of God. For liberal Christians, salvation consisted in a life dedicated to social service that would act as a witness to Christ's teachings. The very diversity of definitions of salvation, I would argue, made evangelical Christianity a powerful instrument of cultural imperialism. Whereas a new adherent may have been attracted by the simplicity of the message of the Atonement, once assent was given to the saving power of Christ, such assent might, according to another version of salvation, involve the acceptance of a whole host of values, practices, and ways of ordering the family and society that were based as much on Western European and North American culture as on biblical precedent.

Case Studies of English and American Women Missionaries

By way of illustrating the theological and institutional background of the missionary movement in general, and the limits and possibilities that the mission field offered to single women missionaries in particular, I analyze the careers of two very successful single women missionaries in south India. Both Amy Carmichael and Eva Swift arrived in India in the 1880s, in the midst of a vast influx of women into the mission field. By this time, Protestant missionary institutions were well established in the Indian field, a large community of Indian Christians was already in place with their own culture at work, and women's missions were at their peak. Although Carmichael was British and Swift was American, the differences in their approach to their vocation were functions not so much of nationality as of denomination. Carmichael, born a Presbyterian, embraced a pietist style of Christianity: she believed her vocation as a missionary consisted in being an obedient instrument of God whose will she attempted to discern through prayer and careful reading of the Bible. This approach set her on a maverick's path, validating a bold, iconoclastic, experimental style of evangelism that did not recognize the authority of any institution, whether Hindu or Christian, above that of God's own directives. Carmichael was a well-known figure in missionary circles by virtue of the numerous books and articles she published from 1895 on. Eva Swift, on the other hand, seems to have assiduously avoided the spotlight. Her approach was much more subdued and far less self-conscious than that of Carmichael. In order to discern Swift's theological and social views, one must read between the lines of the papers she wrote, collected, and deposited toward the end of her life at the missionary archive in the United Theological College in Bangalore. Swift worked within the framework of a form of liberal Christianity that saw the vocation of a missionary as consisting in an exemplary life of service. Although she did not boast of being exemplary herself, she admired and praised those whom she felt were. Even though her style was more moderate than Carmichael's, Swift also drew on her sense of higher authority to challenge patriarchal convention within the American Madurai Mission, of which she was a member. Both women used the empowering potential of Christianity to endorse deviations from established convention in order to secure leadership roles for themselves in very patriarchal missionary institutions. Both used their positions to bring a message of liberation to Indian women, urging them to break with the established norms of patriarchal Indian society. Yet, both women also fostered a certain amount of dependency in the Indians with whom they worked, distrusting the leadership capacities of Indians and tending to favor Westerners over Indians as their successors. This need for dependents to establish their own authority limited the extent of the social message of liberation they sought to bring with them to the women of India.

Amy Carmichael: Indigenous Christianity behind the Ramparts

Amy Carmichael was one of the most famous women missionaries in south India. Notorious among her fellow missionaries for her disdain of conventional evangelistic methods and admired by a vast, worldwide readership for her dedicated work with south Indian orphans, Carmichael was in many ways the epitome of the nineteenth-century "lady missionary." In the over thirty books she wrote describing her missionary endeavors in south India, she appears a true Victorian battle-ax: resourceful, self-sacrificing, dedicated, and willfully oblivious to the disapproval of her peers. This impression is confirmed in the many books written about her and the institution she founded in Tirunelveli district, the Dohnavur Fellowship.[77] Carmichael arrived in Madras in November 1895. She began her career in India working as an itinerant evangelist in the villages of Tirunelveli district, but gained fame (and, in some quarters, notoriety) for the orphanage she founded to "rescue" young girls who had been sold or given to Hindu temples to be trained as *devadasis*, women temple servants whose role was to entertain the deity and preserve the auspicious character of the temple through their ritual work.[78]

Amy Carmichael was born on 16 December 1867 in northern Ireland into a prosperous Scottish family in charge of the local flour mill. Her parents were Presbyterians, members of a church founded by seceders from the official Church of Scotland. She enjoyed a comfortable childhood, but when she was 18 years old her father died from the stress of a large financial loss. His death sent the family into financial and social insecurity.[79] Like many foreign missionaries, Carmichael was informally prepared for her evangelistic work overseas by engaging in philanthropy among the working poor of Britain's many industrial towns. Trained from childhood in the self-sacrificing rigors of noblesse oblige, the future missionary lived in the slums of Belfast and Manchester, where she taught at a night school for boys and established a center called The Welcome that held regular prayer meetings with mill girls (32). In 1886, Carmichael attended her first Keswick Convention. Here she met Robert Wilson, a burly, bearded, taciturn Quaker who was one of the principal leaders of the Keswick movement. He was to become her adopted father and later acted as her patron and mentor.

As mentioned previously, the Keswick movement taught that those who relinquished their own will actually gained power by allowing God's perfect strength, wisdom, and goodness to work through them. Carmichael fully embraced this teaching. In her hands, the idea of sanctification fostered a curious coexistence of deep humility (Carmichael's self-chosen nickname was "Nobody"[38]) with nearly complete confidence in the correctness of her actions. Such a combination of features was particularly advantageous for a woman like Carmichael, who repeatedly challenged and subverted Victorian gender ideology. She aptly described the difficult passage that she had to traverse: "It was a razor edge between faith and presumption, so exceedingly fine" (349). Her life provides an illustration of the ways in which the interpretation of Christianity advocated by the personal holiness movement could authorize alternative visions of social life and legitimate the defiance of convention.

In 1892, after having lived for six years with Wilson and his two grown sons, Carmichael announced that she would join Hudson Taylor's China Inland Mission, scandalizing those who thought she would (and should) remain in England to take care of Mr. Wilson, who by then was quite elderly (52–56). In the end, she was not able to go to China for health reasons, but ended up in Japan with Wilson's reluctant blessing as a member of a multidenominational evangelistic band. She registered with the company under the name Amy Wilson-Carmichael, at Wilson's request. This name remained her nom de plume for many years. Throughout her early years of missionary work overseas, first in Japan and then in Ceylon (Sri Lanka), Wilson periodically issued requests that she come home. In spite of the considerable emotional pressure her domestic obligations must have placed on her, Carmichael remained convinced (and eventually convinced others) that God's will for her was in the foreign missions. In November 1895, she landed in India as a member of the CEZMS and never again left Indian shores.

Once in India, Carmichael regularly scandalized the missionary establishment. In her autobiographical works and the biographies written about her, she is invariably represented as outside the mainstream. Like the Prophets of the Hebrew Bible, Carmichael appeared as a voice crying in the wilderness or, to use the imagery she preferred, a soldier in God's army, urging the reader to join forces with her and God in a fight against "dead" Christianity. Through both her words and her actions she launched devastating critiques of the compromises that the missionary establishment had made in every quarter by the 1890s. In response to the smug racial exclusivism of the hill stations to which Europeans retired in the hot season, Carmichael insisted on bringing her Indian assistant (119). She refused to be carried in a sedan (119), lambasted the use of small material inducements to get people to listen to the gospel (126), and declared that she would rather "live in a mud hut with the people around me than among English people in a bungalow" (122).

In keeping with this rebellious attitude toward British colonial conventions, a constant theme in Carmichael's life and writings is the impulse to break down the linguistic and cultural barriers that separated her from what she perceived to be "the real India." And yet, her relationship to India was deeply ambivalent. Carmichael's sense of integrity was constantly challenged by the Otherness of India. Each time she allowed herself to respond positively to the Indian environment some unsettling reminder that she was in the midst of a land "where Satan held sway" would provoke her to a frenzy of aggressive iconoclasm. The face of a god scratched into the metal surface of the bell she used to call the servants aroused an angry panic: She knocked the bell handle off and pushed it into the fire (121). A walk through the beautiful hills of the

Western Ghats with an Indian companion inspired thoughts of God's immense power and grace, until her reverie was broken by the appearance of an outdoor Hindu tree shrine. Carmichael wrote of this experience: "To see those stupid stones standing there to the honor of the false gods, in the midst of the true God's beauty, was too much for us. We knocked them over and down they crashed and over they rolled forthwith. Oh the shame of it! It makes one burn to think of His glory being given to another" (121–122). Certainly, one would expect that "idolatry" would arouse a particularly vehement response in an evangelical battle-ax like Carmichael, exemplifying as it did a "barbarism" that wrongly located "the sacred in objects instead of in individual consciousness."[80] Scenes like this of zealous Christians knocking over "idols" are a commonplace in the descriptions of and by missionaries.[81] But what else was it about those figures that so horrified Carmichael?

Perhaps it was her discovery that everyday objects, even the physical land-scape, could harbor the meanings of some other system of ordering the world. British colonizers in India were frequently troubled by the realization that India was not a "virgin land" untouched by the effects of human civilization, because such reminders spoiled their fantasies of creating a world anew in a fresh, new land. David Arnold, a historian of colonial India, has written, "Every idyllic spot for a European picnic had been pre-empted by a Hindu shrine or was guarded by the tomb of a Sufi saint. At the foot of each shady tree lay a vermilion-stained stone representing a folk deity, offering protection against smallpox or cholera. The cows that roamed the streets, the peacocks that strut-ted in the parks, the tigers that roamed in the jungle—few aspects of the Indian environment, animate or inanimate, seemed free and unappropriated by some aspect of Indian, especially Hindu, culture."[82]

It is also possible that what frightened Carmichael so and provoked her impulse to destroy was the sensation of being invaded or contaminated by the Indian sensibilities with which these objects—the bell, the shrine in the hills—were so palpably invested. For the meanings that were embedded in the Indian physical environment were not passive entities. In marked contrast to the stress on belief and conscience in evangelical Christianity, the orthopraxic religious assumptions of Hinduism were such that one could find oneself unconsciously acting in a "Hindu" manner.[83] In this way, unthinkingly ringing the bell posed a threat to the integrity of Carmichael's Christian loyalties, for, no matter what the contents of her consciousness, once she had rung the bell, she had ad-dressed the Hindu god whose face adorned it—or so one could imagine. Sim-ilarly, the young missionary's episode in the hills suggests a creeping sensation that she had gotten too close, physically and emotionally, to the religious re-sponses of Indian Hindus. It is possible that Carmichael was moved by the same spiritual thoughts as were the Indians who erected the shrine: admiration for the natural beauty of the surroundings and the sublime workings of the divine. Yet, instead of recognizing that her own responses might be similar to those of Hindus, she vehemently disavowed such a possibility. The fear of being overwhelmed, of being colonized herself by India drove Carmichael to found a fully self-contained institution where she could experiment on her own terms with what seemed to her to be the dangerous, but powerfully attractive, possibilities of indigenization.

Amy Carmichael's first book to gain a wide readership was *Things as They Are: Mission Work in Southern India* (first published in 1901 under the name Amy Wilson-Carmichael). True to her contrary nature, she wrote this book in an attempt to counteract the overly optimistic reports that foreign missionaries tended to send home. Exploding millennial hopes that the times were ripe for the swift conversion of the whole world, she described in painful detail the overwhelming indifference that the vast majority of Indians displayed toward the Christian gospel. The book's reception in England was mixed. By 1901, public opinion on outdoor preaching, bazaar preaching, and other forms of itinerancy was fading and more people were coming to favor types of evangelism that took place in stable institutions such as schools and hospitals.[84] Some readers were thrilled with Carmichael's book, but a few Christians in India were so deeply disturbed that they formed a committee to ask that the young firebrand be sent back to England (161).

Things as They Are was indeed a very bleak description of itinerancy work. From the opening pages, Carmichael established herself as the one truly authentic and reliable source on the Indian missionary project. Promising the reader a glimpse of life "behind the veil," she described experiences that she intimated other missionary authors lacked the moral courage to address. She not only sought to reveal for her readers the atrocities that allegedly went on in the secluded quarters of Indian women in purdah (the accepted role for women missionaries in India); she also wanted to expose the inadequacies of conventional missionary responses to those "crimes".

The Indians in *Things as They Are* respond to her invitations to hear the gospel with derision, indifference, physical threats, and innumerable objections to Christianity, ranging from the philosophical ("You say there is only one true God, but we have heard that you worship three!") to the pathetic ("I can't become a Christian because my husband would beat me"). But the most shocking scenes (from the point of view of an English readership) were those in which she presented an image of herself reflected in the eyes of unsympathetic Indians. In one especially striking vignette, Carmichael described how she finally achieved the attention of a small group of women and was just warming to her sermon when she was interrupted: "I was in the middle of it, and thinking only of it and their souls, when an old lady with fluffy white hair leaned forward and gazed at me with a beautiful, earnest gaze. She did not speak; she just listened and gazed. . . . And then she raised a skeleton claw, and grabbed her hair, and pointed to mine. 'Are you a widow too,' she asked, 'that you have no oil on yours?' . . . Her question had set the ball rolling again. 'Oil! no oil! Can't you even afford a half-penny a month to buy good oil? . . . Don't any white Ammals ever use oil?' " Carmichael's experiences had taught her, she told the reader, that surface appearances in India were not to be trusted. Like the seemingly innocuous marks on the surface of the bell, the expression on the face of an Indian listener could mean something very different from what one expected. In the upside-down world that was the "real India," a countenance lit up with rapt attention meant "nothing more or less than the sweet expression sometimes observed in the eyes of a sorrowful animal."[85]

Carmichael's book disturbed her fellow missionaries and countrymen because it represented the English being openly mocked and insulted by Indians, a distressing reversal of the colonial order of things. She took care to represent the Indian offenders as ignorant, physically unattractive, even bestial, to be sure, but she did not paint herself in the most flattering light either. In another scene, She described the enormous amount of amusement that the arrival of a "Missy Ammal" occasioned in a village. Completely unaccustomed to seeing white women in public, the villagers would ask one another excitedly if the large white creature in the pith helmet (or *sola topee*, the ubiquitous and unmistakable sign of a white sahib) could be a man or a woman: " 'She isn't a man!' 'He is!' 'Not a man, though great and white, and wearing a white man's turban, too! [Is] it not an appalling spectacle?' "[86] Carmichael's transgression of the conventions of missionary literature represented a powerful critique of the missionary strategy of itinerancy, in which the practical futility of the enterprise was revealed in the starkest terms. Even the unique moral properties that genteel white women are supposed to have, which were constantly praised by advocates of women's missions, were revealed in Carmichael's self-portrait as completely irrelevant to the Indian context. On the other hand, her self-denigrating portrayals are perfectly consistent with the tendency of missionaries to represent themselves as martyrs. One discerns a sort of masochistic pleasure in Carmichael's detailed description of her humiliation at the hands of Indian Hindus. But she would be vindicated, or at least she would be within the evangelical religious framework developed in her own books.

How did Carmichael explain the lack of interest in or reverence toward the gospel evidenced by the vast majority of Indians? How did she account for the negative, frequently hostile reception she and her band of fellow evangelists received? When feelings of despair overwhelmed her, Carmichael took comfort in the knowledge that she was not involved in a trivial debate over words or ideas but a terrible battle over matters of ultimate concern. "Our voices grow weary enough, and our hearts grow wearier still, for it seems like fighting shadows, till the remembrance suddenly comes—Not shadow, but substance, the great grim substance of Satanic opposition. And then we take courage—for the battle is the Lord's."[87] Through the metaphor of spiritual warfare, Carmichael consistently interpreted the indifference of Tamils to her entreaties as evidence that they were firmly in the grip of Satan. Because of this, her criticisms of traditional Indian social customs have a certain monotony. Caste prejudice, the immurement of women, poverty, and illiteracy are all traced back to the same fundamental problem, Hinduism, which is equated with the caste system and condemned as demonic, as something fundamentally evil. Carmichael compared the interconnected nature of Indian society to a gigantic spider web, with a malevolent creator (Satan?) at its hub: "One day I looked at a great spider's web several feet in diameter, and saw the mighty Caste system of India. At the outer edges floated almost freely long light threads that caught the morning sun and waved responsively to the morning airs. But nearer to the centre of the web the lines were drawn close—no wandering here; and right in the heart of it crouched the creature who ruled it all. A spider in India can be quite terrific; so can that be which holds the threads of a web woven in the far beginning."[88] That Carmichael would, consciously or unconsciously, select a trope for Indian society with such an important place in Hindu, or at least Upanishadic, religious thought testifies to her remarkable ability to identify with Indian culture. And yet, almost invariably, these empathetic moments turned into their opposite. In Carmichael's case, familiarity did indeed breed contempt, not admiration.

Carmichael's confrontation with "the real India" led her eventually to erect a massive bulwark between herself and the surrounding population. The Dohnavur Fellowship, directly adjacent to the large Tamil village of Dohnavur, sits on 170 square acres of land and is enclosed on all sides by a thick red adobe wall. The doors to the compound are entirely inconspicuous, but once on the other side of them, one enters a unique space that embodies Carmichael's vision for an indigenized evangelical Indian Christianity and reflects her personal creativity, hard work, and talent for fund-raising. I had the good fortune of visiting the Dohnavur Fellowship in May and October 1996. My impressions from these two visits form the basis of the following interpretations.

In the buildings that dot the compound, architectural features from every part of Carmichael's life have been combined in a surprisingly beautiful fashion: The bright red tile roofs so typical of Tamil buildings end in the upturned eaves of Japanese temples (see figure 3.1); teak window frames have been carved into myriad small rectangles that, taken together, form one large cross. The small, free-standing cottages for European visitors, originally built for the foreign volunteers who used to work by the hundreds for the Fellowship, each have a shady verandah and are also equipped with their own private bathrooms. Sometimes non-Western architectural designs are put toward strikingly Victorian uses, as in the 8-foot-tall "moon gate" that separates the boys' side of the compound from the girls' (see figure 3.2). From this charmed space, Carmichael hoped to train an army of young people, the orphans she rescued and was given by Indians in the surrounding areas, to be fresh soldiers in the fight against heathenism.

Carmichael was criticized by some Indians and fellow missionaries for creating an artificial environment that did not prepare the children raised in the Dohnavur Fellowship for life outside its walls (329).[89] The extent to which the Fellowship was cut off from its surroundings is revealed in the fact that the children raised there spoke a uniquely accented Tamil that was hard for outsiders to understand (361).[90] The language question raises a number of issues related to the peculiar form of indigenized Christianity with which Carmichael was experimenting behind the thick walls of the Fellowship. The Western men and women who came to work at Dohnavur were all expected to wear Indian dress, as Carmichael herself habitually did, in violation of the usual custom among nineteenth- and early twentieth-century foreign missionaries.

FIGURE 3.1   Chapel at Dohnavur Fellowship. Photograph by author.

FIGURE 3.2   Moon Gate at Dohnavur Fellowship. Photograph by author.

But the colors she chose for the veshtis and saris were, by contemporary Indian standards, outlandish. "Colours were always significant to Amy—blue for love, purple for service, so the doctors were decked out . . . in violet veshtis with mauve tops" (298). There was no way the staff could not be noticed outside the walls of the Fellowship. This was, as Elliot observes, probably what "Amma," or Mother, as Carmichael came to be known, wanted.

Carmichael insisted that the Fellowship was not an orphanage but a family, and she tried, linguistically and structurally, to make it as much like a Tamil family as possible. The children were housed in groups of ten or so in large round thatched huts, raised off the ground and equipped with a verandah and a red-tiled roof. The foreign and Indian workers who cared for the orphans all had titles based on Tamil kinship terms: Female Indian workers were addressed as *akkā* (Tamil, "elder sister"), female foreigners as *citti* ("mother's younger sister," "aunt"), and men as *aṇṇacci* (Tirunelveli dialect for "older brother") (213, 258).[91] Carmichael wanted to give all the children Tamil names, so the boys received the surname Anandas (derived from *Aṇaṇdaṇ*, "end-less, god" plus *dās* "servant, slave"), and the women the name Carunia (from *kā-ruṇiyam* "grace, compassion, mercy") to signal their affiliation with the Fellowship. In a whimsical addition, Carmichael frequently appended a girl's name with the suffix *pū*, meaning flower. Her laudable effort to give her charges authentically Indian names, however, had the effect of singling out children raised at Dohnavur in wider society, as Tamils didn't normally use these words for personal names.[92]

Carmichael ratified all these innovations in the same way: by drawing on the authority of divine inspiration. Any changes made in the running of Dohnavur were declared part of the pattern that had been "shewn" to her by God in prayer, through her reading of the Bible, and through the circumstances in which God had placed her (198, 235, 268, 351–52). In many ways, the bicultural experiments at Dohnavur produced a culture that was superficially Indian insofar as it featured many details drawn from the local Tamil context—in clothing, naming patterns, and building styles. But the institutional culture at the Dohnavur Fellowship did not alter the colonial dynamics of power on which the institution was based. One problem raised by this kind of partial indigenization was Carmichael's inability to find Indian leaders she deemed suitable for leadership positions at the Fellowship, a point I return to shortly.

Western European and American residents of India may have been more troubled than Indians by the ironies and inconsistencies of Amy Carmichael's efforts to plant Keswick Christianity in Indian soil. Tamil Christian accounts of her life celebrate the extent to which she attempted to blend into the environment. A Tamil novelization of her life, written by a man raised at the Fellowship, opens with Carmichael as a child praying to God to give her beautiful blue eyes like her mother's, instead of her own brown ones. When God answered her prayer in the negative, so the story goes, Mrs. Carmichael assured her daughter that God must have had a reason for creating her as he did. Tilakavati Paul lyrically ventures the hypothesis that many years after her childish prayer, Amy Carmichael received as a substitute for her mother's blue eyes "the sparkling blue uniforms worn by the treasured children raised by Amma and laid like so many blue lilies at the feet of God."[93] Carmichael's lack of blue eyes fascinated her Indian hagiographers. An elderly woman raised in the Dohnavur Fellowship showed me her copy of the lithographic image of its founder and immediately pointed out to me her brown eyes. She explained that Amy Carmichaelamma's brown eyes had been given to her by God so that she could pass as an Indian during the years of her life when she ventured into Hindu temples to find and rescue young devadasi girls.[94]

Keeping in mind the respect, even adoration, shown to Carmichael by many of her Indian followers, it is important also to draw attention to her reluctance to entrust them with leadership positions in the running of the Dohnavur Fellowship. One of the sharpest critics of the Fellowship, Stephen Neill, future bishop of Tirunelveli and missionary historian, lived and worked there for a little over a year. He did not perceive the institution as the harmonious family that Carmichael envisioned. Rather, in his view, the Fellowship was an autocracy equally as riven by racial segregation as any other missionary institution. He remembered the compound as completely detached from village life and "flooded with Europeans," who took their meals separately from Indian workers. " 'Amma,' " he charged, "had no Indian equals, feeling none to be as qualified as Europeans for leadership and responsibility" (268). Neill may not be the most objective of observers, having been dismissed from the Fellowship after months of tension between him and Carmichael. But other indications point to a definite bias in favor of European workers. The inner circle at Dohnavur, those unpaid, unmarried female workers who dedicated themselves wholly to the disciplined, ascetic life of the Fellowship, were called Sisters of the Common Life. During the early years of the Fellowship all European women automatically joined the Sisterhood, but only seven Indian women were invited (239–41).

The Keswick style of Christianity that Carmichael adopted—and her faith that she was divinely guided—gave her the confidence to criticize both Indian and Western bastions of traditional authority and to create her own institutions in which she could blend together diverse strands of culture as she thought aesthetically and pragmatically most appropriate. It even allowed her to transgress the taboo on white women having close relationships with Indian men, a taboo by which, as we saw in the case of Miss Pigot, even missionary women dedicated to a life of chastity had to abide. In *Raj, Brigand Chief* (1927), Carmichael tells the story of her conversion of a fierce bandit, a sort of south Indian Robin Hood who was driven to a life of crime by corrupt Indian officials and who found and embraced the Christian god through Carmichael's personal ministrations. This book contains many of her literary trademarks, including a daring venture in disguise into hostile Indian territory and praise for stalwart Indian heroes who managed to be "almost English" in their honesty, bravery, and physical prowess. In the book's most climactic scene, Carmichael's persona, Carunia, secretly arranges to meet with Raj in a forest clearing. She goes to the appointed spot in disguise, having "stained her hands and face and feet, and, wrapped [herself] in a dark sari" to escape detection by the police. Defying

the taboo against interracial contact, Carmichael depicts the close physical contact she enjoyed with Raj during their clandestine meeting as she urges him
to turn himself into the police. "In a moment Raj had Carunia's hands in his,"
she wrote, "and was fondling them with the eager touch of a loving child." She
deflected criticism of such physical intimacy by casting her relationship with
Raj in a strictly maternal idiom: He called her "Mother," and she in turn regarded him as her spiritual son. Still, the sexual undertones of their encounter
is difficult to avoid, as when Raj asked her to feel the injury he sustained when
he was earlier tortured by corrupt policemen: "Was not my leg broken by
himsa?" Raj asked Carunia/Carmichael, referring to the practice of police tor-
ture which it was the ostensible purpose of the book to expose and condemn,
"and he drew Carunia's hand down gently, till she felt the protruding bone."[95]

That a Tamil audience might find this degree of physicality scandalous or
disturbing is suggested in the Tamil retelling of the story of Carmichael's encounter with the brigand chief. Here, Tilagavati Paul tones down the sexual
element implicit in Carmichael's account by having Cempuli (Red Tiger, Raj's
Tamil eponym) gently touch his eyes to Amma's hands at the climactic moment, instead of taking her hand and having her feel his leg.[96] However, judging from the book's positive reception in its own day, Carmichael's very free-
ness with men may have been taken as proof of her actual chastity, as Hudson
declared of Miss Pigot. In spite of a few tense moments such as those described
above, *Raj, Brigand Chief* won accolades from several distinguished colonial
authorities. Three south Indian bishops provided forewords to her book, as did
the eminent adventurer T. Howard Somervell, member of the 1924 British
expedition to Mount Everest and medical missionary at the LMS mission in
Neyoor, Travancore.

Notwithstanding the book's reception, I think we can still read the narrative as a tale in which Carmichael defuses the frightening sexuality of the
Indian male with Christian charity, sublimating her own sexual attraction into
a socially acceptable maternal mode. It is a story that caught the imagination
of Indian Christians; a movie based on the book circulates in Tamil Nadu in
video form to this day. Carmichael's successful "taming" of the Red Tiger
represents the wish that the shield of Christ could allow women to defy even
the sexual taboos generated by a fear of miscegenation, freeing them from the
constraints that normally hedged in the lives of independent colonial women.
The history of Miss Pigot and her battles with Rev. Hastie suggests that this
wish was realizable only in fiction.

Carmichael ran the orphanage and its attendant institutions (schools, hospital, etc.) in Dohnavur for approximately fifty years as its undisputed spiritual
and organizational leader. In October 1931, while on a preaching tour in a
neighboring temple town (Kalakadu), she experienced a painful fall, incurring
multiple injuries that plagued her for the rest of her life (311). Her mobility
was very much limited after the accident, but she continued to manage the
Dohnavur Fellowship for the next twenty years from her bed in what she called
"the Room of Peace," her bedroom and study in the main bungalow. On 18
January 1951 she died, four years after India gained its independence from

Great Britain. The effect of the movement to transfer leadership of the Christian missions and Indian churches to Indians, which emerged contemporaneously with the Indian Independence movement, was felt even behind the thick walls of Dohnavur.[97] When she died, Carmichael left the leadership of the organization in the hands of four people: an Indian man and woman who had been raised at the Fellowship (Rajappan and Purripu, the daughter of Ponnammal) and an English man and woman, May Powell, a nurse, and John Risk (368, 373).

Eva M. Swift: Congregationalist Piety and the American Madurai Mission

On 12 July 1884, Miss Eva M. Swift arrived in Madurai, then a busy commercial and cultural center in the south of the Madras Presidency. At 22, she was the youngest missionary ever to be sent to a foreign field by the American Board.[98] By 1921 she was the principal of the Lucy Perry Noble Institute for Women (LPNIW), an institution for women's work that consisted of an industrial school, an elementary school, and a college for training Indian women to work as evangelists for the mission. An ambitious experiment in self-sufficiency, the institute covered thirty-one acres of land situated on the outskirts of Madurai and included a garden, orchard, poultry farm, and several acres of rice paddy fields. A juxtaposition of Swift's understanding of her role as missionary with Carmichael's allows us to see how variant interpretations of Christianity could give rise to such different styles of missionary "service" and yet could be turned with equal effectiveness to ratify women's deviations from the patriarchal missionary establishment.

Eva Swift spent the first ten years of her life in Huntsville, Alabama, where her father owned several foundries in addition to a family farm at the edge of town. In a thin photo album describing her life before she became a missionary, Swift traced the beginnings of her vocation to the attraction she felt to the family's black slaves. She referred several times to her desire to get closer to these compelling figures, who were both outside her world and yet familiar, if not clearly defined presences within it. On one page she recalled watching baptisms take place in a nearby spring from the balcony of the Huntsville Hotel: "the Negroes singing 'spirituals' the candidates trembling with excitement and shouting Hallelujah!, and sometimes springing actually over the heads of the crowd into the water." On another page she wrote that one of her favorite childhood pleasures was to accompany the field slaves out for the day; young Eva would carry her own gunny sack over her shoulder and fill it with peas or cotton bolls, just as her companions did.[99] Such memories foreshadow the affectionate interest Swift seems to have taken in the lives of the Indians among whom she worked, as well as the sense of distance that she felt from them as a result of her own privilege.

During the American Civil War, Mr. Swift was financially ruined, a tragedy that led to his premature death around 1872. Swift's widowed mother moved the family to Atlanta, Georgia and then to Dallas, Texas. It was in Dallas that

Eva Swift dedicated herself to the missionary service, having experienced a personal call during a meeting held by Rev. C. J. Scofield in 1883. She applied to the American Board of Commissioners for Foreign Missions in 1884, was accepted, and left Dallas for south India in March 1884.

The ABCFM, founded in 1810, was ostensibly an interdenominational missionary board, but it was heavily dominated by Massachusetts Congregationalists, a denomination deeply rooted in New England Puritanism.[100] By 1860, the Board was sending missionaries to the Native Americans, the Levant (present-day Syria), Burma (Myannmar), Ceylon (Sri Lanka), and India, impelled by the Great Commission to act as a moral beacon for the rest of the world. At the time Swift set sail for India, American missionary boards had been sending single women as missionaries to the foreign countries for about twenty-five years. At first, they were treated as minors in the mission organizations, receiving smaller salaries than those of single men and having no right to vote or attend mission meetings. And yet, unencumbered by many of the responsibilities of married women, unmarried women greatly expanded the range of projects that a missionary society could undertake in a given area. Swift's first responsibility was to take charge of the Madura Girls Boarding School, started in 1835 by the mission founders to be "the first effort for the education of females, other than dancing girls [devadasis], ever made in the district."[101] By 1890 she was superintending all five girls schools run by the AMM.

With her growing responsibility came a desire to participate more fully in the administration of the mission. Swift was one of the principal instigators in 1890 of a movement among the mission's single women to gain a voice in the mission's meetings. In a typescript of her memoirs, she recalled that while a young woman in Texas, she was accustomed to being asked to share in prayer meetings and offer testimony in public meetings. The Protestant churches in the United States with which she was familiar were evidently more liberal than were mission stations in India, and Swift was disappointed to discover that she was expected to keep silent under the patriarchal style of church government within the AMM. In the end, her dismay at the undemocratic and, to her mind, un-Christian nature of this state of affairs outweighed her sense of obligation to established church authority: "After a few years I broke into the even tenor of the men's ideas by speaking in the prayer-meeting. I can clearly recall the sensation it produced. Dr. Jones told me he 'saw visions' all night, Dr. Chester wrote an alarmed query about this startling innovation, and there was a twitter of talk all around the Mission."[102] Swift maintained that her desire to participate in the decision-making life of the mission did not come from a sympathy for "women's rights." Rather, she felt excluded from Christian fellowship and angered by the injustice of having to "abide by and obey rules the reasons for which I knew nothing." Like many women missionaries of the nineteenth century, she distanced herself from the concurrent movements for women's suffrage and property rights in the United States and Britain.[103]

When the decision formally to include women in the mission councils finally took place in 1893, women were granted the right to participate in the mission's meetings and to vote on "women's work," that is, matters having to do with Indian girls or women.[104] However, on an informal level, a certain patronizing attitude toward women prevailed. Swift wrote, "There came a time when the men would open a meeting by saying 'I hope all the ladies will feel free to take part.' This was generally followed by an embarrassed silence on the part of the ladies. What I was thinking about the silence I will not record."[105]

The change in formal mission policy can be traced to the establishment of separate women's missionary boards in the late 1860s. Like the compromise made by the AMM to allow women to vote on matters related to women, the women's boards represented a compromise between advocates of women's full participation in the life of the church and traditionalists who felt the need to abide by the Apostle Paul's injunction that women not teach or lead men (1 Tim 2:11–14). The middle way between full inclusion and full exclusion was to grant women the authority to teach and lead other women, but not men. Through the women's boards, women missionaries were able to promote their own projects to an unprecedented degree.

Swift's visions for women's work were grand and informed by a steady stream of input from her fellow missionaries, both at home and in other foreign fields. She went back to the United States on furlough numerous times in the course of her career, to raise money from home congregations and gather new ideas for improving her projects in Madurai. This was very different from Amy Carmichael's strategies to promote innovation. The Dohnavur Fellowship retained its idiosyncratic features because innovative ideas for changing it came largely from Carmichael's exclusive prayer meetings with her closest inner circle in Dohnavur. Swift, on the other hand, regularly put into practice the insights of Christian social scientists, evangelists, and social workers around the world.

For example, in 1890–1891, Swift returned to the United States on furlough. While there, she met with Sarah Capron, a senior missionary at the AMM who had retired from the foreign missionary service and was working with Dwight Moody in Chicago, helping to establish the woman's work aspect of his Bible Institute. On her way back to India, Swift proposed to the American Board in Boston a plan to create a training school for Indian women on the model of Capron's work with the Bible Institute. The evangelistic workers in Swift's Bible School for women would be trained in a curriculum modeled after seminary education for men, the core consisting of courses on the New and Old Testaments, church history, and theology. Upon graduation, each woman evangelist worker would be given her own "pastorate" so that she could systematically visit with and instruct all people who were willing to accept teachers in the area over which she had been given responsibility.[106] Even though the Board declined to provide funds for Swift's proposal to create a virtual female Indian Christian clergy, Swift persevered. That summer, she managed to raise enough money from her own congregation in Dallas to begin the school with its first three students in the rented rooms of a house in the center of Madurai city. Year after year, the school expanded, attracting students from among the many Christian families in the Madurai area and money from

Swift's numerous connections in the United States In 1916, Swift raised enough money to purchase a large amount of land and she moved the school to the site on Alagar Koil Road.[107]

The Tamil name for the compound, still etched into the main gate on Alagar Koil Road, was Rachanyapuram (Tamil *iraṭsaṇayapuram*, lit. "place of salvation"). It was situated several miles from the institutional center of the AMM in the middle of Kaḷḷar country, an area dominated by a caste whose traditional occupation was said to be thievery or protection from thievery. The relatively remote location of Rachanyapuram allowed for a remarkable degree of self-sufficiency. Under Swift's effective management, the school's residents grew their own rice and vegetables, made their own cloth and furniture, and ran a school and a dispensary for the neighboring population. The majority of its students appear to have been initially the daughters and wives of the local Christian community, but in time the school became known as a refuge for abandoned women, widows, and recent converts "suffering from the opposition of their families." The new "science of missions" being developed in the United States encouraged missionaries to supply social programs to uplift the poor but urged them at all costs to avoid the cycle of dependency that material support often brought in its wake. In accordance with this trend, Swift decided that although her Christian duty to serve the needy prevented her from turning such women away from her doors, the school would not provide them with a free ride. As she put it succinctly, "We felt that we should ask them to give a fair and honest return in labour for what they receive." Indeed, one of the main goals of the Institute was to educate residents in both Christian principles and the principles of "honest work." The need for strong work discipline was articulated in the idiom of moral improvement. "Impertinence to the matrons or teachers directing this work will subject the student to reprimand and punishment, or to dismissal if persisted in," wrote Swift. "A cheerful willing spirit will accompany any real growth or improvement and the absence of it will be proof of a failure to make right use of an opportunity."[108] Residents who did not work in the industrial school helped prepare meals and clean the buildings and grounds, and planted, weeded, and harvested the rice paddy that provided the bulk of their food (see figure 3.3).

The industrial school's main product, stitched clothing, had the double advantage of providing "civilized" raiment for the residents and their customers at the same time that it generated income for the school.[109] Indeed, the sale of "ladies' and children's garments, gentlemen's clothing, household articles of all kinds, servants' suits, coats, etc." was the school's main source of income.[110] Photographs of the school's students, teachers, and employees show men and women decked out in modest yet sophisticated clothes. The man stands in suit and tie, with white shirt and oiled mustaches. The women sit wearing saris over white, high-collared shirts with sleeves to the wrist; noticeably, they lack the abundant jewelry characteristically worn by Tamil women (see figure 3.4).

Although Swift, like Carmichael, was fluent in Tamil, she did not have the

FIGURE 3.3   Students working in rice fields at the Lucy Perry Noble Bible Institute for Women. UTC Archive, AMM, 14e. Courtesy of United Theological College.

FIGURE 3.4   "27th Class of Bible Women (the seven seated) trained at LPNI. Also two matrons and two teachers, with principal (1926)." UTC Archive, AMM 14e. Gnanaprahasiammal is top, second from left; Eva Swift, top, center. Courtesy of United Theological College.

FIGURE 3.5   "Miss Jeyamani Taylor [Headmistress of the Lucy Perry Noble Bible School], trowel in hand, declares the corner-stone well and truly laid. Miss Swift standing on the wall, several feet higher than the assembled company, figures more largely than she would wish." UTC Archive, AMM 14e. Courtesy of United Theological College.

same desire to break past the cultural and social barriers separating herself from Indians. For instance, in the photographs of Rachanyapuram taken in the early twentieth century, Swift is invariably pictured in Western-style dress, including white long-sleeved blouse and ankle-length dress. In the carefully staged "action shots" of the residents of the school at work, she stands at a distance supervising the work in which her sari-clad students or dhoti-clad male workers are engaged (see figure 3.5). A single photograph in the archives of the AMM depicts the young missionary in an Indian sari, but a handwritten note on the back requests that it never be reproduced. As the photograph of Swift teaching outside what appears to be a Brahman household suggests (figure 3.6), her ideas of what it meant to be close to Indians was very different from Carmichael's. She preferred, it seems, the role of a benevolent, if somewhat distant supervisor over the role of a physically and emotionally close mother. Her conception of the ideal role of the missionary as kind but slightly removed moral exemplar is conveyed in her words of praise for her mentor, Sarah Capron. Contrasting Capron's brand of tolerance and sympathy for Indians with that of Swift's own contemporaries, she wrote, "We are hearing very much, these latter days, of sympathy, understanding and friendship. Here were all these, given from a plane of lofty dignity, which never prevented the Hindu or Christian woman from slipping into the room to drop at her feet, to pour out all her sorrows, problems, hopes or joys—a far finer thing than excess of familiarity which sometimes passes for friendship."[111] Though different in tone from the outright contempt that Carmichael sometimes expressed toward Indians in her early accounts of life in the mission field, this empathic but con-

FIGURE 3.6   Eva Swift teaching. UTC Archive, AMM 14e. Courtesy of
United Theological College.

descending approach also relied on an image of Indians as inferior and in need
of strong moral leadership.

Swift's conception of her role as missionary is also conveyed in the institutional culture she forged at Rachanyapuram. On the one hand, she was
clearly influenced by that strain of missionary philosophy that sought to create
a solid foundation for an independent "native church."[112] The necessity that
students pay for or earn the privilege of being at the school marks an enormous
shift from the days when missionaries would offer meals or small amounts of
money to induce students to attend their schools. At the same time, beneath
the school's motto of training Indian women in "honest work" was the implication that Indian indolence and inefficiency (not colonialism) were to blame
for their poverty and degradation. In the practical, pragmatic soteriology of the
LPNIW, what Indians needed to be saved from was this essential character flaw
that led to innumerable further sources of suffering: poor hygiene, illness,
illiteracy, early marriage, and so on. The concept that Indians needed the moral
and practical leadership of Americans (or British) to pull them out of their
spiritual and material poverty came to prominence in Swift's writings precisely
when the indispensability of her leadership was called into question.

When Swift returned from furlough in 1931 she found India "in a disturbed state," rocked by movements, violent and nonviolent, for independence.
With the talk of political independence came plans for the devolution of leadership from the foreign missions to the Indian Church. The mission, Swift
wrote in her annual letter of 1931, "is practically eliminating itself by placing
itself and its workers under the Indian Church." Her reluctance to relinquish
control of the institution that she had worked so hard to build was typical of
many foreign missionaries. Her greatest worry was that the illiterate and poor
women who were the special object of her benevolence schemes at Rachany-

apuram would not receive the attention or resources they deserved from the Indian Church. "Though much has been done in India," she wrote, "so much remains to do, that to talk or dream of missionaries as no longer needed is to close our eyes to facts and live in a world of theory."[113]

Despite her concern for what she saw as the best interests of Indians, the gradual removal of foreign missionaries from India and the transfer of leadership from missionaries to Indian Christian leaders became a reality. This transition, one of the most remarkable developments in the history of Christianity in India, is unfortunately outside the scope of this project. Suffice it to say that the goal of devolution was that all Indian Christians, presently divided among the different foreign missions (the Anglican CMS, the nonconformist LMS, the Congregationalist AMM, and others) would be united under the leadership of the Church of South India. Indian and Western Christians alike worried that nepotism and rivalry among Christians of different castes would replace the benevolent meritocracy enforced by supposedly disinterested foreign missionaries. It is not that these fears were unfounded (indeed, intercaste rivalry hampered the election of an Indian bishop for several years), but the alternative—an indefinite period of "training" of Indian Christians for leadership by American, German, and English missionaries—was plainly unacceptable.[114]

The careers of Amy Carmichael and Eva Swift, though not typical of the time, are nevertheless illustrative of the kind of energetic, productive activity that Victorian women were capable of once they were liberated from the confining social mores of their home countries. Like the first women medical missionaries, who could not practice in their home countries but were able to enjoy successful careers in the colonies, enterprising women missionaries like Swift and Carmichael found in India outlets for their prodigious creative and productive energies.

Summary

The huge involvement of women at the height of the foreign missionary movement is only just being acknowledged. By the first decade of the twentieth century women actually outnumbered men in the mission field: By 1916, 57 percent of American missionaries overseas were women. In India, the ratio of female to male missionaries was 3 to 2, with slightly more women listed as "unmarried" than as "wives of missionaries."[115] One reason women were largely ignored in missionary historiography for so long is the male bias of the missionary archives themselves. Historian Jeffrey Cox confessed that he worked in the archives of the SPG for months before he realized that the mission was predominantly female.[116] The omission of women's work, or its relegation to asides in the published reports of male-centered missionary societies, stems from the fact that many missionaries considered women's work to be trivial. Next to the important debates over whether English education for elites or vernacular itinerating would be more likely to result in the Christianization of

India, women's focus on the transformation of society by small degrees seemed insignificant. But, as we shall see in the next chapters, women's focus on the everyday was a driving force for change in the lives of Indian converts. Missionaries', especially women missionaries', intense interest in the moral basis and soteriological consequences of day-to-day life helps to explain how Western Christian culture, as a social system, and Christianity, as a religious teaching, became inextricably linked in the minds of many people in India, both Indian and Western.

The proper admixture of Christianity seen as a religious teaching and Christianity seen as Western Christian culture, or "civilization," was a perpetual problem for Protestant missionaries in India. Although the conflation of Western culture and Christianity was heavily contested by both Indian Christians and Western missionaries, it is difficult to deny that the two discourses were deeply intertwined in the imagination of both Christians and non-Christians. The history of Christian conversion in colonial south India demonstrates that the intermixture of religious and cultural ideas in this historical context derived from the constant impulse to attribute religious significance to the behaviors and practices of Indian converts, which frequently resulted in the judgment that they were insufficiently Christian. This impulse to discern moral or spiritual meanings in one's habitus is firmly grounded in Protestant thought, in which the pressure to know if one is saved or not and the absence of concrete mechanisms for finding out fuels a powerful drive to produce or find perceptible evidence of a person's ultimate moral condition. Modern Protestant thought has long posited a close relationship between outward gestures and inner meanings. This is particularly true of those movements that had the most direct impact on foreign missions: evangelicalism, the personal holiness movement, and liberal Christianity. Attention to the connections between practice and belief in missionary and Indian Christian writings allows one to see the discursive intermediary steps by which Western sensibilities and patterns of social life were, consciously and unconsciously, surreptitiously and openly, interwoven into Indian forms of Christianity.

The debate over the conjunction of civilization and Christianity at times took shape over the pragmatic question of whether schools or itinerancy was a more effective instrument of conversion, but at bottom it centered on whether "civilization" ought to precede or would naturally follow Christianization.[117] Though the popularity of one position over the other certainly varied over the years, neither argument ever gained complete ascendancy. The argument that changes in the customs, dress, speech, or conduct of converts were evidence of the civilizing power of the gospel itself was complicated by the fact, occasionally recognized and admitted by missionaries, that converts often had their own reasons for adopting new, Westernized habits. This is a dynamic I examine more thoroughly in later chapters. Missionaries who argued for the precedence of civilization, for their part, had to defend themselves against the charge of expediency—the claim that they were simply trying to save their jobs. After decades of hard work building schools and hospitals with only a handful of converts to show for it, the only consolation many missionaries could derive for themselves (and their disappointed financial backers in the metropole) was that they were breaking up the ground of Hinduism, undermining people's faith in traditional religion and preparing them to embrace Christianity. Present-day scholarly consensus claims that what was to missionaries a consolation prize—the transformation of colonized peoples' attitudes toward their own traditions—was, for better or worse, a crucial factor in the modernization of colonial societies. I leave to others the contemplation of the various modernities that are the legacy of colonization and Christianity.[118] What I want to argue here is that, whatever their stated position on the debate over Christianity and civilization, missionaries in the field *could not avoid* becoming enmeshed in the cultural context in which their teachings were preached, nor could they avoid the tendency of their religious teachings to be attached to particular aspects of Western culture. On the one hand, foreign missionaries in south India had to engage with and accommodate indigenous systems of meaning in the effort to translate Christianity into forms and terms meaningful to local people. In this way, Christianity in India had to adapt to Indian culture in order to be understood at all. On the other hand, even the most noble efforts at "indigenization" resulted in a hybrid form of Christianity that would remain "almost Indian but not quite" so long as English and American missionaries were the driving creative force behind it.[119] The selective appropriation of isolated "Indian" features such as dress, architecture, or even Indian words inevitably led to forms of "Indian Christianity" in the nineteenth and early twentieth centuries that had a remarkably English or American cultural sensibility and a largely foreign leadership structure at the highest administrative levels.

Whatever the debates over the extent to which civilizing ought to accompany Christianity, in the field it was practically impossible to achieve the ideal of preaching the gospel without any effort to improve, undermine, or affect in any way the preexisting social or political systems of the people. Yet, some of the most powerful men in the missionary movement were strong advocates of "pure evangelism," as this ideal was called, and were suspicious for a variety of reasons of the ulterior motives of the "civilizing" work in which many missionaries enthusiastically engaged. Rufus Anderson, secretary of the ABCFM from 1832 to 1872, worked for forty years against widespread resistance to his campaign to prune all "inessential" aspects of mission work overseas. In his opinion, English medium schools, boarding schools, and the involvement of missionaries in the restructuring of government (as in the ABCFM mission to the Hawaiian islands) exceeded the simple purpose of preaching the gospel to "heathens" in a form they could understand. Like his English counterpart, Henry Venn, the secretary of the CMS, Anderson felt that vernacular education and preaching would in the long run be the simplest and most effective means of establishing a native church. For advocates of pure evangelism, like Venn and Anderson, the role of missionaries was to plant the seed of the gospel and then move on, leaving the "native church" to grow as it would on its own soil.[120] One problem with this strategy of concentrating on the strictly spiritual evangelical work was that souls were attached to bodies. The response that Amy Carmichael gave to a donor who asked that his contribution be put only toward "soul-work" could stand as the motto of all those, especially liberal Christians, who felt that social work had to accompany any responsible effort at evangelism: "One can't save and then pitchfork souls into heaven. There are times when I heartily wish we could. [But] souls (in India at least) are more or less securely fastened into bodies. Bodies can't be left to lie about in the open, and as you can't get the souls out and deal with them separately, you have to take them both together. What then is to be done?"[121] On the one hand, this kind of frank recognition of the inextricability of the physical and spiritual aspects of human life legitimated a great deal of philanthropic and benevolent work aimed at bettering the lives of Indian Christians. On the other hand, such an approach resulted in the transmission of Western cultural norms and sensibilities through the supposedly culture-free medium of Christian religious teachings.

The women's missionary project had a special role to play in promoting the "revolution in habits" that was to accompany Christianity insofar as it was conceived of as a "civilizing" force in colonial societies.[122] Because women were excluded from participation in the official life of the church, they were encouraged (and encouraged one another) to manifest piety in the mundane and demonstrate devotion in daily life. Perfect obedience to God in every aspect of life, from the sublime to the seemingly trivial, was supposed to effect perfect liberation from the constraints of merely human convention and custom and thereby foster an expansive, joyful, and peaceful outlook on life. By thus giving women a method and a motivation to change their lives to accord with Christian ideals, evangelical Christian thought contributed to the empowerment of women, enlisting their help in a grand, transhistorical venture to transform human society, at home and in the colonies. But, one must concede, the conjunction of civilization and Christianity empowered English and American women by elevating them at the expense of their clients, the less Christianized and supposedly less civilized people among whom they worked. The message of liberation that evangelical Christian women brought to their work among the "heathen" was thus severely limited. Setting themselves up as the exemplars of an ideal Christian life that would lead to immortality among the angels, Christian women cast their clients in the role of inferiors who needed to change, sometimes to the extent of characterizing them as "beasts."

In the following chapters, I examine whether and how Western women missionaries were actually able to get the women to whom they preached, taught, and ministered to change. One of the great ironies of the missionary project is that the message of civilization, broadcast so loudly and persistently through innumerable channels of colonial society, was rarely received in exactly the form that missionaries desired or expected. Low-caste Christian converts had their own motivations to seek out methods of self- and social transformation, and these motives, along with the distinctive cultural and historical context of south India, produced yet other forms of Indian Christianity than those envisioned by Western Christian missionaries.

PART II

The Conversion of Gender

4

Motherhood and the Home: Indian Christian Domesticity

The missionaries' desire to elevate and transform Indian Christians into more "civilized" representatives of humanity coincided with Indian Christian aspirations to improve their status in Indian society, resulting in a negotiated, hybrid amalgam of values and aesthetic and moral concepts that I have termed the discourse of respectability. The area of Indian social life that women missionaries believed most required the beneficent influence of Christian civilization was the complex of beliefs, norms, and practices connected with the home and women's place within it, a complex that Western women missionaries referred to as Indian "home-life." For their part, Indians sought to transform themselves into respectable Christians in a way that would simultaneously signal their new status to missionary patrons *and* non-Christian Indian neighbors. In this way, preexisting elite Indian notions that linked women and the interior of homes were reconstituted along the lines of newly introduced Western ideals of feminine domesticity.

Western domesticity was by no means a monolithic concept even in its first incarnation in Western Europe, and it varied considerably along class, caste, and urban/rural lines as different sectors of Indian society took it up. Men and women situated differently in the social landscape drew on different elements of the vision of moral transformation that entered Indian society through channels created by the Protestant missions. Printed tracts, sermons delivered from street corners and pulpits, mothers' meetings, and individual instruction all carried messages about the need for Indian women to draw on their natural domestic talents to reorganize their homes so that pious, rational, and appropriately bounded selves would flow from them. But the kinds of interventions that were thought necessary to reform those homes (and beliefs about how those Indian women were to exist in relation to them) reveal the microadjustments that were made in the ideology of domesticity in India to account for class and caste.

The first homes that drew the attention of Protestant missionaries were those of the indigenous elite. In the imagined zenāna ("women's quarters," from Persian) of the writings of British and American Christian women, Indian women lived out their days in a sort of extreme expression of the doctrine of separate spheres which so dominated Western discussions of gender and domesticity. Their accounts are filled with images of ignorant and sickly wives, mothers, and daughters who spent their entire lives within the women's quarters of Indian homes, innocent "prisoners" of the zenāna or the *antarmahal* ("inner rooms," "inner fortified area"). As a way to "penetrate" this enclosed, heavily guarded space and bring education and enlightening knowledge of Christianity to these unhappy women, Western women missionaries developed the method of the zenana missions. This style of evangelism usually combined literacy training with lessons in needlework. Missionary wives or their Indian assistants (often called Bible women) would typically visit elite women on a daily or weekly basis to read aloud from the Bible or from printed tracts, asking and answering questions while their students knitted, sewed, or embroidered. Highly celebrated by their supporters in England and the United States as one of the most effective branches of missionary activity, the zenana missions struck a powerful chord in the imagination of the colonizing nations.

Both male and female Western residents of India were fascinated by the idea and institution of purdah (lit. "curtain"), the systems of seclusion used to enforce strict standards of modesty among predominantly high-class and-caste Hindus and Muslims. A single-minded obsession with the status and role of elite Indian women led foreign missionaries to generalize a notion of the Indian woman, and the steps necessary for her reform, based on the model of the *purdashnin*. The Muslim or Hindu lady of this type was located firmly in the home, ideologically and in practice. The ideological work of the zenana missions was to transform the preexisting identification of women with the home such that women were held to be preservers of the home on the basis of their moral rectitude, measured not by sexual purity and isolation from the outside world but by their rational transactions with the world as readers and consumers, and believers in the Christian faith. If women previously had been tied to the home because it was believed that their sexual purity could be guaranteed only so long as they resided entirely within the four walls of the home or the courtyard, now the home was to be the site of their self-fulfillment because it was where their innate propensities and talents as women would thrive. According to the vision of a future ideal Indian society promoted by both Indian and Western Christians involved with the zenana missions, self-controlled women, sexually contained by their own conscience, would supervise the rational upbringing of morally upright, self-regulating Christian boys and girls within the home.

Something important happened when this model was taken up by the low-caste converts to Christianity who in actuality filled the pews of India's Christian churches. When it became clear that they would not be able to win many conversions from within the homes of India's elite classes, Western women missionaries turned their attention to the low-caste converts who had consistently sought out relations with representatives of Western Christianity. Around the turn of the century, the missionaries' disappointment in the low rate of conversion among elite groups coincided with a revival of Methodist theological imperatives to uplift the masses of poor Christians, both spiritually and materially. This movement peaked in the early twentieth century with the rising influence, especially in the United States, of liberal Christianity. As the reforming efforts of women missionaries were directed at low-caste converts, the homes of low-caste women were found to be too porous, the traffic across their boundaries seemingly chaotic. Unlike the purdashnin "trapped" in their sealed chambers, these low-caste converts needed to aspire along a different vector of reform toward the standard of respectability forged from elite Indian notions of female propriety and family honor and Victorian notions of ideal womanhood. Their reform required not an intensification or multiplication of their transactions with the "outside world," but a tightening up of the boundaries of their homes and selves.

To situate the actual work of the zenana missions, I first investigate the ideological underpinnings of the missions as they emerged out of European and North American responses to nineteenth-century discourses of ideal womanhood. I argue that Western women were intrigued by the purdah system in part because it resonated with patterns of gender segregation with which they were familiar. Next I examine the multifaceted and complex institution of purdah from a variety of historical and anthropological angles. I would like to discern which aspects of the gender ideology embodied in purdah were retained in the production of the new hybrid discourse of femininity generated out of the interaction between Protestant missionaries and representatives of elite Indian culture. Finally, I examine the history of the zenana missions, tracking the changes in the strategies for the reform of Indian women and the reconstitution of their relationship to the Indian home as the focus of the missions shifted from elite to low-caste women.

Fascinated by Purdah

In the last three decades of the nineteenth century, Protestant Christian women formed missionary societies in Great Britain and the United States with a new and unique purpose: to proselytize and minister to non-Christian women in foreign lands. In their promotional and fund-raising literature, missionaries in India in the nineteenth century give a variety of reasons for promoting evangelical and teaching work specifically among women: the need to provide Christian men with suitable wives, the desire to reduce resistance among women to social reform, and the wish to direct the energies of Indian wives and mothers toward reorganizing and reforming Indian homes. Women involved in the Protestant missionary project were motivated by Victorian ideas about gender that glorified women's role as the moral guardian of the home. Such ideas informed their conviction that converting mothers and wives was essential to bringing about the spiritual regeneration of a society. U.S. and British women's foreign missionary societies considered the mission field in India especially suited for the efforts of women missionaries because of the particular social organization of gender there. In virtually every region in India, men and women observed some protocols of sex segregation, though they varied considerably in terms of their rigidity and the extent to which they were enforced.[1] The testimony of the returning wives of missionaries regarding the effects of purdah led many to believe that only women could preach the gospel to the women of India.

Indeed, the zenana, or women's quarters, loomed large in the imagination of the Christian West as a condensed symbolic figure for a number of contradictory notions. While authors used lurid descriptions of the dark, cramped, and dirty zenana to illustrate the oppression of Indian women at the hands of their men folk, they deployed images of the zenana as a place where women cared for their children to emphasize the crucial role women played as the primary educators and socializers of the next generation.[2] For Western women missionaries, it became the privileged site of intervention. As E. R. Pitman wrote in 1903 in a tract extolling the importance of the Indian zenana missions, "In the *Zenana* the influence of the mother is all-powerful. She is a devoted adherent of the old idolatry, because she knows no better, and her bitterest invectives are heaped upon the heads of those who were the means of beguiling her son from the faith of his ancestors. But if the *women* were instructed, and led to Christ, what upheavals may we not expect, what numerous confessions, what progress in the faith of Christ?"[3] As this passage makes clear, women missionaries and their supporters rallied around the notion that the women of India had the power either to subvert or promote the civilizing potential of Christianity. This rhetoric drew on a politicized version of the idea that men and women in civilized society occupied complementary spheres of action: Men's proper domain was the world of work and their proper instrument was the intellect; the domain of women was the home and their natural prowess was in matters of emotion and affect. Like the ideal Victorian mother, the Indian woman ruled the roost, as it were, through her moral authority. But an Indian mother's influence was felt to be "perverted" to the extent that it was rooted in a staunch adherence to the "faith of the ancestors" and expressed through myriad "idolatrous" practices.

At times, rather than being conceived of as an active opponent to the civilizing and Christianizing project of imperialism, the zenana was figured as an absence, a lack, which the West would fill. The famous Sanskrit lexicographer Sir Monier Monier-Williams, who in 1887 was the chairman of the CEZMS, declaimed in a speech before the annual meeting of this body:

> True English homes are not to be found in India . . . there exists no word that I know of in any Indian language exactly equivalent to that grand old Saxon monosyllable "home"; that little word . . .

which is the key to our national greatness and prosperity. Certainly the word Zenana—meaning in Persian "the place of women"—cannot pretend to stand for "home" any more than the Persian Mardana, "the place of men," can mean "home." For home is not a mere collection of rooms . . . home is not a place where women merge their personal freedom and individuality in the personality of men; still less is home a place where husbands and wives do not work, talk and eat together on terms of equality. . . . Rather it is a hallowed place of rest and of unrestrained intercourse, where husbands and wives, brothers and sisters, male and female relatives and friends, gather together round the same hearth in loving confidence and mutual trust, each and all working together like the differently formed limbs of one body, for the general good and for the glory of the great Creator.[4]

Monier-Williams's idealized representation of the home summoned up a range of associations. He evoked the idea of the home as the site of women's heroic work of nurture and moral uplift, giving credit to English homes for the material and moral successes of the British Empire. He also played on a notion that came into prominence in the late nineteenth century, expressed very vividly here, of the home as a sheltered space within which companionate marriage would flourish and generate harmonious social interaction around it.

We should bear in mind that not everyone in this period subscribed to this description of the Victorian home. Small but significant numbers of European and American writers and activists were questioning assumptions about women's inherently and exclusively domestic nature. But these early feminists were probably not missionaries or missionary supporters. Patricia Hill has argued persuasively that the vast majority of women involved in the women's foreign missionary movement in the late 1800s did not support the concurrent women's rights movement.[5]

As I touched on in the previous chapter, scholarship on the doctrine of separate spheres, which shaped much of the discourse on gender in Europe and North America from the late eighteenth to the early twentieth century, acknowledges that, from the beginning, the notion of men and women inhabiting two separate but adjoining and complementary spheres of activity was more of a guiding vision than a reality lived out in the everyday. Over the course of the nineteenth century in Europe and North America, as a result of the Industrial Revolution and the resulting accumulation of capital, the activities of production were detached from those of reproduction and assigned to two value-laden spatial domains: the home and the workplace. The home came to be regarded as a site for the rejuvenation and replenishment of men depleted of vital substance through their interactions with a morally unsavory, market-driven workplace.[6] Leonore Davidoff and Catherine Hall consider one of the most influential religious responses to the changed political economic systems which developed as a result of the accumulation of capital to be the identification in early evangelical doctrine of the home as the crucible of character. In the writings of Hannah More, William Wilberforce, and others, the home appeared as a sheltered zone where women were charged with the responsibility to restore their world-weary menfolk and raise proper children by creating a morally and culturally pure environment. Throughout the years of European colonization of Africa, Asia, and Latin America, these ideas were imported into various non-Western societies producing a wide variety of effects. Missionaries were often the agents most responsible for importing these ideas to the non-Western societies, but they were taken up by colonial subjects in diverse, sometimes surprising ways. Literature on domesticity and the doctrine of separate spheres in the colonies has shown that "the natives" did not receive these ideologies in a wholesale or uniform manner.[7]

Similarly, Western proponents of domesticity adapted the doctrine of separate spheres to the conditions they encountered in the colonies. Miss Greenfield of the Society for Female Education deftly deployed the assumptions of this ideology when she argued before the 1883 Missionary Conference in Calcutta that women's gifts of persuasion on the basis of affect (and not reason) were powerful weapons in the battle against a demonic Hindu "heathenism":

> "Higher education," we are told "was to slay Hinduism through its brain"—though it has not done so yet! My sisters, you and I in all our woman's weakness and conscious insufficiency are here in India to strike the death-blow, not at the monster's *head* but at his HEART, and by God's help we shall drain out his lifeblood yet! For I believe that the heart of Hinduism is not in the mystic teaching of the Vedas or Sharsters [sic], not in the finer spun philosophy of its modern exponents, not even in the bigoted devotion of its religious leaders; but enshrined in its homes, in the family life and hereditary customs of the people; fed, preserved, and perpetuated by the wives and mothers of India. . . . Let us in our Master's name lay our hand on the hand that rocks the cradle, and tune the lips that sing the lullabies. Let us win the mothers of India for Christ, and the day will not be long deferred when India's sons also shall be brought to the Redeemer's feet.[8]

Greenfield's exhortations had a strong rhetorical appeal, drawing as they did on an implicit theory of socialization, namely, that the strongest, most deeply felt and fiercely defended commitments are not those articulated in intellectual systems, but those that escape explicit articulation through their inscription on the body and in daily life. Women's importance to the missionary project did not lie in their expertise in "finer spun philosophies," but in their familiarity with the habits of family life—the vehicles best suited for ideologies that penetrate to the depths of the self. Such habits were, in Greenfield's idiom, crucial building blocks in the constitution of a sanctified Christian life.

The rhetoric of both Pitman and Greenfield reflects the influence of Methodism on the missionary movement, which gave greater value not only to the emotions, but also to everyday life as the potential ground of salvation. Although John Wesley's doctrine of the universality of grace was at odds with

John Calvin's view that only the predestined members of the elect would enjoy salvation, Wesley shared with the latter the Protestant dogma that one could not earn salvation through "good works." Salvation from sin, which was also universal, was a gift from God alone, and no amount of human effort could win it. However, though one could not gain salvation by one's own efforts, one could lose it. Methodists saw grace not as a perpetual state, but as a temporary condition that could be squandered through "bad works." The purpose of piety—service to the Church, reading edifying tracts, prayer, hymn singing and other spiritual exercises, and one's disciplined conduct in everyday life—was to prevent the lapse into active sinfulness in the face of the world's many snares and temptations.[9] It was this intense attention to the quotidian and the regulation of everyday habits and behavior that accompanied it that distinguished Methodists and made them a "people apart" from the unsaved.

Although this attention to the quotidian may be traced back to Wesley's theology of sanctification, it was not the exclusive prerogative of Methodists. Evangelicals within the established Church of England, like Hannah More, and women missionaries representing a variety of denominations shared a passionate "intramundane asceticism" that linked domestic practices with redemption. The importance of the quotidian in evangelical and missionary discourse greatly heightened the religious significance of woman's role as guardian of the household, not only in North America and Western Europe but also in the colonized world. As Greenfield's exhortation suggests, women missionaries saw that local women should be enlisted wholeheartedly as vital instruments in a people's salvation because they had the most influence over the customs and practices that made up domestic life, and therefore over the deepest sentiments, the "heart" or what we might call the "consciousness" of a people.

Connected to this desire to influence the customs and consciousness of Indians through their womenfolk, the zenana fascinated Western observers because it represented an uncolonized space within the Indian milieu.[10] It marked in a particularly vivid way the frontier of colonial knowledge and influence—for without knowledge of the "manners and customs" of their subjects, colonizers felt they lacked the understanding necessary to civilize their subjects thoroughly. I would argue that the fascination of Western women with purdah also had something to do with the fact that Indian practices of gender segregation—with women's activities restricted to the interior of the house or courtyard and men's activities ranging outside these spaces—produced a social landscape that on the surface appeared very similar to the vision of the world according to the separate spheres doctrine. It was in some respects a distorted image of themselves that they saw as they gazed out of their carriages and drank tea in the mysterious zenanas of Indian homes during their occasional forays into Black Towns, the sections where the "natives" lived in colonial cities like Madras, Bombay, and Calcutta. However, in the imagined zenana, the protocols of gender segregation and division of labor that felt "natural" and appropriate to Western women were exaggerated almost beyond recognition.

In literature promoting the zenana missions Indian women are consistently characterized as miserable creatures all but wallowing in suffering. This emphasis on misery in descriptions of native life was integral to the imperialist nature of the missionary project. As the Comaroffs have argued in their work on missionaries in colonial sub-Saharan Africa, "In making the other a passive sufferer, the term evoked the conceit of heroic salvation, and simultaneously established an alibi for intervention."[11] The politically conservative nature of the women's foreign missionary movement suggests that by dwelling on the horrors of the treatment of women in India, missionary women deflected attention from the critique of gender relations that was emerging at the same time in Europe and North America. Indeed, one of the ironies of the women's foreign missionary movement is that although the institution of purdah was repeatedly condemned in the movement's rhetoric, the missionaries did very little to eradicate it. Western missionaries' socially constructed image of purdah, it seems, lent force to the notion that only women could teach, heal, and minister to India's women, and thus opened up opportunities for women in India that were not available in their home countries.

Though many of the values associated with the seclusion of women in India were also embedded in Victorian notions of femininity, foreign observers represented the practice of purdah as one among the many forms of mistreatment of women in India that indexed the country's low state of civilization. Like sati and child marriage, the seclusion of women was a clear indicator that Indians, specifically Indian men, were not morally fit to rule themselves. When purdah came under attack in the nineteenth century, its formerly taken-for-granted nature was challenged, and defenders as well as detractors of the custom began to voice the reasons behind it.

Indian Ideas about Purdah

The most common explanation for the practice of secluding women offered by both British and Indian historians in the nineteenth century, as in the contemporary period, was that it was adopted during the Muslim interregnum as a means of preventing miscegenation.[12] As such, it was intricately bound up with Golden Age narratives of the subcontinent in which the decline of Indian civilization is said to have been hastened by the invasion of Muslims from Turkey and Persia, whose marauding hordes sexually assaulted Hindu women (among other alleged atrocities). The social chaos wrought by the Muslim invasions necessitated, historians said, that Hindu men protect their women by taking the extreme measure of severely restricting their social contact and physical mobility.[13] Others suggested that in the late eighteenth century, families newly arrived in the halls of high society adopted the customs and values of the Mughal aristocracy, including that of female seclusion, to distinguish themselves from their unsophisticated, rural neighbors.

Explanations for purdah that assign the blame to an aggressive or imperialist Muslim presence in India and the need to mobilize against an outside Other shift attention from the important ways purdah has long served as a nexus for relations of power *within* the Indian Hindu household. Several contemporary feminist anthropologists have examined the diverse expressions of purdah in Indian society.[14] A common thread in their findings is that the behaviors constitutive of purdah in modern India—veiling, silence, bodily gestures such as seeking a place of lower elevation to sit—are part of a larger complex of norms and behaviors designed to maintain social distance between specific categories of individuals. Which categories of people must keep purdah in front of others varies by religion and region. Among south Asian Muslims, purdah mostly regulates social interaction between men and women, whether related or not, whereas among Hindus, purdah restrictions generally prevent familiar social contact between members of the same joint family. Thus, in a Hindu family, a young bride keeps purdah not only in front of her husband and the affinal male relatives older than her husband; she also keeps purdah in front of her mother-in-law. By observing patterns of who keeps purdah in front of whom, anthropological explanations generally maintain that purdah restrictions regulate social boundaries based on sex and/or age and support authoritative relationships through the strict control of emotionally charged, and hence potentially disruptive, social contact.

In two very different essays, Uma Chakravarti and Nur Yalman have examined the Brahmanical assumptions that undergird purdah ideologies. In a wide-ranging study of classical Indian texts from the Laws of Manu to the epic literature of the Ramayana and the Mahabharata, Chakravarti argues that the roots of purdah can be traced to the emergence in the eighth to sixth centuries B.C.E. of a new political economy in which control over land was held and transmitted patrilineally.[15] In the highly stratified society that resulted from the changes of this period, land-holding groups were anxious to control women's sexuality to ensure the paternity of their descendents. Texts informed by the values of this new Brahmanical culture represent women as innately adulterous and endowed with uncontrollable sexual appetites. For example, a frequently cited line from Manu 9:15 reads, "Good looks do not matter to them, nor do they care about youth; 'A man!' they say, and enjoy sex with him, whether he is good-looking or ugly."[16] According to the gender ideology of Brahmanical patriarchy, women are not simply regarded as creatures of excessive sexuality; they are also represented as crucial linchpins in the structure of caste. Through their reproductive capacities they are regarded as "gateways— literally points of entrance into the caste system," and for this reason they must be zealously guarded, especially against the sexual advances of the lower-caste male.[17] Such sexual encounters between high-caste women and lower-caste men are the dreaded *pratiloma* ("against the hair") unions spoken of in the Laws of Manu. Whatever the limitations of such broad accounts of history, Chakravarti's identification in early Brahmanical texts of purdah-type ideologies provides an important corrective to the idea that purdah is a Muslim import into Indian culture.

In his classic essay, "On the Purity of Women in the Castes of Ceylon and Malabar," anthropologist Nur Yalman developed an influential thesis as to why the upper-caste woman is the object of moral panic both in practice and in

Brahmanical texts. Yalman redefines caste as a basic principle of Hindu social organization whose function is to produce closed kinship structures, castes, which preserve land, women, and ritual quality, that is, the purity of caste, within them. Though caste membership is conveyed to children through both their father and their mother, there is an asymmetry to the system in that men can engage in sexual relations with women of higher or lower ritual status without affecting their purity, whereas women are permanently contaminated by sexual contact with men of a lower caste, thereby threatening the purity of the entire caste.[18]

Through his study of female puberty rites among the high castes of Ceylon (Sri Lanka) and Malabar (the western coast of Kerala), Yalman found that a girl's arrival at puberty is a moment of intense danger for this system because her awakened sexuality creates the potential for breaches within it. Frequently, different castes resolve this danger through different puberty rituals: prepubertal marriage (as among orthodox Brahmans), puberty rites in which a young women is symbolically married to a phallic object, such as an arrow (as among the non-Brahman castes of western India studied by S. C. Dube), or rites in which the young girl is symbolically married to a Brahmin man who will enhance and not contaminate the ritual purity of which she is the vehicle (as among the Nayars of Malabar). Purdah can be thought of as a different solution to the problem of the danger that arises when a woman reaches sexual maturity. Rather than contain this danger through an actual or symbolic marriage, it is contained literally by guarding the woman within the interior space of the house and protecting her from the perceived lascivious gazes and sexual advances of threatening lower-caste men.

These ideas find an echo in the conventions of many different kinds of cultural productions in Indian literary and artistic traditions. In Sanskrit poetics as in the poetics of Indian architecture, the interior space at the heart of the household (the zenana, *antahpuram*, "inner city"; or the *antarmahal*, "inner walls," "fortified area") guaranteed the sexual purity of the women who resided there by isolating them from contact with outsiders. The romance of the story of Nala and Damayanti in the Mahabharata, for example, draws on the tension created by the fact that the love between the young people develops without the two ever having seen each other. Nala communicates with Damayanti, secluded behind the high walls of her father's place, through the mediation of messenger geese. In south India, the organizing principles of early classical Tamil poetics encode an intensely gendered understanding of physical space. A whole series of conventions separate ancient Tamil Sangam poetry into two genres organized around the division between *akam*, the domestic, interior space of the household associated with love and women, and *puṟam*, the public world, a quintessentially male space of heroes, battles, and glory.[19] Though the issue of caste purity does not arise in this ancient Tamil worldview, the chastity of wives is a major concern. According to the martial values first expressed in Sangam poetry and carried forward through centuries of Tamil folk and classical literature, the chastity of a wife protects her husband from harm in battle. As illustrated in the story of Kaṇṇaki (the heroine of the Tamil epic *Cilapati-*

kāram), who brings to ruin the capital city of a king who wrongly condemned her husband to death, the perfect chastity of a wife can provide the moral capital she may leverage to avenge her husband's soiled reputation. These examples illustrate the ways Indian literary contexts present family status and honor as intimately linked to the sexual behavior (or misbehavior) of wives.

Gender ideologies do not stay the same for centuries; rather, the constraints and opportunities posed in a specific historical moment shape the way historical agents adapt them to their needs. But in each of its historical and literary expressions, the practice of purdah has been well-suited to carry meanings that signal prestige. A family whose womenfolk keep purdah demonstrates thereby the delicacy of its women, the absence of compulsion for them to work outside the home, and visible evidence that the women are shielded from any contact with men outside the family that might lead to miscegenation. In the nineteenth century, purdah achieved a certain fashionableness as upwardly mobile families endeavored to signal their improved social status by conspicuously displaying their ability to restrict the physical mobility of women. As Miss Bielby, M.D., a medical missionary, wrote in 1885, "A man's social standing in his own class depends, in a great measure, upon whether he can afford to keep his wife and daughters in Zenana or not. So it has come to pass, that upper-class servants, and other men in similar positions keep their female relations as strictly 'behind the purdah' as a Prince does."[20] The prevalence of the practice of purdah in the nineteenth century among a wider cross-section of social classes than in earlier periods coincided with the interest that Europeans showed in the "exotic" custom of purdah, suggesting that such interest may have given new strength or social significance to this so-called traditional custom. If the testimony of foreign residents of India is to be believed, representatives from Britain, Europe, and the United States became a favored audience for performances of purdah as a sign of the gentility of the family. As one observer wrote, "Occasionally, to make a show of great respectability, native women who have never been secluded, when visited by European ladies pretend that they are not allowed to be seen."[21] Insofar as Westerners were both fascinated and appalled by purdah, such performances tended to elicit an ambivalent reaction. A common response was to lecture Indians about the need to reform these barbarous practices so as to accelerate their entrance into the exclusive club of "civilized" nations. John Murdoch's book *The Women of India and What Can Be Done for Them* (1885) is a collection of excerpts from such lectures, delivered by both Europeans and Indians at the various venues of the social reform movement. In such venues, the "women's question" was an intensely debated topic.[22]

Debates over the emancipation of women forced advocates of the practice of purdah to articulate and defend the previously unstated assumptions behind women's immurement. One such advocate was Balloram Mullick, a judge in the Bengal courts, an admirer of Sir Henry Maine, and author of a collection of essays on *The Hindu Family*. For Mullick, as for many elite Hindu men in the nineteenth century, the issue of purdah was ultimately not about women, but about men. The sexual honor of women was important largely insofar as it reflected back on the prowess of the male members of the family. Mullick's diatribes against emancipation for women vividly evoke the humiliation of men who could not protect their wife: "Emancipation should follow the capability on the part of males of protecting females from insult and injury in the world outside. . . . Nothing is more foolish on the part of a weak husband than to expose his wife to insult and injury which he would be powerless to prevent."[23] Stratification in Indian society turned on (among other things) the difference between socially powerful men who could guard their women and economically and socially weak men, such as low-caste laborers, whose wives were exposed to threats of sexual violence under the feudal system of land ownership. Thus, Mullick's cautionary references to the vulnerability of women, which were largely addressed to men, depended on and reinforced the caste- and class-based divisions of Indian society.

Moreover, Mullick's representation of women as weak creatures who were utterly helpless without the protection of a man obscured a complex set of anxieties about the potential for chaos inherent in women's sexual agency. His concerns about women's sexual propriety did recognize the power that women wielded as gatekeepers of the family honor, but only in a very negative way.[24] His recognition of women's agency as defenders, or potential subverters, of patrilineal order was anxiously brought to the fore with the dystopic fantasy that women released from the physical confinement of the home would immediately run off with other men. Given the worrying possibility that liberated women would cuckold their husbands, Mullick insisted that the emancipation of women should take place only after certain conditions had been met, conditions that the systematic, "modern" education of women could produce. Education would foster the emotional maturity necessary to resist temptation and strengthen virtue by inculcating religious and moral values.

Like Mullick and supporters of social reform, the zenana missions were deeply invested in this vision of mature, educated Indian womenhood. Both the zenana missions and the debates on the women's question were part of a larger transformation of the role of women within the family and society, which covertly hinged on the significance of women's sexuality. In the new paradigm of femininity that arose out of the interaction between missionaries and representatives of high-caste Hindu culture, some of the elements of the high-caste vision of female propriety were retained but were turned in the direction of Victorian gender ideals for women. This new ideal emphasized the value of self-control, a quality that was consistent with the Victorian model of the ideal wife, whose rationality consisted in her ability to control expenditure and sublimate her sexuality into strictly reproductive channels.[25] Indeed, rather than relying on the literal walls of the zenana or antarmahal to protect a woman's chastity, supporters of the vision of the Indian New Woman urged women to exercise sexual self-control and to manifest their interiorized commitment to chastity and fidelity through their dress and demeanor.[26] According to this understanding, the importance of female chastity to the status of the family was by no means diminished, but the site of its articulation shifted significantly, from the architecture of the house to the demeanor of the woman as an expression of the state of her conscience. The literal immurement of a woman reformed along the lines of the discourse produced by the zenana missions would be almost an affront, suggesting that such a woman *needed* outside intervention to defend against possible breaches in her own willpower and self-possession.

However, the transposition of the site of self-control from the exterior walls to the interior conscience should not be understood as an inevitable teleological or evolutionary development from gross outside to subtle, refined inside (however tempting such an interpretation might be). Rather, this shift should be seen in a more structural light as an effect of the variant possibilities available in the juxtaposition of certain consistent elements: women, virtue, sexual vulnerability, walls. The texts of the classical Brahmanical tradition provided ample evidence that the recognition of the need for psychological self-surveillance by women frequently coexisted alongside the impulse to contain potentially wayward females behind the four walls of the home. Hindu social reformers gave new life to the arguments and admonitions contained in these texts, plumbing the depths of their tradition for moral support for new customs and practices. Manu's comment that "women who guard themselves by themselves are well-guarded" (Manu 9:13), for example, was used by social reformers in the service of a new "liberal conservative" notion of proper femininity. Judge Mullick expressed the same sentiment (linking it to the Ramayana and not the Laws of Manu) when he argued that education for women was a necessary prelude to emancipation: "Neither houses, nor vestments, nor enclosing walls are the screen of a woman. Her own virtue alone protects her."[27]

Although the new hybrid discourse of femininity retained the idea of separate spheres of activity for women and men organized along the division between public and domestic, transactions across that boundary were encouraged that would ideally bring women into a limited dialogue with the public world of men. The push for women's literacy was a key element in this transformation. The aim of fostering women's capacity to engage the public sphere through their roles as readers (and occasionally writers) of edifying texts was not to make women into philosophers or competitors for literate men's jobs as clerks in the colonial administration; it was to make them into suitable wives. The ideal modern Indian woman would be a companion for her husband who would not obstruct his education and progress toward "enlightenment." From the point of view of the spiritual cooperation of the conjugal relationship, companionate marriage bore a resemblance to Brahmanical ideals of wifehood insofar as a wife's duty was to support her husband's spiritual progress along the stages of life as defined by his *varnashrama dharma* (religious duties as defined by age and caste).[28]

Christian missionaries would probably not have recognized this similarity, however, because of their deep investment in viewing the Hindu conjugal relationship as the moral opposite of the Christian one: as a relationship of bondage rather than equality, of the force of tradition rather than the freedom of contract. Missionaries reviled the extended Hindu family on the basis of the perception that relations between husband and wife in the Hindu household were subordinated to the relations between the husband and his natal kin. The notion that intimacy between husband and wife was achieved, if at all, only through a struggle against those competing forces was anathema to the missionary conscience. As I explore more thoroughly in the next chapter, Christian missionaries sought tirelessly to undermine this style of family in favor of a nucleated, patriarchal family with the monogamous, heterosexual couple at its center.

One aspect of the new paradigm of femininity offered by the proponents of Christianity proved to be quite problematic, especially for low-caste converts. Missionaries viewed the role of low-caste women in agriculture and small-scale trading with tolerance at best and suspicion at worst. And yet they recognized the need for women to be contributing members to the household economy. In their direct contact with low-caste women, missionaries involved in women's work did not encourage labor in these areas; rather, where possible, they supported money-making activities for women that would produce genteel character. Lady missionaries trained low-caste Indian women in teaching, evangelism, lace work, embroidery, spinning—all vocations in which women could enjoy the "symbolic shelter" characteristic of the purdah system and thus not jeopardize their reputation for respectability and gentility.[29]

How did those involved in the zenana missions contribute to these transformations? How did this discourse take shape out of the multitude of interested actions taken by lady missionaries, their students in the zenana schools, the Indian women who worked in these schools, and the missionary boards that funded them? To address these questions, I trace the history of the zenana missions of several Protestant missionary organizations as they turned their attention from the urban elite among whom they had worked in the mid–nineteenth century, to the rural poor who converted to Christianity in large numbers in mass conversions that took place throughout the nineteenth and twentieth centuries.

History of Zenana Missions

The zenana missions grew out of the difficulties women missionaries encountered in their efforts to enroll elite Indian women in the conventional schools they started beginning in the late eighteenth century. Initially, many women missionaries attributed Indian resistance to women's education to beliefs held by high-caste Hindu men that female education produced widows, encouraged disobedience, and facilitated adulterous liaisons. Meredith Borthwick notes that one particularly alarming worry was that literate women would use their new skill to send their lovers written invitations to secret rendezvous! There was also an economic component to the resistance to women's education. Indians were eager to have their sons educated in schools run by Christian missionaries in the hopes of social and economic advancement, but they balked at the idea of sending their daughters. Education for women, in fact, could be a liability, making it harder to find a suitable groom for an educated bride.[30]

In addition, caste prejudice hindered the expansion of both girls' and boys' schools. In areas where missionaries had been successful at attracting lower-class pupils, members of the "respectable classes" were reluctant to permit missionaries to educate their sons and daughters for fear that they would be associated with a lower social stratum. And in towns where Christian schools had traditionally attracted upper caste students, the admission of a "Pariah" could empty its ranks, at least temporarily.[31]

Even Indian Christians resisted women's education for many decades. Little is known at present about Ziegenbalg's efforts at girls' education in Tranquebar besides the fact that he oversaw "charity schools" for girls beginning in 1710.[32] But the CMS chaplain James Hough reported that the schools for girls that he opened in 1819 in the Christian villages of Tirunelveli, Nazareth, and Mudulur were established only over the objections of the community's leaders.[33] Hough does not elaborate on the reasons Indian Christians gave to support their objections to education for girls, but one can surmise that it had to do with the novelty of instructing girls and with the Christians' concern for their reputation for respectability, especially in the eyes of their neighbors. That the initiative for the schools came largely, perhaps entirely, from Hough is indicated by the fact that three years after opening, the schools lapsed for lack of attendance and remained closed for at least the next seven years.[34]

The zenana missions grew in part out of the failure of girls' schools to attract many students besides the daughters of very low-caste families. The zenana missions, which peaked in popularity and influence in 1850–1890, were focused on high-caste women and took as their field of operation the women's quarters of elite Indian homes. The zenana missions were not so much a part of the concurrent work among low castes that would eventually result in the bulk of conversions to Christianity, but part of larger efforts to recruit converts from among Indian elites in the service of a top-down approach to evangelism. Like the establishment of English medium schools to attract the boys of the Indian elites, the zenana missions were motivated by the belief that Christianity would be more influential and would spread more easily in India if the leaders of Indian society could be induced to accept the Christian religion.

The official histories of the zenana missions generally locate the beginnings of the method in Bengal.[35] The distinctive sociohistorical environment of Calcutta during the early British Raj provided the conditions under which evangelism among elite Indian women could attain some moderate success. The emergence of a class now known as the Bengali *bhadralok* created a demand for the services offered by women missionaries. The Bengali bhadralok were the product of a number of historical forces. The children of men who had gained great wealth in the eighteenth century through their partnerships with and patronage under the agents of the East India Company, the bhadralok often were able to accumulate significant amounts of capital, investing it in both trade and land. Where their fathers had grown rich working for the Company in the capacity of brokers, *dewans* (ministers and managers), *banias* (bankers, financial consultants), translators, and *munshees* (tutors), the sons took advantage of the Western education offered by Christian missionaries to parlay these material resources into greater wealth and positions of responsibility within the colonial administration. By the mid–nineteenth century, the bhadralok was established as the leading faction within the Bengali elite and had both the means and the motivation to pursue lifestyles that blended "traditionally" Indian—Mughal and high-caste Hindu—status markers with those derived from European traditions.[36]

The Scottish Free Church mission started the first zenana mission in Calcutta in 1855, with the assistance of a single lady English missionary named Miss Toogood, but the woman credited with first teaching women in zenanas on a large scale was Hannah Catherine Mullens, who is lionized in missionary histories as "the Apostle of the Zenanas."[37] Daughter of Alphonse Lacroix and wife of an LMS minister and historian, Joseph Mullens, Mrs. Mullens, it was said, opened the zenanas of Calcutta with the "tip of her knitting needle." E. R. Pitman, following missionary lore, relates that in early 1856, a Vaishnavite native doctor in Bhowanipore, a suburb of Calcutta, died, leaving a family of dependent women penniless. When Mrs. Mullens went to his home to comfort the survivors she met his daughter, a 25-year-old widow and only child who had been thoroughly educated in her youth by a traditional Indian pundit. Mullens was impressed with the young woman's intelligence and hired her to teach a small class of students in the widow's own house. The school quickly grew to accommodate twenty-three students who ranged in age from 8 to 20. Among them, several were married and at least one was a mother, but they were all, according to Mullens, the daughters of "respectable Hindu householders." Mullens and other missionary wives visited the school on a regular basis and its reputation rapidly grew through word of mouth.[38]

The strong prejudices against female literacy that held forth in the eighteenth century gradually gave way in the late nineteenth century. According to Borthwick's history of women's education in Bengal, the second half of the nineteenth century witnessed a remarkable increase in the popularity of formal education among middle-class Bengali families. In 1863 there were 95 girls' schools with a total attendance of 2,500, but by 1890 the number of schools had increased to 2,238 with a total of more than 80,000 students. Most of these schools were not run by Christian missionaries, but were the product of a resurgence of reforming activities by Bengali intelligentsia.[39] Crucial to the success of the Christian zenana missions were the Indian women employed by them who actually carried out the bulk of the work of teaching. As in every method used by Western missionaries to reach Indian audiences, the cooperation and initiative of Indians were critical to its success. I return to a discussion of the role of Indian women workers, the "Bible women," in the zenana missions after a brief discussion of the curriculum of these schools.

The Work of the Zenana Missions

The zenana missions were intended to introduce women to a wider conception of the world through Western education and to broaden their minds beyond the "cramped walls of the zenana." But this agenda was always auxiliary to that of sweeping away ideas and concepts considered antiquated by modern sensibilities so that the students would be ready to receive a superior worldview, namely, a Christian one. In the schools run by missionaries and the zenana missions alike, education was always and explicitly bound up with conversion to Christianity understood as a kind of modernization. In a connected fashion, these missions were also intended to draw secluded elite Indian women into dialogue with the agenda for social reform (with the recasting of Indian women at its center) that was heatedly discussed in the emerging public sphere of literary societies and debating clubs. As mentioned before, the goal was not to equip women to enter that sphere on equal footing with men, but to train them to take up their roles as rational mothers and readers of edifying tracts. What kind of activities defined the distinctive style of pedagogy and evangelization of the zenana missions?

The zenana missions were intended to make Indian women into better wives and mothers through the training of both their minds and their hands. The two main components of the curriculum of zenana missions were instruction in reading and training in needlework. Drawing on a long-standing European association between needlework and femininity, Western women missionaries felt that sewing, embroidery, knitting and lace work would inculcate in Indian women a particular style of genteel femininity.[40] In a manner reminiscent of Miss Greenfield's speech before the 1882 Missionary Conference, women missionaries filled the hands of Indian women with knitting needles and embroidery pillows so that they would not be occupied with "idolatrous" objects such as charms or flowers for the worship of gods. Once distracted from "superstitious" or religious practices, Indian women could cultivate through needlework the kind of character that was more suited to the requirements of the Christian faith. As Mala de Alwis argues in her study of Christian boarding schools in colonial Sri Lanka, "Sewing played a crucial role in the very molding of Christian women, in the construction of a particular moral demeanor. It was a practice that insisted on neatness, orderliness, concentration, patience, and precision."[41] In addition, missionaries and Indians alike saw instruction in sewing as an incentive offered to Indian women so that Western women could gain access to the zenana and preach the gospel.[42]

And yet, in the wake of debates over women's education that continued throughout the nineteenth century, the attention given to needlework in the zenana missions attracted considerable criticism. Judge Bulloram Mullick condemned the emphasis paid to "fancy work" in the zenana missions, considering it a pointless diversion from women's attention to household duties. "What is wanted," he wrote, "is knowledge that will fit her for companionship, for bringing up children, for nursing her family, and for taking an interest in the welfare of all women."[43] Though progressive Indian advocates of women's education appreciated the methods of the zenana missions, which allowed respectable women to gain an education while preserving their good name, they were repelled by the overt proselytizing and apparent frivolity of zenana education. Subsequent to the success of Protestant zenana missions, many

Indian reformers began their own institutions for instructing women.[44] Perhaps in response, the missionaries redoubled their efforts to use women's education as a vehicle for spreading the gospel. Mrs. Capron of the AMM reported that she taught no needlework in the zenanas, but relied "solely on God's word."[45] During Amy Carmichael's first years in India, she deplored the suggestion of one of her Bible women, Saral, that she could attract more women to hear the gospel by teaching them to knit. When Carmichael refused the suggestion, Saral objected that "there was nothing in the Bible that bore upon pink wool and knitting needles." Carmichael's thunderous reply, "Indeed there is! Zecharaiah 4:6, 'Not by my power, but by my spirit,' " reflects a growing missionary consensus that zenana education ought to be more serious, more explicitly evangelical, and concentrate more on Bible study.[46]

Instruction in literacy in the zenana missions was organized around tracts, pamphlets, and readers produced in large numbers by missionary society printing presses. These lesson books introduced concepts such as the solar system, germ theory, and the Christian notion of the good life through a series of increasingly difficult chapters. Designed to provoke discussion about the subjects of the lessons, the primers were to guide readers and listeners to an appreciation of the greatness of the Christian god and the superiority of Christianity. In one English-language lesson book, *The Zenana Reader* (1869), written by Charlotte Tucker under the pseudonym A.L.O.E., the fictionalized dialogue between a young Muslim wife (Sukara Bibi) and a Western woman missionary (Miss Ada) gives a highly idealized representation of this style of teaching.[47] For example, a lesson on the rotation of the planets culminates with Sukara Bibi's ecstatic wonder at the marvels of creation and its Creator: "Great—glorious—most wonderful Being, who made all the suns, moons, and planets, who sends them all on their courses, and never lets them go wrong or fall!"[48] Miss Ada brings her student to this rapturous moment through the patience with which she answers Sukara Bibi's questions as well as her skill at improvisation; at one point, Miss Ada sticks a knitting needle through a ball of yarn to illustrate the way the planets rotate on their axes. Like all good pedagogues, she moves from the known to the unknown, from the mundane spherical nature of the ball of yarn to a cosmic vision of the planetary spheres rotating in the heavens. But one wonders how persuasive a real-life Miss Ada might have been, especially if she had to use Miss Tucker's lesson books.

In one lesson, Sukara Bibi expresses some perplexity over the crucifixion of Jesus. Miss Ada attempts to clarify this crucial element of Christian theology through a parable: "There was a Maharani who wanted a tower built that would look to the East to the rising sun, but not West to the setting sun, for that depressed her. Similarly, she wanted to see South to the view of a river flowing, but not North to where the desert was." Miss Ada patiently explains to her student how impossible it would be to build such a structure, and then goes on to compare the necessary four walls of this hypothetical tower to the components of God's nature:

God's nature is to be composed of four parts: Love, Holiness, Justice and Truth are combined. But you can't have one aspect without the other. When God saw that Mankind was full of sin, he knew that he was worthy of death, he must be punished. God's Holiness showed Man to be worthy of death; His Justice pronounced sentence upon us; His Truth required that that sentence should be carried out. But if One as pure as God Himself could be found to endure the punishment of death for others, Justice would be satisfied, Truth be maintained and Love could receive the sinner. The Son of God offered Himself for this great work which He alone could perform. Christ stood in our place, He met our doom, He paid our debt with His blood.[48]

The allegorical and numerical schemes used in this lesson seem more like mnemonic devices than efforts at understanding. Aside from the fleeting and artificial reference to the Maharani, Miss Ada does not create a bridge for Sukara Bibi (or the readers of this text) between her own assumed truths and that of her student. Rather, she erects a rather forbidding tower, a terrifying image of God's absolute power.

In a discussion of Tucker's work, John Murdoch of the Christian Vernacular Education Society reviewed another of her lesson books. In Tamil its title was *Mātarpūccaram* (Women, the garland of flowers), and by 1888 it had been translated and published in several Indian languages. The chapter titles indicate that the point of entry for Christian values was identified as home life: sewing and washing clothes, bathing, cleanliness/hygiene, food and drink, taking care of a sick person, giving medicines, worms and rashes. Murdoch wrote, "The results have been most disheartening. The need of such lessons seems never to have entered the mind of most [Indian] ladies. The book has after all these years had a very limited circulation."[49] The kind of home life envisioned by Western missionaries, both the negative home life that needed reformation and the ideal toward which Indians were encouraged to strive, evidently did not evoke recognition in many Indian women

A more successful reading book for women was Annal Satthianadhan's *Nalla Tāy* (The good mother; 1862), a child-rearing manual that went through four editions and remained in circulation for sixty years. Satthianadhan wrote *Nalla Tāy* as a sort of epistolary mothering manual on the model of U.S. and British English-language advice books (e.g., Mrs. T. Clarke's *Instructions to Christian Mothers*, Mrs. Mullens's *Paranjothi and Kirubei*, and Rev. John Abbott's *The Mother at Home*). John Abbott's *The Mother at Home* was Satthianadhan's model for the overall plan of the book. She organized her "letters" according to Abbott's chapter topics: a mother's duty, a mother's authority, a mother's difficulties, a mother's faults, a mother's instructions, a mother's reward, and a mother's responsibility. Satthianadhan's tract is no pinnacle of Tamil literature, but it is a good example of the hybrid imagination of Indian Christians whose intermediary position between Western and Indian cultures enabled them to communicate Western ideals of feminine domesticity through idioms and illustrations that were meaningful to their Indian audiences.[50]

Although Satthianadhan did establish links in her writing to existing Tamil literary genres, especially proverbs, *Nalla Tāy* represents a departure from established Tamil literature and parenting practice in that nineteenth-century Tamil mothers did not transmit child-rearing information in print. This is not to say that the notion of childhood or the importance of proper parenting was absent in the Tamil cultural milieu. Tamil musical and literary genres contained moral instruction and parenting models that mothers and fathers may well have drawn on to socialize their children. The indulgent treatment of the baby god Krishna described in the *Bhagavata Purāṇa* or the moral lessons espoused in terse, epigrammatic fashion in Tamil ethical literature, for example, may have shaped the way actual parents raised their children. A schema of childhood development through various stages can be seen in the literary conventions of Tamil poets, who draw on a series of "types" of women, organized by age, to define the character of their heroes and heroines.[51] But the concept of directly engaging parents, let alone mothers in particular, to address the recurring challenges of child development by the consistent application of an explicit religious teaching was, to my knowledge, something new to nineteenth-century Tamil culture.

In fact, mothering manuals had been a novelty in the United States and Britain only a hundred years before the publication of Satthianadhan's book. With the social dislocation that accompanied the Industrial Revolution, advice manuals for parents encouraged them to foster strong emotional ties with children, who were likely to move far away from their natal homes, and equip them with strong moral values so that once away from home they would conduct themselves in an upright fashion. By the time Satthianadhan wrote the first edition of *Nalla Tāy* in 1862, English-language advice books for mothers had undergone considerable changes. From guides for parents of both sexes written by Christian ministers that were often based on sermons and took the sermon's directly exhortatory form, by the 1830s they had adopted a more intimate form of address and a more specific focus on women as the primary socializers of young children. Like American domestic literature written from the 1840s on, *Nalla Tāy* is an "amalgamation of fiction, didacticism, and domesticity."[52] The author incorporated narratives from real life, told in a rambling, folksy style, to illustrate Christian moral truths enacted (or woefully disregarded) in the daily lives of common people.

Nalla Tāy, as the title suggests, did not take on the entire edifice of the doctrine of separate spheres, but focused on a woman's maternal duty to create an orderly home to raise self-regulating, intelligent, and god-fearing children. This, Satthianadhan writes, was "a woman's greatest work." Fathers do play a part in her book, especially in the administration of corporal discipline, but mothers bear the greatest responsibility for parenting. From the very first pages of the book Satthianadhan assumes a gendered division of labor whereby women work at home while men work in the world outside the home. "Directing children properly is the special and very important duty of mothers," she writes. "Do not look towards your husband [for help]! Men who go out to the forest or field will not know much about the affairs of the house. The sins and errors of your children will be on your head."[53] Such a division of labor was by no means a *fait accompli* among most nineteenth-century Indian Christians. Nevertheless, Satthianadhan writes as though this ideal were already realized in order to define a specific religious role for Indian Christian women, namely, being the primary moral guides and exemplars for young children.

One of the main themes of the book is that the family is a single moral unit that can be raised up to heaven by the energetic leadership of the mother or plunged down into hell because of her ineffective or lazy parenting. In several of the book's many vignettes from "real life," a mother foolishly permits a child's sinful nature to luxuriate unrestrained until his terrible actions drag him, along with his mother, to hell. To avoid this grim prospect, Satthianadhan taught that the first step in parenting was to establish firm control over one's child. The mother's command over her children should be absolute, she advised, the children's obedience immediate: "When the mother says one word the children should not sing out a hundred words in answer to it."[54] As a way of establishing control over young children when their innately rebellious nature manifests itself, Satthianadhan recommended the old Puritan practice of breaking the child's will. Children are like young saplings which one can bend as one pleases, she writes, but after they mature, no matter how hard you try, you cannot make them budge.[55]

As a fourth-generation Christian whose father, John Devasahayam, was a well-regarded pastor and author himself, Annal Satthianadhan was well-educated in the Tamil literary tradition.[56] We will have occasion in chapter 5 to examine her life as the wife of the prominent south Indian clergyman W. T. Satthianadhan, and her career as a teacher and promoter of women's education. For now, my focus is on her influence as a writer. Satthianadhan's facility with the verbal arts of the Tamil literary tradition (both folk and classical) are apparent in her ability to condense the morals to be drawn from her own narratives into a single proverb borrowed from the vast storehouse of existing Tamil literature. For example, in a section devoted to the importance of teaching children proper moral conduct when they are young, she refers to the proverbial flexibility of saplings: "Maram siru kanrāyirukkum pōtē [atai] valaikkavēṇtum [You can bend a tree only when it is young]."[57] Later, she deploys another proverb with a similar meaning: "Sirumaiyir kalvi silaiyileluttu" [Learning in youth is written in stone]."[58] Whether this is an adaptation or her own invention, it conforms well to the poetic conventions of Tamil proverb in being a pithy single verse with a neat front rhyme. The best-known Tamil proverb that she uses could be regarded as the motto of the whole book: "Tāyaippōla piḷḷai, nūlaippola cēlai [As the mother is so is the child, as the threads are so is the sari]." In her hands, this naturalized image of family resemblance (ambiguously physical, temperamental, or moral) becomes a strong statement about the need for mothers to set a moral example for their children. Through this and other similar applications of popular sayings, Satthianadhan was able to bridge the distance between Christian and Tamil religious teachings by using the forms of traditional literature to present unfamiliar ideas in familiar garb.

One example of Satthianadhan's deft manipulation of Tamil proverbs deserves special attention. She follows Abbott and many authors of early English and American nineteenth-century advice literature in identifying the practical, pragmatic benefits of good mothering: Children will comfort you and take care of you in your old age if you raise them correctly. But the bonds between parents and children, she argues, extend far beyond the exigencies of this world. Disparaging the importance of worldly goods (as did American Puritan writers of a generation before), she emphasizes the ultimate value of the unity of the family as a moral entity: "None of the wealth and prosperity that we spend our lives seeking will come with us [when we die]; not even needles whose eyes have been broken will come in the end. But our children will come with us. They belong to us both in this life and the next."[59] An educated Tamil reader would immediately recognize that the phrase "needles whose eyes have been broken" is a reference to a poem by one of the most famous Tamil Siddhars, Paṭṭiṇattār. This phrase is a quotation from a Siddha poem, the last line of which reads, "Kātaṟṟa ūsiyum vārātu kāṇum kaṭaivaḷikkē." Because kaṭai can mean both "store, bazaar" or "end," the line can be read in two ways: Broken needles (lit. needles without ears) will not come on the way to the marketplace, or Broken needles will not be found on the final way (i.e., the way to salvation).[60] Thus, in the Siddha context, the reference to broken needles alludes to the uselessness of material wealth to the sannyasi, the renunciant who has abandoned everything upon entering onto the "final way." In her improvisation off the original meaning, Satthianadhan retains the image of the broken needle as a symbol of worthless material possessions that one cannot bring on a spiritual journey, but for her, the destination of this journey is the Christian heaven, not release (mukti) from the cycle of death and rebirth. The ultimate end for Satthianadhan is understood in the Christian sense as the reunion of the saved with God. Both Paṭṭiṇattār and Satthianadhan use eschatological visions to promote a particular idea of ethics in this life, and both deny the value of worldly possessions. But Satthianadhan clearly directs the resources of Tamil literature toward new religious purposes by urging her readers to strengthen family ties, not sever them, in order to achieve salvation.

Investigations into advice literature in the United States provide some suggestions about why this concept might have been compelling to Satthianadhan's Indian Christian audience. In the U.S. parenting advice literature that Satthianadhan used as the model for her book, the concern to forge a tight bond between mother and child can be traced to a historical moment of unprecedented physical mobility. Mary Ryan argues that parenting literature took off as a genre in the 1830s because the economic and social changes brought about by the Industrial Revolution meant that sons no longer necessarily followed in their father's footsteps. No longer dependent on their father's approval or beneficence for their material sustenance, male children increasingly pursued their own vocations in cities far removed from their natal homes, where they were subjected to moral temptations undreamed of back home (e.g., alcohol, gambling, prostitution, indebtedness). Ryan observes a link between the emergence of parenting literature and the need to instill strong moral values in children who would live out most of their lives (and raise their own children) far from the direct influence of their parents. Indian Christians in the late nineteenth century were also extremely mobile and thus perhaps likely to need a moral anchor to withstand the temptations to which their unstable lives exposed them. Many educated Tamil Christians traveled far away from their natal villages to teach in distant schools run by missionary organizations. In these new environments, often in isolation from other Indian Christians, the temptation that many young men (and women) faced was not so much the fleeting pleasures of alcohol or gambling, as the comforts of not being in the religious minority. Satthianadhan's *Nalla Tāy* provided a concrete solution to this temptation of apostasy. Mothers who followed her advice could instill firm moral principles in their children (obedience, fear of God, honesty, etc.) that would enable them to conduct themselves in an upright fashion in any environment.

Like *Mātarpūccaram* and *The Zenana Reader*, *Nalla Tāy* was designed to transmit new ideas about proper femininity, conjugality, and motherhood to Indian women. Satthianadhan's book succeeded among Indian Christians where books like A.L.O.E.'s *Mātarpūccaram* failed because it responded to the true conditions of the lives of Indian Christians. They appreciated her book because it provided a concrete solution to the threats to family unity presented by social dislocation. Like all the literature produced by and for the zenana missions, *Nalla Tāy* contributed to the reconfiguration of the Indian Christian family by projecting as real and accomplished an ideal gendered division of labor along the model of the separate spheres doctrine of nineteenth-century European and U.S. gender discourse. It enlisted women in the effort to transform this ideal into reality by providing them with a new religious role as mothers and invested them with the grave moral responsibility of ensuring the spiritual well-being of their children.

This project centered on the image of the mother at home, to be sure, and was therefore closely implicated in the production of a Western-style discourse of domesticity. But it was not a wholesale adoption of the doctrine of separate spheres. The ideal woman in Satthianadhan's vision was an outspoken individual actively engaged in the life of her community, not the meek stay-at-home depicted in socially conservative versions of Western gender discourse. The authorial persona of *Nalla Tāy*, perhaps based on Satthianadhan herself, did not sit at home presiding over the morality of her own privatized household. Still less did she sequester herself in the sheltered space of the home to maintain the family honor by guarding her own modesty as an idealized elite Hindu wife would do. The good mother of Satthianadhan's tract strode about the countryside, visiting families of all walks of life and freely dispensing advice to them on how to train children into morally upright, self-controlled, obedient Christians. She could do so without attracting criticism, I would argue, because of her extraordinary mastery of Christian feminine virtues of self-control and self-restraint. In the next section, I examine the Indian Christian women whom one might regard as the real-life counterparts of Satthianadhan's "good mother."

Indian Bible Women: Intermediaries and Exemplars

Crucial to the ability of Western women to find and communicate with Indian women in the zenanas was the presence of their native assistants, the so-called Bible women who accompanied them on their visits.[61] Though in the English-language histories of the zenana missions the voices that speak loudest are those of Western women missionaries hailing the steady increase in the number of Indian women affected by the "civilizing" influence of Christianity, a different story emerges if we look at the women's missions from the perspective of the Indian Christian women who facilitated the access of Western women to Indian homes. Their story reveals with great clarity the minute changes that took place in the realm of the everyday over the course of conversion to Christianity. Whatever effectiveness these missions had was due largely to the presence of Indian workers such as Bible women, who traversed the racial, religious, and cultural divisions that separated white women missionaries and the Hindu women they sought to contact.[62] Bible women's own writings and self-descriptions suggest that they were involved in a complex process of translation, reducing to a single intelligible level of order the panoply of differences among themselves, their British and American patrons, and their Hindu or Indian Christian audiences. I examine the writings of Bible women in the following discussion of changes in the discourse of domesticity among Indian Christians. First, I provide some historical background to this special "office" of women's work.

Generally speaking, the phrase "Bible women" described literate or semiliterate women who were themselves converts to Christianity and who worked in coordination with foreign missionary women in their visits from house to house, introducing women to the virtues of the Christian faith (and the "dangers" of non-Christian faiths) through reading lessons, sewing and knitting lessons, hymns, and conversation. But it is important to note that Indian Christian women worked as paid agents of missionary stations in a variety of roles, for example, as lay preachers, schoolteachers, and teachers in zenana schools. Sometimes the phrase Bible woman was used to refer to lay preachers, as distinct from "zenana workers," and sometimes the same women shifted from one type of work to another in the course of their association with a mission station. [63]

Most historians have traced the use of Bible women, in the sense of women evangelists who visited other women in their homes, to revivalist missions in Britain whose aim was to bring about the moral and spiritual regeneration of working-class communities. The most celebrated leader of this movement in England was Ellen Ranyard, an influential evangelist who recruited from among London's industrial urban poor. She was born in 1810, the daughter of a cement maker.[64] In her efforts to bridge the social distance between her fellow evangelists, for the most part educated and middle-class women, and their target audience, mill workers and factory girls, Ranyard was motivated in part by anticlerical sentiments. She wrote, "The people are tired of what they call 'parsons' and 'humbug'." She was inspired by the missionary emphasis on "native agency" and in turn inspired many who sought to contest the monopoly on church leadership enjoyed at the time by educated, middle-class men. What the people needed, she felt, was a new kind of agent, "a woman of their own class who could speak as they spoke, understand their difficulties and be as it were like themselves, only transformed by her faith and her Christianity."[65] Instead of class differences, Bible women in India were employed to overcome the vast racial, religious, and cultural differences that separated Western missionary women from their students. And yet, they occupied a decidedly low position in the hierarchy of the missions. They were to carry out the laborious day-to-day tasks of teaching, while the missionary ladies would come once a week or every two weeks to evaluate and supervise their progress.[66] The leaders of the zenana missions strongly encouraged the training of Bible women, in part, no doubt, to relieve themselves of the physically uncomfortable work of walking around in the sun from house to house or village to village. Pitman wrote, "It is a judicious outlay of strength and time to train, at each centre of mission-operations, as many native Bible-women as can be found fit for the work. Being natives they can bear the heat of the climate better, understand the feelings of the people and the modes of daily life far more, and feel a sincere sympathy for their sufferings—not deeper or more true perhaps, than that cherished by English missionaries, but a sympathy born of actual experience."[67]

The aim of Bible women's formal training was, first, to ensure that they could read and write well enough to teach, and second, to see that their conversion to Christianity was as thorough and orthodox as possible. A good Bible woman was one who, through her own conversion, had internalized the urgent goal of converting her fellow Indians. Ideally, the Bible women of India, it was hoped, would not only be more effective at making contact with non-Christians than European or American women, whose grasp of the language and culture was often less than complete, but also would serve as role models, demonstrating in their person the transformative capacity of the Christian faith. As Eva M. Swift wrote, "The people will not come into a Christian church to be preached to, so we must send the preachers to them. And who so fit to go to them, as the people of their own tongue, those who themselves have been brought out of darkness, and can witness to the glory of His marvelous light."[68] Bible women were thus exemplars for the high-caste students of the zenana missions who illustrated the effects of engaging in the kind of transactions with the public sphere that were encouraged by these institutions. They demonstrated in their persons how to achieve the kind of gentility and good character that was necessary for women to engage in the limited dialogue with the public world through education that was envisioned by women missionaries and advocates of social reform (see figures 4.1 and 4.2).

It is not altogether clear what kind of social or economic background most Bible women came from. Although the missionaries of the AMM did not keep

FIGURE 4.1 "Bible Woman instructing her pupils," from *American Madurai Mission: A Cartographical View, Prepared for the Exhibit of the Ecumenical Conference*, New York City, 21 April–1 May 1900. UTC Archive, AMM, 14d. Courtesy of United Theological College.

FIGURE 4.2 "Bible Woman teaching high caste Hindu women," from *American Madurai Mission: A Cartographical View*. UTC Archive, AMM, 14d. Courtesy of United Theological College.

records of the castes of the women who became Bible women, references to
the fact that they should ideally come from respectable families suggest that
many of them gained access to elite households because they shared the same
social background as their students. Yet, in her study of Bible women associated with the LMS in Travancore, Jane Haggis has found that the Indian women
who worked in the zenana missions there were generally from low-caste backgrounds. Many other sources indicate that in general, Bible women were of
lower social and economic status than their students. In her novel *Saguna*
(1895), Krupabai Satthianadhan, the wife of prominent church leader Samuel
Satthianadhan and daughter-in-law of Annal Satthianadhan, suggests that the
poverty of Bible women aroused ambivalence even within segments of the
Indian Christian community. When the eponymous heroine expresses her desire to join a preaching tour, her brothers mock and tease her: "They called me
a Bible woman, and gave me a few tracts and some battered, worn-out books
which they told me to carry under my arm just as the typical Bible woman
did."[69]

Whether Bible women themselves came from high-caste communities (as
the accounts of the AMM suggest) or from those of lower castes (as Haggis's
study suggests), their life stories reveal that many came to the missions after
enduring considerable hardship and were for the most part marginalized from
elite Tamil society. Many were widows or women estranged from their husband, with or without children. Without a husband and thus without the protection of the patriarchal household, widows and abandoned wives were vulnerable to sexual and economic exploitation. One brief example of the
trajectory of a Bible woman is given by Gnanaprahasiammal, one of the most
senior Bible women in Eva Swift's school (see figure 4.3). Gnanaprahasiammal
was alternately abused and abandoned by her husband throughout her married
life. The daughter of a Christian schoolteacher from Tirunelveli, she achieved
a certain degree of literacy through formal education before she reached puberty and her parents removed her from school. The man she was married to
shortly thereafter moved the family to Madurai in pursuit of a clerical government job. After one of his many unannounced departures, Gnanaprahasiammal found work with the AMM. Through independent study of the Bible she
prepared herself to work as a Bible woman for Miss Swift's predecessor in the
department of women's work. Gnanaprahasiammal's biographer, Miss Swift,
notes with some satisfaction that she lived to the ripe age of 71 and outlived
her husband, who died contrite and utterly dependent on her.[70]

As with Gnanaprahasiammal, Bible women's association with the Protestant missions gave them an opportunity to craft new personae for themselves, to develop skills and a degree of independence unusual for women at
the time. And yet, there were firm limits on the extent to which they could
construct new identities. These limits were imposed not only by the ideals of
domesticity promoted by the zenana missions; they also came from pressures
within colonial Indian society. Bible women faced the same kinds of pressure
that successfully banished unmarried female Vaishnavite singers from the zenanas of the Bengali bhadralok. As Sumanta Banerjee has shown in her study

FIGURE 4.3   Gnanaprahasiammal, senior Bible woman. UTC Archive,
AMM, 14e. Courtesy of United Theological College.

of the decline in prestige these female religious specialists experienced in the
nineteenth century, the Vaishnavis were considered at best a bad moral influence on the genteel ladies of the bhadralok, the *bhadramahila*, and at worst
prostitutes. Banerjee writes of their bawdy lyrics, "What used to be innocent
fun, now held a threat to domestic stability, thanks to the 'enlightenment.' "[71]
Unlike Vaishnavi singers, Bible women did not, to my knowledge, spice up
their narratives based on biblical characters with sexual allusions. But, as unattached women who moved around in the course of their work, Bible women
were just as constrained by the new strictures of colonial Indian standards of
respectability as Vaishnavi singers were.

Like Vaishnavis, Bible women had to negotiate the prevailing gender
norms which took a dim view of women who moved outside the safe and
respectable boundaries of the home. Whereas the wandering typical of Bible
women's work was not considered extraordinary for men, for Indian women
of respectable families it was highly unusual. Itinerancy in colonial India was
associated with two groups of Indian women, neither of whom garnered much
social status: working women from lower castes who were engaged in trade,
and wandering religious women who were often associated with prostitution.[72]
At a time when the mark of respectability for women was their restricted mo-

FIGURE 4.4   "Annal Pakiam, a Bible-woman," from *American Madurai Mission: A Cartographical View.* UTC Archive, AMM, 14d. Courtesy of United Theological College.

bility, Bible women had to develop strategies for projecting an honorable, re-spectable image in order to carry out their vocation. One way these women were able to transgress the social codes was by projecting an image of super-chastity. Bible women worked within established definitions of femininity to craft personae that made them nonthreatening guests in the zenanas of elite women. In their style of self-presentation, they went to great lengths to de-emphasize all traces of their sexual desirability or availability: They removed their jewels and wore white saris, drawing on widely recognized markers of virtuous widowhood in its ascetic and asexual mode, and often carried enor-mous cloth-covered Bibles as a visible sign of their vocation as religious women (see figure 4.4). In a fund-raising pamphlet produced in 1916, Eva Swift writes, "When I first came to India I used to hear it said that the chief qualifications for Bible-woman's work was 'age and ugliness.' "⁷³ As was mentioned in my earlier discussion of purdah, the ideology behind the prohibition on women's inhabiting public space in India had to do with protecting their chastity, and thus the honor of their male family members. On account of being physically unattractive or having passed beyond the stage of being perceived as a sexual person, middle-aged Bible women "earned" the right to move freely in public space denied to most Indian women. As ostensibly nonsexual beings, they were neither threats to the dominion of wives in the zenana nor targets for sexual predation in public.

One category of Indian women who fit many of the requirements necessary for carrying out the work of evangelizing and teaching was widows. As the social reform movement turned its attention to the "rehabilitation" of widows, some zenana missions adopted policies restricting their ranks to widows and unmarried women only. At least as early as 1921, Miss Swift's school offered admission *only* to widows and unmarried women. In 1916, Swift acknowledged that elderly widows were the preferred candidates for the work because they had both experience and freedom from domestic obligations: "It still remains true that acceptable workers must have some maturity of age and experience. These are found, presumably, in the widow, who by reason of broken relationships, is set free from the claims of family life."[74] Moreover, the status of many widows as dependents in the household of their deceased husband, and the result that they were delegated to do the most difficult and unpleasant household labor, may have made working for the mission a more attractive option than working for their in-laws.

The plight of widows was a well-known feature of Indian culture among the Christian communities in the United States and Britain. It is possible that the frequent reporting of widows among Bible women in the records available to us, for the most part fund-raising appeals to Christians back home in the United States, is related to the desire to capitalize on this knowledge. Not so well-known is the fact that many non-Brahman communities did not prohibit widows from remarrying. The prohibition was one of the aspects of the Brahmanical lifestyle adopted by upwardly mobile castes in their bid for higher social status. The question of the status of widows in the various communities of nineteenth-century India is one that bears further research. Most missionary sources as well as pamphlets produced by social reformers stress the image of the suffering, abandoned widow, but other colonial sources suggest that in many communities widows were permitted, even encouraged to remarry.[75] The desire to target widows for uplift and rehabilitation may have been yet another example of the tendency of foreign colonizers to generalize for all of Indian culture the practices and beliefs of the Brahman minority.

Bible women's manner of self-presentation is clearly not a straightforward adoption of the notions of female respectability engendered by Western women missionaries. The Bible woman here is not the refined "angel of the house" of the Victorian imagination, but neither is she the genteel bhadramahila of the Bengali bhadralok imagination. By drawing on a variety of sartorial conventions, mainly from the highly stigmatized tradition of Indian widowhood, Bible women conveyed an image of an independent woman who could move between the worlds of the Protestant mission and the local Indian environment.

Reforming the Hut

As I alluded to previously, the fund-raising and promotional materials produced by missionaries in charge of women's work suggest that a dramatic shift
took place around the turn of the century in the nature and function of evangelical work among Indian women. From 1850 to 1890, work specifically
among women was based on the model of zenana missions. The work of the
missions took place in towns, among the homes of the elite and upwardly
mobile families, and was motivated by a desire to gain conversions among the
elite members of society, who tended to observe purdah restrictions more
strictly than nonelites. During this period, the ideology of conquest and conversion through penetration of the domestic sphere is vividly apparent in
English-language missionary fund-raising and promotional literature. This
strategy of top-down social transformation eventually reached a point of diminishing returns. Though zenana visitation had taken pride of place on many
missionary societies' agendas for women's work, by the turn of the century
many missions were beginning to regard it as an inefficient drain on their
resources. Along with schools for girls from high-caste families, the zenana
missions served through emphasis on literacy to bring Indian women into
dialogue with Western notions of feminine propriety, motherhood, and the
organization of domestic space. However, they produced almost no actual converts. The annual reports of many missions reflect an ever more desperate
search for solace in the gains they had made simply in persuading a few women
of the value of Christianity and Western domestic practices. The failure also
produced a new category of Christian in India, the Secret Christian, a woman
who professed a faith in Christianity but was unable to affirm this publicly for
fear of reprisals from her husband.[76]

As the nineteenth century came to a close, the demand for zenana missions decreased for a couple of reasons. First, as the notion of female education
took hold among the liberal elite, many families who previously would not
allow their daughters and wives to leave the house now permitted them to do
so for schooling. Second, the mass movements to Christianity in the early
twentieth century brought many poor people and members of the low castes
into the Protestant fold. As a result, many missions shifted their focus from
towns to village communities, where practices involving gender segregation
and seclusion of women were not as prevalent or observed with the same rigor
as among elite, urban groups. The next phase of women's missionary work,
which can be placed roughly between 1890 and 1940, saw the emergence of
Bible women's training schools, in which Indian Christian women with rudi-
mentary or no formal education could gain sufficient knowledge of the Bible
and techniques of evangelization to find employment in the missions. Liberal
Christianity became influential during this period, evidenced in the efforts
taken to ensure not only the spiritual but also the material well-being of converts. All over India, technical training centers sprang up alongside seminaries
and schools to teach indigent Christian men and women a trade such as weav-

ing or tailoring. The history of women's work in the AMM provides an excellent example of the shift in focus of missions at the turn of the century and helps to illuminate the changes in Indian Christian domesticity as the concern for respectability spread from elite groups to socially more marginalized groups.

Accounts of the zenana missions typically describe the Hindu home as a stumbling block to evangelism, even as its alleged deficiencies are taken as a compelling reason for intervention. In the descriptions of foreign missionaries the Indian home appears at once too porous and too contained. Images of the dark and cramped zenana pervade the literature describing work among elite women.[77] This image helped to convey the idea that women were trapped within the inner compartments of houses and in need of rescue. The strategy for the reform of such homes, and of the women inside them, was to open them up to transactions with the public world of colonial India. Other representations stress the chaotic, uncontrolled movements between inside and outside and deplore the confusion said to arise due to the lack of clear boundaries. One journalist describes the challenges facing Bible women in this way: "Frequently a teacher will be interrupted by the crying of several small children, the barking of a dog or the bellowing of a cow which ordinarily occupies a stall in one of the best rooms of the house. Sometimes the doors are suddenly pushed open by the cow which is just coming in from pasture and the teachers have to grab their books and rush to a place of safety until the cow is placed in the stall."[78] The apparent conflict between these two contradictory views of Indian homes may be resolved by considering the class differences that were being described and reinscribed by these Western observers. Judging from their accounts, the implicit assignment of Bible women in middle-class or elite homes was to pry open the walls of the zenana and expose its inhabitants to the civilizing influence of Christianity, modernity, and Western education. In lower-class homes, on the other hand, Bible women were to bring order by firming up the home's internal and external boundaries and providing a clear center through a commitment to Christianity.

The reports that Bible women connected with the AMM produced for their supervisors reveal a representation of the Indian home that does not exactly correspond to the representations of Western observers. These reports cannot be read as undistorted reflections of the activities engaged in by Bible women, but must be considered representations of their own work in the best possible light. Given the degree of dependence that obtained between Bible women and their employers, it is not surprising that no record survives of Bible women's "backstage" impressions of their involvement with the women's missionary societies. Although these reports were obviously not intended as descriptions of the Indian home per se, they do provide an important counterweight to the negative assessments of the Indian home generated by Western missionaries. These reports convey an image of the home as an entity with relatively fluid boundaries, as a dynamic meeting place, not a static cage. It appears that Bible women addressed a wide range of listeners as people gathered at the thresholds and verandahs of houses to listen to them preach. Traveling *sadhus*, people returning from pilgrimage, and the husbands and male relations of the students all figure as interlocutors in the accounts of the women of the AMM.[79] Though the justification for the zenana missions rested on the notion that only women could reach other women (because of the restrictions of purdah), the descriptions in these reports suggest that in practice, the codes of purdah were capable of negotiation and that Bible women taught and preached to both men and women, to anyone who paused in the course of their paths to listen to them.[80]

Although these comings and goings were sometimes looked down upon by Western observers, the Bible women's accounts show that they took advantage of the unexpected departures and arrivals that enlivened Indian houses to drive home their message about the salvific power of the Christian faith. In fact, this ability to improvise, to think on their feet and respond imaginatively to the questions of their students as well as the random or unexpected events that took place in the course of their visits seems one of the most important evaluative criterion brought to bear on the work by Bible women themselves. The following report, written in 1893 by Y. Jesuvadiyal, a Bible woman who worked for the AMM, shows the skill at speaking persuasively on one's feet that these women refined in their work:

> When I was teaching [several Hindu women] in a house, a girl came bringing water and the holy ash they use to smear on their foreheads and gave it to them. They received it with great care, drank the water and smeared themselves with the ash. When I looked at them and asked what it was, they answered it was holy water [*tirtam*] brought from Ramesvaram by a lady who had gone there. "If we drink it we can obtain merit," they said, "It is water given by a great man." I was astonished to see such ignorance. I said, "When I am sick, if you eat medicine will I become healthy? If she goes to Ramesvaram, how can you obtain merit? Is it possible that water can cleanse our sins? Our sins will not be absolved by the merit performed by an even bigger sinner than ourselves. . . . For the cleansing of sins, this water, these ashes, and pilgrimages will not help. If we believe in the one who came to cleanse our sins and save us, if we confess our sins, and accept forgiveness from him, our sins will be cleansed by the blood that he spilled on the cross."[81]

Jesuvadiyal here displays a remarkable ability to redirect the meaning of local practices in a new direction, a talent similar to Annal Satthianadhan's capacity to redeploy proverbs and quotations from classical Tamil literature for new religious purposes. The author of this report initially denies that there is any connection between her own practices and those of her non-Christian students, but she goes on to subtly suggest that Christian practices work along the same principle as Hindu practices, only more effectively. The symbolism used by Jesuvadiyal and her students to convey spiritual power depends on a similar metaphor. Through their absorptive, liquid properties, both the blood of Jesus and the water from Ramesvaram dissolve and wash away the sins of humanity. But the liquid blood that Jesuvadial refers to gets its power from Christ's redemptive suffering on the cross instead of from the austerities performed by the holy men who reside in Ramesvaram.

As we saw in the previous chapter, between 1892 and 1921, Eva Swift built the Bible women's training school into a complex institution known as Rachanyapuram. Over the course of those thirty years, the overall purpose of the institution—to transform Indian women into model Christian wives and mothers so that they would transform Indian homes, and eventually the Indian nation—remained largely the same as that which had originally motivated the wives of the early missionaries. Swift wrote emphatically, "India needs more Christian homes. The Christian homes need better educated mothers. The nation, the Church, the home, all alike need more women pure in life, earnest in purpose and capable in service."[82] The main change that took place in the early twentieth century was the shift in the focus of intervention from literacy to practical skills.

What kind of practical skills were deemed necessary for poor, low-caste Indian Christian women? Swift definitely considered basic literacy skills a necessity for the women educated at the LPNIW. But in addition, she wanted to train women in modern techniques of "home management." The curriculum of the Department of Home-nursing and Home Management was designed to instruct women in how "to care for clothing, to mend, to patch and darn, to buy, to cook, etc." Besides this formal course work, Swift constructed model houses from locally available materials that were designed "upon a better model for light and air."[83]

Measures as far-reaching as the construction of these homes (valued at $500 apiece, according to Swift's fund-raising material) were regarded as necessary for two reasons. First, Swift deemed the influences and atmosphere of the ordinary home lives of Indians, even Indian Christians, to be "demoralizing" and "impure." Second, the careful management of the everyday lives of students offered instructors and house matrons many opportunities to reinforce the teachings of Christianity. She wrote, "An experience of some years has led us to feel that the women learn comparatively little from their study of general principles of conduct, but when led to apply these principles to particular cases, true training begins." Swift attributed the inability of Indian women to grasp theoretical concepts to the underdeveloped nature of the Indian mind. "With a child's immaturity of mind," she continued, "they too often fail to make this application, and our method of training must be line upon line, and precept upon precept applied to the daily life."[84] Such consistent, thorough attention to the transformation of habits and customs along the lines of Christian principles, or Western sensibilities, was possible in the model homes. Here students lived in an environment built according to Western standards of privacy, hygiene, and order, with separate rooms for different functions and human inhabitants separated from nonhuman inhabitants. In a newspaper article on Swift's work in Madurai, the students are reported describing how they "learned to live" in these artificial homes: "When at home we live in little villages where all the homes are made of mud with roofs of thatch. Too often the cattle live in the best part of the house, for we are afraid they will be stolen from us. Our houses are more like cattle pens than homes. In our school home we are learning to whitewash the mud walls of our cottages, to keep the house in order inside and out. Our cow has its shed at one side, and our fowls are not living in the room with us."[85] Clearly, the first priority on the agenda of the women's missionary project—to reform the Indian home—summoned up vastly different interventions when attention was redirected from the homes of elite Hindu women to the homes of low-caste converts to Christianity. In the case of low-caste "huts," the goal of reform was still to reshape the principles of order that organized the home, but from the opposite direction, as it were. Instead of trying to open up the walls enclosing the high-caste zenana, reformers had to stop the easy traffic across the threshold: Human and non-human inhabitants were to be strictly separated, and the boundary between the home and the surrounding environment had to be clearly demarcated through the technique of whitewashing. To missionaries, and perhaps the converts themselves, these boundaries were the very essence of civilization, their instantiation in the homes of recent converts the visible signs that the inhabitants had been "uplifted" from their former state.

According to the plan of its founders and supporters, the students at the LPNIW would not only be the beneficiaries of the newly introduced ideas about how to set up their homes, they would also teach these ideas to their fellow Indian women. Just as the Bible women of the late nineteenth century were enlisted to act as mediators between the mission and Indian village women, witnessing to the latter about the salvific power of the Christian faith, so in the 1920s they acted as conduits for a form of Christianity now fully informed by a model of development along the lines of modern, Western values and lifeways. Through their involvement with missionary institutions like the LPNIW, convert women from the so-called low castes were exposed to notions of self-sufficiency through cottage industries, as well as to older elite conceptions of female respectability. The curriculum of the new Bible schools suggests that a new creation was under way, a sort of hybrid form of respectability combining a concern with chastity and self-control with notions of maternal self-sacrifice and rational consumption vis-à-vis the family economy. In search of visible signs of their higher status and "advancing civilization," low-caste Christian converts became active participants in the creation of a new ideology of femininity. This involved sartorial changes such as wearing sari blouses (which was a new and highly contested practice among low-caste groups in the Madurai area) and abandoning the heavy gold earrings that signified wealth and stretched the ear lobes sometimes as far as the chin, a subject I take up in chapter 6. The changes that took place through conversion in the direction of a model of femininity based on upper-caste customs and Western values had a strong behavioral component. A missionary from the Tamil Evangelical Lutheran Church who worked with Kallars in Usilampatti (near Madurai), a low-caste community classified as one of India's "criminal castes," wrote, "The women in Kallarnad have a status and an importance not always common. It may, therefore, perhaps be said that the Christian women keep more in the back-ground than their Hindu sisters, probably caused by the higher culture they have received through their Christian training."[86] The price of "higher culture" for many low-caste women was precisely this kind of melting into the background. For low-caste women, conformity to the standard of respectability generated by the zenana missions may have earned for themselves and their communities a quality of self-respect that was vital in their struggles against the oppressive structures of the social hierarchy. However, it also required their voluntary subordination. To become the respectable women held out to them as an ideal by the representatives of the women's missions they had to engage with multiple techniques of psychological and sartorial self-enclosure.

Summary

In the new discourses of gender that emerged out of nineteenth-century India, the suspicion of female sexuality that required the active intervention of males to control women was replaced by women's own internalization of the values of modesty. Though they did not convert in significant numbers, the first students of the zenana missions did absorb some of these values, as evidenced by the confidence with which missionary women could pick them out of a crowd on the basis of their carriage and demeanor many years after their studies were concluded. For low-caste converts, who did convert to Christianity in large numbers, the new discourse of gender they were called on to inhabit was empowering in some ways and debilitating in others. On the one hand, the cultural justifications of the exploitation of low castes—that easy sexual access to low-caste women was at once a cause and a tragic consequence of the group's low status in the Hindu social hierarchy—were eroded by public and visible displays of their new status, including a new style of house, whose well-defined internal and external boundaries were an index of the level of civilization achieved by its inhabitants. On the other hand, the conditions of the lives of low-caste women made their achievement of the ideal of respectability quite difficult. The dire poverty of many low-caste groups required women from these groups to work outside the home. Throughout the nineteenth and twentieth centuries, low-caste women played an important role in agriculture and in the processing into marketable form of raw materials such as palmyra sap and leaves, animal skins, and coir (the tough fibers of coconut husks, used to make various textiles). Though there was a sexual division of labor in the work activities of low castes, it was not immediately apparent to or valued by Western observers in the same way that the sexual division of labor among elites was. The hard physical labor required of low-caste women made the acquisition of literacy and skill in needlework, the marks of female gentility, difficult to attain. Moreover, the dependency of their communities on the dominant castes made them vulnerable to sexual assault and exploitation. This is an aspect of the oppression of low-caste communities that is just now receiving attention by scholars, although hints and suggestions that it was and is a significant element in the structure of domination in Indian society appear occasionally in the oral memory of Hindu and Christian low-caste communities. The fact that low-caste women were not always able to defend themselves against such politically motivated sexual violence made their status as respectable women, that is, women to whom sexual access was strictly limited, easily jeopardized.

5

Civilization and Sexuality: Indian Christian Marriage

When we are seeking to ascertain the measure of that conception which any given race has formed of our nature, there is, perhaps, no single test so effective as the position of women. For, as the law of force is the law of the brute creation, so in proportion as he is under the yoke of that law, does man approximate to the brute; and in proportion, on the other hand, as he has escaped from its dominion, is he ascending into the higher sphere of being, and claiming relationship with Deity.

> —William Ewing Gladstone, prime minister of England, cited in Murdoch, *The Women of India*

Marriage took on a new and politically charged salience in colonial India, where "civilization" was measured by, among other things, gender relations in the domestic sphere. Texts as varied as legal arguments, missionary tracts, and fiction written by Indian Christians denigrated Indian families and the diversity of conjugal forms they made possible. Colonial arbiters of morality such as missionaries, legislators, and jurists applied an evolutionary schema to social life in the colonies and placed at the pinnacle of development the nuclear family with an intimate heterosexual couple at its center. The frequent invocation of the discourse of civilization in discussions of marriage among advocates of very diverse political and social perspectives suggests that conjugality had become a lightning rod for concerns about cultural and racial difference, concerns that in the nineteenth century were invariably filtered through the lens of evolutionism. The debates on Indian Christian marriage were particularly charged because of the apparently ambiguous position of Indian subjects who professed the religion of the colonizers. Indian

Christians were close to the colonizer in terms of religion, but distant in terms of custom and history. In virtually every instance, texts that dealt with the question of marriage can be read as efforts to define the moral status of Indian Christians, and thus their position in colonial Indian society as a whole.

My focus in this chapter is on representations of Indian Christian conjugality created by both Indian Christians themselves and British jurists and missionaries. Much recent scholarship that examines Indian Christianity under colonialism argues or implies that British colonizers set the terms and conditions that Indian Christians, along with other colonial subjects, had to negotiate. When one is examining documents drawn primarily or exclusively from the archives of the colonial state, the argument that the state is the principal shaper of the discourse on marriage and civilization seems almost self-evident.[1] But when we place the representations and arguments of the state alongside those of native Christians, the power of the state is seen to be far from absolute. The definition of prestigious and morally correct marriage alliances and the determination of the grounds on which such alliances could be ended were concerns too integral to the internal structure of the community and its status in the eyes of others to be relinquished to the state. Counter-representations that challenged and in some instances rejected the terms and definitions of marriage dictated by European authorities show that Indian Christians were by no means passive recipients of Western discourse on marriage. At times, Indian Christians forcefully condemned conjugal models based on middle-class British and U.S. gender ideology and exalted forms linked to their claims to royal descent or ancient biblical traditions. Even Indian Christian texts that affirmed Western models of marriage cannot be understood simply as testimony to the unmediated assimilation of the ideals of the West, but should be read as assertions of respectability, in which a community's moral stature was expressed through the common currency afforded by marriage.

In cases of rejection as well as acceptance, I emphasize that I am looking at *representations* of conjugality and the arguments that were made about a group's standards of morality on the basis of them. We can no more know what the actual marriage relationship of any Indian Christian was like by reading these texts than we can know about present-day marriages by reading Harlequin romances. Broadly speaking, two ideals of marriage, both of which advocated monogamy, competed for prominence in Indian colonial society as the most morally upright and respectable form of conjugality. The first ideal was based on Brahmanical forms of marriage, which restricted divorce and remarriage to men and constructed women's sexuality as a threat to community order that needed to be contained. Brahmanical cultural and social forms gained prestige in part because of colonial patronage and in part because of the great value given to indigenous culture by nationalists, as they sought a cultural basis for resistance to colonization in the defense and preservation of tradition. The second ideal was based on Western Christian models of marriage. Accompanying the missionaries' tireless crusade against the diversity of Indian forms of conjugality was a celebration of the Western bourgeois nuclear family as the pinnacle of moral evolution. In this vision of marriage, neither men nor women could divorce and wives were constructed as the helpmeet and supporter of husbands.

In this chapter, I examine representations of conjugality produced in three very different textual genres: the administrative records of the Madras Presidency; the literature produced by educated, urban, high-caste Indian Christians; and the tracts of the first independent Christian church in south India. It is necessary first to establish the legal context of nineteenth-century Indian Christian marriage. In the first section, I provide a brief history of the interactions between missionaries and converts over issues related to marriage, and follow this with a section examining legislation that influenced the colonial discourse on Indian Christian marriage. The last two sections compare the writings of Indian Christians who embraced companionate marriage and the nuclear family with Indian Christians who firmly rejected these models of family life in order to show that in both contexts marriage was a central signifier of the group's converted status. Marriage was an outward sign of the quality of their inner transformation, a signifier of who Indian Christians were in a cultural, religious, and moral sense. Different groups of Christians adopted diverse forms of marriage as their ideal. Whereas the elite Satthianadhans embraced a form of marriage that was explicitly modeled after Western forms of companionate marriage, the founder of the Hindu Christian Church, Rev. Arumai Nayakam Sattampillai, championed a martial form of marriage drawn from conservative elements of the Indian tradition. But both forms of marriage had the effect of broadcasting the message that Indian Christians practiced a high standard of morality that deserved public recognition and respect.

The evangelical image of religious conversion as a moment of transformative insight that radically changed the moral constitution of the subject seldom appears in administrative records. Although this trope was very common in the popular literary genre of conversion narratives, conversion in the imagination of British jurists appeared more frequently as a series of stages in which changes in the external conditions of life, glossed by colonists as "home-life," had a progressive influence on converts' inner moral lives. The legislative debates over Indian Christian marriage between 1850 and 1872 show that British legislators and jurists grafted evolutionist ideas of progress onto the idea of Christian conversion to deal with the liminal position of Christians in Indian society. In the arguments of British jurists, custom is the engine that drives the gradual process of Christianization; changes in custom equip Indian Christians for the moral challenge of living fully under Christian law.

Pliant Pupils and Recalcitrant Rubes

In the first half of the nineteenth century, the colonial state had very little to do with Indian Christian marriage. The state was primarily interested in the institution of marriage to the degree that it involved the transfer of property, and, as Indian Christians had, in general, very little property, they were largely left to carry out their inheritance matters without the assistance or interference of the state. Moreover, the state's interest in the social customs of its subjects was comparatively limited in the period prior to the 1850s, during the rule of the English East India Company. According to the statements of missionaries in legal records and in their reports to missionary boards in the metropole, foreign clergy appear to have been the primary arbiters of moral authority for Indian Christians at this time. However, a closer look at the sources indicates that the extent to which Western churchmen accommodated the laws of their church to local conditions varied considerably. They wielded the most influence in contexts such as boarding schools, where they had almost complete control over their charges from dawn till dusk, and much less influence in rural areas, where a pastor or missionary was lucky to visit outlying congregations twice a year to baptize, sanctify marriages, and offer communion. In the latter situations, foreign clergymen shared power with indigenous authorities over the jural regulation of sexuality and reproduction.

Missionaries took an active role in the marriages of the students in their educational institutions, where they acted in loco parentis in multiple ways.[2] In some of the most extreme examples of paternalism exercised by the missions, the missionaries arranged the marriages of their students themselves, applying in each case their own criteria for what constituted a good marital alliance. A "young bachelor missionary" of the American Board wrote to the home board about his consternation in having to carry out this responsibility: "Among the papers before me is one containing two columns of names. One might be puzzled by the numerous and many colored lines running from one column to the other, each name being attached to two or more in the opposite column. But if one knows the Hindu custom of 'engagements' out here, and if one noted that one column contained male names and the other female names, light might dawn. There are some dozen couples to be 'engaged' and named and I confess to a feeling of embarrassment when I take up the list."[3] The young missionary's displacement of the responsibility for this "custom" onto Hindu practice obscures the extent to which the arrangement of marriage was a central component of a missionary's authority over his or her wards. Just as the arrangement of marriages by Indian parents was an expression of their greater maturity and good judgment compared to that of children, so did the exercise of this prerogative by missionaries convey their moral superiority over *both* the students and their parents. Missionaries of the AMM took over the parental role to such an extent that they provided dowries for the students that graduated or married out of their schools.[4] English missionaries were equally eager to manage the marriages of their students and employees. In 1859, the English missionaries of the Society for the Propagation of the Gospel in Foreign Parts formalized a long-standing rule that Indian catechists and schoolmasters who were employed by the mission must marry a graduate of the mission's boarding schools or forfeit their job.[5] However, most Christians were not subject to the same degree of surveillance and intervention as those who lived directly under the care of the missions.

Well into the late nineteenth century, in rural areas geographically removed from the centers of missionary influence, Indian Christians continued to arrange their own marriages. They adjusted their new faith to the rules and customs they had followed before conversion, generally applying their own caste laws in questions involving age of consent, the appropriate age difference between bride and groom, and distinctions between marriageable and unmarriageable kin. Because missionaries were effectively incapable of exercising much influence in remote areas, rural Indian Christians became the object of considerable anxiety.

The Indian Christian Marriage Act of 1864, though seemingly an act that only regulated the procedures for registering Christian marriages, in fact imposed a number of conditions that brought marriage more firmly under the jurisdiction of the church and state, at least in theory. A marriage had to be performed before an ordained minister, in a house of worship, and the officiant had to speak words to the effect that the marriage did not contravene any of the regulations that defined legal marriage. The parties had to be of a certain age (over 16 years for the groom, over 13 for the bride), could not have a living spouse, and could not be related to each other within the prohibited degrees of affinity and kinship.[6] At the time that the Act was modified in 1872, Rev. Robert Caldwell of the SPG complained that Indian Christians in "the rural districts" were freely performing their own version of the solemnization of marriage. He alleged that in place of a formal wedding in a church, rural Christians often conducted very simple ceremonies in their home that consisted only in reciting the Lord's Prayer and a relative's tying the south Indian symbol of marriage, the *tali*, around the neck of the bride.[7] That these "irregular marriages" could be dissolved as easily as they were made was testified to by a catechist of the AMM. M. Thomas asserted in a memorandum sent to the Madras government that the Indian Christian Marriage Act of 1872 was being virtually ignored by Christians who lived in rural areas. He wrote that among rural Christians the couple would go to the village *panchayat* (traditional ruling council in a Hindu village) to ask for a divorce as soon as disputes arose between them. The panchayat would pronounce divorce and collect the requisite fines from each party. Thomas complained that then "the divorced husband and wife each goes and finds another husband and another wife in the manner of the Hindus."[8]

As Thomas's testimony makes clear, one should not overestimate the extent of power that missionaries had over their Indian congregations. Even in towns, where presumably the physical proximity of the mission stations to their congregations could ensure more effective implementation of their own standards of marriage, Protestant missionaries tended to adjust Christian practices to the expectations of their local congregations, sharing with elders and parents the symbolic and actual authority to create and dissolve marriages. According to one official marriage registrar, Mr. Parry of Jessore, Indian Christians in the period before 1864 followed a divorce procedure that resembled the procedure for accusations of adultery used by village panchayats. Petitions for divorce on account of adultery were granted when the aggrieved party could prove guilt before the minister and the congregation.[9] The minister alone did not grant divorces, nor did he forbid them altogether, nor was divorce granted through petitions to the state. Rather, the congregation and the minister together weighed the evidence and made a judgment, although presumably they did not levy a fine, as the village panchayat did.

The Law of the Land: Civilization and Legal Discourse

From 1850 on, a number of bills were proposed that aimed to bring Indian Christian marriage under the jurisdiction of the state. At least eight bills were proposed between 1850 and 1872 to manage the particular legal challenges presented by the conversion of Hindus and Muslims to Christianity, six of which passed into law (see table 5.1). With one exception (the Lex Loci Act of 1850, which I discuss shortly), all of these created new standards for Indian Christian marriage. This flurry of legislative activism was not restricted to Indian Christians; the colonial state passed dozens of laws during this period that amended or created marriage laws for virtually every different religious community in India. Given the colonial state's repeatedly and emphatically declared intention not to interfere with the personal laws of its Indian subjects, the sustained intensity with which different marriage laws were created is somewhat surprising. One possible reason for this is that once property laws had been regularized according to the conventions of private property, the next frontier of colonial intervention was marriage. Once private property, the hall-mark of a modern capitalist economy, was in place and had restructured the public sphere, it only remained to restructure the private sphere so that private property could descend in a regular manner without the complicated (from the point of view of the British) inheritance patterns that devolved from a plethora of different marriage laws. From this perspective, the project of reforming marriage laws for the different religious communities of colonial India entailed a further intrusion into the nooks and crannies of Indian life, which extended changes wrought by eighteenth-century reforms in property law. Such an analysis, while addressing some aspects of the increase in legislation, also raises the vexing question as to whether the "private sphere" is an appropriate term for describing the arena in which activities related to the reproduction of social life (e.g., child rearing, conjugal relations, cooking, eating) took place within Indian households. Moreover, if it is true that most Indian Christians did not possess much property and the British were largely interested in marriage to the extent that it involved the transfer of property, we must look beyond strictly material interests for additional explanations.

One of the guiding assumptions of the legal debates over Indian Christian marriage was that the law of a people was ideally suited to their moral conditions. Because those conditions could and did change over time, lawmakers constantly had to adapt the law to match the evolving moral constitution of the people. The conversion of Indian Hindus and Muslims to Christianity thus presented a problem to colonial lawmakers: Should these converts be governed by the laws of the community they were born into, or those of the Christian

TABLE 5.1. Legislative Acts Related to Indian Christian Marriage

Act XXI	1850	Caste Disabilities Removal Act (Lex Loci Act)
Act XXV	1864	Indian Christian Marriage Act
Act V	1865	Indian Marriage Act (an amendment to Act XXV of 1864)
Act XXI	1866	Native Convert's Marriage Dissolution Act
Act IV	1869	Divorce Act
Act XV	1872	Indian Christian Marriage Act

community they joined as adults? If Indian Christians were changed by their conversion experiences or by their exposure to the edifying influence of Christianity, had they changed sufficiently to be governed by English law, purportedly the most morally stringent and highly evolved law of all?

A related problem presented by Indian Christian marriage was that the conflicts that most frequently called for the adjudication of the state arose *between* the marriage laws of two religious communities. At the beginning of the period of legislative interest in Indian Christian marriage, calls for the direct intervention of the state arose in response to instances in which the conversion of one party (usually the husband) instigated conflict between husband and wife and their respective families. Considerable difficulties arose over the question of whose marriage law should prevail in such contexts: that of the nonconverted spouse, whether Hindu, Muslim, or Sikh, or that of the converted spouse, the Christian. As Gauri Viswanathan has demonstrated in her ground-breaking study of conversion in colonial India, *Outside the Fold*, the conflict that arose over conversion afforded the colonial state a key opportunity to establish itself as a neutral party above the internal divisions of the general populace. "As disruptive as it might seem," Viswanathan argues, "conversion also brings to a focus an essential role of the state in modernity: the restoration of a fixed, unassailable point of reference from which cleavages within communities are addressed. If conversion precipitates breaches within the fold, it also sets in motion a dynamic social process that confers a new power and role on the state."[10] Disputes related to conversion enabled colonial jurists to exercise their power to assign legal identities to Indian subjects. When faced with any case involving the domestic affairs of Indian Christians, British legislators began with the question, Should they be governed by the laws of Christian Englishmen, or by the customary laws of their ancestral community? Viswanathan argues, rightly, I believe, that although colonial decisions were not wholly consistent, in general they tended to argue that Indian Christians should be governed by the law of the community into which they were born, unless their customs and usages had changed to such a degree that they could be said to have genuinely "attached themselves" to a new community. One overlooked aspect of conversion to Christianity in colonial India is that the way this question was answered reflected both the legislators' view of the moral status of Indian Christians and their understanding of the process of conversion.

One of the most foundational acts passed by the colonial government, the Lex Loci Act of 1845 (forerunner to the Caste Disabilities Removal Act of 1850), secured the state's claim to be a legitimate governing body that could arbitrate the disputes of its subjects from a religiously neutral perspective. This legislation was based on the legal principle that in contractual matters, people ought to be governed by the law of the place in which the rights or responsibilities covered by the contract were acquired. Its intention was to protect converts to Christianity from the most punitive aspects of Hindu and Muslim law, which regarded individuals who changed their religion as legally dead and therefore no longer entitled to a share in the family's property. According to the logic behind the concept of civil death in Hindu legal contexts, if an heir was unable or unwilling to perform the death rituals necessary for the well-being of his deceased ancestors, he should not be allowed to enjoy the property amassed by the latter. Thus, by changing their religion converts forfeited any rights to inherit property from their natal household. British jurists responded to the legal fiction of civil death with their own imaginative use of legal logic. By extending the idea that the law of the place in which rights were acquired should prevail in instances where there was conflict between the law of the land of origin and the law of the land of domicile, Indian Christians were treated as though they were, for the purposes of law, still Hindus, especially if they still retained many of the habits and customs of the Hindu community into which they had been born. Hindu converts to Christianity, in other words, were deemed as never having left the "land" of their birth, even though they claimed to have moved to the "land" of Christianity.

The Lex Loci Act and the Caste Disabilities Removal Act were meant to protect the property rights of converts, but, as Viswanathan argues, they did so by effacing converts' claims to have undergone a genuine and significant moral change as a result of their religious experiences. [11] Although this legislation did not clarify the status of converts with respect to other aspects of their former life, such as their relationship to the wife or husband to whom they had been married prior to conversion, it did establish a line of legal reasoning that maintained that Indian Christians could not, in fact, change their status as moral subjects by the mere profession of Christianity. In subsequent years, rulings that invoked the Lex Loci Act relied on the position that unless converts could show considerable evidence of having transformed their way of life, they would by default be governed by the customary laws of their community.

For example, in the landmark case *Abraham v. Abraham* (1863), the Privy Council settled a dispute between the widow and son and the brother of an Anglo-Indian merchant over whether the deceased's property should be distributed according to Hindu law of a joint family or by the customary practice of "native Christians." The Council ruled that, with regard to "matters with which Christianity has no concern," converting to Christianity did not necessarily entail a change in a person's rights or responsibilities as determined by the law of the class or family to which he or she belonged. Furthermore, the determination of which law should govern an individual should be made "according to equity and good conscience" by "referring the decision to the usages of the class to which convert may have attached himself and of the family to which he may have belonged." [12] That is, one must examine the way of life of the individual to determine which "usages" he or she observes in matters of property and inheritance, life cycle rituals such as weddings and matters such as dress and conduct. One sees a similar pattern of legal hermeneutics in rulings on which notions of kinship should determine marriageable kin for Indian Christians. In *Lopez v. Lopez* (1885), the High Court of Bengal in Calcutta ruled that the prohibited degrees of affinity and consanguinity within which Indian Christians could not marry should be determined by "the customary law of the class to which they belong," not by the ecclesiastical law of England.[13] By 1930 the courts had determined that "customary law" for Indian Christians meant the laws of the church or denomination to which they belonged, but for many years the phrase was frequently interpreted by lawyers, missionaries, and Indian Christian church leaders to mean caste law.[14] In other words, the categories of kinship, replicated over generations through marriage, that would determine the structure of the Christian community should be those of the communities into which converts had been born.[15]

Viswanathan's reading of the Lex Loci Act and the cases that invoked it portrays the Indian state as seeking to fix static categories of identity to minimize the disruptive societal effects that conversion brought in its wake. She also argues, rightly, I believe, that by emphasizing the presence or absence of changes in lifestyle among converts, the British rewrote conversion "from a spiritual to a material act." As she writes, "The least important consideration in judicial rulings was how converts perceived and experienced their new religion."[16] However, I believe a closer examination of the arguments offered by colonial jurists indicates that they regarded the convert's "usages" as a prime site for the expression of an individual's personal will and conscience. In their ruling on *Abraham v. Abraham* the lordships of the Privy Council asked themselves, "If the spirit of an adopted religion improves those who become converts to it, and they reject from conscience customs to which their first converted ancestors adhered, must the abandoned usages be treated by a sort of *fictio juris* as still the enduring customs of the family?" The courts, they argued, "should rather proceed on what actually exists than on what has existed, and in forming their own presumptions have regard rather to a man's own way of life than to that of his predecessors. Though race and blood are independent of volition, usage is not."[17] I agree with Viswanathan in seeing these decisions as supported by an unspoken suspicion of Indian Christian converts' personal testimony, their speech alone, but they did not deny converts' agency. On the contrary, by emphasizing a materialistic model of conversion that gave precedence to faith manifested in action, these rulings communicated a rather liberal notion of human nature evolving over time as new habits are acquired and old ones are lost.

Another legal context in which the ambiguous identity of Indian Christians came to the fore was in legislation allowing Indian Christians to dissolve the marriage they had contracted prior to their conversion. At issue was whether English law, which generally forbade divorce, should be applied to Indian Christians, or whether they should be governed by the laws and practices of the many different castes and communities from which they came. The issue was first raised in 1853 by the Governor General's Council. At the time, English divorce law was stricter than that of any other Protestant nation in Europe. Even a cursory perusal of these laws demonstrates that the British had their own myths and metaphysical theories about affinity, kinship, and marriage. Before the disempowerment of the Ecclesiastical Courts in England in the mid–nineteenth century and the passage of the English Matrimonial Causes Act of 1857, marriage and divorce were understood legally according to a sacramental theory of marriage that held that a husband and wife were joined in the flesh through sexual intercourse, a view that had been abandoned decades before by every Protestant European nation except England.[18] In cases of marital breakdown, the state allowed only two ways to obtain a legal separation enabling one to marry again: by obtaining a divorce through an Act of Parliament or by showing that the marriage was incestuous and therefore null.[19] The Anglican sacramental theory of marriage gave rise to a complicated system of determining the degrees of affinity and consanguinity within which a marriage could legally take place. An odd mixture of "mathematics and mysticism," the convoluted rules defining prohibited degrees, generated a very broad definition of incestuous marriage. Even a very distant consanguineous relative, such as a descendant of one's own great-great-grandparents, was disallowed according to the prescribed degrees of prohibition. The degrees of affinity were even more comprehensive. When a man and woman had sexual intercourse, each party was considered related by law to the other party's relatives because of the doctrine that sexual intercourse joined the couple in the flesh. For example, if a man's wife died, he was forbidden from marrying his wife's sister, because it would be tantamount to marrying his own sister. The prohibition on marrying people who were related, even distantly, to a previous sexual partner was so extensive that in one case, the marriage of a man was nullified because he had had sexual intercourse before his marriage with his wife's third cousin.[20]

But we should not assume that English men and women married only once in their lifetime because of the legal restrictions on divorce. The high death rate combined with the absence of strictures against remarriage for widows and widowers meant that English people could and frequently did have numerous legally sanctioned sexual relationships in succession. Yet both the determination of the prohibited degrees of affinity and consanguinity and the grounds for divorce were equally important components of the construction of English marriage law as a signifier of the strict moral standards maintained by the English. In colonial legal arguments, both issues were treated with a certain reverence, which suggests the power they had to convey England's purportedly advanced state of moral evolution.

In the very first case to consider the question of divorce laws for Indian Christians, in 1853, a member of the Governor General's Council, Sir Barners Peacock, argued that Indian and English Christians ought to be held to the same definition of incestuous marriage. In the face of the prevailing view among colonialists that Indians were morally inferior to English men and women, the controversial nature of Peacock's position lay in its implication that, essentially, Indian Christians were indeed capable of abiding by the strict moral standards enshrined in English matrimonial law. Peacock, who was the chief justice of the High Court in Calcutta, based his legal argument on an Act of Parliament that prevented the solemnization of Christian marriages in India in which the marrying parties were related to each other within the degrees of affinity or consanguinity prohibited in England. The Act was probably intended initially to prevent incestuous marriages between *English* Christians in India, who, under the supposedly deleterious influence of the Indian climate, tended to stray from the moral standards of their home country. In any case, it did not specify to which race of Christians it referred, that is, whether to Christian English people in India or Indian Christian converts. Peacock took the silence on the question of race to mean that the law applied to all Christians. He argued, "The legislature, by extending the impediments depending upon consanguinity or affinity to marriages of Christians in India, have drawn no distinction between Native Christians and others professing the Christian religion, and there does not seem to be any reason in principle for drawing such a distinction; for what is contrary to God's law with regard to the one must be equally so with regard to the other."[21] In the legal question at hand, Peacock's opinion was that Indian Christians should not have the freedom to divorce so long as English Christians did not have it. At a more theoretical level, however, by arguing that all those who professed a belief in the Christian god were obliged to obey his laws, the chief justice strongly implied that Indian Christians should be considered the moral equals of European Christians.

The Court of Directors did withhold the right of divorce from Indian Christians in 1853, but not on the grounds suggested by Peacock.[22] Nevertheless, Peacock's formulation of the issue became almost canonical in the legal literature. In succeeding years, when jurists sought prior legal opinions that articulated the position that English law should apply to Indian Christians, they invariably cited Peacock's stirring words. It seems Peacock's opinion was invoked at times to satisfy the piety of legislators who liked the idea of the moral equality of Indian Christians but balked at its instantiation in law or practice (much as they did the putative political equality of Indian subjects in general).[23] Opponents of Peacock's perspective pointed out that if Indian Christians were to be governed by European marriage laws, they would have to make considerable adjustments in their domestic affairs. One widely cited objection was that cross-cousin marriage and uncle-niece marriage (both explicitly proscribed by the *Book of Common Prayer*) were widely practiced in many of the communities from which Christians were drawn, especially in the south of India. Such jurists repeatedly deferred Indian Christians' achievement of moral status commensurate with British Christians beyond a horizon marked by their *thorough* Christianization.

British jurists buttressed this view of Indian and English moral nature with a secular model of conversion that saw Christianization as a cascading series of changes. Abiding by their commitment to rise above the religious differences that divided Indian subjects, legislators tended to gloss over the first move in the series: Did a person simply change his or her mind, profess to Christianity in a way that could be false or equivocal, or did a change take place in his or her moral disposition because of some supernatural agency? Abjuring the question of the prime mover, legislators argued that the profession of Christianity eventually ought to lead to changes in the ways Indian Christians conducted their lives: Changes in custom would in turn bring about subtle changes in the moral qualities of Indian Christians, which would prepare them for being governed by English law. Until that time, Indian Christians ought to be treated as though they were in a transitional state. According to this gradualist view, conversion was no all-or-nothing affair, achieved through a momentary flash of insight that transformed the self. It took place in stages and involved both inner and outer changes.

Sir Henry Maine, a historian whose acclaimed study of Roman law, *Ancient Law* (1861), led to his appointment as legal advisor to the Governor General's Council in India, applied this notion of conversion when he introduced a bill in 1864 that would legalize the remarriage of native converts to Christianity who had been deserted or repudiated by their wife or husband, revisiting the question initially raised by Peacock.[24] His solution to the problem of how to permit Indian converts to dissolve their previous marriage bonds so that they could remarry as Christians, without violating either Christian, Hindu, or Muslim law, was to construct a secular theory of marriage that would rise above the truth claims of any particular religious perspective. This solution was entirely consistent with Maine's evolutionary theory of law, which predicted a steady progression of legal forms from those based on religious belief to those based on contractual agreement between equal parties. A well-constructed concept of civil marriage as a contract entered into by two people promising certain things to one another would, in Maine's view, effectively rise above all the different sacramental theories of marriage.

In his arguments for the bill, Maine painted a vivid portrait of the plight of the imagined beneficiary of the legislation: a high-caste male convert who was unable to extricate himself from his first marriage by Hindu law and prevented by Christian law from ever marrying again so long as his first wife remained alive. According to the somewhat distorted impression that British jurists had of Hindu law, Hindu jurisprudence lacked not only a procedure for divorce, but the very concept of divorce (as the dissolution of the marriage bond). One legislator, Mr. Prinsep, argued that "although the head of 'divorce' will be found in the Indexes of most of the translated works and English Commentaries on that Code of law, with which alone I have any acquaintance, yet most of the passages cited seem to point rather to *abandonment* of the wife and grounds on which it is justifiable, than to the actual disruption of the tie of matrimony, which Hindu law appears to regard as indissoluble."[25] Prinsep here may be referring to those passages in the ninth chapter of the Laws of Manu that describe the conditions under which a man may supersede his wife (she drinks, is dishonest, rebellious, ill, violent, a spendthrift, or barren). In this same section, Manu also delineates the reasons why a wife may "hate" her husband and differentiates between legitimate and illegitimate reasons. A wife who "transgresses against" a husband who is "infatuated, a drunk or ill" may be deprived of her jewelry and personal property and abandoned temporarily by her husband. A wife with more legitimate causes for dislike (such as impotence, insanity, and "fallenness") "should not be deserted or deprived of her inheritance." Clearly, colonial jurists would have had a hard time extracting from these passages a clear sense of a Hindu remedy for an unhappy marriage approximating the English concept of divorce. But other aspects of Hindu marriage law were easier to discern. In the case of Hindu wives, they were flatly prohibited from marrying more than one man in their lifetime. As Manu said, "A wife is not freed from her husband by sale or rejection; we recognize this as the law formulated by the Lord of Creatures long ago."[26]

With this understanding of the Indian legal environment, Maine reasoned that Hindu men, married at a young age and then converted in the mission schools by "the operation of reason," could not divorce their first wife (because divorce did not exist as a legal category in Hindu law) and could not get married to a new one (because Christianity recognized the previous marriage as legitimate and would not permit polygamy).[27] Maine argued that if the enforced celibacy that such a predicament entailed would create a difficult situation for European men, it would create a wholly intolerable situation for Indian men.

To substantiate the need for legislative intervention, Maine deployed a time-honored instrument of colonial thought, taxonomy, commenting on the fundamental differences between Indians and Europeans and men and women. Discreetly avoiding overt reference to the stereotyped image of the excessive sensuality of "Orientals," Maine simply argued that "all the essential differences between Oriental and Western society tended to augment the immorality of the [existing] law in India." In the West, Maine argued, the natural abhorrence to the state of celibacy was mitigated by the "touch of asceticism" derived from the history of Christian monasticism. But, he maintained, "To an Oriental trained in the zanana [sic], the very conception of such a life was probably unintelligible, monstrous and against nature." If Indian men were hypersexual, constitutionally and morally incapable of celibacy, Indian women were hyposexual, delicate to the point that they could not be forced to join with their convert husbands even if the law compelled them.[28]

Maine's characterization of the differences between Indian men and women with regard to sexuality is certainly at variance with the characterizations of the Indian textual traditions. Whereas Maine portrays Indian women as extremely scrupulous, Manu, for example, depicts them as sexually voracious: " 'A man!' they say, and enjoy sex with him, whether he is good-looking or ugly."[29] Also, where Maine sees Indian men as incapable of celibacy, the Indian tradition testifies to countless instances in which male celibacy (brahmacarya) is upheld as a fundamental condition of moral self-development (because of the self-control it requires) and self-transformation (in part because of the retention of semen).[30] Maine was trying here to establish the hardship that the present legal environment created for Indian converts and their unconverted wives. For this reason, he drew on British colonial stereotypes readily at hand—of the lustful male colonial subject and his frigid female counterpart—regardless of their applicability in the Indian context.

The bill Maine proposed was passed into law on 31 March 1866 as Act

XXI, but not without controversy. A few legislators objected that the law effectively made the wives of converts into widows. It treated the wife according to the usage of Hindu law, whereby the convert was legally dead and therefore his wife legally a widow. The (ex-) wife would retain her right to "maintenance, dower or inheritance," but if she remarried at any time after the granting of the decree permitting her (ex-) husband's remarriage, then she had to forfeit all claims to her former husband's property.[31] In fact, the wives of converts had few viable alternatives to becoming Christians themselves, an issue to which I will return.

Another example of distorted colonial conceptions of Hindu marriage put to use in the service of an evolutionary view of marriage in India is provided by the writings of Justice Lewis Charles Innes, a judge in the Madras Presidency. In an argument opposing a bill that would require that all marriages performed under the Indian Christian Marriage Act involve lifelong monogamy, Justice Innes maintained that because most Christian converts were from the lower castes, among whom divorce and remarriage was generally legal and unrestricted, the imposition of monogamy for life would be a serious hardship to them. He wrote, "Among Hindus marriage is not a monogamous contract, and polygamy, which is practised in the higher castes, is still more general in the lower castes, in which husbands abandon their wives, and wives their husbands, for other wives and husbands, for causes which in a civilized community would be considered very inadequate grounds of separation." Here was a version of the colonial taxonomy of castes according to which high social status was correlated with strict rules governing sexuality and, conversely, low social status correlated with lax sexual rules. Innes unambiguously identified monogamy with higher civilization and nonmonogamy with barbarism and argued that it would be a grave mistake to require Indian Christians, who were drawn mostly from low-caste groups, to adhere suddenly to "national habits and customs appertaining to a far higher standard of civilization."[32]

According to Justice Innes's evolutionary view of society, customs and habits having to do with the family originated out of and were adapted to the moral conditions or environment of a people: "The effect, therefore, of the proposed measure will be to impose upon these converts, marrying since the enactment, restrictions to which their social customs (having their origin in and adapted to their moral conditions) have not habituated them." But a change in customs could in turn affect the conditions from which a people's morality arose. Innes argued that such a change could happen only gradually: "To suppose that the profession of Christianity, or even the practice of it for one or two generations, can work any such radical change in national habits as would fit these castes for the adoption of this view of the marriage contract, is to expect a miracle." As far as Innes was concerned, to forbid remarriage among recent converts to Christianity would be disastrous: "Among a half savage and highly impulsive people such as these lower castes are, the consequence would be simply an increase of murder and concubinage."[33] His logic is characteristic of an understanding of social evolution that arose in response to the "failure" of so-called primitive and backward groups (like the colonized

Indians) to seize opportunities afforded by colonialism to better themselves. Some liberal thinkers explained this puzzling intransigency by arguing that culture put a limit on the extent to which individuals could ascend the ladder of progress, binding them into a particular history and worldview that restricted their ability to grow and evolve. Because of the inhibiting effects of custom, progress along the ladder of social evolution could occur only in small increments.[34]

The concept embodied for the British in the term "civilization" in this evolutionary sense was not a value to which Indians generally subscribed, let alone applied to their own marriages before colonial rule. The idea of civilization, in the sense of living in a city or being cosmopolitan, was embodied in the word *nakarikam* and its derivatives, but the precise evolutionary sense of civilization was particular to nineteenth-century British usage. Rather than the language of civilization, indigenous Tamil discourse on marriage invoked terms like *kaṭṭupāṭu* ("discipline, restraint") and *ōluṇgu* ("order," "propriety") to describe and define morally upright forms of conjugality. Indians had their own scale of values for determining what kind of marriage carried the most prestige and their own systems of classification for determining the moral value of different forms of marriage. The precise way marriage alliances generated social capital and the kinds of alliances that generated the most social capital varied considerably from group to group.

But only those castes accorded the least status by the patriarchal norms of orthodox Brahmanical Hinduism practiced a form of serial marriage that permitted both wife and husband to dissolve their previous marriage ties and marry another partner. As mentioned in the previous chapter, according to Brahmanical sexual morality, men could have multiple wives and sexual partners, but women's chastity was tightly bound up with family honor. Women were considered the conduits of caste and family membership and therefore, in castes that had a stake in preserving their caste purity, could have only one sexual partner. These standards were made at once more rigid and more widely recognized through their codification in the lists of castes ranked in order of precedence, which were published in the 1891 and 1901 Census of India, and in comprehensive catalogues such as Edgar Thurston and K. Rangachari's *Castes and Tribes of Southern India* (1901).[35] As colonial ethnography attempted to classify castes to facilitate British governance of the Indian subcontinent, they tended to apply Brahmanical conceptualizations of caste differences, generalizing and broadening the reach of a perspective that may have actually had less authority in the precolonial than in the colonial period.[36]

We can begin to see how a situation developed in which two ideals of marriage, both of which advocated monogamy, competed for prominence in Indian colonial society as the most morally upright and respectable form of conjugality. On the one hand, there was the elevation of Brahmanical forms of marriage that restricted divorce and remarriage to men and constructed women's sexuality as a threat to community order that needed to be contained. This process, which has been referred to in much of the scholarly literature on nineteenth- and twentieth-century Indian history as Sanskritization, was intensified by the colonial state. Because of their reliance on Brahman pandits, clerks, and other assistants, colonial ethnographers and jurists gave considerable prominence to Brahmanical texts and social forms in their studies and decisions, thereby reinforcing and extending the reach of Brahmanical patriarchal norms. Indian nationalists also attributed great value to Brahmanical discourse, as they sought a cultural basis for resistance to colonialism. At the same time, missionaries were stridently promoting a different model of ideal marriage. British and American missionaries sought to urge on Indian Christians the moral superiority of the Western bourgeois nuclear family, regarding it as the pinnacle of moral evolution. In this model, divorce was prohibited for both men and women, and wives were to occupy a subordinate, helping role while husbands occupied the role of leader and guide.

Like British jurists, American and British missionaries reserved their harshest criticism for nonmonogamy in its many forms, from polygamy and polyandry to serial monogamy facilitated by unrestricted divorce.[37] But colonial moralists found fault even in Indian family forms such as the joint family, which was most often organized around monogamous heterosexual couples. Not directly offensive to legislators, the persistent dampening of intimacy between husband and wife in Indian joint families was anathema to Western missionaries. They saw the cooperative and affectionate relationship between the conjugal pair as essential to the healthy and productive functioning of their preferred family form, the nuclear family. Missionaries of the late nineteenth century ceaselessly trumpeted the superiority of companionate marriage over the diverse forms of conjugality present among non-Western people. Evangelical literature is replete with comparisons of home life across cultures. Among savage people, it was said, wives were silent drudges, dominated by their brutish husbands into a state of virtual slavery. Among civilized people, however, women were said to be effective supporters of their husband, good helpmeets whose natural capacities for intelligence, taste, and good judgment were released under the refined conditions of civilized Christian society.

Stories of Indian Christian Life

Elite Indian Christians were among the first groups in India actively to appropriate companionate marriage as the conjugal ideal. Why? One could argue that it was simply a function of their close proximity to Western missionaries, that the concept and practice of companionate marriage rubbed off on them as a result of natural influences. This is the reason elite Indian Christian authors themselves offered, as we shall see. My contention is that, first of all, companionate marriage was important for Indian Christian converts from high-caste communities because their religious conversion frequently entailed their complete alienation from their natal family. Ending one's engagement with the family religion led to isolation, which could be partially remedied, ideally, by a strong marriage bond to a fellow Christian. Second, companionate marriage was also important as an indicator of a person's elevated moral status and advanced progress along the path of Christianization.

In this section, I discuss the writing of the women who married into the Satthianadhan family, a prominent Indian Christian clan that traced its ancestry back to the first converts at Tranquebar. From the point of view of the early movement to convert elite Indian men through Western education, the Satthianadhans were ideal converts—literate and sophisticated in their appreciation of both Indian and Western classical cultural forms. Many of the men in the Satthianadhan family became prominent leaders in Christian and colonial institutions as ministers, lawyers, and professors, and many of the women made names for themselves as journalists, writers of fiction, and vocal advocates for women's education.[38] Many of the Satthianadhans appeared to accept the missionary view that Indian Christians should make themselves over in the model of Western Christian families. They took their ability to instantiate Western forms of marriage in their own home as a point of considerable pride, evidence that they had achieved an unusual level of refinement. But the model of companionate marriage was not often easily achieved by elite Indian converts. Unlike low-caste converts, who tended to convert in groups connected by bonds constructed of caste or family, high-caste converts to Christianity were frequently "outcasted," ostracized from their natal family and community. Outcasting was a traumatic process, which sometimes culminated in a family performing the death rituals for the convert, demonstrating the extent to which he or she was "dead" in the eyes of Hindu law and family affection. The marital bond thus became important to converts who were essentially deracinated from their family. And yet, if one party was a convert (usually the man) and the other was not (usually the woman), the intimacy held out by visions of companionate marriage was considerably compromised. The writings of Indian Christian women authors represented the achievement of emotional intimacy between husband and wife as the culmination of a long and sometimes rocky journey toward complete conversion, and thus the mark of genuine spiritual change.

Through a close reading of two fictionalized biographical accounts of conversion by a member of the Satthianadhan clan, Krupabai Satthianadhan (see figure 5.1), I argue that the conjugal relationship represented the beginning of the formation of a new, redeemed family, one that was organized around and grounded by love for the Christian god. Some biographical information on the principal members of the family gives an indication of the intense conflict generated within and between families by conversion to Christianity and of the way this conflict gave rise to the significance of the conjugal relationship as a sign of the depth and authenticity of an individual's conversion.

The founding patriarch of the Christian Satthianadhan family was W. T. (William Thomas) Satthianadhan, born Tiruvengadam Naidu into an influential Hindu family in Tirunelveli in 1830.[39] One cannot tell exactly what his caste background was, as his caste name, Naidu, was used by a broad range of Telegu-speaking groups that resided in the southern Madras Presidency. Tiruvengadam's ancestors migrated to Madurai from Trichinopoly for trade,

FIGURE 5.1   Memorial stone for Krupabai Satthianadhan at the Zion
Church in Chintadripet, Chennai. Photograph by author.

and both his grandfather and maternal uncle had government appointments,
the latter as *tahlsidar* (tax collector) of Tirunelveli.[40] Although the family was
devoutly Vaishnavite, his father, a clerk in the collector's office, sent the boy to
a missionary school in Palayamkottai at the age of 14 so that he could learn
English and pass the requirements for obtaining a position in government
service under the British. In this school, Tiruvengadam came under the influence of William Cruikshanks, a charismatic, blind Anglo-Indian teacher, legendary for his role in converting a number of high-caste boys. Tiruvengadam's
baptism in 1847 led to his alienation from his Hindu relatives and caused so
much consternation among the families of his fellow pupils that they boycotted
the school, leaving the building empty for several weeks.[41] He left his family's
home and went to the house of a missionary, where he stayed until the ensuing
controversy subsided. At his baptism, he took the name William after his first
Christian teacher and the name Thomas after the missionary who gave him
shelter from the chaos that resulted from his conversion. Like many Indian
Christians, he also adopted a Sanskrit name that conveyed his devotion to the
Christian god, Satthianadhan, meaning "True Lord" or "Lord of Truth." After
working closely with Rev. Thomas Ragland of the CMS on itinerating tours of

the northern Tirunelveli district, Satthianadhan went on to become a missionary with the CMS and one of south India's most prominent Indian churchmen. He was the chairman of the Native Christian Council for over twenty years and a vigorous promoter of the financial independence of the Indian Church.[42]

According to a biographical sketch initially written for publication in the *Christian College Magazine* by his daughter-in-law, Krupabai Satthianadhan, the impetus for W. T. Satthianadhan's public profession of faith in Christianity was his impending marriage. Of the several accounts of his conversion, Krupabai's narrative is the only one that mentions his engagement, a detail that reflects her interest in marriage as a structure for understanding or charting a person's progress toward complete Christian understanding. In Krupabai's sketch, entitled "A Story of a Conversion," W. T. Satthianadhan's interest in Christianity grew in proportion to his mental and emotional agitation. Krupabai paints a vivid portrait of the conflict the young man faced when he contemplated the prospect of being turned out of his family and caste: "Then the thought of his whole family came on him. The most distant member was bound to him by ties indissoluble, which a foreigner can hardly realize, and the pangs he felt at wrenching himself from his dear ones, breaking their hearts, and of demeaning himself in the eyes of those whose esteem he so cherished, can hardly be described." In Krupabai's portrait, both his rising interest and his rising agitation soon became apparent to his family (particularly his female relatives), who resolved that the best way to contain this trend was to get him married to the girl to whom he had been betrothed since childhood. The night before his wedding his inner conflict came to a head. This setting of the scene conforms to many of the features of popular conversion narratives of the period: It takes place at night, in solitude, and is a moment fraught with great emotional tension. It is precisely this emotional tension (raised to a fever pitch by the author's dramatic description) that ushers in the intervention of the divine: "He was going to be married and thus allowing himself to be more closely bound to his home and his family. No sooner had these thoughts crossed his mind than he felt impelled by a force, which was not his own; a power seemed to take possession of him and gird him with strength and courage. It was the power of the Almighty overshadowing the man, the first equipment of the soul for the warfare of life, a life so new, so utterly unlike the one he had hitherto led. A joy most ecstatic filled him. He rose and fled. The ties that had bound him to the world, all disappeared. There was no fear, no dread of any kind."[43]

He did not marry the woman to whom he had been betrothed, and Krupabai's account does not indicate what happened to her, but focuses on Satthianadhan's experience. According to Krupabai's portrait, when the young Satthianadhan finally made the decision to embrace Christianity he experienced incredible relief at his release from the familiar ties that had restrained him earlier. Rendered by the author as liberation from the constraining bonds of custom, family, and the orthodox notions of propriety and decorum they entail, the moment of initial conversion clears the way for a wholesale change in orientation. Krupabai suggests that the dissolution of ties to one's natal family is regrettable, but their dissolution is precisely what permits the construction of new bonds to a new family, united around a common devotion to the Christian god.[44]

In 1849, two years after his conversion from Hinduism, W. T. Satthianadhan married. His wife, Anna Devasahayam, was descended from a lineage of fourth-generation Tamil Christians who traced their origins to Tranquebar, the site of the first Protestant mission in south India. Anna was the only daughter of the first ordained pastor in the CMS, John Devasahayam, former assistant to the Rev. C. T. E. Rhenius, a German missionary attached to the Anglican CMS, renowned for his support of Indian church leaders and his early advocacy of molding the life of the church to the local culture, a method that would much later be called "indigenization."[45] Anna was her father's pet. According to histories of the family, she used to accompany Rev. Devasahayam on his preaching tours when she was a girl and thereby absorbed the deep understanding of Christian theology and practice for which she was greatly respected by her peers and children.[46] In her later life, she would gain fame as a teacher and writer; she was the author (under the name Annal Satthianadhan) of the child-rearing manual *Nalla Tāy*, which we examined in chapter 4.

It is a measure of W. T. Satthianadhan's perceived talent and potential, and perhaps of the scarcity of Christian bridegrooms of high caste, that he, a recent convert from Hinduism, was able to marry into such a prominent Christian family. Many of the marriage alliances made by the Satthianadhans henceforth were along the lines of caste or status.[47] This allowed for both the consolidation of the relatively few families of high-caste converts to Christianity and for the retention, to a certain extent, of the family's status in Indian society. By marrying exclusively with other high-caste converts (even if they had to transgress lines of caste or *gotra*) they were able to maintain the social boundaries that preserved their social status and created networks of personal contact that helped them to sustain a position of dominance in the numerous institutions founded by the missions.[48]

Nineteenth-century representations of Anna and William Satthianadhan's marriage stressed their professionally collaborative relationship. Their marriage in many ways resembled that of the British and American missionaries in that the conjugal relationship was organized by a gendered division of educational and evangelical labor. When William was summoned to Madras in his capacity as CMS missionary, Anna joined him in the work of evangelization along the gender-segregated lines that missionary wives often followed, organizing and carrying out the instruction of women. She was already engaged in the method of zenana teaching in Madras six years before CEZMS sent its first European agent. For thirty years, she worked for the CEZMS in positions of considerable responsibility, at one time overseeing the personnel of eight schools and supervising zenana teaching in two hundred homes.[49]

The couple also selectively incorporated habits and customs of Europeans in their manner of living. A visitor to their home in Chintadripet, Madras, noted that even though the physical structure of the house was in keeping with Indian architecture, its interior decor reflected the depth of influence of Western manners on the family. The visitor mentioned a verandah where William would entertain male visitors, and a square inner courtyard around which the living quarters of the house was built, in keeping with Indian architectural conventions. However, she also observed, "The front room, with chairs and a sofa and tables and many tokens of refinement, told its own story of the daily life of its occupants. Here was quiet comfort and a place of welcome for friends."[50] The Satthianadhan residence was clearly a home successfully reformed according to the ideas of order described in the previous chapter: While the division of inside and outside allowed for the spatial segregation of the sexes to conform to the expectations of Indian patriarchy, its front room was public enough to accommodate the "mixed doubles" forms of socializing favored by British and Americans. The Satthianadhans had been to England in 1878 as guests of the CMS and had brought back with them numerous souvenirs from this influential journey. In a sense, these souvenirs were more than reminders of a great journey; they bore witness to the couple's active cultivation of the tastes and sensibilities of their English employers.

By their own accounts, the trip to England in 1878 rapidly accelerated this process of cultural, aesthetic, and moral refinement. The CMS sponsored the tour to raise funds from English churches by providing a living example of the civilizing influence of Christianity. Satthianadhan gave forty sermons to forty different congregations, rehearsing the story of his own redemption in parish after parish. But if he had some impact on the perceptions of India held by English men and women, the impact they had on him was far greater. He wrote in a speech given shortly after his return: "It was my privilege to move in the best of Society (in England) and hold communion with Christians of the highest and purest type. . . . In their society, I may say honestly I felt I was moving in a higher and purer atmosphere. It seems a law of nature that association generates assimilation. I felt that in their company I was making an advance in what was higher, nobler and purer."[51] As Satthianadhan's words of praise make clear, some Indian Christians actively desired closer contact with the English as a means of integrating the supposedly pure and noble values that the English embodied into their indigenous way of life.

This strategy of assimilation had a number of effects. On the one hand, the acceptance of a colonial scale of value structured the relationships of elite Indians to Indians who did not have the same privileged access to missionaries. The ability of elite Indians to emulate the lifestyle of English Christians more closely than the average convert was a point of pride, a mark of superiority over the socially "backward" or "underdeveloped" Christian Indian. On the other hand, when Indian Christians accepted and affirmed scales of value and virtue introduced by colonizers and measured their moral progress accordingly, they structured their relationships with the missionaries as one of dependency. The difficulty in maintaining this delicate tension is reflected in a letter that Satthianadhan wrote in 1863, asking the CMS parent committee for a raise in salary (from Rs. 25 per annum) on the grounds that the Church had cultivated in educated Indian Christians like himself tastes and desires the denial of which amounted to cruelty.[52] He began by noting the public nature of the "native pastor's" role and the need for him to maintain a decent standard of living in order to uphold the dignity of the office. "The position of a Native Pastor," he wrote, "as it will be readily allowed, is or ought to be a respectable one." He describes the difficulty of maintaining such a position given rising prices and the fact that the scale of salaries had not kept pace with inflation. Next he turned to the sensitive issue of differences among the classes of Christians:

> I have endeavored till now to avoid making any invidious compari-
> son between members of the same body, but the task I have im-
> posed on myself and the nature of the reasoning necessary to sus-
> tain the case of hardship I have undertaken to elucidate renders this
> impossible. Among the Native clergy, some have been taken from
> the humbler and others from the higher walks of life, words which
> do not import from the meaner and better castes in the Hindu
> sense of the word, but from the lower and upper grades of society in
> the English or Christian sense of the term. This, in the first place,
> suggests a difference in the mode of living to which they have be-
> come accustomed. The former have been used to a mode of life so
> primitive that scarcely anything can be simpler; while being igno-
> rant of English, they require neither English books for the improve-
> ment of their minds in English literature nor experience any of
> those wants incident to a state of mental cultivation imposed by the
> possession of tastes and desires generated by increased civilization.[53]

Two points need to be made to place Satthianadhan's comments about social differences among Indian Christians in perspective. As the first English organization to establish a "native church" through the active cultivation of Indian leadership, the CMS was exceedingly concerned to detect and eliminate caste prejudices among its Indian clergy, more so even than most missionary societies in India. For this reason, Satthianadhan had to define his views about the differences between himself and the rank-and-file Indian Christian church with extreme care. Although the CMS refused to tolerate overt caste prejudice (on the grounds of its connections with Hindu religious views of the social order), they could identify with and even indulge in class prejudice, judging it a social rather than a religious matter. In addition, Satthianadhan was consistently regarded by British missionaries to be the least encumbered by caste prejudice of all the Indian ministers of his generation.[54]

In his letter requesting greater remuneration for his labors as Indian pastor, Satthianadhan scrupulously avoided references to caste and instead couched the differences between himself and other Christians in terms of the "primitive" and the "civilized." His emphasis on the refinement and "superior mental cultivation" that resulted from English education and the deliberate fostering of English tastes and manners in one's home life distanced him from other Indian Christians, elevating him above the latter as their moral superior. It also gave him grounds for appealing for respect and proper treatment from the missionaries. Educated elite Indian Christians like himself, he argued, "from the knowledge of English and consequent superior mental cultivation have tastes and feelings which cannot be refused gratification without inflicting a species of unhappiness too refined to be described, but too real to be unintelligible to those who possess this same mental cultivation and that in a much higher degree than we can pretend to."[55] While appealing to the inflated self-concept of the colonizer, Satthianadhan also aligned himself with them and pursued the prevailing colonial model of conversion to his own advantage. Like the colonial legislators examined in the previous section, he implied that a substantial transformation had taken place in his inner moral constitution *not* at the moment of conversion, but through the cultivation of tastes and sensibilities that were conceptualized as the extension and ultimately the fruit of that conversion.

Thirty-five years later, W. T. Satthianadhan's overt endorsements of Anglicization were very much out of fashion. By at least the 1890s, missionaries and Indian Christian leaders decried the "ugly transitional symptoms" that indicated an underlying imbalance in Indian Christians' aspirations to an ideal shaped wholly by Western cultural standards.[56] The lifestyles of Indian Christian "dandies" who adopted the dress and manners of European gentlemen and ladies came under criticism not only for aesthetic reasons (Western-style clothes were regarded as less "graceful" on Indians than indigenous styles) but also for economic ones.[57] I return in the next chapter to a more thorough consideration of the complex questions of identity and self-transformation at stake in sartorial matters. What needs to be noted here is that so long as conversion was conceived of as something more than merely spiritual, internal, and private but rather as something that manifested itself in virtuous public behavior, it was hard to extricate the standard of virtue against which true conversion was measured from Western precedents.

The writings of Krupabai Satthianadhan, the first wife of W. T. Satthianadhan's son Samuel, illuminate how the conjugal relationship persisted as an important arena within which the depth of one's conversion was measured and manifested. Even while "superficial" cultural adaptations such as dress and manners were downplayed as indicators of the extent of self-transformation, the relationship between Indian Christian wives and husbands was elevated as a site for the cultivation of the spirit of liberty that Christian, and modern, civilization embodied. Companionate marriage, understood as emotional intimacy and mutual appreciation between husband and wife, represented the highest achievement of civilization according to the standard shared by high-caste converts and their missionary patrons.

Krupabai presented an intimate portrait of Indian Christian marriage in *Saguna: A Story of Native Christian Life* (1895), a fictionalized account of the conversion of her mother and father (Radhabai and Haripunt Khisty) to Christianity and of her own love-marriage to the son of a distinguished Tamil Christian family (Samuel Satthianadhan).[58] The novel narrates the spiritual journey of Harichandra, a devout and well-to-do Vaishnava Brahman, who embraces Christianity after a long period of questioning the tenets of his ancestral faith. The theme of liberation rings frequently in this text, liberation characterized (as in "A Story of a Conversion") as release from the snares of family and from that all-enveloping category of meaningful practices, custom. The text describes the traumatic severing of old relationships and the awkward but ultimately liberating efforts to create new bonds with a new family bound together through common allegiance to the god of the Christian religion.

In the novel, after Harichandra announces his intention to convert to Christianity, his entire family and the other Brahmans in the community persecute him relentlessly. The hostility of the household takes shape vividly in Harichandra's mother's attempt at poisoning her son. The author sums up the sentiments bound up in this act of extreme hostility: "Better a dead and honoured son, than a polluted living one" (56). The normally beneficent act of feeding, which restores and strengthens the connections between family members, becomes in the wake of one member's desertion of the family religion an act of murderous hostility. Harichandra resolves to seek shelter in the home of the local missionary. But he is able to get his wife to join him only by exploiting her obedience to his authority as her husband. He and his brother trick Radha into meeting them at a temple far from home where she is coerced into entering the missionary's carriage. Ironically, the patriarchal demand for a Hindu wife's absolute obedience is what in the end, permits, the growth of a purportedly egalitarian Christian marriage between Harichandra and Radha (56–59).

The author renders with great sensitivity the rocky transitional period during which Radha is confined to the missionary's bungalow: "A sense of shame overwhelmed her at the thought that her husband, in her eyes the very perfection of humanity, should have brought her to this disgraceful place" (59). After a few unsuccessful attempts to escape, Radha tries to make the best of things in her new environment among the "polluting" Christians, maintaining her own ideas of domestic order even in the home of the missionary: "She had her idols, kept her fasts and festivals and gave her husband food outside the house." She resists the advances made to her by the Christians, shrinking from the touch of both Indian and European Christians who were drawn to this "attractive young girl, fresh from Brahmanism." Eventually, however, Radha comes to accept her husband's faith. She sees the beneficial effects of this new religion on her husband and feels a growing admiration for the customs of the Christians among whom she unwillingly lives: "She felt she moved in a higher, purer atmosphere. . . . The calm of the Sabbath, the call for morning and evening prayers, her husband's devotion, and the great forbearance shown to her ignorant superstitious ways by those whom she felt were superior to her. These and many other things changed her attitude towards the new religion, and gradually she succumbed to the strong influences of Christianity" (61). Radha's words echo W. T. Satthianadhan's description of his sojourn among the English Christian community in 1878 and reflect the same assumptions about environmental influence. The regular periodicity of the Christian timetable and the "calm" that emanates from the well-ordered spaces of the Christian compound contribute to her conscious sense of the superiority of the Christian way of life. And it seems that at a level below her conscious awareness, the environment in which Radha is contained itself begins to work its influence on her, slowly and steadily displacing or casting into doubt the customs she is habituated to and replacing them with new ones. Among the new customs she takes on is that of an intimate relationship with her husband.

Soon after her reconciliation with her husband, Radha suffers a spiritual crisis. This becomes the occasion for a scene of intimate familiarity between husband and wife, the climax of the narrative of the conjugal relationship between Harichandra and Radha as they heal the bond that had been ruptured by Harichandra's conversion to Christianity: "There was now no feeling of constraint between Harichandra and Radha. The unnatural fetters of custom had fallen away and they met and talked with the freedom of children. . . . She puts her hand in his and exclaims, 'What will you say if I tell you what I think when I feel most happy?' " (62). Although the reader is led to think that Radha will reveal her delight at having discovered Christianity for herself, in fact Radha is preparing her husband (and the reader) for the news that all the joy in her life is overshadowed by her fear of sin. She is convinced that she does not deserve God's love because of her sinful nature. Harichandra assures her that God does not love us with a human love: "He loves you with a love as eternal as the hills. There is no shadow of change in him. Your best is always weak and poor, but His promises are sure." It is not clear from the author's description of Radha's response to her husband's soothing words whether the love she feels is a Christian notion of divine love, Agape, or romantic human love for her husband, Eros. Krupabai writes, "Radha's heart swelled as she listened to the words. The winds murmured loud and seemed to prolong the word, *love*, as they carried it to the flowing river with its deep, solemn voice. She felt the eternal love round her as well as in her heart (63)." As this passage indicates, Radha's deep sense of conviction in the truths of Christianity coincides exactly with her achieving a more profound state of intimacy with her husband. Literary representations such as *Saguna* had an obvious pedagogical intent. By illustrating how Harichandra and Radhabai's marriage survived the trauma of conversion through the patience of the husband and the obedience of the wife, Krupabai provides a model for other marriages rendered unstable by the unevenness of Christianization between the two parties.

Along with her father-in-law's understanding of the significance of environment in cultivating Christian values, Krupabai appears to share something of Justice Innes's perspective on family customs as the "natural" consequence of a people's moral condition. The love between Radha and Harichandra develops out of the moral environment in which they are placed, restoring the couple to the uncomplicated, "natural" innocence of childhood. It dissolves the artificial constraints of custom, which operates here, as in her other writings, as the main obstacle to freedom. And yet, for Krupabai, love is not simply natural, it also has transcendent qualities. In her representation of marriage, love does not simply arise as an adaptation to a change in environment. Love between husband and wife flows from supernatural causes, from the active intervention of God. Krupabai's descriptions of the love between couples in her novel inevitably fuse the love of Christ for humanity or the love of humanity for Christ with the love between husband and wife. She resacralizes the marriage relation, making marriage into a sacrament, a position that had been steadily eroded by the development of modern civil law in the nineteenth century.

Marriage among the "Original Kshatriyas": Rev. A. N. Sattampillai and the Hindu Christian Church

Rev. Arumai Nayakam Nadar's perceptions of European Christians were about as far from those of the Satthianadhan family as Annie Besant's views of Indians were from those of Margaret Mayo. The maverick founder of one of the few independent Christian churches in nineteenth-century south India was known mostly by his honorific appellation, Saṭṭampiḷḷai, which he acquired as a young man for being the monitor, or classroom student leader, at the SPG seminary in Sawyerpuram. His writings reveal how vehemently some Indian Christians rejected the ideas of civilization and moral progress embedded in the prevailing colonial model of conversion as a series of stages. As I discussed in chapter 2, Rev. A. N. Sattampillai was one of the many mission-educated Nadars actively involved in the struggle to gain public and legal recognition of their caste's long-obscured status as twice-born Kshatriyas. Although Sattampillai was a staunch Christian with considerable knowledge of Christian history and biblical literature, central to his activism were calls for a rejection of Western manners and customs and an active appropriation and rejuvenation of the customs of the Nadars' glorious past. By analyzing the view of marriage and divorce that Sattampillai advocated in a series of pamphlets, I argue that his model of civilized marriage was drawn not from European notions of companionate monogamous marriage but from his reconstruction of the Nadars' Kshatriya heritage.

Sattampillai's interpretation of Christianity deserves fuller treatment, but in this section I confine myself to describing the outlines of the history and theology of the church he founded before focusing on the views of the Hindu Christian Church toward marriage. Established in 1857, the immediate setting for Sattampillai's new church was the nearly exclusively Christian towns founded in Tirunelveli district in the early 1800s. Built on largely uncultivated land purchased by the CMS mission, these "model Christian villages" proclaimed their difference from the surrounding countryside not only by their physical planning—cultivated gardens, tree-lined avenues, and streets organized along grids—but also by their names: Mudulur ("First-town," founded in 1799 with a population of twenty-eight), Megnanapuram ("City of good knowledge"), Sawyerpuram, Nazareth, Prakasapuram ("City of light"), Christianagram.[59] The population of these towns was overwhelmingly drawn from the Nadar caste, reflecting the success that Protestant missionaries had had in converting large numbers of people from this group. Its leadership, as we shall see, was composed mostly of wealthy, educated, literate members of this community. Arising out of this unique social setting, the Hindu Christian Church came to be one of the most radical Christian movements in India in appropriating the religion of the colonizers to serve the needs and affirm the values of upwardly mobile converts.

The founder of the Hindu Christian Church was born Arumaināyakam on October 24, 1824. The son of a wealthy Nadar Christian family of Korkai, he finished his education at the mission school in his home town before entering the SPG seminary at Sawyerpuram where he studied under the famous Tamil scholar G. U. Pope.[60] There he excelled in scholarship, learning Greek, Sanskrit, English, Tamil and Hebrew.[61] While in school he won the Monkton catechistship in 1848 and an essay contest in 1849. He was also made a monitor, or Sattampillai (a title he kept throughout his life).[62] As one missionary that he knew later in life testified, he was "far and away the most educated and intelligent man in the whole mission."[63] When Sattampillai began his work as a catechist and teacher with the SPG mission in Nazareth under the supervision of Rev. Augustus Frederick Caemmerer (a German missionary who had been in south India since 1791), he seemed from all accounts to be on the brink of a brilliant career in the church.[64] However, his independent thinking and Caemmerer's domineering nature led to a number of major disagreements. First, Sattampillai raised objections to placing a cross on the altar on the grounds that such treatment amounted to idolatry.[65] Second, he allegedly tried to undermine the appointment of an untouchable Pallar schoolmaster by accusing him of improper conduct toward a woman.[66] Finally, when Caemmerer insisted that Sattampillai marry the girl he had chosen for him, instead of the woman to whom Sattampillai had been betrothed, Sattampillai flatly refused. As Rev. Arthur Margöschis wrote many years later, "In the olden days it was not uncommon for the missionary, to a considerable extent, to arrange the domestic affairs of his flock. The Christians were *in statu* and required many matters to be done for them. In this way, the missionary of Nazareth arranged a marriage for Sattampillai, who . . . had ideas of his own, and some other lady than the one selected by the missionary was in his eye. He refused to marry the girl chosen by the missionary, who thereupon, dismissed him from service."[67] That was in 1850. Sattampillai consequently appealed to the church authorities in Madras but to no avail. One Sunday, he got into a "great dispute" with Caemmerer and was summarily thrown out of church by the sexton at the command of the missionary. After this public humiliation, Sattampillai left Nazareth and went back to Mukuperi, a neighboring town, where he slowly gathered allies among his friends and relatives for his contest with the European church leadership.[68]

At this time, antimissionary sentiment was already brewing among disaffected Nadar Christians. In 1849, Rev. Robert Caldwell had published his influential pamphlet, *The Tinnevelly Shanars*. Presumably to gain support for missionary work among his imagined audience, Caldwell depicted the Nadars in very uncomplimentary terms, describing what he took to be their limited intellectual capacities, litigiousness, and devotion to demons. Hindu Nadars were not the only ones held up as objects of contempt; Christian Nadars also came up short under Caldwell's critical scrutiny. Basing his judgments on the authority of his own personal experience (having spent twelve years in south India, during eight of which he resided in Tirunelveli), Caldwell wrote that those who train catechists and schoolmasters get a most "melancholy idea of the intellectual dullness of the class."[69] As we saw in chapter 2, the publication of this pamphlet enraged many Nadars and generated a cavalcade of counter-histories of the race, several of which were produced by Sattampillai's sons and Nadar relatives in the Tirunelveli area.

In 1857, Sattampillai gained an important ally in his campaign against the European missionaries. In January, Caemmerer suspended another catechist, Swamiadian, who had worked for the mission for twenty years, for the rather bizarre crime of causing "molten lead to be poured down the throat of a live pig with a view of obtaining a certain residuum which he could use as a medicine." During the time of his suspension, Swamiadian grew increasingly bitter toward his employers. By July, he was organizing tumultuous meetings in which he "eulogized himself and his services to the Mission" and urged the people of Mukuperi to demonstrate their loyalty by joining him for Sunday services in the CMS church in Prakasapuram, located less than a mile away, between Mukuperi and Nazareth. After the first meeting, 200 out of the 500–550 congregants at Mukuperi left with Swamiadian. According to Caemmerer, while he was employed by the mission Swamiadian had been consistently dismissive of Sattampillai and his opposition to the European missionaries.[70] But, by mid-1857, they were jointly orchestrating open rebellion against the SPG mission, along with two more disgruntled catechists, Visuvasam (recently dismissed by the SPG) and Maduranayagum (the headman of Prakasapuram, a former member of the CMS church and the uncle of the woman whom Sattampillai was prevented from marrying). Caemmerer wrote that the "rebellion assumed a civil phase" when the four leaders took to raising money from fellow Nadars in the local market, imposing a four *anna* per person "tax" on all Nadars to support the publication of a tract condemning Rev. Caldwell's assertions about the Nadar caste.[71] Caemmerer's attempt to stop the matter by having the district subcollector issue warrants for their arrest only exacerbated the conflict. The four led a decisive breakaway from the congregations of the SPG and began conducting services in a temporary shed in Prakasapuram, led by the charismatic Sattampillai.[72] The schismatic church swiftly gathered large numbers of adherents, at one time claiming a following of 6,000 members, almost all of them Nadars.[73]

Although neither missionary accounts of the period nor the tracts produced by Sattampillai and his family make direct mention of it, the summer of 1857 marked the beginning of a period of extraordinary political upheaval in India, starting with the rebellion of the Indian sepoys in north India, in Meerut, in May of 1857, and extending in south India to many varied disturbances in 1858 occasioned, in part, by the reading of the Queen's Proclamation establishing the Crown's direct rule.[74] It is hard to imagine that Sattampillai and his colleagues were not affected in some way by news of mass defection by fellow Indians formerly loyal to Western mentors. Caemmerer's frequent repetition of the word "seditious" in his report to the SPG secretary suggests that *he* saw similarities between the Meerut sepoys and the Nadar instigators of the Prakasapuram schism. And indeed, Sattampillai and his relatives were, like the sepoys but in a less violent way, trying to establish a new center of power, with their own independent networks of patronage and service and a distinctive ideology that placed their contemporary conflicts with European missionaries in the context of sacred history.

Caldwell wrote of the group five years after their founding, "In their zeal for caste and Hindu nationality, they have rejected from their system everything which appeared to savour to them of a European origin . . . they appeared to be drifting without chart or compass no one knows whither."[75] Yet there was a definite guiding principle to Sattampillai's theology and the reforms that he required at the level of liturgy and practice. The innovative core teaching that Sattampillai preached was that Jesus did not intend for Christians to abandon the laws given in the Hebrew Bible.[76] This he felt was an error promulgated by European Christians, an error, moreover, that represented only one among their numerous moral lapses and transgressions.[77] Sattampillai sought to correct the distortions that European Christians had wrought on the original form of Christianity by returning to the laws of the Hebrew Bible. A trumpet blast from the church tower summoned the faithful to worship, and followers washed their hands and feet before entering the sanctuary, where they punctuated the service with bodily prostration.[78] He denied the efficacy of infant baptism and abandoned the idea of an ordained ministry, declaring that "any one might become a minister of the Gospel."[79] The "Judaizing" elements of the Hindu Christian Church included the celebration of the Sabbath on Saturday, the reckoning of days from evening to evening, and the celebration of new moon days, Passover, Rosh Hashanah, and Yom Kippur (the most important Jewish holy days).[80] Sattampillai also incorporated the purity and pollution regulations of the Hebrew Bible: "It is not enough to follow [the rules for] spiritual purity set down in the ten commandments, [but techniques] of bodily purity which have been taught in God's scriptures publicly for all people in all ages are also necessary for domestic and church-related practices."[81] Notable among the rules for maintaining purity were those having to do with women. Sattampillai's followers observed both menstrual pollution and birth pollution, during which time women could not enter the church. A woman was considered polluted for the seven days of her menses or until it was over (Lev. 15:19–30). If she gave birth to a boy-child, the period of birth-pollution extended for forty days. If the baby was a girl the period of impurity lasted for eighty days (Lev. 12:1–8).[82]

At the same time that Sattampillai taught that the laws of the Hebrew scriptures were still binding on Christians, he also drew on verses from Christian scripture (specifically a verse in Paul's letters to the Corinthians concerning circumcision, 1 Cor. 7:17–20) to argue that converts to Christianity did not necessarily need to abandon their indigenous laws and customs if these did not violate "the righteousness of the law." Thus, as was customary among Hindus but illegal for Indian Christians, members of the Hindu Christian Church celebrated marriage in the home, not in church. Startlingly, they also burned incense and offered "food, drink, and perfumes" to Christ in their services, in a manner similar to the Hindu ritual of puja.[83]

Because many of the laws of the Hebrew Bible that Sattampillai emphasized were also enjoined by Brahmanical Hindu law (such as the observance of menstrual and birth pollution taboos), Sattampillai's version of Christianity facilitated a very high degree of Sanskritization among his fellowers. This was further legitimated by his view that Brahmanical law and custom were his community members' birthright, by virtue of their being Kshatriyas. Thus, in a sense, the Nadars' conversion to Christianity, for Sattampillai, constituted not a step up the ladder of civilization but rather a restoration of their ancestral way of life, long denied to them or forgotten in the course of time. The highly Sanskritized nature of Sattampillai's style of Christianity is particularly evident in the area of gender relations. Most scholars and missionary observers who have discussed the Hindu Christian Church note the fact that they followed the tenets of Hindu law in matters having to do with marriage and inheritance, as enshrined in written texts such as the Laws of Manu, but the significance of Sattampillai's attention to gender relations has been entirely overlooked. For Sattampillai the organization of gender relations, especially through marriage, was a prime indicator of a community's moral worth. He exercised strict discipline to make his own family and community's oluṇgu (moral order) above reproach, and consistently disparaged Europeans and other Christians for their lax sexual morality and lack of control over women.[84] In a series of tracts written in either a hybrid form of Tamil (combining transliterated English and Hebrew words with both high literary, middle literary, and colloquial Tamil words) or a fluent and energetic, if somewhat long-winded English prose style, Sattampillai drummed home his message that Europeans (by which he meant, it seems, mostly English people but also perhaps Americans and Continentals) were "immoral," "depraved," and "whorish." He singled out for particularly harsh censure the "loathsome kind of matrimony" according to which a woman once married to one man was able to remarry subsequent to divorce or widowhood. This Sattampillai objected to as a total violation of the laws laid out in both the Hebrew Bible and the New Testament. Though he based his objections on scriptural citations, he argued against women's ability or right to remarry on grounds that seem more relevant to Brahmanical legal traditions. For example, his main objection to widow remarriage was that it involved the "pollution" of the body of the church and even the wider community through the creation of children whom he considered tantamount to bastards, "an evil and adulterous generation." He taught that if a woman's husband died before giving her any children, she should marry her husband's brother or one of her husband's fraternal kinsmen related by blood (sapintaṉ samōtakaṉ) so that that the dead man's property could descend in proper patrilineal order.[85]

Sattampillai's defense of strict patriliny and levirate marriage in Rūtam-māvai, a retelling of the story of Ruth set to the meter of a popular style of Tamil folk song, explicitly and implicitly depends on Brahmanical ideas of sexuality and reproduction. Here he laid out his defense of the custom of levirate marriage by drawing on citations not only from Hebrew texts but from

Brahmanical *dharmaśāstras* as well. The explanation for Sattampillai's eclectic use of sources, and the basis for his highly Sanskritized form of indigenous Christianity, is found in the narrative he weaves into this mass of citations, a story of the joint history of the ancient Hebrews and Aryans. According to the author, both ancient peoples are direct descendants of Noah, whose ark was stranded in the Aryavartin, "in the region of the Himalayas," when the waters of the great flood subsided. Because of their common ancestry, Sattampillai argued, the rules of the ancient Hebrews and those of the Aryans are in agreement as to the prohibition of widow remarriage and the recommendation of levirate marriage as an acceptable solution to the problem of a man's dying without an heir. Only those who have fallen away from the true teachings— Europeans and the "debased" castes of India—admit the legitimacy of "independent marriage" whereby a divorced or widowed woman may marry any man she pleases, and any man may freely marry her. Sattampillai wrote that Europeans strayed from the true path when Roman kings such as Constantine and Theodorus converted to Christianity and introduced their own immoral rules regarding marriage into the laws of the holy church.[86] Contemporary European missionaries continued to debase Christianity and deceive others; as he wrote: "You have tainted 'the sincere milk of the word' of God (I Pet. 2:2) by mingling with it the poison of your own impure national tradition."[87]

In his attack on widow remarriage and women's right to divorce, Sattampillai undermines the English colonizers' claim to moral superiority on two counts: by accusing them of falling away from the true teachings of their religion and by comparing them directly with the only other group within India who practiced this "loathsome kind of matrimony." He wrote, "The practice of the wicked path according to which one joins oneself to any man's wife as one's own woman has been practiced up to the present day by the morally debased castes who do not follow the Law of Manu as the law for producing progeny, just as it was practiced by wicked Hindu Rakshasas in the original time."[88] With this argument Sattampillai distanced his community from low-caste converts to Christianity, and assimilated the latter to Europeans, by alleging that both shared an unbridled sexuality that led to the degradation of their entire stock.

Sattampillai's assimilation of the Brahmanical perspective on gender and sexuality led him to contest even those elements of European and American Christianity that tended to enhance women's social and religious status. This misogynist tendency was not only reflected in his ban on women's remarriage and the retention of Hindu menstrual and birth pollution observances; it was also apparent in Sattampillai's spirited condemnation of the Salvation Army and other Christian proponents of a more liberal view of women. Sattampillai expressed outright horror at the Salvation Army's willingness to ordain women and even send women preachers out to the missionary field: "The motto 'it is a shame for a woman to speak in the church' is inscribed not by the mere sentiment of St. Paul in accordance with the spirit of his age as the Salvationists erroneously conjecture, but as the permanent divine law perpetually binding the whole human race from the creation of Adam to the end of the world."

Later he dismissed the claim made by the author of a popular book of commentary on the Bible, *Scott's Holy Bible*, that after the birth of Jesus, women were released from the curse that had been placed on them since the Fall to be subjected to the will of their husband. If this were true, he argued, why do women still bear the burden of labor pangs as the physical sign of their state of servitude and accursedness? Why is it that, "even in their so called enlightened Christian Europe," the form of the human body has not changed so as to make men the bearers of children? It must be, Sattampillai concluded, because women are still rightfully subject to the will of their husband and father as a vital part of the divinely ordained social order.[89]

At first glance, Sattampillai's perspective on gender appears to be radically idiosyncratic; I would argue, however, that it draws not only on the patriarchal aspects of the Jewish and Christian scriptures but also on Brahmanical assumptions and values. Whether the Nadars' claim to their Kshatriya heritage is genuine or not, the effort to actualize it through the reorganization of gender relations can be seen as a key example of a more general movement among upwardly mobile Indian Christians who justified claims to respectability and enhanced social status by demonstrating their kaṭṭupāṭu, their ability to control "their" women's behavior. This tendency is seen with particular clarity in Sattampillai's writings, in which marriage—especially widow remarriage—served as the ground on which he could make arguments about the relative moral status of European Christians, Nadar Christians, and Christian or non-Christian low-caste Indians. Conjugality, as in the actual relationship between husband and wife, does not arise as a topic for comparison for Sattampillai, perhaps because of his decidedly chauvinistic attitude toward women: that they were created to serve men. Rather, Sattampillai participates in the general tendency in colonial south India to measure a people's level of civilization by their form of gender relations. Like elite Indian Christian writers such as Krupabai Satthianadhan and the British legislators we examined earlier, Sattampillai too sees custom as a crucial vector of change. But, in another instance of his skillful ability to turn the tables on the colonizers, he condemns Europeans for *their* supposed sexual profligacy and lack of self-control and argues that it is the *Westerners* whose customs have degenerated and who have violated the pure truth of Christianity.

Summary

Law is a significant category in this chapter because marriage was an aspect of life that the state repeatedly attempted to regulate through legislation. The other arenas of practice that I examine in this study—sartorial practice and domesticity—were relatively far removed from the control of the state (with an important exception in the case of the Breast Cloth Controversy of 1858, which I examine shortly). But, often at the insistence of missionaries, the state did take considerable interest in marriage. From the early years of the nineteenth century, missionaries requested British legislators and jurists to adjudicate when marriage laws clashed in instances of interreligious marriage, such as that between a convert and the unconverted spouse to whom he or she had been married in youth. After the state passed several pieces of legislation that set specific conditions for the performance of Indian Christian marriages, clergymen—Indian, English, and American—asked the state to strengthen their hand against Indian Christians who did not change the way they conducted their marriage affairs to conform to the rules of the Christian denomination to which they belonged. In my examination of the arguments made by British jurists, I have shown how deeply influenced these men were by ideas of social and moral progress, often glossed by the term "civilization." I have also tried to show that these ideas were shared by Indian Christians. "Degeneracy" and "progress" were terms common to all parties in the discourse on Christian marriage in India.

Marriage provided a forum in which different conceptions of the Indian Christian community and its location along two very different scales of moral progress could be negotiated. In my discussion of Krupabai Satthianadhan's writing and that of A. N. Sattampillai, I argued that Indian Christians gravitated toward two models of the ideal marriage relationship: companionate marriage, in which women and men worked together to produce and reproduce Christian culture in a hostile environment, and a Sanskritic model, in which women were to be protected and sheltered because they were the vehicles for reproducing the community across generations. Here, the hybrid discourse of female respectability, formed from the interaction between elite Indian and Western gender norms, seems to bifurcate into two distinguishable varieties, one influenced more by Western bourgois ideals and one influenced more by Brahmanical or Kshatriya ideals. Those who adopted the customs and behaviors of Europeans along with their religion tended to celebrate the companionate form of marriage, whereas those who appropriated Christianity but sought to cleanse it of European cultural elements advocated a form of marriage based on high-caste practice. What the two forms have in common is an abhorrence of divorce and remarriage; that is, both the Hindu Christian Church Christians and the high-caste Christians of the Satthianadhan family shared a commitment to lifelong monogamy and thereby distanced themselves from the nonmonogamous practices of the lower castes.

6

Gold and Cholis: Indian Christian Sartorial Style

As I have shown in the preceding chapters, between 1858 and 1910, numerous changes took place in the lives of Indian Christians that contributed to a radical transformation of the gender roles and expectations placed on men and women. The massive influx of low-caste Christians into the Church prompted a redirection of resources such that energy was directed less toward top-down strategies of social change through the conversion of elites and more toward the conversion, reform, and social improvement of large numbers of low-caste converts. By the turn of the century, strategies for the "uplift" of low-caste converts centered on the socialization of these groups to Western Christian modes of behavior, socialization that generally took place in stable institutions such as schools, industrial work programs, and hospitals. Though Paraiyar, Pallar, Chakkiliyar, and other low-caste and "untouchable" converts underwent considerable changes, the role of the "civilizing" component of missionary Christianity in the production of a new, respectable community identity is most readily discerned in changes in Nadar/Shanar Christian lifestyles.[1]

Nadar churches expanded rapidly from the early years of the nineteenth century. With the growth in Christian schools for both men and women, many Nadars ceased to ply their traditional trade of toddy tapping and turned instead to the "cleaner" salary-earning work of teaching, evangelization, or trade (in coir, dry goods, and especially the lucrative coffee business). Formerly, when Nadar social life was organized around the work of toddy tapping, women's work was considered vital to the economic well-being of a household. While Nadar men climbed the thirty-foot-high palmyra trees to collect the sweet sap in small buckets, women of the community stood over fires in temporary huts erected in the groves, boiling the sap down into a thick syrup.[2] After pouring the syrup into coconut shell molds, Nadar women were responsible for marketing the end product, jaggery, in local bazaars or to local traders. With the move of the community's menfolk to trade and salary-earning professions, Nadar women were withdrawn from the public sphere of productivity. Through the educational efforts of women missionaries, Bible women, and others, Indian Christian women were increasingly encouraged to become professional wives and mothers. As I discussed in chapter 4, as more prestige became attached to the elite custom of purdah, many women of newly respectable Nadar Christian families were encouraged to go into seclusion, especially in Nadar urban centers like Sivakasi in north Tirunelveli. The style of femininity that resulted was an amalgam of the chaste helpmeet of the Victorian imagination and the purdah-dwelling elite Indian woman who lived out the days of her life in the symbolic shelter of the home.

One of the most striking ways in which Indian Christians asserted their new identities and claims to respectability was through dress. In nineteenth-century and early twentieth-century south India, visual presentations of the self were key components in the assertion of status. Wherever the mobilization of low castes was made possible by the conditions of colonialism, one sees groups of people staking claims to new identities through changes in their physical appearance and the appropriation of status symbols traditionally reserved for social elites. For example, David Hardiman describes how, in the course of social and religious movements that swept through Western India in the nineteenth century, the women of Dohodiya *adivasi* ("indigenous," "tribal") groups gave up wearing heavy brass ornaments, replacing them, in some instances, with silver jewelry. Bernard Cohn investigates similar movements in north India among the low-caste Noniyas of Uttar Pradesh in the 1950s. When Noniya men began to wear the sacred thread, which was regarded as the ritual prerogative of twice-born castes, they met with violent reprisals from the local elites, whom Cohn calls "the lords of the village."[3]

In nineteenth-century south India, Nadars, along with other groups considered low caste, were subject to a number of social disabilities: They were forbidden to carry umbrellas, to carry pots of water on their hips, to milk cows, to wear sandals or gold or silver jewelry, and, significantly, to wear any garments above the waist or below the knees. These prohibitions systematically denied members of low-caste groups the use of widely recognized symbols of social worth, thus both reflecting and reinforcing the low place that these groups occupied in the caste hierarchy. The historical record indicates that through the late nineteenth and early twentieth century, Nadars defied these taboos where possible in the pursuit of a more respectable identity. The *Tirunelveli District Gazetteer* stated that in 1902 in Ovari, a town in south Nanguneri taluk, "The Shanars decided that their women should no longer carry head-loads and wear beads or leaden bracelets and should not go to market."[4] In Madurai at the turn of the century, the AMM historian John Chandler reported that Nadars in the area "stationed men at the gates of gardens where their wells were frequented and forced every woman of their caste to carry her pot of

water on her hip" instead of on her head (which had previously been the custom) in order to substantiate the community's claims to Kshatriya status.[5]

In this chapter, I discuss the sartorial styles that Indian Christians adopted
in the nineteenth and early twentieth centuries in order to examine the creation
of new or reconfigured social identities that accompanied conversion to Christianity. This chapter does not intend to provide a comprehensive treatment of
changes in Indian Christian dress styles; that important study remains to be
written. Rather, here I analyze specific conflicts that erupted in the nineteenth
and early twentieth century over the issue of Indian Christian dress and style
to show how sartorial style functioned, alongside conjugality and domesticity,
as an arena for displaying and contesting claims about the social and moral
condition of individuals and communities. As in the arenas of domesticity and
conjugality, although American and English missionaries were in some cases
the instigators of new fashions and styles, the agency of Indian Christians was
clearly at work in their selective appropriation of Western Christian cultural
forms. Indian Christians tended to respond most energetically to those aspects
of the social and religious program offered by foreign missionaries that best
suited their own efforts at self- and community improvement; such criteria
were themselves very much a product of indigenous south Indian concepts of
social worth. Moreover, in the arena of sartorial style, we can see with particular
clarity that the process of creating new social identities hinged on the production of new ideals of femininity and masculinity. I focus on how these gender
norms were realized in new forms of visual self-presentation, forms that were
taken, in turn, as arguments about the degree of moral refinement or "civilization" that the group or individual had achieved. As one would expect in the
complex social field that was colonial south India, these visual arguments were
vigorously applauded and supported by some and vigorously condemned, even
violently opposed by others.

In the first section, I argue that the significance of clothing in the status
hierarchies of nineteenth-century south India was deeply influenced by the
cultural dimensions of kingship, in which symbols such as clothing and articles
of adornment were used to honor those people who best approximated the
moral ideal. Kings and *poligars* (*palayakkarars*, regional chieftains who commanded a great deal of power in precolonial south India) promoted their loyal
followers within the local status hierarchy by bestowing on them the honor of
wearing a special garment, carrying a certain banner, or being carried in a
palanquin. British colonialism brought an influx of new rulers, with new concepts of the moral ideal to be emulated. In the second section, I investigate a
particular instance of conflict that erupted when local missionaries intentionally or unintentionally arrogated to themselves the role previously monopolized
by kings and poligars, by insisting that the female members of their congregations wear blouses covering their bosom, in violation of the taboo that prohibited low-caste women (and men) from wearing garments above the waist
or below the knee. The so-called Breast Cloth Controversy of 1858 provides an
excellent example of how the intentions of missionaries to improve the morality of their "wards" were complicated by the varying intentions of Indian

Christians seeking upward mobility and their non-Christian neighbors seeking to maintain the status quo. Given the highly charged political environment of colonial south India, in which the same symbol could generate widely divergent meanings, it is necessary to systematically unpack what the breast cloth represented to missionaries, Nadar Christians, and traditional elites to discern how the donning of a particular garment could explode into violent confrontation.

The strategic use of clothing or adornments was not, however, limited to intercaste conflicts. In the third section, I investigate an episode that took place fifty years after the Breast Cloth Controversy to demonstrate that the multivalent symbolic possibilities of sartorial style were used at times by Indian Christian women to challenge the moral complacency of their own community. In 1909, a group of Indian Christian women deliberately removed their gold jewelry in a small-scale revival movement that shows how Christian values of poverty and simplicity could be mobilized to critique the materialism of the nascent Indian Christian middle class. Finally, in the fourth section, I assert that men's bodies as well as women's served as vehicles for broadcasting new assertions of respectable community identity, an identity that drew on a pool of signifiers from both Western bourgeois and elite Indian culture. Although men's sartorial innovations tended not to arouse as much controversy as women's did, they raised familiar debates among Christians, Indian and Western, as to the relationship between external gestures and the state of one's inner conscience in the process of religious conversion.

Building Up an Honorable Body: South Indian Emblems

The significance of clothing in the status hierarchies of south India cannot be understood apart from the institution of kingship. However much colonial ethnographers tried to represent Indian society as static and rigidly hierarchical, numerous avenues for social change and social mobility made nineteenth-century Indian society extremely complex, fluid, and dynamic. The tendency in Orientalist scholarship to privilege caste over kingship as the major social and political institution in India has obscured the dynamic nature of Indian social relations.[6] In precolonial society and in the princely states of colonial times (though less so), the king's ability to recognize merit in his followers and bestow honors on them provided an important avenue of social mobility.

Pirutus (also spelled *virutus* and *pirudhas* in English-language literature), generally translated by the English word "emblems," refer to the gifts that a sovereign would give to his loyal subordinates in honor of feats of valor performed in the king's service, such as killing wild animals or defeating the king's enemies in battle.[7] Typically, these were objects such as flags decorated with the special insignia of the king, fly whisks (a symbol of kingship), and swords, but the concept of pirutu extended to the right to display such objects in formal processions, along with other perquisites such as the right to a ride in a palanquin and be served by specialists such as dancers, musicians, and torch bearers.

Titles, paradigmatically one of the names of the king, formed another category of pirutu bestowed as a mark of honor. As Nicholas Dirks rightly observes, pirutus may be seen as the counterparts of the honors (*mariyātai*) distributed by the god among his followers in the central ritual of Puranic Hinduism, *pūjā* (examined in chapter 1). Emblems were to the king as honors were to the god, material objects that transmitted the substance of the sovereign from himself to his followers and thereby allowed the followers to partake of a portion of the king's or the deity's sovereignty. In the family histories that Dirks examines in *The Hollow Crown*, the very gestures through which pirutus are exchanged closely resemble the gestures constitutive of puja. For example, in one family chronicle describing the rise of the Madurai Nayakars, the foundational ancestor is said to have intervened at a decisive moment in the king's celebration of Navarattiri (the nine-night festival in honor of Shiva). An enormous buffalo had been selected as the sacrificial victim, but it was so large that no one could slaughter it in the appropriate fashion. Just when everyone had given up hope, Vicuvanata (Viswanatha) Nayakar stepped up and sliced off its head in one blow. Out of gratitude the king embraced him and "presented him with all the valuable jewels and clothes which he had on his person," declaring that the young stranger was worthy to rule on a throne just as the king.[8] As described in this passage, the gestures of the king are structurally identical to those carried out in a temple puja: The devotee/follower performs service for the deity/king, and on being pleased with such service the deity/king shares with the follower part of his substance, as represented and transmitted by his clothes and jewelry. Besides standing as a sign of the king's pleasure, the pirutus also recognize that the subject was acting in a way that approximated the king's heroic, courageous conduct and, further, allow the recipient to approximate the king's conduct even more. An honored subject, by acting virtuously, would get to use a special umbrella or flag or decorated palanquin, just as the king did. In other words, pirutus signified a subject's proximity to the moral ordering center of society, the king, both by recognizing virtuous action and by allowing for the imitation of the sovereign.

In each case, whether garments, jewelry, or flags, the object itself can be seen as more than just a mark of honor. As Joanne Waghorne argues, these objects helped to build up a new "body," a new substantial identity for the recipient, transforming him from what he was into a new, honored and honorable companion of the king.[9] This is especially apparent in the Pudukottai context, where the king himself was transformed from a lowly Kallar (a low-caste community that came to be regarded by the colonial state as a "criminal caste") into a royal entity. "The legend of the Tondaimans' rise to power," argues Waghorne, "likened the acquisition of royal status to a slow process of getting dressed, becoming ornamented with the physical signs of kingship." Once he became king, moreover, he then had the capacity to transform his subordinates as he himself had been transformed.[10]

I would argue that the signs of degradation borne by Nadars and other low castes were like negative pirutus. Their exposed breasts, iron ornaments, and blistered, calloused feet (the result of the taboo against low castes' wearing sandals) were badges of shame, not honor, that built up a body that placed them *outside* the respectable social order, at a distance very far removed from the ordering center of society, embodied in the king. When Nadars began to aspire to a better station in Indian society and aligned themselves with new centers of power in the emerging political landscape of colonial south India, they started to acquire pirutus of their own, from new sources. In the process, they built up new respectable bodies, combining indigenous concepts of virtue and propriety with new notions of the properly bounded and contained Christian body to craft visual self-presentations that signaled to both Hindus and Christians that they were people worthy of considerable respect and regard.

Jewels and Cholis: Refashioning Women's Bodies

The historiography of south India has assigned the name the Breast Cloth Controversy (or, the Upper-Cloth Controversy) to one of the most famous instances of the construction of new identities by low-caste groups through sartorial changes.[11] In 1828–1829, and again in 1858–1859, the princely state of Travancore, on the southern border of the Madras Presidency (now part of present-day Kerala), was rocked by outbreaks of violence. In response to a decision by low-caste Christian women to wear a particular style of garment covering their torsos in open violation of prevailing social norms, male members of the locally dominant caste, the Nayars, burned down chapels, destroyed gardens, and poisoned wells. They also, significantly, publicly stripped the women of Christian Nadar communities, tearing from their bodies the disputed upper cloth, a length of cloth drawn across the breasts and over the shoulder, the wearing of which the Nayars claimed as their own exclusive prerogative.

The Breast Cloth Controversy of 1858

Historians of the Breast Cloth Controversy are virtually unanimous in viewing the upper cloth as a symbol of the social aspirations of Nadars.[12] Although Nadars had been considered a very low caste in the Hindu social order, in the nineteenth century many of them benefited from economic changes that were taking place in the region in response to colonization. Some became quite wealthy, particularly through their involvement with the coffee plantations in the hills of Ceylon (Sri Lanka) and the Western Ghats or through trade along the trunk roads built by the British.[13] Over time, the Nadars' improving economic condition made their ascribed status as a low, ritually polluting caste incommensurate with their perceived self-worth. As Clifford Hospital has written, "The dress styles of the Nadar women themselves are most easily understood as a symbolic portrayal of the fact that they were . . . no longer subject to the dominance of the Nayars, no longer compelled to an attitude of respect."[14]

As a symbol, the breast cloth was interpreted slightly various by the different interested parties. To missionaries it made sense as a symbol of upward mobility through the idiom of modesty. For them, covered breasts were a sign that the wearer possessed a mature and proper shame in nakedness; thus, they perceived the wearing of the upper cloth as evidence of an increasing concern for modesty in people who were gradually being civilized by the Christian gospel. Nadars and Nayars shared a very different understanding of the symbolism behind the cloth. In the Hindu context, a bare chest was a symbol of deference and humility. Just as a Brahman entered a Hindu temple bare-chested, exposing his naked torso in the presence of God, so would a servant in the presence of a person of rank remove the thin cloth that shielded his shoulders from the sun and tie it around his waist. Both the British and Indians perceived a relationship between humility and clothing, but whereas the British read the presence of clothing (on the chest) as a sign of modesty, Indians read the presence of clothing in the company of persons of higher rank as an of-fense.[15] Violence broke out between the two groups of Indians because both recognized that in wearing the upper cloth Nadars were refusing to concede to the Nayars and others their customary inferiority. Nadars believed they were worthy of the honor that wearing such a garment betokened; Nayars did not believe they were worthy and sought to strip them, by force if necessary, of this unearned badge of privilege.

By examining these events in their historical context and looking beyond the confines of traditional historical sources to nineteenth- and early twentieth-century Malayalam literature, I propose a new interpretation of the upper cloth as a symbol of sexual accessibility. One largely unexamined feature of caste oppression in India was the sexual exploitation of low-caste women by higher-caste men. Low-caste Christian converts' desire to craft a more respectable social identity cannot be fully appreciated without an understanding of the effect that the threat of sexual violation, whether realized or not, had on a community's social standing and internal sense of dignity. I hope to demon-strate that the upper cloth was indeed a symbol of the social aspirations of up-and-coming Nadars, but more specifically, it signaled that Nadar women like upper-caste women from the Nayar and Nambudiri communities, possessed sexual honor worth respecting.

Historical Background

The southwestern coast of India was (and is) sociologically one of India's most complex regions. Extremely old Muslim (Muppillai) and Syrian Christian com-munities, founded by immigrants from the Middle East, have existed since the first millennium of the common era. A large community of fisher people, the Mukkuvars, converted to Roman Catholicism in the mid–sixteenth century. However, the majority of the population was Hindu and comprised three main status levels: several castes of heavily indebted (formerly enslaved) agricultural workers, a Brahman land-holding and priestly elite, and a Nayar military caste, many of whose members owned land or worked as managers for Brahman estates.

Up until the early twentieth century, the two locally dominant, landowning castes of the region, Nayars and Brahmans, buttressed their economic inter-dependence with a kind of sexual symbiosis that was unique in the subconti-nent.[16] Exercising a very strict system of patrilineal primogeniture, Nambudiri Brahmans permitted only the eldest son in a family to marry and pass on property to his heirs. Younger sons did not marry, though they could and did establish regular sexual relationships with Nayar women. These relationships were legal and respectable and were formally marked by the exchange of cloth. They were called *sambandhams*, literally "connections." A child produced out of one of these sexual partnerships would not have been raised by his Nam-budiri father, but would have grown up in his Nayar mother's home to be the heir of his mother's brother. For, in a fashion complementary to that of the Brahmans, the Nayars' kinship system was organized around the principle of matriliny. It is important to note that matriliny here denotes only a method of reckoning descent within a family, not a degree of power or autonomy accruing to women (as in matriarchy). The *karanavan*, or mother's brother, was the authoritative figure in a Nayar household (*taravad*) who controlled the family's property and exercised authority over the other members. Malayalam literature frequently represents these individuals as stern and autocratic figures.

In the Nayar household, a woman ordinarily lived out her life in the house of her father or brother. Her children, born of unions with either Nayar or Brahman men, were the heirs of her eldest brother, the karanavan. A variety of sources, from sixteenth-century European travel literature to nineteenth-century Malayalam dramas, testify that even if a Nayar woman was married to a Nayar man, she could and in fact should enter into relations with a Brahman man.[17] A Nayar woman was expected to welcome the sexual advances of a Brahman out of deference to his spiritual authority and because such unions brought prestige to her family.

In marked contrast to the sexual freedom of Nayar women, the chastity of Nambudiri women was intensely guarded. Because only the Nambudiri male head of household, the eldest son, could marry women of his community, there was an excess of unmarried Nambudiri women. In part this was mitigated by the practice of polygamy—most Nambudiri elders married dozens, even hun-dreds of women—but only one or two such women actually lived with her husband and bore his legitimate heirs. Nambudiri women who voluntarily took lovers, or were sexually assaulted were punished by ostracism and death.[18] During the colonial period, the caste hierarchy that developed around the sex-ual, political, and religious collusion between Nayars and Nambudiris was per-ceived as very rigid and deeply entrenched. The dominance of these two groups over the lowest castes was intense. They regarded the lowest castes as ritually polluting on the basis of their traditional occupations, which put them into contact with substances associated with death and decay. According to the tes-timony of a foreign missionary who lived in the region for many years, Samuel Mateer of the LMS, distance taboos prescribed a fixed number of steps within which lower-caste individuals might approach members of the higher castes: "A Nair [Nayar] for example, may approach, but must not touch a Nambudiri Brahman. A Shanar [Nadar] must remain thirty-six paces off, and a Puleyan slave must stay at a distance of ninety-six paces. Other intervals, according to a graduated scale, are appointed to be observed between the remaining castes; thus, for instance, a Shanar must remain twelve steps away from a Nair, a Puleyan sixty-six steps away and so on."[19] To prevent polluting contact between castes from happening inadvertently, a plethora of rules and customs ensured that members of different castes were visibly distinguishable from each other.

Sartorial style was one of the most obvious ways to distinguish among groups. In addition, it also served to indicate the place of each caste or religious community within the social hierarchy. In general, the greater the surface area of the body that was covered, the higher the status. In the estimation of Western observers, none of the indigenous residents of this hot, tropical region wore very much clothing. But one must bear in mind that this assessment comes from people who were advised to wrap themselves in a thick layer of flannel undergarments to protect them from the disease-carrying tropical "miasma" of south Asia.[20] In one of his popular books about the customs and habits of Travancore, Mateer described in an economical though deeply condescending fashion the various styles worn by women of different castes. On entering the region, he noted in the 1880s, one immediately noticed the relative absence of clothing on the bodies of the Indian inhabitants:

> Children perfectly naked are playing about in the blazing sun, and from hence southward one sees great numbers of women going about in nature's garb from the waist upwards. Indeed, one of the first signs of having entered Travancore territory is the sight of half-nude Chogan [an untouchable caste] females watering trees, or otherwise engaged on the banks of the backwaters. Muhammadan women, on the contrary, seem rather cumbered with clothing, wearing both jacket and upper-cloth, often black with filth, or the greater portion dirty, then partly covered with one clean white cloth, making the others appear but the worse by contrast. The Brahman women are always nicely dressed. The inelegant but decent dress of the Roman Catholic fisherwomen appears to be the result of a curious compromise between barbarous laws and female modesty—they cover the bosom straight across with a cloth which runs under each arm. But we are struck with the fact that the Christian jacket seems to occur but too rarely in proportion to the number of converts, and are obliged to hope that this mark of propriety and refinement is not getting forgotten in these days of peace and prosperity. The Christians seem to prefer the respectable "upper cloth," but it is insufficient as a garment for females.[21]

I will return to the matter of the Christian women's predilection for the "respectable 'upper cloth' " over the "mark of propriety and refinement," the jacket proffered by Christian missionaries. Visual sources from the period, along with other works of Mateer, help us to expand on this description.

Below the waist, all women wore some kind of unstitched long cloth, wound numerous times around the waist, with one end sometimes drawn up

FIGURE 6.1   "Namburi Brahman husband and wife, copied from a native drawing," from Samuel Mateer, *Land of Charity: A Descriptive Account of Travancore and Its People* (New York: Dodd and Mead, 1871).

between the legs to allow for greater mobility. The women of the Nayar caste sometimes drew the other end of the cloth up across their breasts and over the shoulder, in a style much like the present-day sari. More frequently, at home they did not cover their torso at all. And in semiprivate settings, such as a posed sitting for a photograph or painting, they pulled a light cotton cloth over their breasts and secured it around the chest, under their armpits.[22] Nambudiri Brahman women had to be much more scrupulous in covering their bodies than women of other castes were, as might be expected given the intense concern for women's modesty generated by their polygamous kinship system. They not only drew one length of the lower cloth across their chest, but they complemented this garment with an undergarment, a short-sleeved blouse of colored cloth tied with a knot in the front (*muditichi-ravakkay*). On the very few occasions that Nambudiri women left the seclusion of their home, they further obscured their bodies from sight by traveling under huge umbrellas, as the drawing from Samuel Mateer's *Land of Charity* indicates (see figure 6.1). The women of Muslim and Syrian Christian communities wore a long-sleeved blouse of white or colored cotton that tied in front with a string or tape, while the low-caste Roman Catholic fisherwomen, the Mukkuvars, wore a strip of coarse cloth tied around their chest, covering the breasts but leaving the shoulders bare.[23] Mateer's figure of a Travancoran Muslim man and woman illustrates the long-sleeved blouse, but it's unclear which of the Muslim communities in Travancore this couple belongs to (see figure 6.2). According to the customs of the region enforced by local caste councils, women of the ritually polluting low castes, including the Nadars, were forbidden to wear anything above the waist or below the knees (see figure 6.3).

What precisely was meant by the disputed "the upper cloth" is actually

MUHAMMADANS.

FIGURE 6.2 "Muhammadans," from Samuel Mateer, *Native Life in Travancore* (London: W.H. Allen, 1883).

PULAYARS.

FIGURE 6.3 "Pulayars," from Samuel Mateer, *Native Life in Travancore* (London: W.H. Allen, 1883).

more difficult to determine than one might think. Was it a separate garment, worn across the breasts and shoulders, or was it one end of the yards-long lower garment, which, being first wound around the waist, could be lifted up and draped across the breasts and over one shoulder (like the present-day sari)? Kooiman regards the latter style as the "so-called upper cloth."[24] But Mateer suggests that although this style did serve "*as* an 'upper cloth' " (emphasis mine), strictly speaking, the upper cloth itself was a separate garment, a "light cotton cloth" worn by "Sudra and other middle-class females . . . loosely across the breast and over one shoulder."[25] In any event, sources of the period are unanimous in stating that custom required women to remove any clothing above their waist in the presence of males of high rank.

In Travancore, a council of "Sudra" (probably Nayar) leaders called the Pidagaikarars was responsible for enforcing these rules, as well as for adjudicating disputes that arose over the transgression of caste rules. Each year villages would send two or three delegates to an annual meeting of the body in Sucindram. This council would discuss whether individuals of their own and other castes "had adopted the costume, food, speech (provincialism or brogue) and general habits of the other class," and would mete out sanctions to transgressors.[26] The Sudra caste council's efforts to police the boundaries of the social order by regulating dress is a striking example of the cross-cultural function of clothing to mark social differences. That such a council existed is evidence that the different styles people wore were not simply "natural" expressions of taste, nor a kind of unconscious habitus through which members of society consistently reproduced the boundaries of the social order. In fact the existence of this policing body indicates that force and coercion were necessary, on a semiregular basis, to quell resistance. It suggests that there was resistance to the rules regarding dress even before the missionaries arrived bearing alternative versions of the ideal social order.

Within six years of their arrival in Travancore in 1806, it appears that Christian missionaries with the LMS were urging the female half of their congregations to cover their bosoms in accordance with Western notions of female modesty. In 1814, Col. John Munro, acting as *dewan* (chief executive minister to the ruler) for the young and politically weak queen, Rani Lakshmibai, issued a circular guaranteeing Indian Christian women the right to cover their bosoms, but only with the *soopayam*, the garment associated with Muslims.[27] In 1829, the rani republished the circular as Proclamation 1004 after rioting between Nadars and Nayars broke out when Nadar women started wearing the upper cloth. It was about this time that the wives of LMS missionaries designed a distinctive garment for Indian Christian converts to wear to meet the demands of Christian decency (see figure 6.4). They modeled this garment on the Muslim style of blouse, though with shorter sleeves, similar to the present-day *choli*, or sari blouse. Sources from the period refer to it with the English phrase "Christian jacket" or with words associated with other local garments, *ravakkay* (the upper garment worn by Brahman women) or *sūppayam* (worn by Muslims).

It appears that Indian Christian converts did not take to the jacket im-

CHRISTIAN FEMALE, WITH JACKET AND UPPER CLOTH.

FIGURE 6.4 "Christian female, with jacket and upper cloth," from Samuel Mateer, *Land of Charity: A Descriptive Account of Travancore and Its People* (New York: Dodd and Mead, 1871).

mediately. Missionary wives went to great lengths to encourage Christian Nadar women to wear this blouse—commissioning the girls in Christian boarding schools to sew hundreds of them, which were made available free or at cost to Christian congregations—but the latter resisted them at every turn.[28] The LMS missionary Charles Mault reported that the Nadars looked on it as "an invidious badge of distinction from which the people turned away with as much abhorrence as respectable farmers in England would from a badge worn in a parish workhouse."[29] It was not until about 1856 that the missionaries succeeded in getting Christian women to wear the garment on a large scale. As Rev. F. Baylis wrote to the missionary board in London, "It has been exceedingly difficult to introduce what to them is a strange custom ... the women generally have been content with putting their cloth over their heads and folding it in front, when they come to service, which is not sufficient covering even then, and on other occasions going about as the heathen women. ... At our last celebration of the Lord's Supper, *for the first time*, every one of the female members, old women as well as young (and the old generally have a great objection to these new-fangled customs) had on the jacket and were thus decently clothed."[30] The manner in which many, if not most, Nadar Christian women sought to meet the demands for modesty was to adopt the style of the Nayar and Nambudri upper cloth (whether by donning a separate garment across their chest, or by pulling the end of the lower cloth up around their shoulders). Missionaries of the LMS, in a petition addressed to the rajah of Travancore in March 1859, argued that the upper cloth was not introduced by Christian Nadars, but had long been in use among the hundreds of Hindu toddy-tapper families who migrated between Tirunelveli and Travancore with the seasonal flow of sap from palmyra trees. In addition, they noted that women of wealthy "heathen Shanar families" also wore the upper cloth, giving further evidence that it was regarded as a mark of status. According to the LMS missionaries, the practice had been spreading among toddy-tapper families for some time without resistance.[31] But, as the missionaries along with other observers at the time note, in 1858, after several events made local elites feel that their traditional privileges were under assault, controversy over the upper cloth resurfaced.

The most important source of information on the disturbances sparked by the breast cloth in 1858 and 1859 is the government papers assembled by J. W. Kaye, secretary in the Political and Secret Departments, and presented before the British Parliament in 1859, which are entitled "Papers Relating to the Recent Disturbances in Travancore." These papers bring together official letters and petitions sent by and to missionaries, the British resident in Travancore, the dewan at Travancore, and colonial administrators in Madras. Along with a large cache of missionary correspondence that R. N. Jesudas has collected from archives in India, they make clear that there were several motivating factors behind this particular outbreak.[32] One theory, particularly favored by the LMS missionaries, linked the unrest to a proclamation made by the Princely State of Travancore in 1855 banning slavery, which led to the dissatisfaction of landowners and an expanded sense of liberty among lower classes.[33] Another theory, favored by the dewan, T. Madhva Rao, saw the precipitating cause to be the Queen's Proclamation of 1858, which formalized the transfer of authority for governing India from the English East India Company to the Crown and committed the Crown to a policy of noninterference in religious matters. Public announcements of the Proclamation sparked disturbances where low-caste groups interpreted the Proclamation's commitment to noninterference in religion as an endorsement of their ambitions to be free from all traditional restraints, while local elites interpreted the proclamation as a statement revoking all the innovations that had taken place in Travancore at the instigation of missionaries.[34] All reports agreed that the destruction was widespread: The resident's bungalow was burned, along with five chapels and schools and twenty-nine houses. In the end, the disturbances were quelled when the Nair Brigade was sent in to restore order by the king.

Sexual Violence and the Politics of Caste

Previous scholarship on the disturbances of 1858–1859 has invested these theories and proposed new ones by contextualizing them in the social and economic history of the region. The careful research that Kooiman, Hardgrave,

Yesudas, and Gladstone have done has contributed immeasurable clarity to the historical background of the riots. But such studies have not given an adequate answer to the question, Why did the *upper cloth* emerge as the object of so much contention? I argue that the events surrounding the upper cloth illustrate something about clothing that we tend to take for granted: its ability to publicly signal changes in one's identity or affiliation with different groups.

Emma Tarlo rightly argues that because of its proximity to the body, clothing is particularly susceptible to symbolic elaboration. Existing at the boundary between self and nonself, clothes, like other impermanent ornaments such as jewelry and cosmetics, are frequently perceived as expressions of the wearer's identity or nature. Moreover, like other symbols, clothing is a multivalent sign, liable to be interpreted in a variety of different ways. For this reason, clothes remain an unstable form of symbolic communication because what the wearer seeks to convey by donning a particular garment for a particular occasion may not be perceived by the audience. Tarlo devotes a great deal of attention to the ambiguity of symbolically charged clothing in her analysis of Mohandas Gandhi's experiments with different sartorial styles from the beginning of his career in South Africa to the controversies over the "loincloth" that he wore for the last twenty-seven years of his life. One of the reasons Gandhi spoke frequently about the meaning of his clothes, Tarlo argues, is that people tended to misinterpret the messages he was trying to convey thereby. Still, the ambiguity of meaning conveyed by clothing made it an ideal vehicle for communicating Gandhi's politically risky calls for noncooperation with the powerful British Raj. This is illustrated nicely by Gandhi's apparent inconsistency in public speeches regarding the simple white khadi cloth cap that he designed, the "Gandhi cap," which became one of the primary symbols of nationalist resistance. In some of his speeches, Gandhi forcefully promoted the cap as a "garment of 'truth' " that embodied the very spirit of nonviolence. If everyone followed the truth, he proclaimed, "the government would be forced either to respect public opinion, to put everyone in jail, or to leave the country." And yet, in other speeches, he dismissed the extreme measures taken by the British to abolish the offensive item. In response to the measure taken by a government official in Gwalior to ban the cap, Gandhi wrote, "I am sorry for this unnecessary prejudice against a harmless and cheap cap."[35]

In the case of Gandhi's resistance of colonial rule, as in the Nadar Christian women's resistance to high-caste hegemony, fashion was an important staging ground for social aspirations because controversial claims could be made under the cover, as it were, of quotidian forms of practice. But why did they choose women's clothing, and why, in particular, the upper cloth? In other words, why didn't Christian Nadars express their aspirations for higher status through the defiance of one of the other taboos to which they were subject, such as wearing sandals, carrying umbrellas, or cutting men's hair into a kudumi (*kutumi*), the distinctive topknot associated with Brahmans and other twice-born castes? In fact, Christian Nadars did assume these various markers of respectable identity in violation of local custom, as we shall see in our examination of the kudumi. The difference was in the degree and amount of opposition they encountered from fellow Indians as a result. A more accurate phrasing of the question guiding our present inquiry would be, Why did the violation of the taboo on the breast-cloth arouse such fierce opposition? To answer this question, we have to locate the breast cloth within the system of signifiers in which it operated in south India.

The tradition of viewing the breast cloth as a symbol of the Nadar woman's respectability or honor goes back to the nineteenth century. On the basis of the association of the breast cloth with honor, Samuel Mateer could argue that the prohibition against low castes covering the torso was a way to "mark their degradation," and conversely, wearing the upper cloth was a statement to the effect that Nadars no longer subscribed to their own degradation.[36] Present-day scholars have tended to reinforce this interpretation. According to this view, the public stripping to which Nadar women were subjected was a sign of their humiliation. Although this interpretation accounts for many of the dynamics generated by this garment, it fails to recognize the specifically sexual dimension of a woman covering or uncovering her breasts.

Certainly, one would not want to impose twentieth-century North American meanings onto the events of the upper cloth controversy. There is no reason to assume that breasts were as sexualized in nineteenth-century Kerala as they are in our day. Nevertheless, literary sources from the period do suggest that a woman's breasts did function in some ways as a sign of sexuality. Viewed in this light, the violent reprisals against Nadar women who wore the upper cloth appear to be a form of symbolic sexual violation. The absence of direct references to sexual assault during the disturbances causes one to be somewhat cautious in asserting this interpretation. One thing that is striking about the accounts of the upper cloth controversies is that even though they are filled with accounts of women being stripped, beaten, and publicly humiliated by Nayar men, there is not one clear description of sexual assault. This silence could be due to Victorian discretion, insensitivity, or the desire on the part of Indian Christians to protect the reputation of their women and their community.[37] I believe it is important to question this silence because it obscures the specifically gendered nature of power relations in ethnic or caste-based communities, in this context as in others. In feudal environments such as nineteenth-century Travancore, one expects to see a pattern of sexual exploitation, as the power and authority of the elites is at least partially enforced through demonstrations of their ability to command the sexual services of the less privileged. One Keralan historian does find such a pattern. Kunjun Pillai Elamkulam wrote, "The law of 'droit seignur' characteristic of the feudal system in Europe was not enforced by the Nambudiris among their tenants. There was no necessity of any such law. Not only on the first night of the marriage, but even before and after it, the tenant's women were but the playthings of the jenmis [landowning castes]."[38] Such statements strengthen the interpretation of the removal of the breast cloth as signifying sexual availability or vulnerability.

Literary sources outside the usual domain of historians working in English-language archives suggest that this reading is not improbable. One does not have to look far for Indian literary references to bare chests as well as bare breasts that connote submission and humility. For example, in the great Indian epic, the *Mahabharata*, when Yudhisthira loses himself and his brothers in the gambling match with Duryodhana, the Pandava brothers are humiliated by being made to strip and bare their chests in court. The example of the *Mahabharata* suggests that a *woman's* disrobing had additional meanings. Notably, the next event in the narrative after the dicing match is the stripping of Draupadi, the beautiful and noble wife shared by the five Pandava brothers. Draupadi is wagered and lost by Yudhisthira, who is caught up in a reckless frenzy of gambling madness, and she is dragged out of the interior chambers of the palace by one of the more despicable characters of the Kaurava side, Duhsasana. Draupadi's humiliation at Duhsasana's hands is made still more excruciating by the fact that she is in her menses. When she is thus exposed before the entire assembly of men, Duhsasana takes the edge of the cloth wrapped around her body and pulls, threatening to render her naked. But, at the last moment, Lord Krishna preserves her from this final disgrace by producing one cloth after another so that her body is never exposed. Even though her body remains concealed by an endless stream of cloth, Draupadi is shamed nevertheless, and her desire for revenge drives the Pandava brothers into an all-out war against their cousins. Reinforced by a subsequent scene in which Duryodhana slyly exposes his "thigh" to Draupadi in the presence of her humiliated and powerless husbands, the scene of Draupadi's disrobing functions in the narrative as a symbolic rape. Even if the Kauravas do not actually violate the Pandava queen, they threaten to, and her being very nearly stripped bare is a suggestion that they could have, if not for the miraculous intervention of Lord Krishna.

Closer to the Travancore context, we can consider the Malayalam novels, plays, and poetry of the nineteenth century, produced by and for a literate Nambudiri Brahman elite. In this literature, one gets a sense of the potential meanings of the upper cloth within the intricate dynamics of shame and honor that animated relations between the dominant-caste communities of south Travancore. Amusing portraits of lusty Nambudiri males were a staple of fashionable, high-flown, literary poetry of the time. Judging from this literature, the relationships between Nayar women and the Brahman men with whom they were connected were not ones of stark exploitation. Nayar mistresses had to be wooed; women of this community had the right to refuse the advances of a Nambudiri who expressed sexual interest, and they certainly could and did play off one lover against another. But an element of coercion is evident in that they could not choose *not* to participate in the circulation of Nayar women among Brahman men. This was simply an aspect of the taken-for-granted structure of social authority: A Nayar woman should acquiesce to the sexual advances of Nambudiri men, because the latter were her spiritual superiors and by gracing her with their company, they could enhance the status of her family. In O. Chandu Menon's nineteenth-century drama, *Indulekha*, a Nayar woman tells her daughter, who is apprehensive at the arrival of a Nambudiri man seeking a sambandham relationship with her, that she must tolerate his attention: "These Nambudiris are a curious lot, daughter. It is up to us to behave ourselves."[39] Another, less consequential way that Nayar women showed their respect for Brahman men was to remove their upper cloth in the men's company.

Thus, whereas the missionaries considered covering the breasts good, civilized conduct, Hindus considered covered breasts a sign of lack of respect. A Nayar woman would keep her upper cloth on in public, as in the paintings and drawings of the period, concealing her bosom from the gaze of low-caste men, but if such a woman covered her chest in the presence of a man of rank, she would appear to be the opposite of modest—she would seem insolent and irreverent. As one Nayar gentlemen, K. P. S. Menon, wrote in his reminiscences, "If by chance a woman had a cloth over her shoulders, she would remove it at the sight of a respectable person lest she should seem impertinently overdressed."[40] The expectation that a Nayar woman would expose her breasts in the presence of men of higher rank (and conceal them in the presence of men of lower rank) is related to the question of sexual access. Given the combination of the normative sexual accessibility of Nayar women to Brahman men, and the mandatory display of the torso at their approach, one can conjecture that the upper cloth symbolized, among multiple other meanings, sexual access or lack thereof. The perception of defiance in Nadar women wearing an upper cloth in the presence of Nayar men must be understood in this light. The upper cloth certainly denoted status. The Nadar women appropriating it for themselves certainly was taken as an encroachment on the traditional privileges of women of the upper castes, but it also constituted, I would argue, a woman's assertion of her own claims to chastity (*karpu*). The highly valued feminine virtue of karpu had been considered the exclusive possession of chaste women of the upper caste, and in fact was their exclusive possession so long as low-caste women like Nadars, Chogans, and Pulayars were subject to sexual predation by upper-caste men. In the context of the sexual politics of nineteenth-century south India, wearing the breast cloth came to symbolize not only improved social status but also the closely related capacity of a woman to refuse sexual access.

One objection to this interpretation is that the pollution taboos of the region were so intense that even if high-caste men had had a kind of feudal privilege to the sexuality of their low-caste tenants, they would have eschewed sexual contact with such women. The pollution taboos maintaining separation between people of different castes were indeed notoriously strict in nineteenth-century Travancore. Francis Buchanan, an Englishman who traveled through the Indian princely states of Mysore, Canara, and Malabar, attested that, in fact, men who had sexual relations with women of "inferior" caste had to pay severe penalties: "A Nair man, who is detected in fornication with a Shanar woman, is put to death, and the woman is sold to the Moplays [Mupillais]. If he have connection with a slave girl, both are put to death; a most shocking injustice to the female, who in case of refusal to her lord, would be subject to all the violence of an enraged and despised master." The corporal punishment delivered to Brahman men who transgressed their community's sexual taboos was extremely harsh, though it did not extend to execution: "A Nambudiri who condescended to commit fornication with a Tiati [a female of the Tiyyar caste], would formerly have been deprived of his eyes, and the girl and all her relations would either have been put to death, or sold as slaves to the Moplays, who sent them beyond the sea."[41] As a foreigner with no personal knowledge of any Indian languages, Buchanan's testimony should be taken with a grain of salt.[42] If true, it suggests that there were strong legal disincentives to miscegenation, even though, as Buchanan indicates, women at the bottom of the social hierarchy did not have much choice in the matter.

Because of the fears of pollution and the taboos against miscegenation to which these fears gave rise, many Brahmans and Nayars probably never capitalized on their privilege of sexual access to low-caste women. The pollution discourse leads one to believe that this was due to the fact that low-caste women were sexually repugnant to upper-caste men. Such is the assumption undergirding the response of the descendants of participants in the Breast Cloth Controversy, who insist that caste scruples prevented Nayar men from actually raping or sexually assaulting Nadar women.[43] Yet, as Freud taught, taboos are not created to prohibit behavior that people find naturally repugnant; rather, they are made to stop people from engaging in socially disruptive, but nonetheless somehow very attractive behaviors. I would argue that the taboos on miscegenation reflected and helped to construct an image of the sexually desirable but socially dangerous low-caste woman, which in some cases made the prospect of sexual encounter more rather than less attractive. As innumerable studies of politically motivated rape have shown, this configuration may receive additional force when buttressed by the idea that by raping the women of a group considered "inferior" one is punishing them for other transgressions.

Whether or not actual sexual violation accompanied the other violent reprisals against Nadar women who wore the breast cloth, I hope to show that the appropriation of the garment by Christian low-caste women was part of a more general effort on the part of the community to signal to its neighbors that its women were no longer fair game. In this light, wearing the upper cloth meant that Nadar women had a sexuality that ought to be concealed, guarded, and protected in the way that Nambudiri women protected theirs. The flipped-up turn of the end of the sari cloth broadcast the message, We are modest women; we have sexual honor worth protecting. As members of an honorable, respectable community, they were off-limits to the sexual depredations of the high-caste landlords, threatened, symbolic, or real. Nadar Christian men as well as women had something to gain from this claim, because their masculinity was enhanced by the perception that they were willing and able to defend "their" women and preserve the "purity" of their bloodlines. Men who fought to protect their women from physical assaults are given an important place in Indian Christian accounts of the period, as in the story of Catechist Apollos, of the LMS. His obituary states, "He was a great sufferer for Christ's sake during the 'Upper cloth Riots' in 1858. . . . He did much in getting the riots suppressed and in protecting women against their Sudra persecutors, and as a result was frequently beaten and otherwise ill-treated."[44] Warriors in the battle for self-respect, Nadar men, like Apollos, embodied in their physical bravery the truth of the claims that Nadars would soon bring before the colonial world, namely, that the Nadars were Tamil Kshatriyas, descendants of the original ruling caste of south India.

The Crystallization of "Modesty"

After about two years of increasingly violent and disruptive clashes between Nadars and Nayars, the dispute over the breast cloth reached a legal resolution. The legal side to the affair illustrates how, in the colonial context, status conflicts such as these could be quickly absorbed within the rhetoric of modernity, such that people on all sides articulated their interests in terms of a contest between tradition and modernity, backwardness and civilization. The Nayars, supported by the royal government of the Travancore, argued that the breast cloth was a part of a traditional system of caste markers that helped to differentiate the population into their respective hereditary classes and thus was crucial to preserving the established way of life of the region. It is possible to see the position of the Travancore government as less a rigid advocacy of an archaic system of allocating status or dignity on the basis of heredity than a defense of the king's power to endow his subjects with "bodies" that reflected their distance or proximity from the ordering center of society (namely, himself). Rulers in Travancore had, in fact, previously bestowed on select members of the elite class of Shanars (the Nadars proper) the privilege of wearing the breast cloth.[45] What they objected to was the usurpation of this right by Christian missionaries, who gave Nadar women new kinds of garments and (according to the perception of the defenders of the status quo in Travancore) encouraged them to take up a style of clothing reserved for the higher classes.

For its part, the British government in Madras, impelled in part by the pressure put on them by the English-language press and the LMS missionaries, insisted that universal human rights were at issue. The governor of Madras conveyed the gravity of the colonial government's responsibility to reform this "barbaric" transgression of natural human liberty in a letter to the British resident in Travancore: "I have seldom met with a case, in which not only truth and justice, but every feeling of our common humanity are so entirely on one side. The whole civilized world would cry shame upon us, if we do not make a firm stand on such an occasion."[46] In the eyes of the colonial state, which at least in theory was bound by liberal political principles, the universal human subject was endowed with natural rights, including the liberty to meet the demands of modesty in any way he or she saw fit. Modesty is, in fact, a key issue here, for it is the existence of this sentiment that differentiates the human from the nonhuman. If such delicacy of feeling exists in a person (conventionally, a woman), the obligation of the law is to protect it.

Letters to the editor in English-language newspapers from south India provide a vivid picture of how the news about riots over the upper cloth was interpreted through the discourse of "civilization." Contributors to the *Madras Times*, the *Overland Bombay Standard*, and the *Cochin Courier* were vehement, seeing the outrages against Indian Christian women who sought to wear "clothes such as civilized nations declare essential to decency" as evidence of the "backwardness" and "barbarity" of indigenous rulers.[47] Educated Nadars, possibly in cooperation with their missionary patrons, reinforced this reading of events as a contest between oppressive, tyrannical tradition and modern government based on liberal, enlightenment values. In petitions they sent to the "Right Honorable Governor in Council," the British resident in Travancore, and the queen of England, which were published in the *Overland Bombay Standard*, educated Christian Nadar men represented their conversion experiences through the familiar metaphors of civilizational discourse as a movement from darkness to light, from animal baseness to civilized refinement. Writing explicitly on behalf of their wives and daughters, they begin by noting the long history of systematic oppression of their community by high castes in Travancore, "The poor, degraded, dull, and debased Shanars yielded to the tyranny of the custom with all the stolid indifference of beasts of burden; while the Shanar women passed through a life of constant drudgery, with minds unawakened by a gleam of truth, careless of their modesty as the animals of the field and jungle." In a manner deeply reminiscent of the writings of LMS missionaries, they identify the crucial turning point, which marked the emergence of their benighted ancestors from this state of passive capitulation, with the introduction of Christianity: "From a very early period, the contact with Christianity and civilization, little as it may have been, performed [its] wonted work. A glimmering consciousness dawned upon the Shanar mind; and at length one end of the cloth ordinarily worn by the Hindoo female was drawn over the shoulder in the ordinary Hindoo fashion."[48]

It is ironic that the assertion of modern subjectivity, through which an individual freely exercises her right to personal liberty, should be articulated in language that evacuates the subject in question, the "Shanar Hindoo female," of so much agency. In this petition, the Nadar women who defied the ban on the upper cloth disappear and are replaced by a ghostly cloth "drawn over the shoulder in the ordinary Hindoo fashion." Perhaps the writers adopted this highly ambivalent tone, mixing firm self-assertion with stark self-abnegation, because they thought it would elicit sympathy for their cause more effectively. But it is hard not to see in it an effacement of the active role of Nadar Christian women in the struggle for their own liberation.

In the end, after several communications among the governor, the resident, and the maharaja's dewan, the maharaja of Travancore relented to the Madras government's pressure and proposed "to abolish all rules prohibiting the covering of the uppers parts of the person of Shanar women, and to grant them perfect liberty to meet the requirements of decency in any way they may deem proper, with the simple restriction, that they do not imitate the same mode of dress that appertains to the higher castes."[49] The British accepted the stipulated condition. On 26 July 1859, the maharaja issued a proclamation: "We hereby proclaim that there is no objection to Shanar women either putting on a jacket, like the Christian Shanar women, or to Shanar women of all creeds dressing in coarse cloth, and tying themselves round it as the Mukkavattigal

[Mukkavar, fisherwomen] do, or to their covering their bosoms in any manner whatever; but not like the women of high caste."[50]

Curiously, what appears to have been a *de jure* resolution in favor of the traditional elite of Travancore turned into a *de facto* victory for the Nadars. It seems that the proclamation did little to dissuade Nadar Christian women from continuing to wear the breast cloth, but the violent reprisals against them ceased. Oral history of the area corroborates the colonial record in attesting to the absence of further disturbances over the breast cloth after 1859. Perhaps the unresolved tensions were displaced into other regions. In Madurai, conflicts over women's dress erupted well into the twentieth century. Bible women and other Christian workers testify that as late as the 1940s, terrible conflict could be sparked in a village or region if untouchable Christian convert women started wearing blouses and upper cloth, as they were encouraged to do by their Christian teachers.[51]

Evidently, the presence of the upper cloth across the bosom of a low-caste woman generated many different meanings: To missionaries, it connoted modesty deriving from heightened moral sensibilities; to Nayars, insolence; to Nadars, it was a means of conveying defiant self-respect; and to this twentieth-century scholar looking back over 150 years, the upper cloth's forced removal symbolized vulnerability to sexual assault. The very multiplicity of meanings attached to this object, this gesture, is indicative of the historically and socially volatile climate of the times, as this somewhat isolated corner of the subcontinent became more and more thoroughly enmeshed with global flows of capital and commodities, as well as so-called modern ideas and attitudes. During such turbulent times, signifiers do not have a transparent, univocal meaning equally apparent to every audience member. As Jean and John Comaroff have written, history reveals that the work of power under such conditions is to try to contain symbols' multiple meanings and generate a stable field of signification: "While signs, social relations, and material practices are constantly open to transformation—and while meaning may indeed become unfixed, resisted and reconstructed—history everywhere is actively made in a dialectic of order and disorder, consensus and contest. At any particular moment, in any marked event, a meaning or a social arrangement may appear free-floating, underdetermined, ambiguous. But it is often the very attempt to harness that indeterminacy, the seemingly unfixed signifier, that animates both the exercise of power and the resistance to which it may give rise." The controversies over the breast cloth in nineteenth-century south India represent just such a struggle to contain ambiguity, to emphasize one meaning of this symbol and suppress others. But, as the Comaroffs go on to argue, the opponents in such a struggle are rarely evenly matched. Conflict over meaning thus does not generally continue ad infinitum: "Such arguments and struggles, though, are seldom equal. They have, *pace* postmodernism, a political sociology that emerges from their place in a system of relations. And so, as the moment gives way to the medium-term, and some people and practices emerge as (or remain) dominant, their authority expresses itself in the apparently established *order* of things—again, in the dual sense of an edifice of command and a condition of being."[52] It is an indication of the weakness of the native states relative to the colonial government that in this instance, the orders of the Madras government prevailed over the proclamation of the maharaja. The meaning of the breast cloth that gained ascendancy in the end was that given by Christian missionaries and their fellow thinkers in Madras: Covering the breasts was a sign of modesty, and modesty was the proper mode of respectable, modern femininity.

The conflict over the breast cloth, though it must have enlisted the energy of Nadar women themselves, eventually became subsumed by the more general conflict between modernity and tradition, displacing the physical attacks on women onto a conflict among groups of men. Women's own voices were entirely lost in the fray. Like Catechist Apollos, the Nadar women who wore the breast cloth in violation of local custom also were beaten in the struggle for respectability, a fact that is seldom acknowledged directly in accounts of the conflict. And yet the ideal feminine body that emerged from the controversies is not the warrior-queen, bravely fighting for her people, but the enclosed, modest body of the modern feminine subject. Women's agency is more apparent in a second episode of conflict over clothing, one that took place *within* the Christian community some fifty years after the disturbances in Travancore.

Jewelry in Tirunelveli

By 1909, the Nadars were well-established as the dominant Christian community in Tirunelveli. To a certain extent, they were still embroiled in conflicts with rival castes, such as the military Maravar caste. But many of the conflicts of the nineteenth century were well behind them, and some families of Nadar Christians were relatively well-to-do, particularly coffee plantation owners, traders, and landowners. The issue of the breast cloth had been practically, if not legally, resolved in their favor, and Nadar women wore it regularly without being molested. One of the signs of the community's increased wealth and status was that women would appear in public, including at church services, with the wealth of their family displayed on their body in the form of gold.

Missionaries objected to such displays of wealth as a sign of pride. Since at least the 1830s, regularly recurring campaigns to dissuade Christian women from wearing jewelry had taken place among evangelical Christians in England and the United States, where "jewels" referred to all the gold and silver ornaments worn by women. Many of the missionaries who came to India shared with their peers in the metropole the assumption that jewelry was morally questionable. In a pamphlet published in 1833, the renowned American Baptist missionary to Burma, Rev. Henry Judson, urged Christian women in the United States to sell their jewelry and use the proceeds to support the foreign missions. The pamphlet not only exemplifies the tendency of evangelical Christians to locate the everyday as the arena in which one should properly manifest piety (as we saw in chapter 3), it also illustrates how American Christians put women's jewelry in the service of civilizational arguments, associating abundant adornment with savagery and "plainness" with elevated moral sentiments and civilization.

Judson was appalled by the profusion of jewels worn by Asian converts. To him, the abundance of jewelry layered on a woman's ears, nose, neck, head, and torso signified decadence and barbarism. Such sartorial excess was, in his view, the chief obstacle to "raising up a Church of Christ in this heathen land, and in laboring to elevate the minds of the female converts to the standard of the gospel." Judson found a scriptural basis for his reaction in the Apostle Paul's first letter to Timothy: "I will also that women adorn themselves in modest apparel, with shamefacedness and sobriety, *not with broidered hair, or gold, or pearls, or costly array.*" Appealing to American women's sense of duty to act as moral exemplars for their less fortunate "heathen" sisters, he urged his readers to adopt plain dress so as not to tempt the morally weak new converts of Asia into indulging their vanity. In one passage he vividly evoked the intense interest Indian Christians took in newly arrived female foreign missionaries: "The female converts will run around them, and gaze upon them, with the most prying curiosity, regarding them as the freshest representations of the Christian religion, from the land where it flourishes in all its purity and glory." Such women had better conform to the expectations that Judson raised in his Indian congregations about the elevated moral character of Western women, he warned, or else, when Indian Christians see "the gold and jewels pendent from their ears, they will cast a bitter, reproachful, triumphant glance at their old teachers, and spring with fresh avidity, to repurchase and resume their long neglected elegancies."[53]

As Frank Prochaska has shown, women's societies for social reform and evangelization raised thousands of pounds (and dollars) through the accumulation of small contributions, the "widow's mite" so often celebrated in nineteenth-century fund-raising literature.[54] But such celebration may have been making a virtue of necessity. Before the married women's property rights acts of the late nineteenth century, women in England and the United States had no independent legal claim to immovable property such as land or shares in a business. Thus, at this time, the jewelry worn by American and English women, like that of Indian women, constituted the only form of wealth they controlled. Given its importance as insurance against financial insecurity, one wonders how many women actually responded to Judson's appeal. The legal or customary limitations on the extent to which women could dispose of this property as they wished is a topic that bears further inquiry. For now, I concentrate on the powerful symbolic connotations of Judson's request that women sell their jewels to support good works such as the temperance movement, the abolitionist movement, and the overseas missionary movement.

Judson recommended the renunciation of jewelry not only as a way for European women to set a good example for non-European Christians in foreign lands, but also as the instrument and index of women's own spiritual improvement. By selling their jewelry and using the profits to benefit foreign missions, Christian women could thereby enact and demonstrate at one blow their humility, their elevation of Christ above worldly goods, and their willingness to sacrifice everything in the service of the gospel. This small gesture, removing jewels and putting their value toward the promotion of foreign missions, could have enormous, even cosmic consequences, Judson claimed. In a manner typical of his tendency to link mundane gestures to grand, soteriological consequences, he wrote, "How easy to conceive, from many known events, that the single fact of a lady's divesting herself of a necklace, for Christ's sake, may involve consequences, which shall be felt in the remotest parts of the earth, and in all future generations to the end of time."[55] In an era in which women's contribution to the public life of a nation was practically nil, an invitation to join in this international, even cosmic venture must have been thrilling to hear.

Movements among Christian women to forswear vanity and the love of jewelry were not confined to England and the United States. As Judson had hoped, the example of American and English Christian women was taken up by some Indian women in the colonies. Missionaries periodically reported with satisfaction the occurrence of fads for removing nose jewels among the girls in their boarding schools. One such movement was deliberately instigated in 1889 by a young American missionary, Miss G. A. Chandler, founder of the Anti-Nose-Jewel Society in the Battlagundu girls' boarding school. "Desiring to create a sentiment against the fashion of wearing a pendent from the nostrils, Miss Chandler proposed that each member give up her nose jewel for benevolence, and sign a promise never to wear one in her nose again." Evidently, several students joined the society, much to the consternation of their families. This indignation arose from the fact that in south Indian culture, even among Christians, jewelry meant something very different from decadence, excess, and vanity. In addition to being the sole property that most women had the right to control, women's jewelry was a powerful indicator of the status of a woman and her community, signaling her auspicious married state and her family's caste and level of material well-being. For, among the caste-based restrictions prevalent in the nineteenth century was the rule that only members of nonpolluting castes could wear gold and silver jewelry. In this context, one can imagine why the fiancé of one of the members of the Anti-Nose-Jewel Society, a young Christian schoolteacher, objected to his betrothed's decision to remove her jewel: "I shall never marry a girl without a nose jewel, so it behooves you to put yours back in its proper place." The missionary historian John Chandler conceded that the specific movement initiated by the Anti-Nose-Jewel Society was neither widespread nor long-lasting. But, in general, he noted a decline in the practice of wearing heavy jewelry among Indian Christians.[56] Many Indian Christian leaders supported the views of the missionaries and expressed their disapproval of excessive jewelry among Indian Christians, viewing it as a "relic of savagery."[57] This did not, however, stop the majority of Indian Christians from taking great pleasure and pride in displaying their wealth on the bodies of their women (a fact that may be deduced from the persistence with which Christian leaders doggedly pursued the issue).

Like the pirutus that I examined earlier in the chapter, for the majority of

Indians a woman's jewels were physical tokens of prestige and self-worth that built up a certain kind of body and projected a certain kind of identity. From a specifically Hindu point of view, a heavily jeweled woman was well protected and cared for. The cultural associations connected to women without jewelry illustrate the importance of this idea particularly well. Three kinds of women generally did not wear gold or other valuable jewelry: widows, women from very low-caste communities, and women from extremely poor families. One of the taboos to which widows were subject was the removal of their jewelry on their husband's death. Very low-caste women were forbidden from wearing jewels as a part of the bundle of social disabilities that marked their distance from the ordering center of society. And because jewels were often the first thing pawned in a time of crisis, such as famine or drought, women experiencing a temporary or permanent state of poverty would also not wear jewels, although they were not categorically denied the privilege of wearing them. Thus, a woman without jewelry appeared to be one of three very marginalized types of women: an inauspicious widow, a polluting untouchable, or a pitiable indigent.

In this context, in 1909 a small band of unpaid women evangelists working in the western Tirunelveli district set off their own controversy by voluntarily removing their jewels as a sign of their unrivaled devotion to God. My source for this event is the missionary reportage produced in great quantities by Amy Carmichael. As we saw in chapter 3, this Scots Irish missionary and founder of an independent mission in Tirunelveli district was, by all accounts, something of a firebrand. By 1909, she had practiced the principles of "plain dress" (which included the renunciation of jewels and fine clothes) for twenty-two years, ever since she was "saved" at a missionary convention when she was 19 years old.[58] In concert with the prevailing attitude among evangelical Christians, jewelry for Carmichael represented vanity and an excessive concern for the good opinion of others, a weakness that could easily tempt one into lax observance of God's commands. Removing jewelry meant that one valued God above all things, that nothing rivaled one's love for God.

Carmichael gave the fullest description of the incident that sparked this controversy in *Ponnammal* (1917), the biography of one of the most dedicated Indian workers in the Dohnavur Fellowship. Around 1897, Carmichael and five Indian women began their itinerating ministry, traveling through the villages of Tirunelveli district in a bandy cart. Often, the members of the "Starry Band," Carmichael's name for the group, traveled by themselves. As the first women's evangelist band in the district, Carmichael reported, they had to proceed "circumspectly . . . like a cat on the top of a walk . . . for there seemed to be no end to the occasions on which 'it was necessary to be careful.' "[59] Some of the time, however, they traveled in the company of an independent missionary recently retired from the CMS, Rev. Thomas Walker, and his wife.

One day the Starry Band and the Walkers were accompanied by an Indian man, a young husband who had asked the women to take on his wife as one of their members so that she might learn about Christian charity and evangelism. As Carmichael described it, "As we rumbled along the road, the husband, who had been talking to the Walkers, who were in the bandy ahead of us, now dropped back to ours, and asked his wife to give him her jewels . . . which he did not think became anyone who wanted to live the kind of life he desired for her." Even though the gesture was prompted by a kind of patriarchal command, it acted as an inspiration in the mind of a young widow in the band, Ponnammal. She had not removed her jewels at the time of her husband's death, as per Indian Christian custom, but the young man's suggestion made her consider other reasons for abandoning these symbols of pride and vanity. A piercing vision of how she would appear in the eyes of her peers—"unjew-elled, a marked woman among her own people; an eyesore, an offense"—gave her a moment's hesitation. But the allure of this challenge to demonstrate the extent of her commitment to Christ conquered her fear. According to Carmi-chael, Ponnammal was motivated in part by the concern that if she continued to wear jewels while doing her evangelical work, she might unwittingly give the wrong impression to young people who might be more attracted to her jewels than to the message of "good news" that she was trying to send. In very poor villages the jewels on these women may well have inspired admiration and perhaps the hope that Christianity would lead to greater material well-being, Ponnammal feared. Additionally, as Ponnammal's parents-in-law sug-gested, in well-to-do villages, a woman's jewels may have assured the inhabi-tants that the women were not poor untouchables, but rather women of their own social station.[60]

Whatever the impulse that inspired Ponnammal to take off her jewels, her bold gesture set off a revival. Carmichael described its beginnings in her char-acteristic purple prose: "A few—how few! but still to the startled and indignant eyes that watched it was ominous—'inebriated with Divine love,' eager to for-sake and defy the spirit of the world, stripped themselves of every weight that they might the less laden run the race that lay before them; and they either returned their jewels to their families, or, if free to do so, gave them to be sold for China."[61] The women's antiestablishmentarian acts remind one of the me-dieval women about whom Caroline Walker Bynum has written, who rebelled against their newly wealthy families by rejecting riches and comfort in favor of the asceticism of Cistercian monasteries.[62] Here, too, a dramatic act of as-ceticism might have served as a cloaked critique of the excesses of the com-munity, exposing hypocrisy through the socially sanctioned medium of reli-gion.

The possibility that the community did interpret the women's act of taking off their jewels as criticism is suggested by their immediate, intense disap-proval. "It broke the conventions of life," they charged. "It would lead who knew how far? It was therefore unnatural, disgraceful; worse it was pharisaical. 'Be not righteous overmuch,' was the word flung at Ponnammal." Ponnammal and her fellow workers were pressured by their families to take back their act of renunciation and go back to wearing the jewels. A few succumbed to this pressure, but Ponnammal did not. Looking back on her life, she remembered the trials she underwent as a result of her decision as a defining moment of her life as a Christian. "It was to me a new emancipation," she told Carmichael.

"A new sense of spiritual liberty is bound up in my mind with that experience; it affected everything in such an unexpected way; it set my spirit free."[63]

For up-and-coming Nadar Christians, that their women would spontaneously abandon their jewelry—a public marker of the community's newly won social status—was something like a slap in the face. As in the breast cloth controversy, we see the modes of modesty and shame at work in the production of sensibilities that ensure conformity. But now, Christian women were considered shameless when they did not display on their body the status symbols recognized by their community. Once again, we see a challenge to the status quo under the guise of quotidian practice, through a gesture seemingly innocuous but potentially controversial. These ambiguous gestures generated conflict because they were vaunted by one set of values as proper and reviled according to another set as scandalous and disrespectful. By taking off their jewels the women of Tirunelveli gave notice on one level of their primary allegiance to God; on another level, I argue, they were broadcasting their disapproval of the values of the newly configured Indian Christian patriarchal family in an idiom recognized clearly by their community.[64]

Tempest over a Topknot: Refashioning Men's Bodies

By wearing the breast cloth and reducing the amount of jewelry they wore, Indian Christian women sought to signify an inner change: the yielding of their mind, heart, and conscience to Christian ideals of modesty and humility. What is interesting in the conflicts raised by these efforts is how the Christian meanings attributed to these gestures by the women (and/or their advocates) became complicated by the coexistence of Hindu meanings attached to these same gestures. A similar, if less intense dynamic is evident in changes that Indian Christian men undertook as they endeavored to display their new identities through new forms of sartorial self-expression. Just as Indian women struggled to construct a new female Christian identity through the adoption of the breast cloth, a garment that would represent such women as self-restrained, sexually unavailable, and modest, so did Indian Christian men craft new visual self-presentations through clothing and style. The kinds of sartorial changes that Indian Christian men undertook included wearing boots, hats, and various forms of Western dress. The men encountered some resistance in their sartorial experiments: Low-caste Christians were accused (generally by high-caste Christians) of putting on airs; others found themselves ridiculed for appropriating Western clothing in a piecemeal fashion, rather than appearing in complete suits of Western clothes as elite Indians did.[65] But because the articles of clothing that Christian men adopted—hats, boots, and trousers—generally did not carry preestablished connotations in the Indian cultural context, whatever resistance they encountered was rather limited in scale.

One sartorial experiment of Indian Christian men that did raise controversy involved a certain hairstyle that had a history in the Indian cultural context. In contrast to incidents involving Christian women, the people who objected to this style the most were not Indians, but Europeans, and their objections were not based on concerns that important signals of group identity, whether class- or caste-based, were being muddied, but on concerns about the religious significance of style.

At a gathering of European, British, and American missionaries held in Bangalore in 1879, a small controversy erupted over the issue of whether a particular men's hairstyle was a sign of residual adherence to Hinduism among Indian Christians. The style in question, the *kudumi*, or "topknot," involved shaving the head so as to leave a tuft of hair at the back of the head (among Tamils) or toward the front (among Malayalis), a style associated most closely with Brahmans. Indeed, the subject came up at a panel formed to consider whether a resolution should be adopted by the conference to ban caste from the Indian Christian Church. The kudumi arose as an example of the many different kinds of practices through which caste differences were manifested. Rev. E. H. Baierlain, of the Evangelical Lutheran Mission, started the discussion with a reference to the kudumi as a metaphor for enforced external changes in behavior that would do nothing to change Indian Christians' actual feelings of caste prejudice or pride. Invoking the commonly stated opinion that caste prejudice was the form of sinful pride most particular to Indians, Baierlain said, "Caste is but the old Adam in a Hindu garb, and lives not in the *kudumi* that it might be cut off, or in dress that it might be changed." He referred to the practice of a colleague of his who used to insist that candidates for the position of catechist shave off the kudumi: "As he expressed it, the devil is in the *kudumi*. Well, I only wish it were so, then the scissors would be the best and cheapest exorcist. But he is far too wise to take up his abode in that lofty dangling extremity. He has chosen a much warmer place for this abode, even the heart of man, and there no external proceedings can touch him. Inasmuch as the Spirit of Christ enters the heart of man, the spirit of caste will leave it, and not otherwise. And if the spirit of caste remains in the heart, is there anything gained by cutting off the *kudumi*, by eating and drinking and the like?"[66] Here Baierlain argued, in the tradition of pietism, that external gestures are not as significant as internal feelings, that the only changes that matter in terms of spiritual development or well-being are those that take place in the heart. The impulse to sin would be eradicated, he asserted, only after a transformation of the *conscience*, which he located, significantly, in the heart, the seat of emotion, not in the head, the seat of reason.

Hairstyle may seem at first glance to be a rather trivial affair in light of grand questions like the genuineness of religious conversion, but one does not have to look far to see that style serves frequently as a powerful coded form of communication. Consider Gandhi's skillful use of the symbiotic ambiguity of the khadi cap, at once a "garment of 'truth' " and a "harmless and cheap cap," which makes clear that articles of clothing, haircuts, and other forms of style are useful vehicles for carrying "transgressive" meanings precisely because such a message can be immediately denied with the retort that it is "only" a style.[67] Like the British officers trying to contain Gandhi's movement for independence, European and American missionaries were vulnerable to dark suspicions about many elements of Indian culture because of, among other things, their relative unfamiliarity with the meaning and history of prevailing cultural codes. The debates among missionaries as to whether the topknot indicated some residual adherence to Hinduism shed considerable light on the theories of conversion they implicitly or explicitly carried, specifically with respect to the relation between culture and Christianity, belief and behavior.

It is by now well-established that definitions of conversion are highly dependent on the cultural context in which they are devised. Lewis Rambo argues, "Varied use of the word by many people in many situations leads one to believe that it means just what a given individual or group wants it to mean, neither more nor less."[68] Yet, it has not been sufficiently recognized that not all models of conversion are created equal. Conflict between groups and individuals over what constitutes conversion, especially "authentic conversion," has frequently been a significant element in processes of religious change.[69] In south India as elsewhere, heated battles erupted among missionaries and between foreign missionaries and local Christians over which version of conversion would actually be implemented through the disciplinary procedures of the mission.

The dispute over the kudumi at the 1879 South India Missionary Conference was but one in a long series of conflicts among missionaries and between missionaries and converts over the degree to which different cultural practices conflicted with adherence to Christianity. The enduring importance of the topknot, in particular, as a signifier of the more general issue of Christianity and culture in India is reflected in Samuel Mateer's lengthy summary of the various positions possible on the debate, which he published in 1883.[70] The question of the "propriety, or otherwise, of Native Christians retaining the *kudumi*" was the kind of issue, it seems, on which everyone felt compelled to comment. This was because the debate over the kudumi, though ostensibly about hairstyle and the retention of caste markers, was really about the nature of conversion itself: how it worked, what made it genuine, and what made it false. Here I examine a few of the positions articulated by missionaries and Indian Christian leaders at the Bangalore Conference and in Mateer's book, highlighting those in which the speaker's implicit theory of conversion is most obvious.

Baierlain's remarks about the necessity for a change of heart before a change in practice could take place were characteristic of the pietist styles of Christianity transmitted especially by the German-speaking missionaries trained at Halle, many of whom worked for English missionary societies. In particular, Baierlain's question, "And if the spirit of caste remains in the heart, is there anything gained by cutting off the *kudumi*, by eating and drinking and the like?", is reminiscent of the arguments of an earlier generation of elite Vellalar Indian Christians, converted to Christianity by the original German Lutheran missionaries stationed in Tranquebar. These relatively high-caste Christians maintained rules of caste purity on the grounds that the gospel did *not* consist of food and drink.[71] Yet the Vellalar Christians' vision of a harmonious yet hierarchically ranked social body did not conflict with their German mentors' view of the world. In the eyes of the latter, as with Baierlain, conversion did not necessarily entail a radical transformation of customs but took place in the heart.

A very different view of conversion, and the relation between culture and Christianity implied by it, is evident in the response of Rev. C. W. Arden of the low church Anglican Church Missionary Society: "As the existence of caste prejudice in the mind exhibits itself in outward actions, and as the latter are the natural expression of the former, we cannot condemn one without condemning the other; we are bound to condemn both equally."[72] Arden here articulated a position on the question of the relationship between actions and belief that became prominent in colonial India with the ascendance of missionaries trained in the Methodist and Calvinist traditions after 1850. These "new missionaries," as Dennis Hudson refers to them, tended to argue that outward actions were an index of the inner state and thus could be read as reliable indicators of an individual's spiritual condition. This stance had considerable potential for legitimating interventions in the lives of converts. Positing a one-to-one correspondence between outward actions and the prejudices of the mind provided a simple but powerful rationale for active reform.

Yet another view of the matter was that hairstyle functioned as a signifier of religious identity in a more sociological sense, where the inner life of faith was largely irrelevant. Rev. Burgess, of the Wesleyan Methodist Missionary Society, asserted, "As the clean shaven head is an undoubted sign of Mohammedanism and the kudumi an unmistakable sign of a Hindu, so the grown hair almost invariably points at least to the nominal profession of the Christian faith." For him, what was necessary for genuine conversion was not a simple change of habits, or even of heart, but a vigorous program of moral reform that rested on awakening Indians to the nature and significance of sin. Without this, the nascent Indian Christian community risked becoming just another sociological subgroup among others. As Burgess wrote in a different context at the conference, "We have as a rule to deal with those who have no sense of sin, no realization whatever of pending evil, and consequently no yearning desire to flee from the wrath to come. It is not difficult to understand how such a people, naturally apathetic, and almost devoid of the power of perceiving spiritual truth should content themselves with the bare fact of being connected with a Christian community and attending religious services."[73]

Some twelve years prior to the Bangalore Conference, Bishop Robert Caldwell of the high church Anglican SPG had taken up an investigation into the history of the kudumi in which he echoed the sociological view of the hairstyle taken by Burgess. His article on the kudumi, initially written in 1867 for a newspaper and reprinted by the *Indian Antiquary* in 1875, maintained that the kudumi was simply a fashion, a style with no latent religious meaning. Therefore, whether converts to Christianity kept it or cut it was of no importance from a religious point of view. He traced the history of the kudumi back to the conquest of the indigenous peoples of India by the Aryans, citing as his authority an English translation of the Sanskrit *Vishnu Purana*. According to Caldwell's reading, when the invading Aryans vanquished the indigenous peoples of India they imposed on them different modes of wearing the hair or shaving the beard: The victorious king "made the Yavanas shave their heads entirely; the Sakas he compelled to shave the upper half of the heads; the Paradas wore their hair long, and the Pahnavas let their beards grow." The king also prohibited the conquered tribes from partaking in the rituals of the Vedic religion, the oblations to fire, use of the Vedas, or services of Brahman priests. Caldwell, however, saw these two sets of injunctions as separate: While the religious prohibitions made the indigenous people ritually polluting, the hair and beard styles were enjoined upon them so that they could be distinguished from the ritually pure Aryans.[74] Interestingly, the hairstyle associated with Brahmans and twice-born castes, with the hair shaved into a tuft at the back of the head, was not mentioned in these passages from the *Vishnu Purana*, a silence that Caldwell took as evidence that the kudumi was the default hairstyle of the Aryans themselves.

And yet, he argues, over time, the fashion did spread outside of the twice-born fold. In his day, wealthier members of non-twice-born castes adopted the hairstyle, seemingly without resistance. That those who did so were *still* not admitted into Hindu temples was proof, for Caldwell, that the style had no religious meaning. The kudumi had been from the beginning and remains, he argued, merely a fashion, one that people of his day had come to regard as "a sign of respectability." In fact, he writes,

> A large majority of the Christian Shanars, including nearly all the adherents of the missions of the Society for the Propagation of the Gospel, have adopted the kudumi together with Christianity never supposing for a moment that the fashion they adopted when they became Christians could be regarded by any one as a sign of the heathenism they had left, but on the contrary regarding it, if a sign of any religion at all, rather as a sign of Christianity,—at least in their case, in so far as Christianity favored the adoption of more cleanly, more civilized usages, and taught them, among other minor proprieties, that "it was a shame for a man to have long hair."[75]

In other words, when Nadar men, who ordinarily wore their hair long and tied back in a bun, converted to Christianity, they shaved their head into a kudumi in the manner of high-caste men of the region and wealthier members of their own caste. Here we have another of those moments in the history of Christianity in India when a custom is adopted, or retained, by Christians that has different meanings within two different sets of cultural codes or signs: According to Christian concepts of proper conduct as transmitted through the biblical text, it is "a shame for a man to have long hair," and thus to Christians, whether Indian or Western, wearing the kudumi communicates a willingness to conform to Christian values of propriety and cleanliness. But at the same time, the adoption of the kudumi signals to Indian Hindus, according to their universe of signs, that the converts are claiming a status equivalent to members of twice-born castes and the wealthier members of their own caste. Caldwell took the coincidence of conversion to Christianity and the adoption of the kudumi as further proof that the hairstyle was not a sign of Hinduism. But I would argue that it could equally be taken as another indication that to Indians in the nineteenth century, Christianization was very much like Sanskritization, a move toward more respectable modes of behaving and conducting one's life based on an ideal embodied by the higher castes. One can begin to see why this fashion became the object of power struggles between missionaries and converts, as converts were asked or commanded to relinquish a signifier of status only recently acquired.

In 1883, Mateer took issue with Caldwell's characterization of the style as a matter of "personal taste," a merely "national and respectable usage," arguing instead that the kudumi reflected the wearer's desire to retain or aspire to high-caste status, and therefore was incompatible with true Christianity. He wrote, "Hindu caste and the kudumi appear to be closely associated. Those who retain the former invariably also retain the latter." In his survey of the range of opinion on the issue, Mateer noted that the missionaries of virtually every society in India, except those associated with the German Lutherans' Tranquebar and Tanjore mission, the CMS and SPG in Tirunelveli (under Bishop Caldwell's influence), and the LMS in Travancore, insisted on the removal of the kudumi prior to baptism "as a sign of sincerity."[76] Drawing on the testimony of Sir Monier Williams and an essay written by Mr. V. Samuel, an Indian Christian from Nagercoil, Mateer established that the kudumi was, in fact, invested with considerable religious significance: The tonsure of a male child at 3 years old is one of the necessary *samskāras* that effect the transition of an individual from one stage of life to the next; it covers the soft crown of the head, regarded as sacred, and is to be shaved off only by the eldest son at the funeral of his father.

Interestingly, it seems that Indian Christian men encountered opposition from other Indians only when they shaved off the kudumi, not when they adopted it. Mateer cites an unidentified source who states that during the breast cloth controversies of 1858, Sudra mobs scrutinized the men who attended public markets, "examining the heads of the [men] to ascertain whether they had cut off the kudumi, or lock of hair which is a mark of heathenism, and to assault them if by its absence they were found to be professors of Christianity."[77] On the other hand, as I noted earlier, low-caste men *wearing* the kudumi did not arouse violent opposition—as did low-caste women wearing the breast cloth—even though in both cases the assumption of this particular style of self-presentation made it more difficult to distinguish the caste identity of strangers. The historical record does not contain any incidents, to my knowledge, of men's kudumis being forcibly removed in instances of intercaste conflict involving Christians. Indeed, the only people who called for its removal were Christian missionaries.

How can one account for this absence of controversy, for the fact that, as in Arthur Conan Doyle's Sherlock Holmes mystery novel *The Hound of the Baskervilles*, the dog didn't bark? It seems unlikely that the kudumi did not arouse opposition because it was, as Caldwell argued, just a fashion, with little to no social or religious significance. It may be that Indians did not react violently to Indian Christian men, some of whom must have been of low caste, wearing the kudumi because the style came into fashion during a period when tensions between caste groups were not very high. Unfortunately, Caldwell gave only the vaguest sense of the chronology of the kudumi fashion. A more precise and accurate tracking of the actual spread of the practice of Christians wearing the kudumi would enable one to determine whether its use slipped under the radar, as it were, of high-caste vigilance. But it bears mentioning that nineteenth-century south India was peppered with intercaste and communal conflicts, from the burning of churches in David's time (1802–1803), the breast cloth controversies of 1825–1826 and 1858–1859, to the conflicts over roads in 1858 and the full-scale riots between Nadars and Maravars in Sivakasi in 1899. The third and most plausible explanation is that the practice had to do with men's heads rather than women's bodies. As Nur Yalman noted over thirty years ago, in spite of the predominantly patrilineal nature of kinship in south India, women are perceived as the carriers of a people's bloodline. His investigations into puberty rituals in Sri Lanka and south India showed that the vigilant policing of women of childbearing age can be traced to the conviction that the purity of the caste depends on the sexual purity of its women.[78] I would extend this claim to argue that it was not only women's wombs that carried the essence of a group's identity in nineteenth-century south India; the surfaces of the body were also mobilized to fulfill this function. Because women were perceived as the actual carriers of a people's bloodline they bore a disproportionate responsibility for displaying on their person the markers of community identity. Thus, changes in women's dress styles aroused more conflict than did changes in men's dress styles.

Summary

The examination of sartorial styles taken up by Indian Christians, like the examination of Indian Christian domesticity and conjugality, demonstrates that Christianity was not imposed by missionaries on Christian converts in a unilateral direction. Rather, Indian Christians had their own reasons for adopting particular styles or fashions, which followed a fairly clear pattern of selection. When we situate the innovations undertaken by Indian Christians in the matrix of meanings that circulated in nineteenth-century south Indian society, we can see that those styles or habits that could buttress their claims to enhanced social status in the eyes of their non-Christian Indian neighbors were favored over those that did not. The adoption of the upper cloth over the ravikkay, the wearing by women of gold jewelry and by men of topknots all were styles of self-presentation that sought to construct and inhabit a newly "honorable" and "respectable" identity for communities that had been marked as decidedly on the margins of the social body. When sartorial styles, such as the wearing of the breast cloth by low-caste Travancoran Christian women, were interpreted as infringements on the traditional privileges of the indigenous elite, they could arouse intense opposition, but they did not always do so. When Indian Christian men adopted the kudumi, for example, the only group among whom this seems to have elicited a negative response was Western missionaries.[79]

That Christianity was understood by Indians as a system of practices and beliefs rather than a system exclusively of beliefs is perhaps not surprising given the orthopraxic tendencies of Indian religions, particularly Hinduism. What is more striking is the extent to which missionaries and colonial administrators, in the midst of the Age of Belief, when belief was congealed regularly into new creeds requiring explicit affirmation, helped to construct Christianization as a process involving the renovation of everyday practices. In this context, changes in Christian men's and women's dress and jewelry need to be seen not simply as reflections of transformations in the social organization of gender in Tamil communities undergoing Christianization. Rather, sartorial practices, along with other pedestrian forms of praxis—domestic labor, physical comportment, conjugality—provided the very ground on which the cultural codes that give meaning to social life were fought over and negotiated.

Conclusion: Indian Christianity and Conversion

Karratu kaiyaḷavu, kallātatu kaṭalaḷavu
(What we have learned is a handful, what we have not learned fills the ocean).

—Tamil proverb

This is a crucial moment in the history of the study of Indian Christianity. Once, historians of Indian Christianity, especially Protestant Christianity, were content to sift through the voluminous holdings of the many missionary societies to document the efforts of the men and women sent to India over the course of the past four centuries. Now, each new study of Christianity in India pays more attention than the last to the voices of Indian men and women who encountered these missionaries and responded in innumerable ways to the messages they brought. To give depth to these voices, scholars have increasingly turned to new sources: printed books and pamphlets in Indian languages, handwritten reports, oral histories, photographs, ephemera, and material culture. This long overdue attention to the experiences of Indian Christians in studies of Indian Christianity has also required new theoretical and methodological approaches. The encounter between missionaries and Indians has proved to be a particularly ripe harvest for scholars interested in the subtleties of power exercised through language, education, law, and literature. They have contributed enormously to our understanding of the "long conversation" between Christian evangelists and emissaries of Western "civilization" and those who responded to them.[1] And yet, there remains much we don't know, and may never know, about the transmission of Christianity in India and how individuals and groups accepted it, transformed it, and made it their own. By way of conclusion, I would like to summarize the contributions this study makes to the study of Indian Christianity, both in terms of its place within the larger religious landscape in India and in terms of what Indian Christianity has to teach us about broader issues in the comparative study of religion.

Religion in India

Religion in India has often been seen as synonymous with Hinduism, particularly the elite, literate Hinduism enshrined in a few now canonical sacred texts. But, as many scholars have recently pointed out, Hinduism itself is a vast, sprawling religious tradition not easily reducible to a single, unified "ism."[2] Like any great religious tradition, it has come to be what it is through a long history of interaction with many other traditions, both those that have arisen in south Asia and those that were brought in by traders, soldiers, and missionaries from other parts of the world. This is not to say that Hinduism is an incoherent jumble of contradictory beliefs and practices. On the contrary, there are themes, texts, and traditions that lend considerable consistency to the many varieties of Hinduism. But, given the rising social and political influence in India of what historian Romila Thapar has called "syndicated Hinduism," it is important to provide scholarly perspectives on the Indian religious landscape that foreground the diversity of India's religions such that their distinctiveness is given as much importance as their long history of interaction and mutual influence.[3] One of the best ways to make the variegated nature of religion in India visible is through close analyses of minority religions in the larger social, cultural, religious, and political contexts in which they take shape, such as this study undertakes.

In addition, to the extent that many (but by no means all) of the adherents of the minority religions in India have been drawn from nonelite segments of Indian society, such an emphasis also entails seeing Hinduism in a new way— from below, from the margins, from outside the channels where prestige and power circulate most richly. Indian history reveals a long tradition of marginalized groups mobilizing under the sign of the sacred, from the *śramanas* (renouncers) of the sixth century B.C.E. Gangetic valley, who gave rise to heterodox religions like Jainism and Buddhism, to the low-caste devotees of Vishnu and Shiva in medieval Maharashtra, Karnataka, and Tamil Nadu, whose songs celebrated a new, passionate way of relating to God that was open to everyone. The history of religions in India is replete with instances where new visions of the cosmos supported new formulations of collective identity and new social formations gave rise to new cosmologies. The conversion of Protestant Christians in the nineteenth and early twentieth centuries ought to be seen as another instance of this pattern in the history of religions in India. Given the politicized nature of religion and the sacralized nature of politics in India that I described in chapter 1, we can see with special clarity that the process of a group's distinguishing itself as a new religious community did not come without a struggle. With its potential to bring about a realignment in the web of

relations of dependence and patronage that make up society, religious conversion often troubled those who benefited most from the reproduction of the
status quo through the maintenance of inherited identities, whether colonial
administrators or indigenous elites.

Religion in Colonial India

This study helps to clarify the complex role of the colonial state in shaping
religious identities. Several important studies of religion in colonial India have
drawn attention to the ways in which forms of governance introduced by the
British, such as the All-India Census, altered the place of religion in Indian
society and laid the groundwork for the modern-day politicization of religion.[4]
This was by no means a simple matter of British rulers dictating to Indian
subjects how to manage their religious affairs, but a complex series of negotiations and interactions, such as I describe in chapter 2, among missionaries,
British administrators, and Indians both elite and nonelite. Of critical importance was the way colonial forms of knowledge, exemplified in texts such as
Thurston and Rangachari's compendium of the castes and tribes of southern
India, reified caste identities, reinforcing Brahmanical notions of the relationship among social status, occupation, religious practices, and the regulation of
sexuality. My analysis of the conflict between Rev. Robert Caldwell and Nadar
spokesmen over the representation of the latter in Caldwell's book *The Tinnevelly Shanars* indicates clearly the heavily contested nature of this process.
Conversion movements of the nineteenth and early twentieth century and the
lengthy process of Christianization that followed were deeply informed by converts' desire to distance themselves from the images of the "degraded castes"
that took new shape in colonial discourse. They sought, in part, to rise up
toward what were widely regarded, in both Brahmanical and British scales of
value, as more refined, morally upright modes of being. As this study demonstrates, the drive to become "respectable" had manifold consequences, especially for Indian Christian women.
    Missionaries and representatives of the colonial state clashed over many
issues. Missionaries were a highly diverse lot, and the colonial state's relationship to Hinduism was by no means uniformly negative, and neither was its
relationship to Christianity wholly positive. And yet most missionaries and
administrators shared both a strong commitment to the civilizing rhetoric of
colonial rule and a paternalistic attitude toward Indians. The impulse to raise
up and civilize and yet guide that process with a firm hand led to complex, at
times contradictory results. On the one hand, colonial legislators and administrators desired that converts become moral subjects equivalent to European
Christians, and they held out the promise that they would treat them as such
after seeing visible evidence of change in the lives of converts; on the other
hand, the state wished to minimize the disruptive effects that conversion to
Christianity would bring about and decried such change as "denationalization."
In the legal arena, this ambivalence took shape in the application of the prin-

ciple of Lex Loci in Indian Christian family law. In matters such as inheritance and the definition of marriageable kin, the state governed Indian converts according to the traditions of their natal community, but paid lip service to the idea that over time, Indian Christians would "evolve" to a status in which they could be governed by English Christian family law through the gradual adoption of new habits and values and the abandonment of old ones. It is difficult to ascertain the degree of influence that such laws had on Indian Christian social organization. Did these laws directly promote the reproduction of kinship structure according to inherited caste categories while simultaneously encouraging the emulation of Western Christian lifestyles? Or did they reflect or accommodate preexisting pressures within the Indian Christian community to retain caste identities while adopting a more "respectable" caste lifestyle? More scholarship on Indian Christian personal law during the colonial period could shed light on the issue of the retention of caste-based differences by Indian Christian communities and provide greater insight into the related issue of the relationship between law and religion in colonial India.

The study of the intricacies of conversion in the nineteenth and early twentieth century may also have something to teach us about what Gerald Larson has called India's present-day "agony over religion."[5] It is important to bear in mind the differences between the relationship of politics and religion in contemporary India and under the British Raj. With the transition to Independence, beginning with the Morley-Minto Reforms (also known as the Indian Councils Act, 1909) and the Montagu-Chelmsford Reforms of 1918, religion in India became politicized in a new way such that religious identity came to coincide increasingly with citizenship. These constitutional reforms were designed to transfer more political power to Indian subjects, but they ended up making census categories (especially those having to do with religion) the basis for political mobilization as elections were conducted on the principle of separate electorates for different classes of subjects (Muslims, Hindus, etc.). The politicization of religious identity in present-day India, evident in, for example, affirmative action in public education and employment given to dalits depending on religious identity and the rallying of vote banks around religious identity, was present in a nascent form at most during the period of this study. There are, nonetheless, striking continuities between the resistance to conversion in contemporary India and in the nineteenth century. In particular, one sees a distinct commonality in the view that religious conversion entails the enticement of vulnerable members of society to leave the Hindu fold. The fear that conversion will destabilize society, then and now, is vividly conveyed by the image of the missionary "subjecting the living body of India to a cultural and national vivisection."[6] Efforts to limit the extent and impact of conversions on the integrity of the traditional social fabric have included legislation in some Indian states that grants authority to the state government to regulate conversion. The so-called Freedom of Religion Bills passed in Orissa (1967), Madhya Pradesh (the Dharma Swatantraya Adhiniyam Act [1968]) and Tamil Nadu (Prohibition of Forcible Conversion of Religion Ordinance [2002]), do guarantee an individual's right to change religion, but require that such individuals gain government consent before doing so. In 1977 the Supreme Court of India in *Stanislaus v. the State of Madhya Pradesh* upheld the Madhya Pradesh law, arguing that the Constitution's guarantee of the right to "freedom of conscience" and "freedom to profess, practice and propagate religion" (Article 25) did not extend to the right to convert another person against his or her free will, using force, fraud, or inducement. The state's desire to protect its citizens from being coerced or tricked into conversion under false pretenses is certainly understandable. However, none of these laws define "fraud, force or inducement" with any specificity. Who, then, is to determine what constitutes "fraud" or "inducement"? This is especially important in the context of religious conversion, in which, from the point of view of believers, the successful attainment of conversion's most important benefit (eternal salvation) is neither verifiable or falsifiable in this plane of existence. Leaving these terms undefined means that the laws regulating conversion primarily serve the interests of those who profit most from the status quo, rather than those who have historically employed conversion for gaining increased self-respect, spiritual satisfaction, social mobility, and a host of other benefits, tangible and intangible.

Indian Christianity

Histories of Christianity in India that focus exclusively on the role of missionaries and neglect the equally significant contribution of Indian Christians have, regrettably, reinforced the perception that missionaries duped or coerced low-caste converts into embracing Christianity. The process of conversion to Christianity, as I have sought to show in this study, was never simply a matter of the imposition of a foreign religion on socially weak, vulnerable elements of the Hindu social body. By focusing on the process from the point of view of Indian Christians, one sees that, from the beginning, Indians understood Christianity through indigenous categories and selectively appropriated those aspects of it that corresponded to local values and scales of social worth. At the same time, the distinctiveness of Christianity from indigenous religions was important insofar as it permitted low-caste Indian Christians to make a symbolic or material break from preexisting social systems, so that they could create a new, respectable community identity. It is clear that in the dynamic political field of colonial south India some low-caste converts found Christianity a useful instrument for differentiating themselves from old orders of power and status and of forging new identities as a way of escaping old patterns of degradation and marginalization. Like scholars such as Gauri Viswanathan and Uma Chakravarty, I see conversion to Christianity, especially by women and people from the so-called low castes, as entailing an implicit (and sometimes explicit) critique of dominant Hindu society's patriarchal or hierarchical tendencies.[7] There is a liberatory, critical edge to conversion, a declaration that I will be someone new, I am already someone new. But this study also indicates that through their association with the missions, Indian Christians did not necessarily achieve perfect freedom; more frequently they became enmeshed in new networks of dependency, patronage, and submission.

The analysis of individual and collective responses to Christian teachings illuminates the resourcefulness and resiliency of groups facing pressure from both colonial patrons and high-caste Hindu masters and landlords. Converts often attempted to indigenize Christianity so that it was intelligible and viable within the cultural meanings of local society. They put the practices that they were encouraged or, not infrequently, compelled to adopt in the service of their own interests and bids for social mobility, as the example of the Breast Cloth Controversy reveals with special clarity. Where the tendency to use conversion as a way to differentiate oneself from the mainstream can be seen as a critique of prevailing local hegemonies, the tendency to indigenize Christianity, both by attaching Hindu meanings to Christian practices and by recasting Hindu symbols with Christian meanings (such as Rev. Sattampillai of the Hindu Christian Church attempted), may be seen as a form of resistance to the dominance of foreign missionaries within the institutions of the Church.[8]

And yet, the interests of all the members of the groups undergoing conversion in the nineteenth century were not identical or completely harmonious. Women, it seems, paid a higher price than men did for pursuing a more respectable social identity when they capitulated to an intensified moral surveillance in exchange for the promise of protection and the social regard that being a "protected woman" garnered. The interpretation of Christianity that evangelical missionaries, both men and women, brought with them to India was profoundly influenced by the idea that Christianity could be an instrument of social and moral reform that would "civilize" Indian converts and shape them into proper and respectable middle-class subjects. Combined with the selective appropriation of those aspects of Christianity that conformed to the ideas of social value contained in Sanskritic Hinduism, the dominant form of Christianity that emerged in the mid- to late nineteenth century was fairly conservative. Although it won for many adherents a heightened sense of their own social and moral worth, a sense that was, in some cases, reflected in better treatment by others, the appropriation of Christianity along these lines profoundly affected the gender roles and expectations to which Indian Christian men and women were expected to conform. It produced a notion of respectability that tended to efface previous traditions of women's autonomous power in favor of an ideal of femininity that was contained, restrained, self-regulating, and, above all, sexually chaste. On the other hand, Christianization opened up new roles for independent women—Bible woman, teacher, matron—by which some women established footholds from which to create new possibilities for social mobility, for both themselves and their descendants. When one looks closely at the effects of Christianization in India, especially for women, it is impossible to conclude that its influence was either wholly beneficial or wholly harmful.

Comparative Study of Religion

As scholars of women's history have long known, when one begins to include gender in one's analysis, the old models and narratives may need to be revised. Joan Scott asks, "Can a focus on women 'add a supplement to history' without also 'rewriting history'?"[9] In the context of the history of Indian Christianity, a focus on women not only provides a corrective that illuminates the under-described role of women, both Indian and foreign, in the process of conversion to Protestant Christianity in colonial India. It also entails a new approach to the study of conversion. Women's exclusion from many leadership roles in Christian institutions and the value given to the quotidian by evangelical theology motivated both women missionaries and prominent Indian Christian women to make the reform of everyday practices central to conversion efforts. The focus on women's experience in India thus necessitates a reconceptualization of the process of conversion itself, from seeing it primarily as a function of changing the content of the faith statements to which one gives assent, to seeing it as a transformation of practices and people's complex negotiations over the meanings of such practices.

Classic models of conversion offered by scholars such as William James and Alfred Nock, with their focus on the interior, personal dimension of conversion, are simply not capable of capturing the interplay between "inner" beliefs and "outer" practices that were a consistent theme in the conversion movements of nineteenth- and early twentieth-century India. Indian Christians, missionaries, and non-Christian Indians all expounded on the relationship between practices and inner states on subjects ranging from the nature of a proper Indian home to Christian marriage and the way that Indian Christian men wore their hair. Moreover, while men and women took the public expression of belief to be a vital component of authentic conversion, those same practices—cutting the hair or wearing a particular style of garment—were immediately subject to multiple interpretations. Conversion has too often been seen as an individual, deeply private, subjective experience. It is also deeply social. How does one signal that internal change in a way that is intelligible to others? How do people then interpret these signals or signs? We need more studies that are attuned to the historically and culturally situated nature of conversion to draw out distinct patterns. One pattern that this study reveals is this: When notions of authentic conversion are accompanied by the idea that one's actions or behaviors are indexes of the true state of the soul, then religious conversion can become an effective instrument of radical societal change, giving grounds for the transformation of practices, lifestyles, and lifeworlds to make the outer expression of inner belief conform to what counts as the standard of authenticity. It seems that religious conversion has a less dramatic effect on the structures of social life when people believe that actions have only an indirect or inessential relationship to the inner state. And yet, the transformation of lifeworlds that result from religious conversion does not *necessarily* have a single meaning, such as the increasing penetration of Western culture into indigenous cultures. Because of the inherently ambiguous and multivalent nature of human communication, the same changes in behavior can have vastly different meanings in different contexts. As this study illustrates, the notion that actions are a reliable index of the state of the soul also enhanced converts' capacity to signal their improved social status to non-Christian Indian neighbors in social codes that were immediately intelligible.

Conversion entails a utopian desire for freedom and greater truth expressed in manifold ways. It is rarely, if ever, a once-and-for-all event, but remains an ongoing quest to remain true to the moment when "truth" was most deeply understood, and to realize and embody that truth more fully in everyday life. In that sense, indeed, conversion is bound to transform and unsettle the accepted structures of social life in any society.

Notes

INTRODUCTION: GENDER AND CONVERSION IN COLONIAL INDIA

1. As a result of the highly charged nature of caste politics in India, the terms used to describe the castes who are most marginalized from the centers of social, religious, and economic power in Indian society have changed significantly over the past hundred years. Known as "untouchables" and "outcastes" in British colonial discourse, they were renamed *harijans* ("children of God") by Mahatma Gandhi in the course of their mobilization in the early twentieth century. Contemporary Indian political discourse refers to them with the bureaucratic terms "backward castes" and "scheduled castes and tribes," making reference to government policies of affirmative action taken on their behalf. Politicized members of these castes refer to themselves as *dalits*, from a Marathi word that means "ground down," "oppressed." In this study, I generally refer to them as "low castes" in order to include a range of groups who occupied "low" positions in the social and religious hierarchy in the nineteenth century. Frequently, for reasons of clarity, I use the specific caste (*jāti*) name used at the time to refer to the group, names whose connotations and usages have themselves changed overtime (e.g., Paraiyār, Paḷḷār, Cāṇār [Shanar]/Nāṭār [Nadar]).

2. Robert E. Frykenberg, "The Impact of Conversion and Social Reform upon Society in South India during the Late Company Period: Questions Concerning Hindu-Christian Encounters with Special Reference to Tinnevelly," in *Indian Society and the Beginnings of Modernization, c. 1830–1850*, ed. C. H. Philips and M. D. Wainwright (London: School of Oriental and African Studies, 1976); Robert E. Frykenberg, "On Roads and Riots in Tinnevelly: Radical Change and Ideology in Madras Presidency during the 19th Century," *South Asia* 2 (1982): 34–52; Geoffrey A. Oddie, *Hindu and Christian in South-East India: Aspects of Religious Continuity and Change, 1800–1900* (London: Curzon, 1981).

3. Peter van der Veer, ed., *Conversion to Modernities: The Globalization of Christianity* (New York: Routledge, 1996); Gauri Viswanathan, *Outside*

the Fold: Conversion, Modernity, and Belief (Princeton: Princeton University Press, 1998).

4. Van der Veer, *Conversion to Modernities*, 4.

5. Talal Asad, "Comment on Conversion," in Van der Veer, *Conversion to Modernities*, 263–74.

6. William James, *The Varieties of Religious Experience* (1902, New York: Penguin Books, 1985), 189.

7. See A. D. Nock, *Conversion: The Old and the New in Religion from Alexander the Great to Augustine of Hippo* (Oxford: Oxford University Press, 1933), along with James, for primarily psychological theories of conversion that have contributed to the "interiorist" bias in studies of conversion.

8. For example, Rev. Strachan of the Society for the Propagation of the Gospel did not require from converts who embraced Christianity in groups a verbal statement testifying to their inner experience of conversion, then a staple of evangelical practice in England. Having defended this omission on the grounds that "people whose minds have been from their very infancy steeped in ignorance and superstition" cannot be expected to verbalize their "subjective" conversion experience, he asserted that, from such people, "the best expression [of spiritual experience] is in the life rather than with the lips." "Solution of the Tinnevelly Harvest Problem," *Madras Mail*, 12 July 1878.

9. Robert W. Hefner, "Introduction: World Building and the Rationality of Conversion," in *Conversion to Christianity: Historical and Anthropological Perspectives on a Great Transformation*, ed. Robert W. Hefner (Berkeley: University of California Press, 1993), 17.

10. Pierre Bourdieu, *Outline of a Theory of Practice*, vol. 16 of *Cambridge Studies in Social Anthropology*, trans. Richard Nice (Cambridge, UK: Cambridge University Press, 1977), 94, 90, 164–165.

11. Michel de Certeau, *The Practice of Everyday Life* (Berkeley: University of California Press, 1984); James Scott, *Domination and the Arts of Resistance: The Hidden Transcripts* (New Haven Yale University Press, 1990).

12. Joan W. Scott, "Gender: A Useful Category of Historical Analysis," in *Feminism and History*, ed. Joan W. Scott (Oxford: Oxford University Press, 1996), 167, 168–69.

13. Ashis Nandy, *The Intimate Enemy: Loss and Recovery of the Self under Colonialism* (Delhi: Oxford University Press, 1983); Mrinalini Sinha, *Colonial Masculinity: The "Manly Englishman" and the "Effeminate Bengali" in the Late Nineteeth Century* (Manchester, UK: Manchester University Press, 1995).

14. Peter van Rooden, "Nineteenth-Century Representations of Missionary Conversion and the Transformation of Western Christianity," in van der Veer, *Conversion to Modernities*, 71.

15. See Lata Mani, "Contentious Traditions: The Debate on *Sati* in Colonial India," in *Recasting Women*, ed. Kumkum Sangari and Sudesh Vaid (New Delhi: Kali for Women, 1989), 88–126.

16. John L. Comaroff and Jean Comaroff, *Christianity, Colonialism, and Consciousness in South Africa*, vol. 1 of *Of Revelation and Revolution* (Chicago: University of Chicago Press, 1991), and *The Dialectics of Modernity on a South African Frontier*, vol. 2 of *Of Revelation and Revolution* (Chicago: University of Chicago Press, 1997); Marshall Sahlins, *Islands of History* (Chicago: University of Chicago Press, 1987).

17. Comaroff and Comaroff, *Of Revelation and Revolution*; John Kelly, *A Politics of*

Virtue: Hinduism, Sexuality, and Countercolonial Discourse in Fiji (Chicago: University of Chicago Press, 1991); Nicholas B. Dirks, ed., *Colonialism and Culture* (Ann Arbor: University of Michigan Press, 1991).

18. See Vicente L. Rafael, *Contracting Colonialism: Translation and Christian Conversion in Tagalog Society under Early Spanish Rule* (Ithaca, NY: Cornell University Press, 1988).

1: INTO THE FOLD

1. J. S. Ponniah et al., *An Enquiry into the Economic and Social Problems of the Christian Community of Madura, Ramnad and Tinnevelly Districts* (Madura: American College, 1938).

2. Robert L. Hardgrave, *The Nadars of Tamilnad: The Political Culture of a Community in Change* (Berkeley: University of California Press, 1969).

3. The name Paraiyar, derived from the leather *parai* drum which members of this caste played at religious festivals and weddings, became the English word "Pariah," a blanket term for all so-called outcastes. Edgar Thurston and K. Rangachari, "Paraiyan," in *Castes and Tribes of Southern India* (Madras: Government of Madras, 1909), 6:77, 80.

4. The census counted a total of 1,793,742 Roman Catholics and Protestants out of a population of 47,166,602. *Census of India, 1931: Madras, Part 1: Report*, (Madras: Government Press, 1932), 14:329. The percentage of Christians among the total Indian population has remained quite small, from 2.5 percent to 3 percent.

5. Louis Dumont, *Homo Hierarchicus* [first English edition] (London: E.T., 1972), 25, cited in Duncan B. Forrester, *Caste and Christianity: Attitudes and Policies on Caste of Anglo-Saxon Protestant Missions in India* (London: Curzon, 1980), 103, n. 20.

6. I use "Sanskritzation," a term coined by M. N. Srinivas in the 1960s, to refer to the process of cultural change initiated by upwardly mobile castes in the colonial and post-Independence periods in which claims to higher social status were made by adopting the practices of local dominant castes, such as wearing the sacred thread and reciting Sanskrit or Vedic verses at weddings. See M. N. Srinivas, *Religion and Society among the Coorgs* (Oxford: Oxford University Press, 1952), *The Cohesive Role of Sanskritization and Other Essays* (New Delhi: Oxford University Press, 1984), and *The Dominant Caste and Other Essays* (New Delhi: Oxford University Press, 1987).

7. Forrester, *Caste and Christianity*, 77; Dick Kooiman, *Conversion and Social Equality in India: The London Missionary Society in South Travancore in the 19th Century* (New Delhi: Manohar, 1989), 8.

8. Arjun Appadurai and Carole A. Breckenridge, "The South Indian Temple: Authority, Honour and Redistribution," *Contributions to Indian Sociology*, n.s. 10 no. 2 (1976): 187–211.

9. Burton Stein, *Peasant State and Society in Medieval South India* (Delhi: Oxford University Press, 1994), 452.

10. For analyses of the political symbolism of *mariyātai* and gift giving and the interrelationship between temples and kingship in Vijayanagara, Nayaka, and colonial "little kingdoms" in the Tamil country, see also Pamela G. Price, *Kingship and Political Practice in Colonial India*, vol. 51 of *University of Cambridge Oriental Publications* (Cambridge, UK: Cambridge University Press, 1996), 13–19; Nicholas B. Dirks, *The Hollow Crown: Ethnohistory of a Little Kingdom in South India* (Cambridge, UK: Cambridge University Press, 1988).

11. Appadurai and Breckenridge, "The South Indian Temple," 191.

12. Henry Whitehead, *The Village Gods of South India* (London: Oxford University Press, 1916), 51.

13. The case of Nandanār, the only untouchable among the Saiva bhakti saints celebrated in the medieval text *Periya Purāṇam* by Cekkiḷār, illustrates this prohibition quite poignantly. Cekkilar writes that in spite of his intense devotion to Lord Shiva, Nandanar was unable to approach the lingam at Chidambaram in his normal state. Mercifully, Shiva granted him purification in a fierce trial by fire, from which he emerged endowed with a sacred thread. In other words, he was granted access to the inner sanctum of the temple only by being miraculously (and painfully) transformed into a Brahman. See M. Arunachalam, *The Saiva Saints* (Tiruchitrambalam: Gandhi Vidyalayam, 1985), 74–77; C. K. Subramaniya Mudaliyar, *Cēkkiḻār Cuvāmikaḷ eṉṉum Aruṇmoḷittēvar aruḷiya Periyapurāṇam eṉṉum Tiruttoṇṭar purāṇam*, [The sacred history of the devoted slaves of God, known as the great sacred history, by Cekkilar, known as the master of graceful speech] (Coimbatore: Kōvait Tamiḻc Caṅkam, 1968) vol. 2.

14. Carol A. Breckenridge, "From Protector to Litigant: Changing Relations between Hindu Temples and the Raja of Ramnad," *Indian Economic and Social History Review* 14, no. 1 (January–March 1977): 102.

15. John C.B. Webster, "Christians and the Depressed Castes in the 1930s," in *Economy, Society and Politics in Modern India*, ed. D.N. Panigrahi (New Delhi: Vikas Publishing House, 1985), 332.

16. Breckenridge, 99–104.

17. Price, *Kingship and Political Practice in Colonial India*, 17.

18. More conservative scholars maintain that the earliest Syrian Christian outposts were not founded until the fourth century C.E. For a fascinating account of the evidence for the Thomas tradition, see Stephen Neill, *A History of Christianity in India: The Beginnings to AD 1707* (Cambridge, UK: Cambridge University Press, 1984), 26–49.

19. M. N. Pearson, *The Portuguese in India* (Cambridge, UK: Cambridge University Press, 1987), ch. 4; Neill, *History of Christianity in India*, 118.

20. In fact, as Dennis Hudson relates, on the first day that young Ziegenbalg and Plütschau arrived on the shores of India, they received a most hostile welcome from the Danish officers, who threw them out of the fort into the Tranquebar marketplace. Evidently, when the Danish king, Frederick IV, commissioned the missionaries to go to India he failed to consult with the directors of the Danish East India Company in Copenhagen. In response, they sent a secret message ahead of the missionaries instructing the Company servants to obstruct their efforts in every way. Even fourteen months after their arrival, Ziegenbalg wrote in a letter that the Europeans in Tranquebar "have shewn us all the Spite and Malice they ever cou'd." D. Dennis Hudson, *Protestant Origins in India: Tamil Evangelical Christians, 1706–1835* (Grand Rapids, MI: Eerdmans Studies in the History of Christian Missions, 2000), 1, 22.

21. Stephen Neill, *History of Christianity in India, 1707–1858* (Cambridge, UK: Cambridge University Press, 1985), 28–49.

22. Hudson, *Protestant Origins in India*, 34–42.

23. As I discuss more thoroughly later in this chapter, throughout the eighteenth century, very few European women resided in India. Only the most senior officers of the English or Danish East India Company were able to afford the high cost of maintaining a European wife. As a result, many European men kept concubines, a practice that was widely accepted until the early decades of the nineteenth century.

24. Neill, *Christianity in India, 1707–1858*, 31; Daniel Jeyaraj, "Halle-Danish

(Tranquebar) Mission and Western Protestant Missionary Tradition," *Zeitschrift für Missionswissenschaft und Religionswissenschaft* 84, no. 1 (2000): 11.

25. Hudson, *Protestant Origins in India*, 20.

26. Neill, *Christianity in India, 1707–1858*, 42, n. 56; Hudson, *Protestant Origins in India*, 29.

27. Neill, *Christianity in India, 1707–1858*, 38, 37; E. Arno Lehmann, *It Began at Tranquebar*, trans, and ed. M. J. Lutz (Madras: Christian Literature Society, 1956), 63–64; Hudson, *Protestant Origins in India*, 50, 90, 108.

28. Hudson, *Protestant Origins in India*, 173–84.

29. Lehmann, *It Began at Tranquebar*, 63.

30. Saskia C. Kersenboom-Story, *Nityasumangali: Devadasi Tradition in South India* (Delhi: Motilal Banarsidass, 1987); Leslie C. Orr, *Donors, Devotees, and Daughters of God: Temple Women in Medieval Tamilnadu* (New York: Oxford University Press, 2000).

31. Geoffrey A. Oddie, "Christian Conversion in the Telegu Country, 1860–1900: A Case Study of One Protestant Movement in the Godavery-Krishna Delta," *Indian Economic and Social History Review* 12, no. 1 (January–March 1975): 67, 78. For a concise description of several recurring patterns in religious conversion, see Lewis R. Rambo, *Understanding Religious Conversion* (New Haven: Yale University Press, 1993).

32. For example, Emma Rauschenbusch-Clough writes of the influence of a bhakti teacher, Yogi Nasriah, on Madiga converts in nineteenth-century Andhra Pradesh; *While Sewing Sandals; or Tales of a Telegu Pariah* (London: Houghter and Stoughton, 1899). Saurabh Dube shows that American missionaries in Chhattisgarh built on the successes of the Satnami religious movement; *Untouchable Pasts: Religion, Identity and Power among a Central Indian Community, 1780–1950* (Albany: State University of New York Press, 1998). Geoffrey Oddie has examined the mass conversion of Kartabhajas in Bengal, in "Old Wine in New Bottles? Kartabhaja (Vaishnava) Converts to Christianity in Bengal, 1835–1845," *Indian Economic and Social History Review* 32, no. 3 (1995): 189–224. Whereas Oddie regards these converts as Vaishnavas, Hugh Urban emphasizes the Tantric aspects of their belief and worship in his important study, *The Economics of Ecstasy: Tantra, Secrecy and Power in Colonial Bengal* (New York: Oxford University Press, 2001).

33. Robert Caldwell, *Records of the Early History of the Tinnevelly Mission* (Madras: Higgenbotham, 1881), 55–59.

34. These are the *panchamakara* (five *ms*): *matsya* (fish), *madya* (liquor), *mudra* (parched grain), *mamsa* (flesh), and *maithuna* (sexual intercourse, usually between a high-caste man and a low-caste woman). See Mircea Eliade, *Yoga: Immortality and Freedom*, trans. Willard R. Trask (Princeton: Princeton University Press, 1969); Douglas Renfrew Brooks, *The Secret of the Three Cities: An Introduction to Hindu Sakta Tantrism* (Chicago: University of Chicago Press, 1990); Urban, *Economics of Ecstasy*.

35. Like the Bauls of Bengal, Siddhas used ordinary, sometimes coarse or crude language in their poetry and criticized the prevailing "priestocracy," features that had a wide appeal to the low-caste masses of south India from the thirteenth through the eighteenth century. T. N. Ganapathy, *The Philosophy of the Tamil Siddhas* (New Delhi: Indian Council of Philosophical Research, 1993).

36. Robert Caldwell, *A Political and General History of the District of Tinnevelly in the Presidency of Madras, from the Earliest Period to Its Cession to the English Government in A.D. 1801* (Madras: Government Press, 1881), 247; Paul Appasamy, *The Centenary History of the C.M.S. in Tinnevelly* (Palamcottah: Palamcottah Press, 1923), 46. In several letters sent to Rev. J. C. Kohlhoff in 1803–1805, Rev Satyanāthan, an Indian pas-

tor in the employ of the SPCK, detailed the abuse to which Christians of Tirunelveli were subject. Under the pretense that the Christians did not pay sufficient tax to the *sirkar* (government), they were beaten, tortured, put in stocks, and made to sit in the blazing sun without respite for days at a time by the peons of the village overseers (*maṇiyakkārar*). Evidently, they did not passively submit to this mistreatment. David organized a group of men who called themselves *taṭi-kampu-kārar* ("club-men"), who "went about from place to place redressing the wrongs of the native Christians by force." Caldwell, *Records of the Tinnevelly Mission*, 100–106.

37. Hugald Grafe, *The History of Christianity in Tamilnadu from 1800 to 1975*, vol. 5 of *CHAI History of Christianity in India* (Bangalore: Church History Association of India, 1990), 121–22; Hardgrave, *Nadars of Tamilnad*, 44–45.

38. For later developments in these Christian villages, see ch. 5.

39. Thurston and Rangachari, *Castes and Tribes of Southern India*, 6: 137.

40. C. M. Agur, *Church History in Travancore* (Madras: S.P.S. Press, 1903), 426.

41. The possibility that Murugan cults were a focus of low-caste restlessness in nineteenth-century south India has not been well explored. But another nineteenth-century religious movement among devotees of Murugan, which was started in the 1830s at Tiruchendur, suggests that such cults were instrumental in articulating the aspirations of low-caste groups in the area under the aegis of religion. See M. S. S. Pandian, "Meanings of 'Colonialism' and 'Nationalism': An Essay on Vaikunda Swamy Cult," *Studies in History*, n.s. 8, no. 2 (1992): 167–85; Tiru Ponnilan, "Vaikuntar kāṭṭiya vālkkai neṟ," (The code of ethics created by Vaikunda), in *Nāṭṭār valakkārri-yalāyvukaḷ* (Studies in folklore), ed. S. D. Lourdes (Tirunelveli: Parivel Pathipagam, 1981), 233–50.

42. Agur, *Church History in Travancore*, 432, 427–58; Grafe, *History of Christianity in Tamilnadu*, 28.

43. Kooiman, *Conversion and Social Equality*, 52–53.

44. In the second volume of his *History of Christianity in India*, James Hough, the CMS chaplain in Tirunelveli, wrote of Ringeltaube, "Scarcely an article of his dress was of European manufacture. He seldom had a coat to his back, except when furnished with one by a friend . . . in his occasional visits to Palamcotta. Expending his stipend upon his poor people, his personal wants seem never to have entered into his thoughts." Cited in Caldwell, *Records of the Tinnevelly Mission*, 167. Though it raised eyebrows among the local European population, perhaps Ringeltaube's style of self-presentation helped him gain acceptance among the local Indian population by making him recognizable as a *sannyasi*, or religious ascetic.

45. Neill, *Christianity in India, 1707–1858*, 457.

46. Agur, *Church History in Travancore*, 458.

47. Ibid., 447.

48. See, for example, the historical novel based on her life by A. Madhaviah, *Clarinda: A Historical Novel* (Tirunelveli: Nanbar Vattam, 1992), which was originally published in English in 1915. A Tamil translation done by Satyananda for the Christian Literary Service in 1979 was widely received, and a new critical edition by Lakshmi Holstrom will be published shortly by the Sahitya Akademia of India.

49. Ann Laura Stoler, "Carnal Knowledge and Imperial Power: Gender, Race and Morality in Colonial Asia," in *Gender at the Crossroads of Knowledge: Feminist Anthropology in the Postmodern Era*, ed. Miceala di Leonardo (Berkeley: University of California Press, 1991), 51–101. See also Anne McClintock, *Imperial Leather: Race, Gender and Sexuality in the Colonial Context* (New York: Routledge, 1995).

50. David Packiamutthu, "Royal Clarinda," unpublished manuscript, Bishop Ste-

phen Neill Archives, St. John's College, Palayamkottai, Tamil Nadu, 2; W. Germann, *Missionar Christian Friedrich Schwartz: Sein Leben und Wirken aus Briefen der Halleschen Missionsarchiven* (Erlangen: A. Deichert, 1870), 304; Caldwell, *Records of the Tinnevelly Mission*, 6–8.

51. Schwartz's journal translated in *Neure Geschichten*, cited in Packiamutthu, "Royal Clarinda," 1–2.

52. Thomas Williamson, *The East India Vade-Mecum; or, Complete Guide to Gentlemen Intended for the Civil, Military, or Naval Service of the Hon. East India Company* (London: Black, Parry, and Kingsbury, 1810), 1:457.

53. Suresh Chandra Ghosh, *The Social Condition of the British Community in Bengal, 1757–1800* (Leiden: E.J. Brill, 1970), 74.

54. Stoler, "Carnal Knowledge and Imperial Power," 54–55.

55. Ibid., 57, 53.

56. Williamson, *East India Vade-Mecum*, 337.

57. Christopher J. Hawes, *Poor Relations: The Making of a Eurasian Community in British India, 1773–1833* (Surrrey, UK: Curzon 1996), 8, 9.

58. Ibid., 8, citing T. O. Dunn, "An Anglo-Indian Romance," *Calcutta Review* 295, (January 1919): 56–71.

59. Hawes, *Poor Relations*; Ghosh, *Social Condition*.

60. Stoler, "Carnal Knowledge and Imperial Power," 66.

61. Personal communication, Amanda Hamilton, 15 April 1999.

62. Caldwell, *Records of the Tinnevelly Mission*, 9–12.

63. Packiamutthu, "Royal Clarinda," 5. It is unclear whether the junior Henry Littleton was born out of her relationship with the senior Littleton or was the result of a previous relationship Littleton may have had, or was adopted in some other way.

64. Caldwell, *Records of the Tinnevelly Mission*, 16, citing Germann, *Missionar Christian Friedrich Schwartz*.

65. Caldwell, *Records of the Tinnevelly Mission*, 17.

66. Packiamutthu, "Royal Clarinda," 8, citing Indian Christian historian Paul Kadambavanam, *The Origins of the Tinnevelly Diocese* (1967), 54.

67. Caldwell, *Records of the Tinnevelly Mission*, 16; Germann, *Missionar Christian Friedrich Schwartz*, 325.

68. Packiamutthu, "Royal Clarinda," 8, citing F. J. Western, *The Early History of the Tinnevelly Church*. Germann relates that Schwartz "admonished [*strafen*] Clarinda about her pride [*stolz*] and foolishness [*Leichtsinn*]" (*Missionar Christian Friedrich Schwartz*, 325.

69. Packiamutthu, "Royal Clarinda," 8, citing Western.

70. Caldwell, *Records of the Tinnevelly Mission*, 6–7.

71. Hawes, *Poor Relations*, 15.

72. Caldwell, *Records of the Tinnevelly Mission*, 7.

73. Frykenberg, "On Roads and Riots," 45; Robert E. Frykenberg, "Constructions of Hinduism at the Nexus of History and Religion," *Journal of Interdisciplinary History* 23, no. 3 (winter 1993): 542–45.

74. See Eugene Irschick's discussion of Lionel Place's involvement in the Kanchipuram temple festivals and the shock it elicited among Christians, in *Dialogue and History: Constructing South India, 1795–1895* (New Delhi: Oxford University Press, 1995), 79–86.

75. Ainslie Thomas Embree, *Charles Grant and British Rule in India* (London: George Allen and Unwin, 1962), 270–73.

76. William R. Ward, *The Protestant Evangelical Awakening* (Cambridge, UK:

Cambridge University Press, 1992), and "The Evangelical Revival in Eighteenth-Century Britain," in *A History of Religion in Britain: Practice and Belief from Pre-Roman Times to the Present*, ed. Sheridan Gilley and W. J. Shiels (Oxford: Oxford University Press, 1994).

77. The name Clapham Sect was coined by Sydney Smith in reference to the fact that many in the group lived in the Clapham parish. The members, including John Venn, Zachary Macaulay, Hannah More, James Stephen, Henry Thornton, and William Wilberforce, were also active in movements to abolish the slave trade, the establishment of Sierra Leone for freed slaves, poor relief, and Sunday schools. James Hough, *The History of Christianity in India*, (London: Church Missionary House, 1860), 5:36; Jerald C. Brauer, ed., "Clapham Sect," in *Westminster Dictionary of Church History* (Philadelphia: Westminster Press, 1971), 206.

78. Charles Grant, *Observations on the State of Society among the Asiatic Subjects of Great Britain, particularly with respect to Morals, and on the means of Improving It. Written chiefly in the Year 1792*, 5–25. Page references used here are to the copy in House of Commons, *Sessional Papers*, 1812–1813, Papers Relating to East India Affairs, vol. 10, paper 282, 31–143. Embree writes that Grant formally presented the tract to the Court of Directors in 1797, only after circulating it among his friends for several years. "It did not become well known, however, until it was printed in 1813 in connection with the renewal of the Company's Charter. At that time, Wilberforce gave Grant's ideas wide publicity by quoting them in Parliament and urging people to read the *Observations*." By 1820 it was well-known and regarded as authoritative in evangelical circles and remained for many years a significant reference book for writers on India. Embree, *Charles Grant*, 142.

79. Thomas R. Trautmann, *Aryans and British India* (New Delhi: Vistaar Publications, 1997), 101–11.

80. Embree, *Charles Grant*, 142.

81. Grant, *Observations on the State of Society*, 55, 70, 74.

82. Ibid., 110, 133, 106; Embree, *Charles Grant*, 152.

83. Embree, *Charles Grant*, 155. That Grant's program for reform included not only missionaries but also state-sponsored education in English rather than the Indian vernaculars is significant, but beyond the bounds of this study. See Gauri Viswanathan, *Masks of Conquest* (New York: Columbia University Press, 1989), 71–76, for the resonance Grant's ideas would have among colonial educators who argued for using English literature to inculcate in elite Indians both strong moral values and admiration for the civilization of their conquerors.

84. Stanley Wolpert, *A New History of India*, 4th ed. (New York: Oxford University Press, 1993), 208.

85. See, for example, John Bebb's letter to the Board arguing against support for the Pious Clause. House of Commons, *Sessional Papers*, 1812–1813, East India Affairs, vol. 10, 151.

86. See the answers that Bengal magistrates gave to Governor-General Wellesley in 1801 in response to a request for their opinions on the moral conditions of the Indian people. Parliamentary Papers, 1812–1813, vol. 8, paper 166, "Answers to interrogations by Governor-General, 1801," cited by Embree, *Charles Grant*, 150, n 7.

87. David Kopf, *British Orientalism and the Bengali Renaissance 1773–1835* (Berkeley: University of California Press, 1969); Trautmann, *Aryans and British India*, especially chs. 2 and 3.

88. Grant, *Observations*, 122–27.

89. Embree, *Charles Grant*, 272.

90. Grafe, *History of Christianity in Tamilnad*, 30, n. 31.

91. Hawes, *Poor Relations*, 15; Trautmann, *Aryans and British India*, 109–10.

92. Bishop Thomas Middleton, paraphrased by Hough, *The History of Christianity*, 5:10.

93. Embree, *Charles Grant*, 273.

94. Kooiman, *Conversion and Social Equality*, 56–58.

95. Paul Jenkins, "The CMS and the Basel Mission," in *The Church Mission Society and World Christianity, 1799–1999* ed. Kevin Ward and Brian Stanley (Grand Rapids, MI. Eerdmans, Studies in the History of Christian Missions, 2000), 43–65.

96. John S. Chandler, *Seventy-Five Years in the Madura Mission: A History of the Mission in South India under the ABCFM* (Madras: American Madura Mission, 1910), 36.

97. Viswanathan, *Masks of Conquest*.

98. There is an enormous literature on the Hindu reform movement, especially in Bengal, much of which discusses the influence of evangelical Christian missionaries. Of special interest are David Kopf, *The Brahmo Samaj and the Shaping of the Modern Indian Mind* (Princeton: Princeton University Press, 1979); Kenneth Jones, *Socio-Religious Reform Movements in British India* (Cambridge, UK: Cambridge University Press, New Cambridge History of India III.1, 1989); Geoffrie A. Oddie, *Social Protest in India: British Protestant Missionaries and Social Reforms* (Delhi: Oxford University Press, 1979).

99. Dennis Hudson, "The Life and Times of H. A. Krishna Pillai (1827–1900)" (Ph.D. diss., Claremont Graduate School, 1970); Antony Copley, *Religions in Conflict: Ideology, Cultural Contact and Conversion in Late-Colonial India* (Delhi: Oxford University Press, 1997), chs. 7 and 8; Uma Chakravarti, *Rewriting History: The Life and Times of Pandita Ramabai* (New Delhi: Kali for Women, 2000).

100. Copley, *Religions in Conflict*.

101. Oddie, "Christian Conversion in the Telegu Country, 1860–1900," 65.

102. Several of the most dramatic increases in adherence to Christianity took place in south India during famine years: 1810 (Tirunelveli), 1860–1861 (Travancore), 1870 (Travancore), 1878 (Tirunelveli, Madras, and Andhra Pradesh), and 1881 (Travancore). See Dick Kooiman, "Change of Religion as a Way to Survival," in *Religion and Development: Towards an Integrated Approach*, ed. Quarles van Ufford (Amsterdam: Free University Press, 1988), 167–85, and "Mass Movement, Famine and Epidemic," *Indian Church History Review* 22, no. 2 (1988): 109–131.

103. Since the nineteenth century, the mass movements have been the object of considerable scholarly attention. From Bishop Pickett's massive sociological study of 1933 to a historian's reconceptualization of the movements from the perspective of dalit theology, the phenomenon has attracted both interest and controversy. See John C. B. Webster, *Dalit Christians: A History* (New Delhi: ISPCK, 1992); Forrester, *Caste and Christianity*, ch. 4; Sundararaj Manickam, *The Social Setting of Christian Conversion in South India: The Impact of the Wesleyan Methodist Missionaries on the Trichy-Tanjore Diocese with Special Reference to the Harijan Communities of the Mass Movement Area, 1820–1957* (Wiesbaden, Germany: Steiner, 1977); Oddie, "Christian Conversion in the Telegu Country."

104. J. Charles Molony, *Census of India, 1911: Madras, Part 1, The Report of the Census* (Madras: Government of India, 1912), 57.

105. *Baptist Missionary Magazine* 59 (July 1879): 240; "The Accessions in Tinnevelly: Vindication of the C.M.S." [reprinted from the *Madras Church Missionary Record* for August], *Madras Mail*, 29 July 1878.

106. George Pettitt, *The Tinnevelly Mission of the Church Missionary Society* (London: Seeleys, 1851), 516, cited in Grafe, *History of Christianity in Tamilnadu*, 94; Caldwell, *Records of the Tinnevelly Mission*, 156–57.

107. Rev. Spencer, letter to the editor, "The Tinnevelly 'Harvest,'" *Madras Mail*, 22 June 1878.

108. J. Waskom Pickett, *Christian Mass Movements in India: A Study with Recommendations* (New York: Abingdon, 1933), 330–335.

109. Peter Van der Veer, *Religious Nationalism: Hindus and Muslims in India* (Berkeley: University of California Press, 1994), 26; Arjun Appadurai, "Number in the Colonial Imagination," in *Orientalism and the Postcolonial Predicament*, ed. Carol A. Breckenridge and Peter van der Veer (Philadelphia: University of Pennsylvania Press, 1993), 314–40.

110. Susan Billington Harper, *In the Shadow of the Mahatma: Bishop V. S. Azariah and the Travails of Christianity in British India* (Cambridge, UK: Curzon, 2000), 297–318.

111. The phrase is borrowed from Benedict Anderson's characterization of patriotism in *Imagined Communities: Reflections on the Origin and Spread of Nationalism* (London: Verso, 1991), 143.

112. Kooiman, "Change of Religion as a Way to Survival," 167–85. See also Caldwell's discussion of the numerous apostasies that took place in 1810 among the Shanars of Tirunelveli, who had converted in large numbers in 1800–1802. These relapses, like those that Kooiman studied, took place in the midst of a severe epidemic. Caldwell, *Records of the Tinnevelly Mission*, 76–78.

113. Kooiman cites a letter from the local missionary, who wrote, "Such a large proportion of our people being of course very ignorant are very liable in times of sickness and disease, if not carefully attended to, to offer sacrifices to the Devil and thus return to Heathenism. Many I need not say oodles return every year" ("Mass Movement, Famine and Epidemic," 124).

114. Kooiman, "Change of Religion as a Way to Survival," 82.

115. George T. Washburn and E. Webb, *Christian Lyrics for Public and Social Worship*, 5th ed. (Nagercoil: Madras Tract and Book Society, 1875).

116. C. Joseph, "Koḷḷainōyaip parṟiya viṇṇappam" (Prayer in a time of pestilence), in ibid., 272 (translation mine).

2: COLONIAL KNOWLEDGE

1. In this, I endorse the views of scholars like Nicholas Dirks, Arjun Appadurai, Bernard S. Cohn, Robert Frykenberg, Gyan Pandey and Partha Chatterjee, who argue that "caste" and "Hinduism" were not invented out of whole cloth, but were preexisting formations that were nonetheless radically transformed under the influence of the colonial state.

2. Ronald Inden, *Imagining India* (Oxford: Blackwell 1990); Bernard S. Cohn, *Colonialism and Its Forms of Knowledge: The British in India* (Princeton: Princeton University Press, 1996); Edward W. Said, *Orientalism* (New York: Vintage, 1979).

3. Nandy, *The Intimate Enemy*; Sinha, *Colonial Masculinity*.

4. Comaroff and Comaroff, *Of Revelation and Revolution*, 1:118–25.

5. G. J. Metzger, preface to *Geneaology of the South Indian Gods: A Manual of the Mythology and Religion of the People of Southern India*, by Bartholomaeus Ziegenbalg, trans. G. J. Metzger (1713; Madras: Higgenbotham, 1869), xv.

6. Robert Caldwell, *The Tinnevelly Shanars: A Sketch of Their Religion, and Their Moral Condition and Characteristics as a Caste* (Madras: Christian Knowledge Society Press, 1849); Samuel Mateer, *Land of Charity: A Descriptive Account of Travancore and Its People* (London: J. Snow and Co., 1871); Samuel Mateer, *Native Life in Travancore* (London: W.H. Allen, 1883); Gustav Oppert, *On the Original Inhabitants of Bharatavarsha or India* (Westminster: Constable, 1893); Whitehead, *The Village Gods of South India*; W. T. Elmore, *Dravidian Gods in Modern Hinduism* (1913; New Delhi: Asian Educational Services, 1984).

7. Nicholas B. Dirks, *Castes of Mind: Colonialism and the Making of Modern India* (Princeton: Princeton University Press, 2001), 173, n. 1.

8. Ponnilan, "Vaikuṇṭar kāṭṭiya vāḻkkai neṟi," 234–35.

9. Appasamy, *The Centenary History of the C.M.S. in Tinnevelly*, 40; Agur, *Church History in Travancore*, 572; R. N. Yesudas, *A People's Revolt in Travancore: A Backward Class Movement for Social Freedom* (Trivandrum: Kerala Historical Society, 1975).

10. Frykenberg, "On Roads and Riots in Tinnevelly," 41, 34–52.

11. *The Harvest Field*, July 1886–June 1887; *LMS Reports of Zenana and School Work 1894* (Tittuvelei district, Travancore) (Madras: Addison, 1895); G.O. 417–18, Public, 5 June 1906 (regarding the Indian Christian Marriage Act XV of 1872 and granting licenses to female missionaries).

12. Though the most influential statement of this linguistic discovery was Rev. Robert Caldwell's *Comparative Grammar of the Dravidian or South Indian Family of Languages*, 3d ed. (1913; Madras: Asian Educational Services, 1987), the subject had been explored by British scholars in India for decades. As Thomas Trautmann has demonstrated, the idea of the distinctiveness of Dravidian languages from both Sanskrit and Indian "aboriginal" languages was a topic hotly debated for seventy-five years by British Orientalists based in Bengal and Madras. Trautmann credits not Caldwell but Francis White Ellis, "one of the unknown greats of British Orientalism," with first proving in 1816 that the languages of southern India were not corrupt derivations of Sanskrit, but members of a distinct language family (*Aryans and British India*, 149–50). V. Ravindran discusses the contribution of a loose circle of scholarly missionaries and administrators known as the Madras School of Orientalism in enhancing understanding of the distinctiveness of south Indian peoples from the Aryans of the North: "Discourses of Empowerment: Missionary Orientalism in the Development of Dravidian Nationalism," in *Nation Work: Asian Elites and National Identities*, ed. Timothy Brook and Andre Schmidt, (Ann Arbor: University of Michigan Press, 1999). Nicholas Dirks also has discussed Caldwell's contribution to Dravidian Nationalism in *Castes of Mind*, 134–148.

13. The following brief account of Caldwell's life is drawn from memoirs that he wrote for his family, which were edited and published by his son-in-law, Rev. J. L. Wyatt: *Reminiscences of Bishop Caldwell* (Madras: Addison, 1894).

14. Ibid., 77.

15. Caldwell, *Tinnevelly Shanars*, 12, 13; subsequent references are cited in parentheses.

16. Elmore, *Dravidian Gods in Modern Hinduism*; Whitehead, *The Village Gods of South India*.

17. Sāmiyāṭi is better translated as "god dancer," insofar as *sāmi* is a Tamil word used to describe many different kinds of divine beings. I discuss the implications of Caldwell's inattention to the distinction between pēy and sāmi later in this section.

18. The bows that Caldwell describes were very likely the precursors of the *viḷ* of

the bow-song (viḷpāṭṭu) tradition in contemporary Tamil Nadu. See Stuart Blackburn's well-documented study *Singing of Birth and Death: Texts in Performance* (Philadelphia: University of Pennsylvania, Press 1988).

19. For present-day descriptions of Tamil ritual, see Stuart H. Blackburn, "Death and Deification: Folk Cults in Hinduism," *History of Religions* 24, no.3 (1985): 255–74; Louis Dumont, *A South Indian Subcaste: Social Organization and Religion of the Pramalai Kallar*, trans. Michael Moffatt et al. (Delhi: Oxford University Press, 1986), part 3; Karin Kapadia, *Siva and Her Sisters: Gender, Caste, and Class in Rural South India* (Boulder, CO: Westview, 1995), ch. 6; Marie-Louise Reiniche, *Les Dieux et Les Hommes: Étude des cultes d'un village du Tirunelveli Inde du Sud* (Paris: Mouton Editeur, 1979).

20. Y. Ñāṉamuttu Nāṭār (Gnanamuthoo Nadar), *Cāṉār Cattiriyar* (A polemical treatise maintaining that the Shanars are Kshatriyas, together with a Christian tract, *Irakṣippiṉ piḷāṉ* [Plan of salvation], by the same author) (Madras, 1889), 124 (in English in the original). Located in British Library.

21. This analysis draws on two essays by the Belgian anthropologist Robert Deliège, "Replication and Consensus: Untouchability, Caste and Ideology in India," *Man* 27 (1992): 155–73, and "The Myths of Origin of the Indian Untouchables," *Man* 28 no.3 (1993): 533–49.

22. Thurston and Rangachari, "Paraiyars," in *Castes and Tribes of Southern India*, 6: 89.

23. David Ludden, *Peasant History in South India* (Delhi: Oxford University Press, 1989), 86.

24. Caldwell, *Tinnevelly Shanars*, 40.

25. Ludden, *Peasant History in South India*, 90–91.

26. Ibid., 91.

27. Ibid., 82.

28. Ibid. Ludden cites *Selections from the Records of the Madras Government*, vol. 6, *Correspondence Relative to Proposals for Organizing a Permanent Corps of Coolies* (Madras, 1855), 2–10.

29. After 1750, during Muslim rule of the area, the Arabic term *miras* was used to translate *kāṇi* in the sense of "hereditary rights." The British adopted this usage when they moved into the region. Irschick, *Dialogue and History*, 32; Ludden, *Peasant History in South India*, 86.

30. Irschick, *Dialogue and History*, 32–33; Dharma Kumar, *Land and Caste in South India: Agricultural Labour in the Madras Presidency during the Nineteenth Century* (Cambridge, UK: Cambridge University Press, 1965), 21–22.

31. Samuel Mateer wrote of the Travancore Pulayer slaves in the period before emancipation, "When bought and sold, the agreement specified 'tie and beat, but do not destroy either legs or eyes' " (*Native Life in Travancore*, 58).

32. See James Scott, *Weapons of the Weak: Everyday Forms of Peasant Resistance* (New Haven: Yale University Press, 1985).

33. Stein, *Peasant State and Society*, 212; Irschick, *Dialogue and History*, 55.

34. Mateer, *Native Life in Travancore*, 34.

35. D. Kumar, *Land and Caste in South India*, 48, 232.

36. Forrester, *Caste and Christianity*, 74. For a detailed discussion of the ryotwari settlement, see Ludden, *Peasant History in South India*, 104–114.

37. Mani, "Contentious Traditions," 95.

38. Lloyd I. Rudolph and Susanne Hoeber Rudolph, *The Modernity of Tradition: Political Development in India* (Chicago: University of Chicago Press, 1967); Dirks,

Castes of Mind; Frykenberg, "Constructions of Hinduism," 533–35; Chakravarti, *Rewriting History.*

39. Bernard S. Cohn, "The Census, Social Structure and Objectification in South Asia," in *An Anthropologist among the Historians and Other Essays* (Delhi: Oxford University Press, 1987), 243. Cohn's pioneering work on the Indian census has been extended and expanded by several of his former students, including Arjun Appadurai and Nicholas Dirks. See Appadurai, "Number in the Colonial Imagination," and Dirks, *Castes of Mind,* 198–227. Notwithstanding the profound influence of British colonial rulers and their Brahman pandits, they were not the first or the only people on the Subcontinent to try to fit multiple jatis onto the fourfold varna system. As Wendy Doniger argues, Manu was in essence trying to do the same thing when he identified individual castes as the offspring of intervarna sexual unions (e.g., the "charioteer" [Māgadha] is the son of a "ruler" [Kshatriya] conceived in the daughter of a "priest" [Brahman], while the "fierce untouchable" [Caṇḍāla] is the offspring of a "servant" [Shudra] conceived in the daughter of a "priest"). See book 10 of *The Laws of Manu,* trans. Wendy Doniger and Brian K. Smith (New York: Penguin Books, 1991), 234–40.

40. The fact that British officers were highly dependent on large staffs of "high-caste and learned local assistants, consultants, informants, and investigators" has led historian Robert Frykenberg to conclude that the results of colonial scholarship should be seen as a joint venture. Which parties had the most influence on the final product remains difficult to determine, because, as he notes, the contributions of Indian assistants were often not credited. Frykenberg, "Constructions of Hinduism," 533, 535. Frykenberg introduced this thesis in his ground-breaking book, *Guntur District, 1788–1848: A History of Local Influence and Central Authority in South India* (New York: Oxford University Press, 1965).

41. Eugene Irschick, *Politics and Social Conflict in South India: The Non-Brahman Movement and Tamil Separatism, 1916–1929* (Berkeley: University of California Press, 1969); V. Ravindran, "The Unanticipated Legacy of Robert Caldwell and the Dravidian Movement," *South Indian Studies* 1 no.1 (1996): 83–110; Dirks, *Castes of Mind,* 134–48.

42. Cohn, "Census, Social Structure and Objectification."

43. Appadurai, "Number in the Colonial Imagination," 329.

44. Mateer, *Native Life in Travancore,* 24–25. Mateer's description of the turmoil provoked by the announcement that the census would take place is reminiscent of self-destructive passions unleashed by millennialist movements that announce that the apocalypse is close at hand.

> The enumeration itself caused considerable commotion amongst the people, especially the lower castes. For some months previously the rural population were in a state of complete ferment, dreading that advantage would be taken of the occasion to impose some new tax or to exercise some bitter oppression, as was often done on various occasions in the old times of cruelty and injustice. . . . The Sudras sought to frighten by the report that the Christians were to be carried off in ships to foreign parts, in which the missionaries and their native helpers would assist. When numbers were stamped upon all the houses, people thought that soon they themselves would be branded and seized by the Sirkar. Absurd reports were raised. Some said the Maharajah had promised to supply inhabitants for a country which had been desolated by famine. Others said that a certain number would be shipped off on the 18th May. Till that date the people were whispering "Today or to-morrow

we shall be caught." . . . Many of the people left their gardens uncultivated during the panic, ate up the seed corn, sold their cattle and sheep. One man had ten fowls, and, taking them to a river, he cut off their heads, and threw them away. So dreadful is the ignorance of the people through want of education.

45. E.g., Thomas Turnbull, "Statistical and Geographical Memoir, Maravar or Ramnad, the Isle of Ramiseram and Tondaiman's Country, surveyed in 1814," Mss. India Office Library, London.

46. Hardgrave, *Nadars of Tamilnad*, 275–277, 71–94. This was not a movement restricted solely to India. According to Sattampillai's son, the outraged former catechist translated Caldwell's pamphlet into Tamil and sent it to Shanar communities throughout India, Burma, and Ceylon to make prominent members of this community everywhere aware of the insults to which they had been subjected. A. C. Asiratanadar and T. T. Thomas Nadar, *Shandrar Ethnography* (1912), cited in B. J. M. Kulasekhara-Raj, *Nadar Kula Varalaru: A Brief Account of the Nadar Race* (Palamcottah, 1918), 94–95, cited in Hardgrave, *Nadars of Tamilnad*, 75, n. 10.

47. Most European scholars derived the caste name Shanar from a Tamil word for toddy, *cāṟu*. For a more complete discussion of the various etymological arguments given to explain the name, see Hardgrave, *Nadars of Tamilnad*, 81.

48. S. Winfred, *Shandror Kula Marapu Kattala* (Madras, 1875), 213, cited in ibid., 80. The careers of Rev. Winfred and Rev. A. N. Sattampillai are strikingly similar. Winfred, the first Indian pastor with the AMM, resigned just three years after his ordination in a dispute with the mission over how much "affectionate paternal supervision" the latter should exercise over their Indian pastors. He formally offered his resignation on 15 December 1858, and his relation with the mission was terminated in June of the following year, around the same time that Sattampillai began his Hindu Christian Church in Tirunelveli. Chandler, *Seventy-Five Years in the Madura Mission*, 180–83.

49. CMS Archives, Birmingham University, C I 2/O136/27.

50. Hardgrave, *Nadars of Tamilnad*, 71.

51. The recipients of these letters included W. E. Gladstone, prime minister of England, the archbishop of Canterbury, home secretary of the SPG, viceroy and governor general of India in Council in Calcutta, and the maharaja of Travancore. Gnanamutthoo Nadar, *Cānār Cattiriyar*, 130–140.

52. Ibid., *Cāṇār Cattiriyar*, 4–5, 91–92.

53. Gnanamuthoo to Rev. Robert Caldwell, 14 January 1880, Palamcottah; 123.

54. Gnanamuthoo to Rev. H. W. Tucker, secretary of the SPG, 19 May 1883, Palamcottah; 129.

55. Correspondence between Rev. F. N. Alexander, MA and Y. Gnanamuthoo Nadar, printed in the *Travancore Times*, 20 April, 1 May, and 1 June 1880; 116. See also Birmingham Library archive, C I 2/ O 25/104, for handwritten copies of the original.

56. Gnanamuthoo to Rev. H. W. Tucker, secretary of the SPG, 19 May 1883, Palamcottah; 129.

57. Ibid., 125, citing *CMS Record* for February 1880, 51.

58. Gnanamuthoo to Rev. F. N. Alexander M.A., printed in the *Travancore Times*, 20 April, 1 May, and 1 June 1880, 114, 117.

59. Samuel Sarguner, *Bishop Caldwell and the Tinnevelly Shanars* (Palamcottah: Subramania Pillai, 1883), 5, Gnanamuthoo Nadar included this tract as supplemen-

tary material to a petition asking Prime Minister of India J. W. Gladstone to give his opinion on the issue. Tamil Nadu State Archives, G.O. 1362, Public, 12 July 1883.

60. B. Shobanan, *The Temple Entry Movement and the Sivakasi Riots* (Madurai: Raj, 1985); Breckenridge, "From Protector to Litigant."

61. Hardgrave, *Nadars of Tamilnad*, 92.

62. Kooiman, *Conversion and Social Equality in India*, 155, 156.

63. Rev. Herman Jensen, *A Classified Collection of Tamil Proverbs* (1897; New Delhi: Asian Educational Services, 1997), 44.

64. Dirks, *Castes of Mind*, 71–72.

65. The tendency for the British to reify official Brahmanical understandings of caste was by no means limited to the Madras Presidency. Building on Hiroshi Fuzukawa's history of politics and society in the Deccan, according to which Brahmanical dominance was strengthened by transformations within the precolonial state, Uma Chakravarti makes a compelling case that the further reinforcement of Brahmanical power under colonial rule intensified the oppression of women. Here, too, codes of conduct for women that tended toward the restriction of women's autonomy and mobility were deeply implicated in the ranking of castes in relation to one another. Hiroshi Fuzukawa, *The Medieval Deccan: Peasants, Social Systems and States, Sixteenth to Eighteenth Centuries* (Delhi: Oxford University Press, 1991); Chakravarti, *Rewriting History*.

66. Thurston and Rangachari "Chakkiliyar," in *Castes and Tribes of Southern India*, 2:2.

67. Chakravarti, *Rewriting History*, 52.

68. Mateer, *Land of Charity*,42.

69. Sarguner, *Bishop Caldwell and the Tinnevelly Shanars*, 37.

70. Mateer, *Land of Charity*, 125–126.

71. Caldwell, *Tinnevelly Shanars*, 56.

72. Kooiman, *Conversion and Social Equality in India*, 179.

73. B. S. Baliga, *Tirunelveli*, vol. 13 of *Madras District Gazetteers* (Madras: Government Press, 1957–), 128.

74. Thurston and Rangachari, "Shanars," *Castes and Tribes of Southern India*, 6: 366,363.

75. *Caṭṭampiḷḷai Aiya Kutumbattin piramaccariyamum mangalaviśēśamum* (The celibacy and marriage of Rev. Sattampillai Aiya's family) (Palamcottah: CMS Press, 1905), 13.

76. Hardgrave, *Nadars of Tamilnad*, 133–135.

3: WOMEN'S MISSIONARY SOCIETIES

1. Antoinette Burton, *Burdens of History: British Feminists, Indian Women, and Imperial Culture, 1865–1915* (Chapel Hill: University of North Carolina Press, 1994).

2. Max Weber, *The Protestant Ethic and the Spirit of Capitalism*, trans. Talcott Parsons (1920; New York: Scribner, 1976).

3. Larry Collins and Dominique Lapierre, *Freedom at Midnight* (New York: Simon and Schuster, 1975), 15.

4. See the bibliography for works by Burton, Ramusack, Jayawardena, Grewal, Strobel, Stoler, Forbes, Sinha, and Haggis.

5. Patricia Grimshaw, *Paths of Duty: American Missionary Wives in Nineteenth-Century Hawaii* (Honolulu: University of Hawaii Press, 1989); Jane Hunter, *The Gospel of Gentility: American Women Missionaries in Turn-of-the-Century China* (New Ha-

ven: Yale University Press, 1984); Maina Chawla Singh, *Gender, Religion, and the "Heathen Lands": American Missionary Women in South Asia, 1860s–1940s* (New York: Garland, 2000).

6. Margaret Strobel, "Gender and Race in the Nineteenth- and Twentieth-century British Empire," in *Becoming Visible: Women in European History*, ed. Claudia Koonz et al. (Boston: Houghton-Mifflin, 1987).

7. Percival Spear, *The Nabobs: A Study of the Social Life of the British in Eighteenth Century India* (London: Oxford University Press, 1963), 140, cited in Stoler, "Carnal Knowledge and Imperial Power," 65. Among the most interesting and serious scholarly examples of this approach is Kumari Jayawardena's *The White Woman's Other Burden: Western Women and South Asia During British Rule* (New York: Routledge, 1995).

8. Naupur Chaudhuri and Margaret Strobel, eds., *Western Women and Imperialism* (Bloomington: Indiana University Press, 1992).

9. Jane Haggis, "White Women and Colonialism: Towards a Non-recuperative History," in *Gender and Imperialism*, ed. Clare Midgley (Manchester, UK: Manchester University Press, 1998), 58–60. See also " 'Good Wives and Mothers' or 'Dedicated Workers'? Contradictions of Domesticity in the 'Mission of Sisterhood,' Travancore, South India," in *Maternities and Modernities: Colonial and Postcolonial Experiences in Asia and the Pacific*, ed. Kalpana Ram and Margaret Jolly (Cambridge, UK: Cambridge University Press, 1998): 81–113.

10. Studies that examine the opening up of new career opportunities for educated white women in colonial India include Maneesha Lal, "The Politics of Gender and Medicine in Colonial India: The Countess of Dufferin's Fund, 1885–1888," *Bulletin of the History of Medicine* 1 (1994): 29–60; Patricia R. Hill, *The World Their Household: The American Woman's Foreign Mission Movement and Cultural Transformation, 1870–1920* (Ann Arbor: University of Michigan Press, 1985); Janaki Nair, "Uncovering the Zenana: Visions of Indian Womanhood in Englishwomen's Writings, 1813–1940," *Journal of Women's History* 2 (1990): 8–34.

11. Stoler, "Carnal Knowledge and Imperial Power," 69–73, 70.

12. For a succinct analysis of the place of female sexual honor in the context of British patriarchy, see Mary Poovey, *The Proper Lady and the Woman Writer* (Chicago: University of Chicago Press, 1984), ch. 1.

13. Kenneth Ballhatchet, *Race, Sex and Class under the Raj: Imperial Attitudes and Policies and Their Critics, 1793–1905* (London: Weidenfeld and Nicolson, 1980).

14. Thomas R. Metcalf, *The Aftermath of Revolt: India, 1857–1870* (Princeton: Princeton University Press, 1964), 290.

15. Mrinalini Sinha, " 'Chatams, Pitts, and Gladstones in Petticoats': The Politics of Gender and Race in the Ilbert Bill Controversy, 1883–1884," in Chaudhuri and Strobel, *Western Women and Imperialism*, 98–117.

16. Joseph E. Carpenter, *The Life and Work of Mary Carpenter* (London: Macmillan, 1879), 299, cited in Burton, *Burdens of History*, 555.

17. Ballhatchet has provided a fascinating analysis of this case in his *Race, Sex and Class under the Raj*, 112–16.

18. In her brief consideration of the case, Mrinalini Sinha argues that Miss Pigot was not a Eurasian. Sinha asserts that Hastie identified her wrongly as an illegitimate Eurasian (perhaps as part of his attempt to malign her character). According to newspaper sources of the period, she was the daughter of a planter, James, and his legal wife, Dorothy ("Politics of Gender and Race in the Ilbert Bill Controversy," 105, n. 41).

19. Ibid., 105.

20. Ballhatchet, *Race, Sex and Class under the Raj*, 115, 116.

21. Ibid., 115.

22. *The Harvest Field* (November 1883): 144.

23. Ibid.

24. Gayatri Chakravorty Spivak, "Three Women's Texts and a Critique of Imperialism," in *"Race," Writing and Difference*, ed. Henry Louis Gates Jr. (Chicago: University of Chicago Press, 1986), 263.

25. For a survey of the transformations the idea of separate spheres has gone through, both in U.S. women's history and in scholarship on U.S. women's history, see Linda K. Kerber, "Separate Spheres, Female Worlds, Woman's Place: The Rhetoric of Women's History," *Journal of American History* 75, no. 1 (1988): 9–39.

26. Catherine Hall and Leonore Davidoff *Family Fortunes: Men and Women of the English Middle Class, 1780–1850* (Chicago: University of Chicago Press, 1987).

27. Women's involvement in a number of political and social causes, from temperance to settlement houses, was legitimated by the extension of the concept of separate spheres. For the North American context, see Ian Tyrrell, *Woman's World/ Woman's Empire: The Woman's Christian Temperance Union in International Perspective, 1800–1930* (Chapel Hill: University of North Carolina Press, 1991); Estelle Freedman, "Separatism as Strategy: Female Institution Building and American Feminism, 1870–1930," *Feminist Studies* 5 (fall 1979): 512–29; Kathryn Kish Sklar, "Hull House in the 1890s: A Community of Women Reformers," *Signs* 10 (summer 1985): 658–77.

28. The title of Patricia Hill's history of the women's foreign missionary movement, *The World Their Household*, explicitly makes reference to this.

29. Joan W. Scott, " 'Experience,' " in *Feminists Theorize the Political*, eds. Judith Butler and Joan W. Scott (New York: Routledge, 1992), 22–40.

30. Nayan Shah, "Cleansing Motherhood: Hygiene and the Culture of Domesticity in San Francisco's Chinatown, 1875–1900," in *Gender, Sexuality and Colonial Modernities*, ed. Antoinette Burton (London: Routledge, 1999), 19–34.

31. Mary Carpenter, *Six Months in India* (London: Longman's, Green, 1868), 2: 80, cited in Antoinette Burton, "Fearful Bodies into Disciplined Subjects: Pleasure, Romance, and the Family Drama of Colonial Reform in Mary Carpenter's Six Months in India," *Signs* 20, no. 3 (1995): 564.

32. Elizabeth Cady Stanton, *The Woman's Bible* (1898; Salem, NH: Ayer, 1988).

33. Mrs. E. R. (Emma Raymond) Pitman, *Indian Zenana Missions: Their Need, Origin, Objects, Agents, Modes of Working, and Results* (London: John Snow., n.d. [before 1903]), 26.

34. Annie Wittenmeyer, *Women's Work for Jesus*, 6th ed. 1873; (New York: Garland 1987), 206.

35. Ibid., 208.

36. Jocelyn Murray, "The Role of Women in the Church Missionary Society, 1799–1917," in *The Church Mission Society and World Christianity, 1799–1999*, ed. Kevin Ward and Brian Stanley (Grand Rapids, MI: Eerdman, 2000), 78.

37. For an example of this dimension of women's roles in the mission field, see Hannah Catherine Mullens's portrayal of a genteel missionary wife whose tidy drawing room is itself a witness to the virtues of Christian civilization: *The Missionary on the Ganges: What Is Christianity?* (Calcutta: Calcutta Christian Tract and Book Society, 1856).

38. Patricia Grimshaw, "Conflicts in Roles of American Missionary Women in Nineteenth Century Hawaii," *Feminist Studies* 9, no. 3 (1983): 489–521.

39. Pitman, *Indian Zenana Missions*, 21; Helen Barrett Montgomery, *Western Women in Eastern Lands* (1910; New York: Garland, 1987), 21–23.

40. For instance, the Female Seminary started at the Arcot Mission of the ABCFM was aimed "not to develop excellent scholarship as to fit the girls to become the wives of the Native Christian helpers and teachers and the mothers of a more enlightened Christian generation to come." Mary Chamberlain, *Fifty Years in Foreign Fields: A History of Five Decades of the Women's Board of Foreign Missions Reformed Church in America* (New York: Women's Board of Foreign Missions 1925), 26.

41. Wittenmyer, *Women's Work for Jesus*, 19, 106.

42. Hill, *The World Their Household*, 40.

43. Chamberlain, *Fifty Years in Foreign Fields*, 8; Hill, *The World Their Household*, 36.

44. Geraldine H. Forbes, "In Search of the 'Pure Heathen': Missionary Women in Nineteenth Century India," *Economic and Political Weekly* 21, no. 17 (1986): WS2–WS8; Cecillie Swaisland, "Nineteenth Century Recruitment of Single Women to Protestant Missions," in *Women and Missions: Past and Present*, ed. Fiona Bowie, Deborah Kirkwood, and Shirley Ardener (Oxford: Berg, 1993), 70–84.

45. Swaisland, "Recruitment of Single Women," 72.

46. Appasamy, *The Centenary History of the C.M.S. in Tinnevelly*, 100.

47. Spivak, "Three Women's Texts," 268–69; Hill, *The World Their Household*, 13–18.

48. Jeffrey Cox, "Religion and Imperial Power in Nineteenth-Century Britain," in *Freedom and Religion in the Nineteenth Century*, ed. Richard J. Helmstadter (Stanford: Stanford University Press, 1997), 366.

49. Chandler, *Seventy-Five Years in the Madura Mission*, 310; Hill, *The World Their Household*; F. K. Prochaska, *Women and Philanthropy in Nineteenth-Century England* (Oxford: Clarendon, 1980).

50. At the close of the American Civil War in the 1860s, several U.S. women's missionary societies were formed along denominational lines as extensions of women's church auxiliary groups. These included the Baptist Ladies Missionary Society, Free Baptist Women's Missionary Society, Women's Board of Missions of the Congregational Churches, Methodist Episcopal Women's Foreign Missionary Society, Ladies' Board of Missions (Presbyterian), Women's Union Missionary Society, Women's Foreign Missionary Society (Presbyterian). In England, the societies that supported "women's work" included the London Missionary Society, Baptist Missionary Society, Indian Female Normal School and Instruction Society, Society for Promoting Female Education in the East, and Ladies' Association for Promotion of Female Education (in association with the SPG). Pitman, *Indian Zenana Missions*, 45.

51. *Historical Sketch of the Woman's Board of Missions* ([S.l.]: Woman's Board of Mission co-operating with the American Board of Commissioners for Foreign Missions, [1874],) 12, 15. Available in the History of Women Microfilm Series, reel 939, number 8283.

52. Oddie, *Hindu and Christian in South-East India*, 10.

53. Robert Caldwell, *Reminiscences of Bishop Caldwell* (Madras: Addison 1894), 4–5.

54. R. H. Tawney, *Religion and the Rise of Capitalism* (Gloucester, MA: Peter Smith, 1962), 115, 116–118.

55. E. P. Thompson, *The Making of the English Working Class* (New York: Vintage, 1966), 38.

56. Wittenmyer, *Women's Work for Jesus*, 127.

57. After many years of debate and delay, dissenters won these rights in 1828, Catholics in 1830, and Jews in 1845. Viswanathan, *Outside the Fold*, 5–12; Cox, "Religion and Imperial Power."

58. William Wilberforce, *A Practical View of the Prevailing Religious System of Professed Christians in the Higher and Middle Classes in This Country Contrasted with Real Christianity* (London: T. Cadwell Junior and W. Davies, 1797), 298, cited in Catherine Hall, "The Early Formation of Victorian Domestic Ideology," in *Fit Work for Women*, ed. Sandra Burman (New York: St. Martin's, 1979), 17.

59. Henry Judson, *Mr. Judson's Letter to the Female Members of the Christian Churches in the USA* (Philadelphia, 1832), 7, in Birmingham Library CMS archive, C I 2/o 14 (Tracts and Pamphlets) 5.

60. Information on the millenarian expectations of many missionaries can be found in Charles Forman, "A History of Foreign Mission Theory in America," in *American Missions in Bicentennial Perspective*, ed. Robert Pierce Beaver (South Pasadena, CA.: William Carey Library, 1977), 76; Copley, *Religions in Conflict*; William R. Hutchinson, *Errand to the World: American Protestant Thought and Foreign Missions* (Chicago: University of Chicago Press, 1987).

61. For a discussion of the disagreements of premillennialists and postmillennialists in missionary theory in the United States, see Hutchinson, *Errand to the World*, 112–18; for similar debates in Britain, see Boyd Hilton, *The Age of Atonement: The Influence of Evangelicalism on Social and Economic Thought, 1795–1865* (Oxford: Clarendon, 1988), ch. 1.

62. See, for example, Mrs. Weitbrecht, *Missionary Sketches in North India with Reference to Recent Events* (London: James Nisbet., 1858), ix.

63. See, for example, John S. C. Abbott, *The Mother at Home* (Boston: Crocker and Brewster, 1833), 126.

64. Copley, *Religions in Conflict*, 9.

65. Richard Carwardine, *Transatlantic Revivalism: Popular Evangelicalism in Britain and America, 1790–1865* (Westport, CT: Greenwood, 1978).

66. Hilton, *The Age of Atonement*, 7–8.

67. Copley, *Religions in Conflict*, 8; Hutchinson, *Errand to the World*, 47.

68. Rev. I. W. Charlton, cited in Amy Wilson-Carmichael, *Things as They Are: Mission Work in Southern India* (London: Morgan and Scott, 1904), 111.

69. Melvin E. Dieter, *The Holiness Revival of the Nineteenth Century* (Metuchen, NJ: Scarecrow, 1980), 4.

70. J. C. Pollock, *The Keswick Story* (London: Hodder and Stoughton, 1964), 80.

71. Ibid., chs. 1, 4; Dieter, *Holiness Revival*, 158–62.

72. Quoted in Dieter, *Holiness Revival*, 161.

73. Elisabeth Elliot, *A Chance to Die: The Life and Legacy of Amy Carmichael* (Grand Rapids, MI.: Fleming H. Revell, 1987), 51.

74. Hutchinson, *Errand to the World*, 104.

75. Brauer, "Social Gospel," in *Westminster Dictionary of Church History*, 775.

76. Hutchinson, *Errand to the World*, 104–6.

77. Elliot, *A Chance to Die*; Frank Houghton, *Amy Carmichael of Dohnavur: The Story of a Lover and Her Beloved* (London: SPCK, 1953); Nancy E. Robbins, *Not Forgetting to Sing* (London: Hodder and Stoughton, 1967); Sam Wellman, *Amy Carmichael: A Life Abandoned to God* (Uhrichville, OH: Barbour, 1998); Janet Benge, *Amy Carmichael: Rescuer of Precious Gems* (Seattle, WA: YWAM, 1998); David Jackson, *The Hidden Jewel* (Minneapolis: Bethany House, 1992); Tilakavati Paul, *Emi Kārmaikkal Ammaiyār* (Amy Carmichael the mother) (Vēppēri: Cuvicēśa ūriya nūl nilaiyam, 1980).

78. In the nineteenth century, devadasis were widely reputed to be prostitutes. I cannot go into the controversies over whether or not they should be considered so, but I refer to the reader to three excellent studies: Amrit Srinivasan, "Reform and Revival: The Devadasi and Her Dance," *Economic and Political Weekly* 20, no. 44 (1985): 1869–76; Kersenboom-Story, *Nityasumangali*. Orr, *Donors, Devotees, and Daughters of God*.

79. Elliot, *A Chance to Die*, 29–30; subsequent citations appear in parentheses in the text. All the following biographical information on Amy Carmichael comes from Elisabeth Elliot's excellent biography. Like Carmichael, Elliott was herself was a missionary (in South America) and the author of many books. She thus shares many of Carmichael's theological commitments, but her biography is by far the most comprehensive and critical of all the many books written about Carmichael.

80. Rooden, "Nineteenth-Century Representations of Missionary Conversion and the Transformation of Western Christianity," 71.

81. Even Bartholomaeus Ziegenbalg, with his relatively open attitude toward Indian religion, had at least one outburst of iconoclasm, which has been analyzed with great insight by Hudson in *Protestant Origins in India*, 17–20.

82. David Arnold, *The Problem of Nature: Environment, Culture and European Expansion* (Oxford: Blackwell, 1996), 171.

83. Compare Carmichael's experiences to Hindu stories of "accidental salvation." Narratives of this type characteristically describe how a morally unsavory individual achieves heaven by inadvertently fulfilling the requirements for salvation, often on a special day such as Navarattiri. J. Bruce Long, "Mahasivaratri: The Saiva Festival of Repentance," in *Religious Festivals in South India and Sri Lanka*, ed. Glenn Yocum and Guy Welbon (New Delhi: Manohar, 1982), 189–218; Wendy Doniger, "The Scrapbook of Undeserved Salvation," in *Purana Perennis: Reciprocity and Transformation in Hindu and Jaina Texts*, ed. Wendy Doniger (Albany: State University of New York Press, 1993), 59–64.

84. Copley, *Religions in Conflict*.

85. Carmichael, *Things as They Are*, 8–9.

86. Ibid., 6.

87. Ibid., 8.

88. Amy Carmichael, *Ponnammal: Her Story* (London: Society for Promoting Christian Knowledge, 1918), 20.

89. For example, the authors of the American College survey of Christian communities from the 1930s compared Dohnavur unfavorably with an orphanage founded by one Rev. Athistam in Usilimpatti: "The indigenous methods of life and work that one sees in this orphanage are in striking contrast with what one sees at the settlement of the Dohnavur Fellowship." Ponniah et al., *An Enquiry into the Economic and Social Problems of the Christian Community of Madura*, 179.

90. Interview with Preenapu Carunia, Inba Illam Rest Home, Madurai, 7 October 1996.

91. Ibid.

92. Ibid.

93. Paul, *Emi Kārmaikkal Ammaiyār*, 5.

94. Interview with Preenapu Carunia.

95. Amy Carmichael, *Raj, Brigand Chief* (London: Seeley, Service, 1927), 235–36.

96. Paul, *Emi Kārmaikkal Ammaiyār*, 247.

97. Susan Billington Harper's recent study of the career of the first Indian

bishop, V.S. Azariah, *In the Shadow of the Mahatma*, is far and away the best account of the complex nature of this transfer of authority.

98. *Dallas Morning News*, Sunday Magazine, 21 February 1921, United Theological College Archives, Bangalore (henceforth UTC), Box AMM E/6 13/ folder 3, "Biographical Notes."

99. UTC, "Biographical Notes."

100. Hutchinson, *Errand to the World*, 45.

101. Chandler, *Seventy-Five Years in the Madura Mission*, 306, 56.

102. UTC/ AMM E/6/ 13/ folder 6, "Miss Eva Swift's Notes from her album."

103. Hill, *The World Their Household*, 35.

104. Chandler, *Seventy-Five Years in the Madura Mission*, 309.

105. "Miss Eva Swift's Notes from her album."

106. Ibid.

107. Eva Swift, *The Lucy Perry Noble Institute for Women, 1892–1921*, pamphlet, UTC/ AMM 19/ folder 6, p. 7.

108. Ibid., 6, 7, 32.

109. As studies of missionaries in other colonized countries have shown, the production of Western-style clothing by and for recent Christians served the purposes of colonial expansion both materially and ideologically. See Comaroff and Comaroff, *The Dialectics of Modernity on a South African Frontier*, ch. 5; Cohn, "Cloth, Clothes and Colonialism," in *Colonialism and Its Forms of Knowledge*, 143–44; and ch. 6 of this book.

110. Swift, *The Lucy Perry Noble Institute for Women, 1892–1921*, 17.

111. "Miss Eva Swift's Notes from her album."

112. The philosophy of mission behind this kind of institutional indigenization was articulated most forcefully, and influentially, by Henry Venn, secretary of the CMS from 1841, and Rufus Anderson, secretary of the ABCFM from 1832, although both men had to contend with considerable resistance to their programs from within their institutions. See Hutchinson, *Errand to the World*, 77–90, C. Peter Williams, *The Ideal of the Self-Governing Church: A Study in Victorian Missionary Strategy* (Leiden: E. J. Brill, 1990).

113. Eva Swift, *Miss Swift's Letter No. 11* (Bangalore: Scripture Literature Press, 1931), pamphlet in UTC/ AMM 26, p. 6, 8.

114. Susan Billington Harper, "Ironies of Indigenization: Some Cultural Repercussions of Mission in South India," *Bulletin of Missionary Research* 19 (January 1995): 13–20; Harper, *In the Shadow of the Mahatma*.

115. Harlan P. Beach and Burton St. John, eds., *World Statistics of Christian Missions* (New York: Foreign Missions Conference of North America, 1916), 59. In 1916, 24,039 "foreign staff" were sent around the world by the U.S., British, and European missionary societies. Of these, 7,041 were ordained men, 3,283 were unordained men, 6,992 were wives of missionaries, and 6,727 were unmarried women. Of the 5,465 foreign missionaries stationed in India, 1,629 were ordained men, 414 were unordained men, 1,501 were wives, and 1,921 were unmarried women.

116. Jeffrey Cox, "Independent English Women in Delhi and Lahore, 1860–1947," in *Religion and Irreligion in Victorian Society*, ed. Richard J. Helmstadter (London: Routledge, 1992), 170.

117. Copley, *Religions in Conflict*; Hutchinson, *Errand to the World*.

118. van der Veer, *Conversion to Modernities*.

119. See Homi Bhabha's use of the phrase "not quite/ not white" to convey the

interstitial, hybrid status of educated Indian elites: "Of Mimicry and Men," in *The Location of Culture* (London: Routledge, 1994), 92.

120. Hutchinson, *Errand to the World*, 77–90.

121. Elliot, *A Chance to Die*, 247.

122. Comaroff and Comaroff, *The Dialectics of Modernity on a South African Frontier*, 8.

4: MOTHERHOOD AND THE HOME

1. Hanna Papanek and Gail Minault, eds., *Separate Worlds: Studies of Purdah in South Asia* (Delhi: MO: Chanakya Publications 1982).

2. Nair, "Uncovering the Zenana." Writing of the work that her mother, Kamala Satthianadhan, engaged in as a tutor in the zenanas of royal families in south India in the years after 1906, Padmini Sengupta renders the stereotyped image of the zenana that remained current until at least the 1950s, if not to the present time: "One can imagine especially the dark dismal realm of women, containing child-wives, widows, illiteracy, superstition and ignorance, and the veiled hushed quarters of Purdahnashins into which Kamala literally penetrated, and, to a great extent, dispelled the gloom." Padmini Sengupta, *Portrait of an Indian Woman* (Calcutta: YMCA Publishing House, 1956), 5.

3. Pitman, *Indian Zenana Missions*, 28.

4. Cited in John Murdoch, *The Women of India and What Can Be Done for Them* (Madras: Christian Vernacular Education Society, 1888), 3; also cited in Haggis, " 'Good Wives and Mothers,' " 108.

5. Hill, *The World Their Household*, 35.

6. Davidoff and Hall, *Family Fortunes*.

7. Much of the scholarly literature that addresses the significance of Western ideals of domesticity in colonial settings has been done by Africanists. Jean Comaroff and John Comaroff's theoretically sophisticated essay, "Homemade Hegemony," in *Ethnography and the Historical Imagination* (Boulder, CO.: Westview, 1992) serves as a good introduction to this body of work. A volume of essays collected by Karen Tranberg Hansen provides several excellent case studies examining the reorganization of African society under the influence of Western notions of separate spheres for men and women: *African Encounters with Domesticity* (New Brunswick, NJ: Rutgers University Press, 1992). Work on domesticity in colonial south Asia includes Mary Hancock, "Gendering the Modern: Women and Home Science in British India," in *Gender, Sexuality and Colonial Modernities*, ed. Antoinette Burton (London: Routledge, 1999), 148–60; Malathi de Alwis, "The Production and Embodiment of Respectability: Gendered Demeanours in Colonial Ceylon," in *Sri Lanka: Collective Identities Revisited*, ed. Michael Roberts (Columbo: Marga Institute [Sri Lanka Center for Development Studies], 1997), 105–43.

8. *Report of the Second Decennial Missionary Conference Held in Calcutta, 1882–83* (Calcutta, 1883), 210–11.

9. Thompson, *The Making of the English Working Class*, 365. See also Tawney, *Religion and the Rise of Capitalism*, 109.

10. See Partha Chatterjee, "The Nationalist Resolution of the Women's Question," in *Recasting Women: Essays in Indian Colonial History*, ed. Kumkum Sangari and Sudesh Vaid (New Delhi: Kali for Women, 1989).

11. Comaroff and Comaroff, "Homemade Hegemony," 291.

12. See, for example, Murdoch, *Women of India*, 91.

13. Leigh Minturn, *Sita's Daughters: Coming Out of Purdah* (New York: Oxford University Press, 1993), 75.

14. Papanek and Minault, *Separate Worlds*; Minturn, *Sita's Daughters*; Gloria Goodwin Raheja and Ann Grodzins Gold, *Listen to the Heron's Words: Reimagining Gender and Kinship in North India* (Delhi: Oxford University Press, 1996); Lindsey Harlan, *Religion and Rajput Women: The Ethic of Protection in Contemporary Narratives* (Berkeley: University of California Press, 1992).

15. Uma Chakravarti, "Conceptualizing Brahmanical Purity in Early India: Gender, Caste, Class and State," *Economic and Political Weekly* 28, no.14 (3 April 1993): 581.

16. Doniger and Smith, *The Laws of Manu*, 198.

17. Chakravarti, "Conceptualizing Brahmanical Purity," 579.

18. Nur Yalman, "On the Purity of Women in the Castes of Ceylon and Malabar," *Journal of the Royal Anthropological Institute of Great Britain and Ireland* 93, no.1 (1963): 42.

19. A. K. Ramanujan, *The Interior Landscape* (Bloomington: Indiana University Press, 1975).

20. Quoted in Murdoch, *Women of India*, 95.

21. Quoted in ibid., 91.

22. There are now several significant studies of the "women's question" in the Indian social reform movements. The essys in the volume edited by Kumkum Sangari and Sudesh Vaid, *Recasting Women: Essays in Colonial History* (New Delhi: Kali for Women, 1989) represent a high point in this scholarship; in this volume, Partha Chatterjee's "The Nationalist Resolution of the Women's Question" has been especially influential in providing a compelling explanation for why questions having to do with women dropped out of the nationalist agenda after 1890. Also excellent is Radha Kumar's *The History of Doing: An Illustrated Account of Movements for Women's Rights and Feminism in India, 1800–1990* (New Delhi: Kali for Women, 1993).

23. Quoted in Murdoch, *Women of India*, 92.

24. While Mullick seems to suggest that purdah was a necessary and effective means of protecting women, others argued that it only provided the appearance of propriety. In his "Observations on the State of Society among the Asiatic Subjects (1792)," Charles Grant wrote, "Imperious dominion, seclusion and terror, are the means . . . used to enforce the fidelity of the wife. But opportunities of guilt are not wanting. In the hours of business, men are generally at a distance from the retirements of the women; they are often, and for considerable periods, far from home; females, who are the great instruments of corrupting their own sex, are permitted access to the zenanas; besides the Hindoo laws allow women to converse with Soneassees [*sannyasis*], a set of vagrant devotees, some them most indecent in their appearance. The consequences are such as might be expected" (60).

25. Poovey, *The Proper Lady and the Woman Writer*, ch. 1.

26. For Judge Mullick, another of the "conditions" necessary for the emancipation of women was a change in dress styles. Decrying the gossamer-thin fabrics then fashionable in Bengal, he wrote, "Emancipation is impossible, so long as the female is not decently clad. As it is, the dress of our females [only] partially covers their nudity." Cited in Murdoch, *Women of India*, 93.

27. Ibid., 95.

28. Julia Leslie, *The Perfect Wife: The Orthodox Hindu Woman According to the Stridharmapaddhati of Tryambakajivan* (New Delhi: Oxford University Press, 1989).

29. The phrase "symbolic shelter" is Hanna Papanek's, in Papanek and Minault, *Separate Worlds*.

30. Meredith Borthwick, *The Changing Role of Women in Bengal, 1849–1905* (Princeton: Princeton University Press, 1984), 61.

31. John Anderson, an educationist and minister of the Free Church of Scotland in Bengal, described the caste prejudice that prevented intercaste schools as "a wall of brass [that was] not to be scaled in the present state of the country." (Miss) C. Rainey, *A Visit to Our Indian Mission Field* (Paisley, Scotland: J. and R. Parlane, 1887), 71.

32. Jeyaraj, "Halle-Danish (Tranquebar) Mission," 11.

33. Hough, *The History of Christianity in India*, 5: 366.

34. Caldwell, *Records of the Early History of the Tinnevelly Mission*, 209, 220.

35. Although the distinctive combination of needlework and literacy training does seem to have been initiated by the zenana missions in Bengal, the official narrative belies the importance of earlier experiments that took place in the south perhaps as early as the eighteenth century. In 1844, Rev. John Devasahayam (an Indian Christian pastor whose daughter's influential book, *Nalla Tāy*, we shall examine shortly), suggested to Miss C. C. Giberne of the CMS, the first single lady missionary to Tamil Nadu (who had worked previously in Sri Lanka with the Society for Female Education), that she employ elderly Christian women to evangelize to non-Christian Indian women in their homes. This method had evidently enjoyed some success earlier in the Christian coastal settlement of Tranquebar. Appasamy, *The Centenary History of the C.M.S.*, 101.

36. S. N. Mukherjee, "Class, Caste and Politics in Calcutta, 1815–1838," in *Calcutta: Essays in Urban History* (Calcutta: Subarnarekha, 1993), 125–28.

37. Mrs. Winter, "Missions to Women, by a Missionary's Wife," in *Report of the General Missionary Conference, Allahabad, 1872–73* (London: Seeley, Jackson, and Halliday, 1873), 153; Pitman, *Indian Zenana Missions*, 20.

38. Within a few months the school expanded to other households so that Mullens could claim 150 students, 80 women and 70 girls. Pitman, *Indian Zenana Missions*, 21. Mrs. Mullens herself was the author of numerous books that were translated into Indian vernaculars and became staples of the zenana missionary curriculum: *Phulmani and Karuna* (1852), *What Is Christianity?* (1856), and *Daybreak in Britain* (n.d.).

39. Borthwick, *Changing Role of Women in Bengal*, 105, 73.

40. For a thoroughly engaging examination of the place of needlework in European gender discourse, see Rozcika Parker, *The Subversive Stitch: Embroidery and the Making of the Feminine* (London: Women's Press, 1984).

41. Alwis, "The Production and Embodiment of Respectability," 119.

42. Mary Chamberlain, *Fifty Years in Foreign Fields: A History of Five Decades of the Women's Board of Foreign Missions Reformed Church in America* (New York: Women's Board of Foreign Missions, 1925), 28.

43. Cited in Murdoch, *Women of India*, 52; see also Eleanor McDougall, "A Tour of Enquiry into the Education of Women and Girls in India, 1912–1913," in *International Review of Missions, 3, 1914* (Edinburgh: International Review of Missions, 1914), 117–18.

44. Borthwick, *Changing Role of Women in Bengal*, 73–85.

45. Henry Stanley Newman, *Days of Grace in India: A Record of Visits to Indian Missions* (London: S.W. Partridge, n.d.), 315.

46. Elliot, *A Chance to Die*, 100.

47. A.L.O.E. [Charlotte Tucker], *The Zenana Reader* (Madras: Christian Vernacular Education Society for India, 1880); A.D., *Until the Shadows Flee Away: The Story of the CEZMS in India and Ceylon* (London: Church of England Zenana Missionary So-

ciety, 1912), 69. Miss Tucker's pseudonym stood for "A Lady of England." In addition to being a CEZMS missionary in Batala, she authored a popular series of English children's books which shared with much children's literature of the time a propensity for sentimentality and simple moral lessons. Many thanks to Mari Shopsis for alerting me to A.L.O.E.'s metropolitan significance.

48. A.L.O.E. [Charlotte Tucker], *Zenana Reader*, 15, 34.

49. Murdoch, *Women of India*, 27–28.

50. One of my Tamil teachers in India refused to read the text with me after two sessions. Given by the author's ungrammatical use of Tamil and many awkwardly forced translations, he regarded the book as a poorly written collection of clichés and generalities.

51. Tamil poetry has established schemas for distinguishing the different stages of life of a female heroine. According to one of them the stages proceed in this way: *pētai* (5–7 years old), *petumbai* (8–11), *maṅkai* (12–13), *maṭantai* (14–19), *arivai* (20–25), *terivai* (26–31), *pērilampeṇ* (32–40). M. Winslow, "*paruvam,*" in *A Comprehensive Tamil and English Dictionary* (1862; New Delhi: Asian Educational Series, 1987).

52. Mary P. Ryan, *The Empire of the Mother: American Writing about Domesticity, 1830–1860* (New York: Haworth, 1982), ch. 2, 21–29, 34.

53. Annal Satthianadhan, *Nalla Tāy* (The good mother) (1862; Madras: Christian Literature Society for India, 1921), 6, 1 (my translation).

54. Ibid., 7: "Tāyvārttaiyai mīrakūṭātu; taṭuttu maruttu tarkkam pēcakkūṭātu; tāy oru vārttai pēca, piḷḷaikaḷ ataṟku nūṟu vārttai pāṭakkūṭātu."

55. Ibid., 2: "Maram siru karnāyirukkumpōtē [atai] valaikkavēṇṭum; muṟṟiṉapiraku eṉṉa pirayācappaṭṭālum valaiyamāṭṭātu."

56. John Devasahayam was a minister with the CMS and an accomplished scholar who was literate in both German and English. He translated several works from German into Tamil, including "Christ's Passion," "Golden Treasury," and "Spiritual Refreshment." Krupabai Satthianadhan, *Miscellaneous Writings* (Madras: Srinivasa, Varadachari, 1896), 78.

57. Satthianadhan, *Nalla Tāy*, 2. Rev. Herman Jensen collected a similar proverb (number 3303): "Ceṭiyilē vaṇaṅkātatu, marattil vaṇaṅkumā?" (Can you bend in the tree what was not bent in the sapling?) *A Classified Collection of Tamil Proverbs*, 366.

58. Satthianadhan, *Nalla Tāy*, 5.

59. Ibid., 3: "Nām tēṭukiṟa āsti bāsti aṉrum nammōṭukūṭa varamāṭṭātu; kātarunta ūciyum nammōṭu kaṭaiciyil varātē. Āṉāl nammuṭaiya piḷḷaikaḷ māttiram nammōṭukūṭa varuvārkaḷ; avarkaḷ immaikkum maṟummaikkum nammuṭaiyavarkaḷ."

60. Many thanks to P.R. Subramaniyan for this insight.

61. See Rainey, *Visit to Our Indian Mission Field*, 71.

62. This point is made effectively in the two existing scholarly studies of Bible women in English: Forbes, "In Search of the 'Pure Heathen';" Haggis, " 'Good Wives and Mothers,' " See also Eliza F. Kent "Tamil Bible Women and the Zenana Missions of Colonial South India," *History of Religious* 39, 2 (November 1999): 117–149.

63. Mary Chamberlain makes a distinction between zenana workers and Bible women in her history of Women's Board of Foreign Missions (WBFM), "The Bible woman went out into the villages, preached by the roadside, talked to the women who gathered to draw water from the tanks and wells. The Zenana worker went into the homes, had regular pupils, taught secular studies, plain and fancy needle-work and gave lessons in the Bible." *Fifty Years in Foreign Fields*, 57. In her novel, originally entitled *Saguna: A Story of Native Christian Life* (Madras: Srinivasa, Varadachari; 1895), Krupabai Satthianadhan suggests that Indian Christian women employed by the mis-

sion worked as both outdoor preachers and zenana teachers and represents them as powerful public speakers who brought the gospel to life in a compelling fashion, even if they were not themselves above gossiping about their Western missionary patrons. Chandani Lokugé, ed., *Saguna: The First Autobiographical Novel in English by an Indian Woman* (Delhi: Oxford University Press, 1998), 102–106.

64. Prochaska, *Women and Philanthropy* 126.

65. E. Platt, *The Story of the Ranyard Mission, 1857–1937* (London: Hodder and Stoughton, 1937), quoted in Peter Williams, "The Missing Link: The Recruitment of Women Missionaries in Some English Evangelical Missionary Societies in the Nineteenth Century," in *Women and Missions: Past and Present Anthropological and Historical Perceptions*, ed. Fiona Bowie, Deborah Kirkwood, and Shirley Ardener (Oxford: Berg, 1993), 47.

66. Among the most illuminating descriptions of Bible women's work are those given by women missionaries at the decennial General Missionary Conferences, which brought together missionaries from a wide spectrum of societies to share techniques, philosophies, and methods of evangelization. Miss Winter, Miss Brittan, and Rev. D. Herron, "Missions to Women," in *Report of the General Missionary Conference, Allahabad, 1872–1873*, (London: Seeley, Jackson and Halliday, 1873), 153–169; Miss Etherington, Miss Greenfield, Miss Joseph, and Mrs. Lewis, "Work among Women," in *Report of the Second Decennial Missionary Conference, Calcutta, 1882–83*, 197–216; Mrs. Bissel, "Work among Women," in *Report of the Third Decennial Missionary Conference, Bombay, 1892–1893* (Bombay: Education Society's Steam Press, Byculla, 1893), 322–24.

67. Pitman, *Indian Zenana Missions*, 38.

68. Eva M. Swift, *A Bible School in Madura, S. India* (Madras: Addison, 1895), pamphlet, UTC, AMM 19/ folder 6.

69. Krupabai Satthianadhan, *Saguna*, 102.

70. UTC/AMM 19/Folder 6.

71. Sumanta Banerjee, "Marginalization of Women's Popular Culture in Nineteenth Century Bengal," in Sangari and Vaid, *Recasting Women*, 153.

72. Besides the Vaishnavis of Bengal, consider, for example, the descriptions of Basavis of Kannada-speaking regions and the Matangis of the Telegu-speaking regions in Thurston and Rangachari, *Castes and Tribes of Southern India*, vol 5. 1–7.

73. Eva M. Swift, *The Madura Letter No. 4* (April 1916), pamphlet, UTC/ AMM 19/ folder 6.

74. Ibid.

75. See Thurston and Rangachari, *Castes and Tribes of Southern India*.

76. Speaking of a village in the Madras Presidency around 1910, Mary Chamberlain writes, "There seemed to be many secret disciples in Chittoor, people who confessed in their hearts that Jesus was the true Son of God, but who had not the courage to give up home, husband, children, kindred, reputation, and everything that they held dear in life for this new religion" (*Fifty Years in Foreign Fields*, 163). One finds a wealth of information on Secret Christians in the dissertation on Nadar women in Sivakasi by A. Nageswari, "A Study of Social Change among the Nadars of Tamil Nadu (with Special Reference to Women)" (Ph.D. diss., Bangalore University, 1994).

77. Nair, "Uncovering the Zenana."

78. *Dallas Morning News*, 21 February 1921, newspaper clipping, UTC/ AMM E/ 6/ folder 3 (biographical notes).

79. Handwritten Bible women's reports in UTC/ AMM 26.

80. See Ann Gold's exploration of how one Rajasthani woman defines purdah

according to her changing needs and life circumstances: "Purdah Is as Purdah's Kept: A Storyteller's Story," in Gold and Raheja, *Listen to the Heron's Words*, 164–81.

81. Handwritten report by Y. Jesuvadiyal, UTC/ AMM 26 (translation mine).

82. Eva Swift, *The Lucy Perry Noble Institute for Women, 1892–1921*, pamphlet, UTC/ AMM 19/ folder 6, p. 38.

83. Ibid., 17, 35

84. Eva Swift, *A Bible School in Madura, S. India* (Madras: Addison, 1895), pamphlet, UTC/ AMM 19/ folder 6, p. 9.

85. *The Missionary Herald*, November 1931, newspaper clipping, UTC/ AMM E/ 6/ folder 3 (biographical notes).

86. Mrs. E. Himmelstrand cited in Ponniah et al., *An Enquiry into the Economic and Social Problems of the Christian Community of Madura*, 50.

5: CIVILIZATION AND SEXUALITY

1. See recent works by Viswanathan, *Outside the Fold*, ch. 3, and Meera Kosambi, "Gender Reform and Competing State Controls over Women: The Rakhmabai Case (1884–1888)," in *Social Reform, Sexuality and the State*, ed. Patricia Uberoi (New Delhi: Sage, Contributions to Indian Sociology Occasional Studies No. 7 1996), 265–90.

2. For an insightful Foucauldian analysis of mission boarding schools in Sri Lanka, see Alwis, "The Production and Embodiment of Respectability."

3. Mr. Chamberlain cited in Mary Chamberlain, *Fifty Years in Foreign Fields*, 87.

4. John Chandler reports that in 1847 the dowry provided for students was fixed at Rs. 45. The following articles could be substituted for a money payment: 1 large brass pot for water, Rs. 5; 1 brass sembu, Rs. 1–8; 1 brass lamp, Rs. 3; 2 brass plates, Rs. 3; 2 couches, Rs. 10; 2 cloths, Rs. 8; 1 hardwood chair, Rs. 3–8; 2 chairs, Rs. 6; cash Rs. 5; total, Rs. 45. A Bible and two hymn books were given in addition (*Seventy-Five Years in the Madura Mission*, 58).

5. Archives of the SPG, Rhodes College, Oxford, D5, Madras, 1855–1859.

6. In the Indian Christian Marriage Act of 1872, the age of consent for both parties was raised to 18. Tamil Nadu State Archives (henceforth TNSA), G.O. 539–540, Public Dept., 28 July 1909, Memorandum on Marriage and Divorce Laws of Native Christians (henceforth Memorandum on Marriage and Divorce), 29.

7. TNSA, G.O. 5–11, Legislative Dept., 9 April 1872, Christian Marriage Bill: The Opinions of the Advocate General, the Lord Bishop of Madras, the Rev. Dr. Caldwell, and certain Roman Catholic Bishops on the Native Christian Marriage Bill, and the observations of Govt. thereon, submitted to the Govt. of India.

8. TNSA, G.O. 165, Ecclesiastical Dept., 17 December 1888, Indian Christian Marriage Act, 1872.

9. Memorandum on Marriage and Divorce, 4.

10. Viswanathan, *Outside the Fold*, 17.

11. Ibid., 77–82, 103.

12. "Hindoo Converts to Christianity," *Weekly Reporter, Appellate High Court, containing decisions of the Appellate High Court in all its branches, viz, in Civil, Revenue and Criminal Cases, as well as in Cases referred by the Mofussil Small Cause Courts; together with Letters in Criminal Cases, and the Civil and Criminal Circular Orders, issued by the High Court; also Decisions of H.M.'s Privy Council in cases heard in appeal from the Courts of British India*, ed. D. Sutherland (Calcutta: Messrs Thacker, Spink., 1864), 1:1.

13. *Lopez v. Lopez* (1885) Indian Law Reports, Calcutta Series, Vol. 12, 724, 730.

14. *Saldanha v. Saldanha.* (1929) I.L.R. 54 Allahabad 288.

15. In his unpublished dissertation, Chandra S. Mallampalli argues that *Abraham v. Abraham* was an exception to the Madras High Court's trend of applying fixed legal standards to Indian Christians from a variety of different communities: "Contending with Marginality: Christians and the Public Sphere in Colonial South India," (Ph.D. diss., University of Wisconsin-Madison, 2000). He looks mainly at the understanding of the necessary components of a valid Christian marriage ceremony, as specified by the Indian Christian Marriage Act (XV) of 1872. We are in agreement that the courts struggled constantly with the problem of where to locate Indian Christians within the emerging categories of personal law devised over the decades for different communities within India. In addition, it could be that at least the judiciary came to see the Indian Christians as completely "Christianized" around the turn of the century. But according to my research, as late as 1908 the Public Department of the Madras Presidency issued an order upholding the ruling in *Abraham v. Abraham* that the personal law that should govern the definition of "incestuous marriage" ought to be the personal law of the communities to which the marrying parties belong, not the ecclesiastical law of England. TNSA G.O. 122, Public 1906, 19 February 1906 and G.O. 675, Public, 12 September 1906, Marriage among Native Christians under the Indian Christian Marriage Act XV of 1872.

16. Viswanathan, *Outside the Fold*, 80, 82.

17. "Hindoo Converts to Christianity," 7.

18. For a lucid discussion of the history of English divorce law, see Colin Gibson, *Dissolving Wedlock* (London: Routledge, 1994), chs. 1, 2, and 3.

19. In his novel *Hard Times* (1854; New York: Penguin, 1995), Charles Dickens conveyed a poignant sense of the difficulties English divorce law presented for people in unhappy marriages through the character of good, hard-working Stephen Blackpool inextricably bound to a drunken wretch of a wife (67–80).

20. Joseph Jackson, review, *Law Quarterly Review* (1969), cited in Gibson, *Dissolving Wedlock*, 10.

21. Memorandum on Marriage and Divorce, 2.

22. Ibid., 5.

23. Consider, for example, the furious response of the lieutenant governor of the Northwestern Provinces in 1878 to the claim that censorship acts explicitly directed at the native press were contrary to liberal principles of government because they were prejudiced against Indians: "The time has come for us to cease from putting our heads in a bush and shouting that black is white. We all know that in point of fact black is *not* white. . . . That there should be one law alike for the European and Native is an excellent thing in theory, but if it could really be introduced in practice we should have no business in the country." Quoted in Anil Seal, *The Emergence of Indian Nationalism* (Cambridge, UK: Cambridge University Press, 1968), 144.

24. Memorandum on Marriage and Divorce, 7–10.

25. Ibid., 6.

26. Doniger and Smith, *The Laws of Manu*, 9: 80–85, 77–79, 45.

27. Memorandum on Marriage and Divorce, 17.

28. Ibid., 17, 19.

29. Domger and Smith, *The Laws of Mann*, 9:14.

30. See Joseph Alter's essay on present-day advocates of celibacy, "Celibacy, Sexuality and the Transformation of Gender into Nationalism in North India," *Journal of Asian Studies* 53 no.1 (1994): 45–66.

31. Memorandum on Marriage and Divorce, 21.

32. TNSA, G.O. 94, Ecclesiastical Dept., 16 April 1875, Opinions solicited re: bill to punish breaches of monogamous marriage contracts.

33. Ibid.

34. See Peter J. Bowler, *The Invention of Progress: The Victorians and the Past* (Oxford: Basil Blackwell, 1989).

35. See Nicholas Dirk's discussion of H. H. Risley's decision to list the castes enumerated in the Census of India according to rank or precedence and the controversies that ensued: *Castes of Mind*, 212–224.

36. Nicholas B. Dirks, "The Original Caste: Power, History and Hierarchy in South Asia," *Contributions to Indian Sociology*, 23 no. 1 (1989): 59–77.

37. See Janaki Nair's excellent discussion on the passage of Acts that gradually undermined the legal and material basis of matriliny under the Marumakkathayam and Aliyasanthana law in Malabar and South Canara: *Women and Law in Colonial India* (Delhi: Kali for Women, 1996), 146–163.

38. For a concise historical survey of the family, see Eleanor Jackson, "Caste, Culture and Conversion from the Perspective of an Indian Christian Family based in Madras, 1863–1906," available at www.multifaithnet.org/mfnopenaccess/research/online/drafts/ejcaste.htm.

39. Paul Appasamy, *The Centenary History of the C.M.S. in Tinnevelly*, 102.

40. Samuel Satthianadhan, *The Rev. W. T. Satthianadhan: A Brief Biographical Sketch* (Madras: Society for the Propagation of Christian Knowledge, 1893), 2.

41. D. S. Batley, *Indian Christians: Biographical and Critical Sketches* (Madras: G.A. Natesan, 1928), 42.

42. S. Satthianadhan, *W. T. Satthianadhan*, 16. As an old man, W. T. Satthianadhan returned after the death of his wife to live in his ancestral village, Sindapundari, to witness to his relations, who for the most part had remained Hindu. He even bequeathed his ancestral home to the CMS to be used as a base for evangelizing among his relations. It's tempting to hypothesize that he wanted to restore some of the familial bonds that had been compromised through his conversion 33.

43. Satthianadhan, *Miscellaneous Writings*, 55, 61.

44. The new family constituted through conversion to Christianity is reminiscent of the "family" of devotees so important in Saiva and Vaishnava Bhakti traditions. In Bhakti as well, an individual's connections to his or her biological family are severed in favor of new bonds that connect him or her to the family of devotees organized around the worship of Vishnu or Shiva. See Norman Cutler, *Songs of Experience: The Poetics of Tamil Devotion* (Bloomington: Indiana University Press, 1987), 132.

45. Rhenius was actually fired from the CMS after a protracted dispute over many ecclesiastical and theological issues, particularly his unauthorized ordination of several Indian ministers, contrary to the Anglican practice of granting only bishops the right to ordain. Appasamy, *The Centenary History of the C.M.S. in Tinnevelly*, 61–68.

46. Satthianadhan, *Miscellaneous Writings*, 81.

47. W. T. and Anna Satthianadhan arranged two such prestigious marriages for their son, Samuel, a professor of law and prolific writer who was educated in England. In 1881 Samuel married Krupabai (the author of the works we are examining), the daughter of the first Brahman converts to Christianity in the Bombay Presidency. In 1898, several years after his first wife's death, he married Kamala, the daughter of English-educated Brahman converts to Christianity from the Telegu-speaking part of the Madras Presidency, who was also an author. Kamala Satthianadhan wrote, with

her husband, *Stories of Indian Christian Life* (Madras: Srinivasa, Varadachari, 1898) and was a contributor to the English-language periodical *Indian Ladies Magazine*.

48. See Lionel Caplan's incisive sociological analysis of the ramifications in Madras in the 1980s of the hegemony of high-caste Christians within the Church: *Class and Culture in Urban India: Fundamentalism in a Christian Community* (Oxford: Clarendon, 1987).

49. Batley, *Indian Christians*, 45.

50. Ibid., 46.

51. S. Satthianadhan, *Rev. W. T. Satthianadhan*, 25.

52. S. Satthianadhan, *Rev. W. T. Satthianadhan*, 56-61. Conflict between Indian clergy and the missionaries surfaced continually over the question of salaries. Not only were Indian clergy paid far less than Western missionaries were, but educated Indian clergy were paid far less than were their peers who worked for the state. See Graham Houghton's investigation of this issue within the CMS. *The Impoverishment of Dependency: The History of the Protestant Church in Madras, 1870-1920* (Madras: Christian Literature Society, 1983), 26-29.

53. S. Satthianadhan, *Rev. W. T. Satthianadhan*, 58.

54. CMS Archives, Birmingham University, Birmingham, letter from Robert Meadows to Corresponding Committee, 7 February 1871, C I 2/ O 162/10; and his personal file C I 2/ o 211/ 1-42.

55. S. Satthianadhan, *Rev. W. T. Satthianadhan*, 59.

56. Satthianadhan and Satthianadhan, *Stories of Indian Christian Life*, v.

57. For example, Miss Greenfield, missionary in Lodiana, in the pamphlet *Sons of God, Slaves of the Money Lender: An Appeal to Indian Christians against Getting into Debt* (Madras: Christian Literature Society, 1893), bemoaned the fact that "recently baptized converts think that the clothes they wore as heathen are coarse and ugly, and instead of the useful homespun cloth they formerly wore, they want to air themselves in fine muslin or calico of the English make."

58. Chandani Lokugé has recently edited the novel, providing an excellent preface that locates the author in the context of postcolonial literature: *Saguna: The First Autobiographical Novel in English by an Indian Woman*. The work was originally published in serial form in the *Madras Christian College Magazine* in 1887-1888. It was published as a book by the Madras publishing company Srinivasa, Varadachari, and Company in 1895, one year after her death, as *Saguna: A Story of Native Christian Life* by Mrs. S. Satthianadhan. In 1896 it was translated into Tamil. In subsequent citations, I cite the page numbers from the more accessible 1998 edition.

59. Hardgrave, *The Nadars of Tamilnad*, 45-46.

60. Vincent Kumaradoss, "Negotiating Colonial Christianity: The Hindu Christian Church of Late Nineteenth Century Tirunelveli," *South Indian Studies* 1, no. 1 (1996): 39. Korkai holds a significant place in Tamil history as the legendary site where the three brothers Cēran, Cōlan, and Pāṇṭiyan (personifications of the three great Tamil dynasties) were said to have been born. To non-Brahman activists it is thus important as the "cradle of South Indian civilization." Caldwell, *A Political and General History of the District of Tinnevelly*, 283.

61. Arthur Margöschis, "Christianity and Caste," *Indian Church History Review* 6. (October 1893): 540.

62. M. Thomas Thangaraj, "The History and Teachings of the Hindu-Christian Community Commonly Called Nattu Sabai in Tirunelveli," *Indian Church History Review* 5, no. 1 (1971): 46. The role of *saṭṭampiḷḷai*, or monitor, derived from the English

method of education, whereby a senior boy in a classroom would be assigned to supervise and tutor his juniors.

63. Margöschis, "Christianity and Caste," 540.

64. Neill, *A History of Christianity in India*, 214.

65. Kumaradoss, "Negotiating Colonial Christianity," 40.

66. Hardgrave, *Nadars of Tamilnad*, 73.

67. Margöschis, "Christianity and Caste," 539–40.

68. Thangaraj, "History and Teachings," 47.

69. Caldwell, *The Tinnevelly Shanars*, 63.

70. Archive of the SPG, Rhodes College, Oxford (henceforth SPG archive), C/IND/MADRAS/8, Caemmerer, copy of letter to C. S. Kohlhoff, secretary of the Madras Diocese Corresponding Committee, Nazareth, 8 August 1857. Other sources confirm this impression of Rev. Swamiadian as a powerful leader not above using force or coercion. The author of a tract condemning idolatry by "backsliding" members of the various churches in Nazareth area wrote that in 1851, Swamiadian "knocked out the teeth of the last sorcerer who was left in Mukkuppiri, plundered his property, and drove him out of town." Sintr Sandana Nadar, *Māntiriya avapaktiyaip parriya ōr upaniyāsam* (A lecture on witchcraft), (Palamcottah: Darling Press, 1915), 10

71. Hardgrave, *Nadars of Tamilnad*, 74; SPG archive, C/IND/MADRAS/8, Caemmerer, copy of letter to Kohlhoff.

72. *Report of the Proceedings of the Church Missionary Society for the Year 1858* (London: Church Missionary Society, 1859), 271.

73. Appasamy, *The Centenary History of the C.M.S. in Tinnevelly*, 130. Scholars as well as missionary observers have noted the decline of the church even before its founder's death in 1918. The schismatic community was itself divided by a number of internal schisms, which are narrated with great poignancy in the later tracts of the founder. In 1893, Margöschis reported that it had only nine hundred adherents. However, as a testament to the continuing relevance of some part of Sattampillai's message, whether the extreme caste solidarity or the "syncretic," "indigenized" understanding of Christianity, the Hindu Christian Church continues to exist to the present day, under the name of the Indian Church of the One Saviour. It has been known by several names in the course of its history: the *Nāṭṭār sapai* (the National Church), *Eka Irakṣasiya Intiya sapai* (The Indian Church of the One Savior), *Sattampiḷḷai Vēdam*, Jehovah Messianism, and the Hindu Christian Church. Vincent Kumaradoss notes that there are four active congregations in Tirunelveli district and branches in Coimbatore, Madras (Chennai), and Salem ("Negotiating Colonial Christianity," 39). With Prof. Kumaradoss's help, I had the privilege of attending Saturday Sabbath service in the branch church in Chennai in January 1997.

74. Cohn, "Clothes Caste, and Colonialism," 141; Frykenberg, "Roads and Riots in Tinnevelly."

75. Caldwell cited in Joseph Mullens, *A Brief Review of Ten Years' Missionary Labour in India, between 1852–1861* (London: James Nisbet, 1863), 52.

76. Sattampillai cited as scriptural basis for this view Matthew 5:17–19 and Luke 24: 44–48. A. N. Sattampillai, *A Brief Sketch of the Hindu Christian Dogmas* (Palamcottah: Shanmuga Vilasam, 1890), 1.

77. *Caṭṭampiḷḷai Aiya kuṭumbattin piramaccariyamum maṅgalaviśēśamum* (The celibacy and marriage of Rev. Sattampillai Aiya's family, henceforth, *Celibacy and Marriage*) (Palamcottah: C.M.S. Press, 1905), 2. All translations from this text are my own.

78. Hardgrave, *Nadars of Tamilnad*, 77; *Celibacy and Marriage*, 2.

79. *CMS Report for 1858*, 272.

80. Appasamy, *Centenary History*, 130; *Celibacy and Marriage*, 2.

81. *Celibacy and Marriage*, 2.

82. *Ekkālap pirastāpam: Mūkkupīri-Pirakāsapuram Intia Eka Iraṭcakar Sabai Narceyti ēṭu* (The good news magazine of the Mukuperi-Prakasapuram Indian Church of the Only Saviour), (March–April 1990), 3.

83. Sattampillai, *A Brief Sketch of the Hindu Christian Dogmas*, 3–4, 11–12 (in English in the original). Sattampillai appears to justify this on the basis of Christ's fully divine and human nature. Even though Jesus was perfectly united with the almighty, he still had his "human frame"; therefore, it was appropriate to offer him "sacrificial nourishments" just as his followers did during his lifetime.

84. The author of the history of the family's "celibacy and marriage" writes that because suitable marriage partners could not be found, Sattampillai's eldest son, P. V. Pandian, remained celibate and unmarried until he was 45 years old, and his two daughters never married. Of the daughters he writes, "these women remained in the state of perpetual asceticism (*satā turavu nilaimai*) in the model of the holy virgins (*parisuttayāṭṭikaḷ*) of the ancient Christian church." Anonymous, *Celibacy and Marriage*, 2, 3.

85. Sattampillai, *Hindu Christian Dogmas*, 5, 6–7; A. N. Sattampillai, *Rūttammāvai* (Song of Ruth) (Palamcottah: Church Mission Press, 1884), 26.

86. Sattampillai, *Rūttammāvai*, 28, 30.

87. Sattampillai, *Hindu Christian Dogmas*, 30.

88. Sattampillai, *Rūttammāvai*, 31: "Evan peṉcātiyaiyun taṉakkup peṉṉcātiyākac cērttukkoḷḷukira tuṉmārkka natapaṭikkaiyāṉatu ātikākattil ārkkarmutalān tuṣṭa indukkaḷāl naṭantēri vantatupōla maṉuneri muraiyaic cantativaraṉ muraiyāyk kavaṉittu naṭavāta nīcacātikaḷukkuḷḷē nāḷtuvaraikkum naṭantēri vantutāṉikkiratu" (my translation).

89. Sattampillai, *Hindu Christian Dogmas*, 23, 39.

6: GOLD AND CHOLIS

1. The decision about which name to use to refer to this community is complicated by the very same political and social movements that this chapter endeavors to describe and analyze. In some ways, it is anachronistic to refer to members of this caste as Nadars before 1857, when the movement to change public perceptions of the caste got under way, but in the interest of consistency and out of respect for contemporary usage, according to which Shanar carries negative associations, I use the term Nadar except when it occurs in quoted texts.

2. Caldwell, *The Tinnevelly Shanars*, 56.

3. David Hardiman, *The Coming of the Devi: Adivasi Assertion in Western India* (New Delhi: Oxford University Press, 1995), 145–46; Bernard S. Cohn, "The Changing Status of a Depressed Caste," in *An Anthropologist among the Historians*, 279.

4. B. S. Baliga, *Tirunelveli*, vol. 13 of *Madras District Gazetteers* (Madras: Government Press, 1957–), 128.

5. Chandler, *Seventy-Five Years in the Madura Mission*, 24; Mateer, *Native Life in Travancore*, 203.

6. In *Castes of Mind*, Nicholas B. Dirks has consolidated and expanded on much of his previous scholarship on this subject, arguing against unitary theories of caste

proposed by colonial administrators and postcolonial anthropologists (such as Louis Dumont) that attempt to generalize about the workings of "the caste system" throughout India.

7. Several scholars have dealt with the subject of pirutus, including Joanne Punzo Waghorne, "From Robber Baron to Royal Servant of God? Gaining a Divine Body in South India," in *Criminal Gods and Demon Devotees: Essays on the Guardians of Popular Hinduism*, ed. Alf Hiltebeitel (Albany: State University of New York Press, 1989), 405–26, and *The Raja's Magic Clothes: Re-Visioning Kingship and Divinity in England's India* (University Park: Pennsylvania State University Press, 1994); Dirks, *The Hollow Crown*. Susan Bayly briefly discusses the importance of emblems among Paravar Roman Catholics in *Saints, Goddesses and Kings: Muslims and Christians in South Indian Society, 1700–1900* (Cambridge, UK: Cambridge University Press, 1989).

8. Dirks, *Hollow Crown*, 47, 100, 98.

9. Waghorne, "Gaining a Divine Body in South India."

10. Waghorne, *Raja's Magic Clothes*, 226, 227. Waghorne and Dirks have examined the significance of pirutu in a rather limited context, the Hindu princely state of Pudukottai, but a similar dynamic may be observed in other Indian contexts. Cohn has described how Mughal emperors expressed their acceptance of the loyalty of followers by bestowing sets of garments. These *khilats*, or "robes of honor," represented the transmission of authority from sovereign to subordinate. The most powerful khilat, Cohn writes, "was a robe or garment that the Mughal himself had worn, and on occasion he would literally take off a robe and place it on one of his subjects, as a particular honor." Bernard S. Cohn, "Clothes, Caste and Colonialism," in *Colonialism and Its Forms of Knowledge*, 114–115.

11. Tamil scholarship tends to refer to the disturbances with the more decorous phrase *tōḷcīlaip pōrāṭṭam* (shoulder-cloth struggle). See P. S. K. Paktavatsalan, "Teṉ tiruvitāṅkūr tōḷcīlaip pōrāṭṭam" *Arāycci* 4, no. 1 (October 1973): 83–94.

12. In alphabetical order: Cohn, "Clothes, Caste and Colonialism," 114–115; J. W. Gladstone, *Protestant Christianity and People's Movements in Kerala* (Trivandrum: Seminary Publications, 1984); Joy Gnanadason, *A Forgotten History: The Story of the Missionary Movement and the Liberation of People in South Travancore* (Madras: Gurukul Lutheran Theological College and Research Institute, 1994); Robert L. Hardgrave, "Breast Cloth Controversy: Caste Consciousness and Social Change in South Travancore," *Indian Economic and Social History Review* 5, no. 2 (1968): 171–87; Clifford G. Hospital, "Clothes and Caste in Nineteenth Century Kerala," *Indian Church History Review* 13, no. 2 (1979): 146–56; Robin Jeffrey, *The Decline of Nayar Dominance: Society and Politics in Travancore, 1847–1908* (New Delhi: Vikas, 1994), 53–62; Kooiman, *Conversion and Social Equality in India*, 148–67; Yesudas, *A People's Revolt in Travancore*.

13. Hardgrave, *Nadars of Tamilnad*; Kooiman, *Conversion and Social Equality in India*, 117–135; Dennis Templeman, *The Northern Nadars of Tamil Nadu: An Indian Caste in the Process of Change* (Delhi: Oxford University Press, 1996).

14. Quoted in Clifford G. Hospital, "Clothes and Caste in Nineteenth-Century Kerala," 156.

15. This point is made most clearly in ibid., 146–56.

16. Jeffrey, *The Decline of Nayar Dominance*, 10–16.

17. R. Nandakumar, "The Missing Male: The Female Figures of Ravi Varma and the Concepts of Family, Marriage and Fatherhood in Nineteenth Century Kerala," *South Indian Studies* 1 no. 1 (1996): 58–59.

18. Yalman, "On the Purity of Women," For a vivid evocation of Nambudiri fam-

ily life in the late nineteenth and early twentieth centuries, see the short stories written by Lalithambika Anterjanam, which have recently been translated and collected by
Gita Krishnankutty in *Cast Me Out If You Will* (New York: Feminist Press, 1998).

19. Mateer, *The Land of Charity*, 32.

20. Cohn, "Clothes, Caste and Colonialism," 153–56; According to Mateer, "On
his first arrival in the country a European must be greatly shocked by seeing so large
a proportion of the population going about in a state thus nearly approaching to nudity, and it requires a long time to become familiar with such a state of things." With
a peculiar racial twist he adds, "The dark complexion of the natives, perhaps, makes
this custom seem less unnatural than it would be amongst Europeans" (*Land of Charity*, 61).

21. Mateer, *Native Life in Travancore*, 15.

22. Nandakumar, "The Missing Male," 67.

23. Mateer, *Land of Charity*, 61–62; Letter from Rev. E. Lewis to the resident, 21
January 1859, cited in Yesudasan, *A People's Revolt*, 192.

24. Kooiman, *Conversion and Social Equality*, 148.

25. Mateer, *Land of Charity*, 61–62.

26. Agur, *Church History in Travancore*, 570.

27. House of Commons, "Papers Relating to the Recent Disturbances in Travancore," *Sessional Papers* 1859-II, vol. 25, 355. These papers are available in the TNSA as
a separate file, "Copies of the Official Papers sent from India touching the Recent
Disturbances in Travancore," by J. W. Kaye, and in microprint as part of the British
Sessional Papers. The page numbers I use here correspond to the British Sessional
Papers. Readers who wish to consult the print version in the TNSA should note that
page 1 corresponds with page 353 of the Sessional Papers.

28. Jeffrey, *Decline of Nair Dominance*, 54.

29. Quoted in Kooiman, *Conversion and Social Equality*, 158.

30. Cited in Jeffrey, *Decline of Nair Dominance*, 54.

31. House of Commons, "Papers Relating to the Recent Disturbances in Travancore," *Sessional Papers* 392–93.

32. Yesudas, *People's Revolt in Travancore*.

33. House of Commons, "Papers Relating to the Recent Disturbances in Travancore," 353.

34. For a thorough discussion of the events in Tirunelveli, see Frykenberg, "On
Roads and Riots in Tinnevelly."

35. Emma Tarlo, *Clothing Matters: Dress and Identity in India* (Chicago: University
of Chicago Press, 1996), 16; Gandhi paraphrased by Tarlo, 84, 85.

36. Mateer, *The Land of Charity*, 41.

37. In this light, one could compare the silence surrounding the question of sexual assault in this context with that surrounding the rape of women caught in the
chaos of Partition. See Veena Das, "National Honour and Practical Kinship: Of Un-
wanted Women and Children," in *Critical Events: An Anthropological Perspective on
Contemporary India* (Delhi: Oxford University Press, 1996).

38. P. N. Kunjan Pillai Elamkuluam, *Studies in Kerala History* (Kottayam, Kerala:
N.B.S., 1970), 315–16, cited in Yesudas, *A People's Revolt in Travancore*, 9, n. 15.

39. Nandakumar, "The Missing Male," 60, 59.

40. Ibid., 67.

41. Francis Buchanan, *A Journey from Madras through the Countries of Mysore,
Canara and Malabar* (1807, Madras: Asian Educational Service, 1988), 412, 414–16.

42. See Thomas Trautmann's description of the negative review Buchanan's

book received from the Orientalist Alexander Hamilton, in *Aryans and British India*, 33–34. Hamilton wrote, "We have no hesitation in stating the faculty of conversing with them as an indispensable qualification [of knowing a people]; and of this Dr. Buchanan was totally destitute."

43. Mr. and Mrs. Jesunadan [pseudonym], interview by author, Chrompet, Tamil Nadu, 27 January 1999.

44. *Annual Report of the Trevandrum District, South Travancore, in Connection with the Malayalam Mission of the London Missionary Society* (Madras: Addison, 1896), 8.

45. Hardgrave, *Nadars of Tamilnad*, 62; "The Petition to the Right Honorable the Governor in Council from the Shanars of South Travancore," reprinted in *Bombay Standard*, 11 February 1859; "Petition of the Missionaries of the London Missionary Society, stationed in South Travancore, to his Highness the Rajah of Travancore," in House of Commons, "Papers Related to the Disturbances in Travancore," 391.

46. House of Commons, "Papers Related to the Disturbances in Travancore," 395.

47. Letter to the editor by "Observer," *Overland Bombay Standard*, 9 February 1859, 9.

48. "The Late Riot at Travancore—Petition of the Shanars," *Overland Bombay Standard*, 11 February 1859. It seems that the British resident, Lieutenant General William Cullen, did receive this petition, but "returned it as a matter of local usage and caste, with which the Government declined to interfere." House of Commons, "Papers on the Recent Disturbances in Travancore," 357.

49. House of Commons, "Papers on the Recent Disturbances in Travancore," 356.

50. Hardgrave, *Nadars of Tamilnad*, 69, citing V. Nagam Aiya, *The Travancore State Manual*, 3 vols. (Trivandrum: Government Press, 1906), 1: 531.

51. Interview with Miss M. P. Pappanellaiya (daughter of Mary Pappanellaiya, Bible woman), 70 years old, Artikulam, Madurai, 19 September, 1996.

52. Comaroff and Comaroff, *Christianity, Colonialism and Consciousness*, 18.

53. CMS Archive, Birmingham Library, Birmingham, UK, C I 2/ O14 [Tracts and Pamphlets]/ 5, Henry Judson, "Mr. Judson's Tract to the Female Members of the Christian Churches in the USA and earnestly recommended to the serious and prayerful consideration of all Christian Women in India" (Philadelphia, 1833) [henceforth Mr. Judson's Tract], 1, 2, 4 (emphasis in original). Judson here used the King James translation of the Bible, citing from the infamous chapter in 1 Timothy in which, in addition to condemning women's adornments, Paul bars women from teaching men in church.

54. Prochaska, *Women and Philanthropy in Nineteenth Century England*.

55. Mr. Judson's Tract, 7.

56. Chandler, *Seventy-Five Years in the Madura Mission*, 400, 401.

57. Mrs. S. Satthianadhan [Krupabai], *Saguna*, 31; see also A. Satthianadhan, *Nalla Tāy*, 12, 49–51.

58. Elliot, *A Chance to Die*, 17.

59. Carmichael, *Ponnammal*, 12–13.

60. Ibid., 19, 22, 24.

61. Ibid., 21.

62. Caroline Walker Bynum, *Holy Feast and Holy Fast: The Religious Significance of Food to Medieval Women* (Berkeley: University of California Press, 1987), ch. 1.

63. Carmichael, *Ponnammal*, 21, 26.

64. To this day, Indian Christian women I would argue, tend to have an ambivalent relationship toward jewelry. The Christian Nadars of Sivakasi, for instance, are
famous for their large dowries, consisting of multiple pieces of thick gold chains and
heavy earrings. Concurrently, however, many (generally older) women who identify
themselves as evangelical make a point of not wearing any jewelry, thereby position-
ing themselves in a marginal, critical stance vis-à-vis Indian Christian society. For
dowries in Sivakasi, see Nageswari, "A Study of Social Change among the Nadars of
Tamil Nadu."

65. See the short stories by Samuel and Kamala Satthianadhan, *Stories of Indian
Christian Life*, which illustrate and comment on the "transitional symptoms" of Indian Christian life. Tarlo astutely analyzes the potential risks and rewards for Indian
men of wearing a mixture of Indian and Western clothing styles, (*Clothing Matters*, 48–
52).

66. Papers, Discussions and General Review, Vol. 1 of *The Missionary Conference:
South India and Ceylon, 1879* (Madras: Addison, 1880), 403.

67. Tarlo, *Clothing Matters*, 84. A more recent example is the fad among young
Afghani men for the "Titanic" haircut (modeled after Leonardo di Caprio's coiffure)
in Taliban-ruled Afghanistan, where, according to the Taliban's reading of Shariah,
men are to dress, shave, and wear their hair as the Prophet Muhammad did in the
seventh century. Arguably, the Titanic craze, which persisted in spite of considerable
risk of persecution, can be read as a kind of nonverbal resistance to the Taliban's extremely harsh interpretation of Islam. For some helpful discussions of the political
and religious symbolism of clothing cross-culturally, see Linda B. Arthur, ed., *Undressing Religion: Commitment and Conversion from a Cross-Cultural Perspective* Oxford: Berg
2000).

68. Rambo, *Understanding Religious Conversion*, 3.

69. This point was made clear in many of the presentations given at the conference "Converting Cultures: Religion, Ideology, and Transformations of Modernity,"
held at the Humanities Institute, Dartmouth College, 1–3 December 2002, papers
from which should soon be available as an edited volume.

70. Mateer, *Nature Life in Travancore*. 188–199.

71. Hudson, *Protestant Origins in India*.

72. *Missionary Conference: South India and Ceylon, 1879*, 403.

73. *Missionary Conference: South India and Ceylon, 1879*, 294, 317, cited in Copley, *Religions in Conflict*, 24

74. Robert Caldwell, "Observations on the Kudumi," *Indian Antiquary* 4 (1875):
167–68.

75. Ibid., 169.

76. Mateer, *Native Life in Travancore*, 188, 189.

77. Ibid., 198.

78. Yalman, "On the Purity of Women."

79. Conflict between Indian Christians and Western Christian missionaries over
style and the form that Indian Christian identity would take continued into the twentieth century, as Susan Billington Harper demonstrates brilliantly in her analysis of
the power struggles over the vestments that Bishop V. S. Azariah would wear as the
first Indian bishop of the Church of England (*In the Shadow of the Mahatma*, 139–
46).

CONCLUSION

1. The phrase "long conversation" comes from Comaroff and Comaroff's massive and influential study of missions in southern Africa, *Of Revelation and Revolution*, vols. 1–2.

2. For a well-articulated demonstration of this argument, see Frykenberg, "Constructions of Hinduism at the Nexus of History and Religion." For a many-sided exploration of its ramifications for the study of Hinduism, see the special issue of the *Journal of the American Academy of Religion*, "Who Speaks for Hinduism?" 68, no. 4 (December 2000).

3. Romila Thapar, "Syndicated Hinduism," in *Hinduism Reconsidered*, ed. Gunter-Dietz Sontheimer and Hermann Kulke (New Delhi: Manohar, 1997), 54–81.

4. Bernard S. Cohn, "The Census, Social Structure and Objectification in South Asia" in *An Anthropologist among the Historians*, 224–54; Appadurai, "Number in the Colonial Imagination"; Dirks, *Castes of Mind*, ch. 10.

5. Gerald Larson, *India's Agony over Religion* (Albany: State University of New York Press, 1995).

6. Statement attributed to P. R. Raghuraman, secretary of the Harijan Sevak Sangh in Chingleput district, in "Work of Christian Missionaries; Rev. Maclean's Reply to Sangh Secretary," *The Hindu*, 11 June 1936, 7.

7. Gauri Viswanathan, "Religious Conversion and the Politics of Dissent," in *Conversion to Modernities: The Globalization of Christianity*, ed. Peter van der Veer (New York: Routledge, 1996), 89–114; Chakravarti, *Rewriting History*.

8. In advancing a notion of indigenization as resistance to missionary hegemony, however, one needs to exercise caution against overgeneralization. As Susan Billington Harper has argued in "Ironies of Indigenization," as indigenization at the level of symbols and liturgy became fashionable within missionary circles in the twentieth century, it became more difficult to read the appropriation of Hindu symbols by Christians as forms of critique of missionary dominance.

9. Joan W. Scott, *Gender and the Politics of History* (New York: Columbia University Press, 1988), 17.

Bibliography

TAMIL SOURCES

A.L.O.E [Charlotte Tucker]). *Mātarpūccaram* (Women, the garland of flowers [A reading book for zenanas and advanced classes in boarding schools]). Nagercoil: London Mission Press, 1869.

Caṭṭampiḷḷai Aiya kuṭumbattiṉ piramaccariyamum maṅgalaviśēśamum (The celibacy and marriage of Rev. Sattampillai Aiya's family). Palamcottah: C.M.S. Press, 1905.

Ekkāḷap pirastāpam: Mūkkupīri-Pirakāsapuram Intia Eka Iraṭcahar Sabai Narceyti ēṭu (The good news magazine of the Mukuperi-Prakasapuram Indian Church of the Only Saviour). (March–April 1990).

Nadar, Sintr Sandana. *Māntiriya avapaktiyaip parriya ōr upaniyāsam* (A lecture on witchcraft). Palamcottah: Darling Press, 1915.

Ñāṉamuttu Nāṭār, Y. *Cāṇār Cattiryar* (A polemical treatise maintaining that the Shanars are Kshatriyas, together with a Christian tract, *Irakṣapiṉ piḷaṉ* [Plan of salvation], by the same author). Madras, 1889.

Paktavatsalan, P.S.K. "Teṉ tiruvitāṅkūr tōḷcīlaip pōrāṭṭam (South Travancore Shoulder cloth Struggle)" *Arāycci* 4 no. 1 (October 1973):83–94.

Paul, Tilakavati. *Emi Kārmaikkal Ammaiyār* (Amy Carmichael the mother). Vēppēri: Cuvicēśa ūriya nūl nilaiyam, 1980.

Ponnilan, Tiru. "Vaikuṇṭar kāṭṭiya vāḻkkai neṟi" (The code of ethics created by Vaikunda). In *Nāṭṭār vaḷakkārriyal āyvukaḷ* (Studies in folklore), ed. S. D. Lourdes, 233–250. Tirunelveli: Parivel Pathipagam, 1981.

Samuel, (Mrs.) A.M.P. *Illara iṉpa irakasiyam* (The secret to a happy home). Madras: Christian Literature Society, 1909.

Sattampillai, A. N. *Rūttammāvai* (Song of Ruth). Palamkottah: Church Mission Press, 1884.

Satthianathan, Annal. *Nalla Tāy* (The good mother). 1862; Madras: Christian Literature Society for India, 1921.

Subramaniya Mudaliar, C. K. *Cēkkiḻār Cuvāmikaḷ eṉṉum Aruṇmoḻittēvar aruḷiya Periya-purāṇam eṉṉum Tirutoṇṭar purāṇam* (The Sacred History of the Devoted Slaves of God, known as the Great Sacred History, by Cekkilar known as The Master of Graceful Speech). Vol. 2. Coimbatore: Kōvait Tamiḻc Caṅkam, 1968.
Washburn, George T., and E. Webb. *Christian Lyrics for Public and Social Worship*, 5th. ed. Nagercoil: Madras Tract and Book Society, 1875.

SOURCES IN WESTERN LANGUAGES

Official Records and Papers

Aiya V. Nagam. *The Travancore State Manual*. 3 vols. Trivandrum: The Government Press, 1906.
Census of India, 1931: Madras. Part 1: Report. Vol. 14. Madras: Government Press, 1932.
Mackenzie, Gordon. *Manual of the Kistna District in the Presidency of Madras*, Madras: Government of Madras, 1883.
Memorandum on Marriage and Divorce Laws of Native Christians. TNSA, G.O. 539–540, Public Dept., 28 July 1909.
Molony J. Charles. *Census of India, 1911: Madras* Part 1: *The Report of the Census*. Madras: Government of Madras, 1912
Opinions solicited regarding a bill to punish breaches of monogamous marriage contracts. TNSA, G.O. 94, Ecclesiastical Dept., 16 April 1875.
Pate, H. R. *Tinnevelly Gazetteer*. Vol. 1. Madras: Government of Madras, 1917.

Sources in Western Languages, 1800–1940

Abbott, John S. C. *The Mother at Home*. Boston: Crocker and Brewster, 1833.
A.D. *Until the Shadows Flee Away: The Story of the CEZMS in India and Ceylon*. London: Church of England Zenana Missionary Society, 1912.
A.L.O.E. [Charlotte Tucker]. *The Zenana Reader*. Madras: Christian Vernacular Education Society for India, 1880.
Agur, C. M. *Church History in Travancore*. Madras: S.P.S. Press, Vepery, 1903.
Annual Report of the Trevandrum District, South Travancore, in Connection with the Malayalam Mission of the London Missionary Society. Madras: Addison, 1896.
Appasamy, Paul. *The Centenary History of the C.M.S. in Tinnevelly*. Palamcottah: Palamcottah Press, 1923.
Batley, D. S. *Devotees of Christ: Some Women Pioneers of the Indian Church*. London: Church of England Zenana Missionary Society, 1937.
————. *Indian Christians: Biographical and Critical Sketches*. Madras: G. A. Natesan, 1928.
Beach, Harlan P. and Burton St. John, eds. *World Statistics of Christian Missions*. New York: The Foreign Missions Conference of North America, 1916.
Bissell, Mrs. "Work among Women." In *Report of the Third Decennial Missionary Conference, Bombay 1892–1893*. Bombay: Education Society's Steam Press, Bycolla, 1893.
Buchanan, Francis. *A Journey from Madras through the Countries of Mysore, Canara and Malabar*. 1807; Madras: Asian Educational Service, 1988.
Caldwell, Robert. *The Tinnevelly Shanars: A Sketch of Their Religion, and Their Moral Condition and Characteristics as a Caste*. Madras: Christian Knowledge Society Press, 1849.

_____. "Observations on the Kudumi." *Indian Antiquary* 4 (1875): 166–173.

_____. *On Reserve in Communicating Religious Instruction to Non-Christians in Mission Schools in India.* Madras: S.P.C.K. Press, 1879.

_____. *A Political and General History of the District of Tinnevelly in the Presidency of Madras, from the Earliest Period to Its Cession to the English Government in A.D. 1801.* Madras: Government Press, 1881.

_____. *Records of the Early History of the Tinnevelly Mission.* Madras: Higgenbotham, 1881.

_____. *Reminiscences of Bishop Caldwell.* Ed. J. L. Wyatt. Madras: Addison, 1894.

_____. *A Comparative Grammar of the Dravidian or South Indian Family of Languages.* 3d ed. 1913; Madras: Asian Educational Services, 1988.

Carmichael, Amy Wilson. *Things as They Are: Mission Work in Southern India.* London: Morgan and Scott, 1904.

_____. *Ponnammal: Her Story.* London: Society for Promoting Christian Knowledge, 1918.

_____. *Raj, Brigand Chief.* London: Seeley, Service, 1927.

Carpenter, Joseph E. *The Life and Work of Mary Carpenter.* London: Macmillan, 1879.

Carpenter, Mary. *Six Months in India.* 2 vols. London: Longman's, Green, 1868.

Chamberlain, Mary. *Fifty Years in Foreign Fields: A History of Five Decades of the Women's Board of Foreign Missions Reformed Church in America.* New York: Women's Board of Foreign Missions, 1925.

Chandler, John S. *Seventy-Five Years in the Madura Mission: A History of the Mission in South India under the ABCFM.* Madras: American Madura Mission, 1910.

Clough, Emma Rauschenbusch. *Social Christianity in the Orient: The Story of a Man, a Mission and a Movement.* New York: Macmillan, 1914.

Clough, John E. *From Darkness to Light: The Story of a Telegu Convert.* Boston: W.G. Cornell, Mission Rooms, 1882.

Dickens, Charles. *Hard Times.* 1854; New York: Penguin, 1995.

Digby, W. *The Famine Campaign: Southern India.* Madras, 1878.

Dubois, Abbe J. A. *Character, Manners and Customs of the People of India.* Trans. G. U. Pope. 1820; New Delhi: Asian Educational Services, 1992.

Downie, David. *The Lone Star: A History of the Telegu Mission of the American Baptist Foreign Mission Society.* Philadelphia: American Baptist Publication Society, 1924.

Freud, Sigmund. *Totem and Taboo.* 1913; New York: Norton, 1989.

Gell, F. *Inquiries Made by the Bishop of Madras Regarding the Removal of Caste Prejudices and Practices in the Native Church of South India.* Madras: Christian Knowledge Society's Press, 1868.

Germann, W. *Missionar Christian Friedrich Schwartz: Sein Leben und Wirken aus Briefen der Halleschen Missionsarchiven.* Erlangen: A. Deichert, 1870.

Greenfield, Miss. "Paper on Zenana Education." In *Report of the Second Decennial Missionary Conference Held in Calcutta, 1882–83.* Calcutta, 1883.

Hossain, Rokeya Sakhawat. *Sultana's Dream and Selections from* The Secluded Ones. Trans. and ed. Roushan Jahan. 1905; New York: The Feminist Press, 1988.

Hough, James. *The History of Christianity in India.* Vol. 5. London: Church Missionary House, 1860.

Jensen, Herman. *A Classified Collection of Tamil Proverbs.* 1897; New Delhi: Asian Educational Services, 1997.

LMS Reports of Zenana and School Work 1894 (Tittuvelei district, Travancore). Madras: Addison, 1895.

Mackenzie, Col. J. S. F. "Caste Marks of Madras." Tanjore, 1830.

Madhaviah, A. *Clarinda: A Historical Novel.* Tirunelveli: Nanbar Vattam, 1915.

Maine, Henry Sumner. *Ancient Law: Its Connections with the Early History of Society and Its Relation to Modern Ideas.* 9th ed. London: J. Murray, 1883.

Margöschis, Arthur. "Christianity and Caste." *Indian Church History Review* 6 (October 1893).

Mateer, Samuel. *Land of Charity: A Discriptive Account of Travancore and Its People.* London: J. Snow and Co., 1871.

———. *Native Life in Travancore.* London: W.H. Allen, 1883.

McDougall, Eleanor. "A Tour of Enquiry into the Education of Women and Girls in India, 1912–1913." In *International Review of Missions, 3, 1914.* Edinburgh: International Review of Missions, 1914.

Montgomery, Helen Barrett. *Western Women in Eastern Lands.* 1910; New York: Garland, 1987.

Mullens, Hannah Catherine. *The Missionary on the Ganges: What Is Christianity?* Calcutta: The Calcutta Christian Tract and Book Society, 1856.

Mullens, Joseph. *A Brief Review of Ten Years' Missionary Labour in India, between 1852–1861.* London: James Nisbet, 1863.

Mullick, Bulloram. *Essays on the Hindu Family in Bengal.* Calcutta: W. Newman, 1882.

Murdoch, John. *The Women of India and What Can Be Done for Them.* Madras: Christian Vernacular Education Society, 1888.

Nelson, J. H. *The Madura Country: A Manual.* Madras: Madras Government, 1868.

Newman, Henry Stanley. *Days of Grace in India: A Record of Visits to Indian Missions.* London: S.W. Partridge, n.d.

Oppert, Gustav. *On the Original Inhabitants of Bharatavarsha or India.* Westminster: Constable, 1893.

Pascoe, C. F. *200 Years of the SPG: An Historical Account of the Society for the Propagation of the Gospel in Foreign Parts, 1701–1900.* London: SPG Office, 1901.

Papers, Discussions and General Review. Vol. 1 of *The Missionary Conference: South India and Ceylon, 1879.* Madras: Addison, 1880.

Pettitt, George. *The Tinnevelly Mission of the Church Missionary Society.* London: Seeleys, 1851.

Pickett, J. Waskom. *Christian Mass Movements in India: A Study with Recommendations.* New York: Abingdon, 1933.

Pitman, Mrs. E. R. (Emma Raymond). *Indian Zenana Missions: Their Need, Origin, Objects, Agents, Modes of Working, and Results.* London: John Snow, n.d. [before 1903].

Ponniah, J. S., et al. *An Enquiry into the Economic and Social Problems of the Christian Community of Madura, Ramnad and Tinnevelly Districts.* Madurai: American College, 1938.

Rainy, C. *A Visit to Our Indian Mission Field.* Paisely, Scotland: J. and R. Parlane, 1887.

Ramabai, Pandita Saraswati. *The High-Caste Hindu Woman.* Philadelphia: The American, 1887.

Rauschenbusch-Clough, Emma. *While Sewing Sandals: or Tales of a Telegu Pariah.* London: Houghter and Stoughton, 1899.

Report of the General Missionary Conference, Allahabad, 1872–1873. London: Seeley, Jackson and Holliday, 1873.

Report of the Proceedings of the Church Missionary Society for the Year 1858. London: Church Missionary Society, 1859.

Report of the Second Decennial Missionary Conference Held in Calcutta, 1882–83. Calcutta: J.W. Thomas, Baptist Mission Press, 1883.

Report of the Third Decennial Missionary Conference, Bombay, 1892–1893. Bombay: Education Society's Steam Press, Byculla, 1893.

Sarguner, Samuel. *Bishop Caldwell and the Tinnevelly Shanars.* Palamcottah: Subramania Pillai, 1883.

Sattampillai, A. N. *A Brief Sketch of the Hindu Christian Dogmas.* Palamcottah: Shanmuga Vilasam, 1890.

Satthianadhan, Annal. *A Brief Account of Zenana Work in Madras.* London: Seeley, 1878.

Satthianadhan, Mrs. S. [Krupabai]. *Saguna: A Story of Native Christian Life.* Madras: Srinivasa, Varadachari, 1895.

_____. *Miscellaneous Writings.* Madras: Srinivasa, Varadachari, 1896.

Satthianadhan, Samuel. *The Rev. W. T. Satthianadhan: A Brief Biographical Sketch.* Madras: Society for the Propagation of Christian Knowledge, 1893.

Satthianadhan, Samuel, and Kamala Satthianadhan. *Stories of Indian Christian Life.* Madras: Srinivasa, Varadachari, 1898.

Smith, Sydney. "Publications Respecting Indian Missions." *Edinburgh Review* (April–July 1808): 151–81.

Stanton, Elizabeth Cady. *The Woman's Bible.* 1898; Salem, NH: Ayer, 1988.

Taylor, Col. Meadows. *The People of India: A Series of Photographic Illustrations of the Races and Tribes of Hindustan,* Vol. VIII. Ed. J. Forbes Watson and Sir John William Kaye. London: India Museum, 1875.

Thurston, Edgar, and K. Rangachari. *Castes and Tribes of Southern India.* Vols. 1–7. Madras: Government of Madras, 1909.

Weber, Max. *The Protestant Ethic and the Spirit of Capitalism.* Trans. Talcott Parsons. 1920; New York: Scribner, 1976.

Weitbrecht, J. J. *The Protestant Missions in Bengal.* London: John F. Shaw, 1844.

Weitbrecht, Mrs. *Missionary Sketches in North India with Reference to Recent Events.* London: James Nisbet & Co., 1858.

Whitehead, Henry. *The Village Gods of South India.* London: Oxford University Press, 1916.

Wilder, R. G. *Mission Schools in India of the American Board of Commissioners of Foreign Missions.* New York: A.D.F. Randolph, 1861.

Williamson, Thomas. *The East India Vade-Mecum, or, Complete Guide to Gentlemen Intended for the Civil, Military or Naval Service of the Hon. East India Company.* Vol. 1. London: Black, Perry, and Kingsbury, 1810.

Winslow, M. *A Comprehensive Tamil and English Dictionary.* 1862; New Delhi: Asian Educational Series, 1987.

Winter, Mrs. "Missions to Women, by a Missionary's Wife." In *Report of the General Missionary Conference, Allahabad, 1872–73.* London: Seeley, Jackson, and Halliday, 1873.

Wittenmeyer, Annie. *Women's Work for Jesus.* 6th ed. 1873; New York: Garland, 1987.

Ziegenbalg, Bartholomaeus. *An Account of the Religion, Manners, and Learning of the People of Malabar, in several letters written by some of the most learned men of that country to the Danish Missionaries.* Trans. Jenkins Thomas Philipps. London: W. Mears, 1717.

_____. *Thirty four Conferences between the Danish Missionaries and the Malabarian Brahmans (or Heathen Priests) in the East Indies, Concerning the Truth of the Chris-*

tian Religion: Together with some Letters written by the Heathens to the said Mission-aries. Trans. J. Thomas Philipps. London: H. Clements, W. Fleetwood, and F. Ste-phens, 1719.

———. *Geneaology of the South Indian Gods: A Manual of the Mythology and Religion of the People of Southern India.* Trans. G. J. Metzger. 1713; Madras: Higgenbotham, 1869.

Secondary Historical, Comparative, and Methodological Sources

Alter, Joseph. "Celibacy, Sexuality, and the Transformation of Gender into Nationalism in North India." *Journal of Asian Studies* 53, no. 1 (1994): 45–66.

Alwis, Malathi de. "The Production and Embodiment of Respectability: Gendered De-meanors in Colonial Ceylon." In *Sri Lanka: Collective Identities Revisited*, vol. 1, ed. Michael Roberts, 105–43. Colombo: Marga Institute (Sri Lanka Center for De-velopment Studies), 1997.

———. "Maternalist Politics in Sri Lanka: A Historical Anthropology of Its Condi-tions of Possibility." Ph.D. diss., University of Chicago, 1998.

Anderson, Benedict. *Imagined Communities: Reflections on the Origin and Spread of Na-tionalism.* London: Verso, 1991.

Anterjanam, Lalithambika. *Cast Me Out If You Will.* Ed. Gita Krishnankutty. New York: Feminist Press, 1998.

Appadurai, Arjun. "Kings, Sects and Temples in South India, 1350–1700 A.D." *Indian Economic and Social History Review* 14 (January–March 1977): 47–74.

———. *Worship and Conflict under Colonial Rule: A South Indian Case.* Cambridge, UK: Cambridge University Press, 1981.

———. "Number in the Colonial Imagination." In *Orientalism and the Postcolonial Predicament*, ed. Carol A. Breckenridge and Peter van der Veer, 314–40. Philadel-phia: University of Pennsylvania Press, 1993.

Appadurai, Arjun, and Carol A. Breckenridge. "The South Indian Temple: Authority, Honour and Redistribution." *Contributions to Indian Sociology*, 10, no. 2 (1976): 187–211.

Archer, Mildred, and Graham Parlett. *Company Paintings: Indian Paintings of the Brit-ish Period.* London: Victoria and Albert Museum, 1995.

Armstrong, Anthony. *The Church of England, the Methodists and Society, 1700–1850.* To-towa, NJ: Rowman and Littlefield, 1973.

Arnold, David. "Famine in Peasant Consciousness and Peasant Action: Madras 1876–78." In *Subaltern Studies III*, ed. Ranajit Guha. Oxford: Oxford University Press, 1976.

———. *The Problem of Nature: Environment, Culture and European Expansion.* Oxford: Blackwell, 1996.

Arthur, Linda B. ed. *Undressing Religion: Commitment and Conversion from a Cross-Cultural Perspective.* Oxford: Berg, 2000.

Arunachalam, M. *The Saiva Saints.* Tiruchitrambalam: Gandhi Vidyalayam, 1985.

Asad, Talal. *Genealogies of Religion: Discipline and Reasons of Power in Christianity and Islam.* Baltimore: Johns Hopkins University Press, 1993.

———. "Comment on Conversion." In *Conversion to Modernities: The Globalization of Christianity*, ed. Peter van der Veer, 263–74. New York: Routledge, 1996.

Babb, Lawrence A. *Popular Hinduism in Central India.* New York: Columbia Univer-sity Press, 1975.

Balasundaram, Franklyn J. *Dalits and Christian Mission in the Tamil Country*. Bangalore: Asian Trading Corporation, 1997.

Ballhatchet, Kenneth A. *Race, Sex and Class under the Raj: Imperial Attitudes and Policies and Their Critics, 1793–1905*. New York: St. Martin's Press, 1980.

Banerjee, Himani. "Attired in Virtue: The Discourse on Shame (lajja) and Clothing of the Bhadramahila in Colonial Bengal." In *The Seams of History: Essays on Indian Women*, ed. Barati Ray, 67–106. New Delhi: Oxford University Press, 1995.

Banerjee, Sumanta. "Marginalization of Women's Popular Culture in Nineteenth Century Bengal." In *Recasting Women: Essays in Colonial History*, ed. Kumkum Sangari and Sudesh Vaid. Delhi: Kali for Women, 1989.

———. *The Parlour and the Streets: Elite and Popular Culture in 19th Century Calcutta*. Calcutta: Seagull, 1989.

Bate, John Bernard. "Metaittamil: Beauty and Power in Tamil Speech and Society." Ph.D. diss., University of Chicago, 1999.

Bayly, Susan. *Saints, Goddesses and Kings: Muslims and Christians in South Indian Society, 1700–1900*. Cambridge, UK: Cambridge University Press, 1989.

Beaver, R. Pierce. *All Love's Excelling: American Protestant Women in Foreign Missions*. Grand Rapids, MI: Eerdman, 1980.

Bell, Catherine. *Ritual Theory, Ritual Practice*. New York: Oxford University Press, 1992.

Benge, Janet. *Amy Carmichael: Rescuer of Precious Gems*. Seattle: YWAM, 1998.

Berreman, Gerald D. "The Brahmanical View of Caste." *Contributions to Indian Sociology* (1971): 16–23.

Bhabha, Homi. *The Location of Culture*. London: Routledge, 1994.

Blackburn, Stuart. "The Kallars: A Tamil 'Criminal Tribe' Reconsidered." *South Asia* 1 (1978): 38–51.

———. "Death and Deification: Folk Cults in Hinduism." *History of Religions* 24, no. 3 (1985): 255–274.

———. *Singing of Birth and Death: Texts in Performance*. Philadelphia: University of Pennsylvania Press, 1988.

Borthwick, Meredith. *The Changing Role of Women in Bengal, 1849–1905*. Princeton: Princeton University Press, 1984.

Bourdieu, Pierre. *Outline of a Theory of Practice*. Vol. 16 of *Cambridge Studies in Social Anthropology*. Trans. Richard Nice. Cambridge, UK: Cambridge University Press, 1977.

Bourdieu, Pierre, and Loic J. D. Wacquant, *An Invitation to Reflexive Sociology*. Chicago: University of Chicago Press, 1992.

Bowler, Peter J. *The Invention of Progress: The Victorians and the Past*. Oxford: Basil Blackwell, 1989.

Brauer, Jerald C., ed. *Westminster Dictionary of Church History*. Philadelphia: Westminster, 1971.

Breckenridge, Carol A. "From Protector to Litigant: Changing Relations between Hindu Temples and the Raja of Ramnad." *Indian Economic and Social History Review* 14, no. 1 (1977): 75–106.

Brockway, K. Nora. *A Larger Way for Women: Aspects of Christian Education for Girls in South India, 1712–1948*. Madras: Oxford University Press, 1949.

Brooks, Douglas Renfrew. *The Secret of the Three Cities: An Introduction to Hindu Sakta Tantrism*. Chicago: University of Chicago Press, 1990.

Brumberg, Joan Jacobs. *Mission for Life*. New York: Free Press, 1980.

Burton, Antoinette. *Burdens of History: British Feminists, Indian Women, and Imperial Culture, 1865–1915.* Chapel Hill: University of North Carolina Press, 1994.

———. "Fearful Bodies into Disciplined Subjects: Pleasure, Romance, and the Family Drama of Colonial Reform in Mary Carpenter's Six Months in India." *Signs* 20 no. 3 (1995): 545–574.

Butler, Judith. *Gender Trouble: Gender and the Subversion of Identity.* New York: Routledge, 1990.

Butler, Judith, and Joan W. Scott, eds. *Feminists Theorize the Political.* New York: Routledge, 1992.

Bynum, Caroline Walker. *Holy Feast and Holy Fast: The Religious Significance of Food to Medieval Women.* Berkeley: University of California Press, 1987.

Caplan, Lionel. *Class and Culture in Urban India: Fundamentalism in a Christian Community.* Oxford: Clarendon Press, 1987.

———. *Religion and Power: Essays on the Christian Community in Madras.* Madras: Christian Literature Society, 1989.

Carman, John B., and P. Y. Luke. *Village Christians and Hindu Culture: Study of a Rural Church in Andhra Pradesh, South India.* London: Lutterworth, World Studies of Churches in Mission, 1968.

Carroll, Lucy. "Law, Custom, and Statutory Social Reform: The Hindu Widows' Remarriage Act of 1856." *The Indian Economic and Social History Review* 20, no. 4 (1983): 365–88.

Carwardine, Richard. *Trans-atlantic Revivalism: Popular Evangelicalism in Britain and America, 1790–1865.* Westport, CT: Greenwood, 1978.

Certeau, Michel de. *The Practice of Everyday Life.* Berkeley: University of California Press, 1984.

Chakrabarty, Dipesh. "The Difference-Deferral of a Colonial Modernity: Public Debates on Domesticity in British Bengal." In *Subaltern Studies VIII: Essays in Honour of Ranajit Guha,* ed. David Arnold and David Hardiman, 50–88. Delhi: Oxford University Press, 1996.

Chakravarti, Uma. "Pativrata." *Seminar* 318 (1986): 17–21.

———. "Conceptualizing Brahmanical Purity in Early India: Gender, Caste, Class and State." *Economic and Political Weekly* 28, no. 4 (3 April 1993): 579–85.

———. *Rewriting History: The Life and Times of Pandita Ramabai.* New Delhi: Kali for Women, 2000.

Chatterjee, Partha. "The Nationalist Resolution of the Women's Question." In *Recasting Women: Essays in Indian Colonial History,* ed. Kumkum Sangari and Sudesh Vaid. New Delhi: Kali for Women, 1989.

———. *Nationalist Thought and the Colonial World: A Derivative Discourse.* Minneapolis: University of Minnesota Press, 1993.

———. *The Nation and Its Fragments: Colonial and Postcolonial Histories.* Princteon: Princeton University Press, 1993.

Chaudhuri, Nupur, and Margaret Strobel, eds. *Western Women and Imperialism: Complicity and Resistance.* Bloomington: Indiana University Press, 1992.

Clarke, Sathianathan. *Dalits and Christianity: Subaltern Religion and Liberation Theology in India.* Delhi: Oxford University Press, 1998.

Claus, Peter J. "Oral Traditions, Royal Cults, and Materials for a Reconsideration of the Caste System in South India." *Journal of Indian Folkloristics* (Mysore) 1 (1978): 1–25.

Cohn, Bernard S. *An Anthropologist among the Historians and Other Essays.* Delhi: Oxford University Press, 1987.

_____. *Colonialism and Its Forms of Knowledge: The British in India*. Princeton: Princeton University Press, 1996.

Collins, Larry, and Dominique Lapierre. *Freedom at Midnight*. New York: Simon and Schuster, 1975.

Comaroff, John L., and Jean Comaroff. *Christianity, Colonialism and Consciousness in South Africa*. Vol. 1 of *Of Revelation and Revolution*. Chicago: University of Chicago Press, 1991.

_____. "Homemade Hegemony." In *Ethnography and the Historical Imagination*, Boulder, CO: Westview, 1992.

_____. *The Dialectics of Modernity on a South African Frontier*. Vol. 2 of *Of Revelation and Revolution* Chicago: The University of Chicago Press, 1997.

_____. "Revelations upon *Revelation*: After Shocks, Afterthoughts" *interventions* 3, no.1 (2001): 100–126.

Copley, Antony. *Religions in Conflict: Ideology, Cultural Contact and Conversion in Late-Colonial India*. Delhi: Oxford University Press, 1997.

Cox, Jeffrey. "Independent English Women in Delhi and Lahore, 1860–1947." In *Religion and Irreligion in Victorian Society*, ed. R. J. Helmstadter. London: Routledge, 1992.

_____. "Religion and Imperial Power in Nineteenth-Century Britain." In *Freedom and Religion in the Nineteenth Century*, ed. Richard Helmstadter. Stanford: Stanford University Press, 1997.

_____. *Imperial Fault Lines: Christianity and Colonial Power in India, 1818–1940*. Stanford: Stanford University Press, 2002.

Cutler, Norman. *Songs of Experience: The Poetics of Tamil Devotion*. Bloomington: Indiana University Press, 1987.

Das, Veena. *Critical Events: An Anthropological Perspective on Contemporary India*. Delhi: Oxford University Press, 1996.

Davidoff, Leonore, and Catherine Hall. *Family Fortunes: Men and Women of the English Middle Class, 1780–1850*. Chicago: University of Chicago Press, 1987.

Deliège, Robert. "Replication and Consensus: Untouchability, Caste and Ideology in India." *Man* 27 (1992): 155–73.

_____. "Myths of Origin of the Indian Untouchables." *Man* 28, no.3 (1993): 533–49.

Dieter, Melvin E. *The Holiness Revival of the Nineteenth Century*. Metcuhen, NJ: Scarecrow, 1980.

Dietrich, Gabrielle. "Dalit Movements and Women's Movements." In *Reflections on the Women's Movement in India*. New Delhi: Horizon India Press, 1992.

Dirks, Nicholas B. *The Hollow Crown: Ethnohistory of a Little Kingdom in South India*. Cambridge, UK: Cambridge University Press, 1988.

_____. "The Original Caste: Power, History and Hierarchy in South Asia." *Contributions to Indian Sociology*, 23, no. 1 (1989): 59–77.

_____. "From Little King to Landlord: Colonial Discourse and Colonial Rule." In *Colonialism and Culture*, ed. Nicholas B. Dirks, 175–208. Ann Arbor: University of Michigan Press, 1992.

_____. "The Conversion of Caste: Location, Translation, and Appropriation." In *Conversion to Modernities: The Globalization of Christianity*, ed. Peter van der Veer. New York: Routledge, 1996.

_____. *Castes of Mind: Colonialism and the Making of Modern India*. Princeton: Princeton University Press, 2001.

_____, ed. *Colonialism and Culture*. Ann Arbor: University of Michigan Press, 1991.

Doniger, Wendy [O'Flaherty]. *Dreams, Illusions and Other Realities.* Chicago: University of Chicago Press, 1984.

———. "The Scrapbook of Undeserved Salvation." In *Purana Perennis: Reciprocity and Transformation in Hindu and Jaina Texts,* ed. Wendy Doniger. Albany: State University of New York, Press, 1993.

———. *The Implied Spider: Politics and Theology in Myth.* New York: Columbia University Press, 1998.

Doniger, Wendy, and Brian K. Smith, trans. *The Laws of Manu.* New York: Penguin, 1991.

Dube, Saurabh. *Untouchable Pasts: Religion, Identity and Power among a Central Indian Community, 1780–1950.* Albany: State University of New York Press, 1998.

Dumont, Louis. *Homo Hierchicus: The Caste System and Its Implications.* Trans. Michael Moffatt. Chicago: University of Chicago, 1980.

———. *A South Indian Subcaste: Social Organization and Religion of the Pramalai Kallar.* Trans. Michael Moffatt et al. Delhi: Oxford University Press, 1986.

Dutt, R. C. *Economic History of India.* London: Routledge and Kegan Paul, 1903.

Eaton, Richard M. "Conversion to Christianity among the Nagas, 1876–1971." *Indian Economic and Social History Review,* no. 21 (1984): 1–44.

Eliade, Mircea. *Yoga: Immortality and Freedom.* Trans. Willard R. Trask. Princeton: Princeton University Press, 1969.

Elliot, Elisabeth. *A Chance to Die: The Life and Legacy of Amy Carmichael.* Grand Rapids, MI: Fleming H. Revell, 1987.

Elmore, W. T. *Dravidian Gods in Modern Hinduism.* 1913; New Dehli: Asian Educational Services, 1984.

Embree, Ainslie Thomas. *Charles Grant and British Rule in India.* London: George Allen and Unwin, 1962.

———. "Christianity and the State in Victorian India: Confrontation and Collaboration." In *Religion and Irreligion in Victorian Society,* ed. R. J. Helmstadter. London: Routledge, 1992.

Engels, Dagmar. *Beyond Purdah? Women in Bengal, 1890–1939.* Delhi: Oxford University Press, SOAS Studies on South Asia, 1996.

Estborn, S. *Our Village Christians: A Study of the Life and Faith of Village Christians in Tamilnad.* Madras: Christian Literature Society, 1959.

Fitzgerald, Rosemary. "On the Delhi Mission and Zenanas." In *Missionary Encounters,* ed. Robert Bickers and Rosemary Seton. London: Curzon Press, 1996.

Flemming, Leslie A. "New Humanity: American Missionaries' Ideals for Women in North India, 1870–1930." In *Western Women and Imperialism: Complicity and Resistance,* ed. Nupur Chauduri and Margaret Strobel. Bloomington: Indiana University Press, 1992.

Forbes, Geraldine H. "In Search of the 'Pure Heathen': Missionary Women in Nineteenth Century India." *Economic and Political Weekly* 21, (no. 17 1986): WS2–WS8.

Forman, Charles. "A History of Foreign Mission Theory in America." In *American Missions in Bicentennial Perspective,* ed. Robert Pierce Beaver, 69–140. South Pasadena, Ca.: William Carey Library, 1977.

Forrester, Duncan B. *Caste and Christianity: Attitudes and Policies on Caste of Anglo-Saxon Protestant Missions in India.* London: Curzon, 1980.

Foucault, Michel. *The Order of Things: An Archeology of the Human Sciences.* New York: Vintage Books, 1973.

――――. *Discipline and Punish: The Birthplace of the Prison*. Trans. Alan Sheridan. New York: Vintage Books, 1979.

――――. *The History of Sexuality, Volume 1*. Trans. Robert Hurley. New York: Vintage, 1980.

――――. *Power/Knowledge: Selected Interviews and Other Writings 1972–1977*. Trans. and ed. Colin Gordon. New York: Pantheon, 1980.

――――. *The Care of the Self. History of Sexuality, Volume 3*. Trans. Robert Hurley. New York: Vintage, 1988.

Freedman, Estelle. "Separatism as Strategy: Female Institution Building and American Feminism, 1870–1930." *Feminist Studies* 5 (fall 1979): 512–29.

Frykenberg, Robert E. *Guntur District, 1788–1848: A History of Local Influence and Central Authority in South India*. New York: Oxford University Press, 1965.

――――. "The Impact of Conversion and Social Reform upon Society in South India during the Late Company Period: Questions Concerning Hindu-Christian Encounters with Special Reference to Tinnevelly." In *Indian Society and the Beginnings of Modernization, c. 1830–1850*, ed. C. H. Philips and M. D. Wainwright. London: School of Oriental and African Studies, 1976.

――――. "On the Study of Conversion Movements: A Review Article and a Theoretical Note." *Indian Economic and Social History Review* 17, no. 1 (1980): 121–138.

――――. "On Roads and Riots in Tinnevelly: Radical Change and Ideology in Madras Presidency during the 19th Century." *South Asia* 2 (1982): 34–52.

――――. "Caste, Morality and Western Religion under the Raj." *Modern Asian Studies* 19 (1985): 321–352.

――――. "Modern Education in South India, 1784–1854: Its Roots and Its Role as a Vehicle of Integration under Company Raj." *American Historical Review* 91 (1986): 37–65.

――――. "The Concept of 'Majority' as a Devilish Force in the Politics of Modern India," *Journal of Commonwealth History and Comparative Politics* 25, no. 3 (1987): 267–274.

――――. "Constructions of Hinduism at the Nexus of History and Religion," *Journal of Interdisciplinary History* 23, no. 3 (1993): 523–50.

Fuller, C. J. *The Camphor Flame: Popular Hinduism and Society in India*. Princeton: Princeton University Press, 1992.

Fuzukawa, Hiroshi, *The Medieval Deccan: Peasants, Social Systems and States, Sixteenth to Eighteenth Centuries*. Delhi: Oxford University Press, 1991.

Ganapathy, T. N. *The Philosophy of the Tamil Siddhas*. New Delhi: Indian Council of Philosophical Research, 1993.

Geeta, V. "Gender and Political Discourse" *Economic and Political Weekly* (16 February 1991).

Ghosh, Suresh Chandra. *The Social Condition of the British Community in Bengal, 1757–1800*. Leiden: E.J. Brill, 1970.

Gibson, Colin. *Dissolving Wedlock*. London: Routledge Press, 1994.

Gilley, Sheridan, and W. J. Shiels. *A History of Religion in Britain: Practice and Belief from Pre-Roman Times to the Present*. Cambridge, MA: Blackwell, 1994.

Gladstone, J. W. *Protestant Christianity and People's Movements in Kerala*. Trivandrum: The Seminary Publications, 1984.

Gnanadason, Joy. *A Forgotten History: The Story of the Missionary Movement and the Liberation of People in South Travancore*. Madras: Gurukul Lutheran Theological College and Research Institute, 1994.

Grafe, Hugald. *The History of Christianity in Tamilnadu from 1800 to 1975.* Vol. 5 of *CHAI History of Chrisitanity in India.* Bangalore: Church History Association of India, 1990.

Gramsci, Antonio. *The Modern Prince and Other Writings.* Trans. Louis Marks. New York: International Publishers, 1957.

Greenblatt, Stephen. *Renaissance Self-Fashionings: From More to Shakespeare.* Chicago: University of Chicago Press, 1986.

———. *Marvellous Possessions: The Wonder of the New World.* Chicago: University of Chicago Press, 1991.

Grewal, Inderpal. *Home and Harem: Nation, Gender, Empire and the Cultures of Travel.* Durham, NC: Duke University Press, 1996.

Grimshaw, Patricia. "Conflicts in Roles of American Missionary Women in Nineteenth Century Hawaii." *Feminist Studies* 9, no. 3 (1983): 489–521.

———. *Paths of Duty: American Missionary Wives in Nineteenth-Century Hawaii.* Honolulu: University of Hawaii Press, 1989.

Haggis, Jane. " 'Good Wives and Mothers' or 'Dedicated Workers'? Contradictions of Domesticity in the 'Mission of Sisterhood,' Travancore, South India." In *Maternities and Modernities: Colonial and Postcolonial Experiences in Asia and the Pacific,* ed. Kalpana Ram and Margaret Jolly, 81–113. Cambridge, UK: Cambridge University Press, 1998.

———. "White Women and Colonialism: Towards a Non-recuperative History." In *Gender and Imperialism,* ed. Clare Midgley. Manchester, UK: Manchester University Press, 1998.

Hall, Catherine. "The Early Formation of Victorian Domestic Ideology." In *Fit Work for Women,* ed. Sandra Burman. New York: St. Martin's, 1979.

Hancock, Mary. "Gendering the Modern: Women and Home Science in British India." In *Gender, Sexuality and Colonial Modernities,* ed. Antoinette Burton, 148–160. London: Routledge, 1999.

———. "Home Science and the Nationalization of Domesticity in Colonial India." *Modern Asian Studies* 35, no. 4 (2001): 871–903.

Hansen, Karen Transberg, ed. *African Encounters with Domesticity.* New Brunswick, NJ: Rutgers University Press, 1992.

Hardgrave, Robert L. "Breast Cloth Controversy: Caste Consciousness and Social Change in South Travancore." *Indian Economic and Social History Review* 5, no. 2 (1968): 171–87.

———. *The Nadars of Tamilnad: The Political Culture of a Community in Change.* Berkeley: University of California Press, 1969.

Hardiman, David. *The Coming of the Devi: Adivasi Assertion in Western India.* New Delhi: Oxford University Press, 1995.

Harlan, Lindsey. *Religion and Rajput Women: The Ethic of Protection in Contemporary Narratives.* Berkeley: University of California Press, 1992.

Harper, Susan Billington. "Ironies of Indigenization: Some Cultural Repercussions of Mission in South India." *Bulletin of Missionary Research* 19 (January 1995): 13–20.

———. *In the Shadow of the Mahatma: Bishop V. S. Azariah and the Travails of Christianity in British India.* Cambridge, UK: Curzon, 2000.

Hawes, Christopher J. *Poor Relations: The Making of a Eurasian Community in British India, 1773–1833.* Surrey, UK: Curzon, 1996.

Hefner, Robert W., ed. *Conversion to Christianity: Historical and Anthropological Perspectives on a Great Transformation.* Berkeley: University of California Press, 1993.

Hewitt, Glenn A. *Regeneration and Morality. Chicago Studies in the History of American Religion*. Brooklyn, NY: Carlson., 1991.

Hill, Patricia R. *The World Their Household: The American Woman's Foreign Mission Movement and Cultural Transformation, 1870–1920*. Ann Arbor: University of Michigan Press, 1985.

Hiltebeitel, Alf, ed. *Criminal Gods and Demon Devotees: Essays on the Guardians of Popular Hinduism*. Albany: State University of New York Press, 1989.

Hilton, Boyd. *The Age of Atonement: The Influence of Evangelicalism on Social and Economic Thought, 1795–1865*. Oxford: Clarendon Press, 1988

Hines, Herbert Waldo. *Clough, Kingdom-Builder in South India*. Philadelphia: Judson, 1929.

Hjele, Benedicte. "Slavery and Agricultural Bondage in South India in the 19th century." *Scandanavian Economic History Review* 15 (1967): 75–86.

Holmes, Janice. *Religious Revivals in Britain and Ireland, 1859–1905*. Portland, OR: Irish Academic Press, 2000.

Horton, Robin. "African Conversion." *Africa* 61, no. 2 (1971): 91–112.

Hospital, Clifford G. "Clothes and Caste in Nineteenth Century Kerala." *Indian Church History Review* 13, no.2 (1979): 146–156.

Houghton, Frank. *Amy Carmichael of Dohnavur: The Story of a Lover and Her Beloved*. London: SPCK, 1953.

Houghton, Graham. *The Impoverishment of Dependency: The History of the Protestant Church in Madras, 1870–1920*. Madras: Christian Literature Society, 1983.

Howes, Christopher. *Poor Relations: The Making of a Eurasian Community in British India, 1773–1833*. Surrey, UK: Curzon, 1996.

Hudson, Dennis. "The Life and Times of H. A. Krishna Pillai (1827–1900)." Ph.D. diss., Claremont Graduate School, 1970.

———. "Christians and the Question of Caste: The Vēḷḷāla Protestants of Pālayamkōt-ṭai." In *Images of Man: Religion and Historical Processes in South Asia*, ed. Fred Clothey, 244–258. Madras: New Era, 1982.

———. *Protestant Origins in India: Tamil Evangelical Christians, 1706–1835*. Grand Rapids, MI: Eerdman, Studies in the History of Christian Missions, 2000.

Hunter, Jane. *The Gospel of Gentility: American Women Missionaries in Turn-of-the-Century China*. New Haven: Yale University Press, 1984.

Hutchinson, William R. *Errand to the World: American Protestant Thought and Foreign Missions*. Chicago: University of Chicago Press, 1987.

Inden, Ronald. *Imagining India*. Oxford: Blackwell, 1990.

Irschick, Eugene. *Politics and Social Conflict in South India: The Non-Brahman Movement and Tamil Separatism, 1916–1929*. Berkeley: University of California Press, 1969.

———. *Dialogue and History: Constructing South India, 1795–1895*. New Delhi: Oxford University Press, 1995.

Jackson, David. *The Hidden Jewel*. Minneapolis: Bethany House, 1992.

Jackson, Eleanor. *Caste, Culture and Conversion from the Perspective of an Indian Christian Family based in Madras 1863–1906*. Available at www.multifaithnet.org/mfnopenaccess/research/online/drafts/ejcaste.htm [accessed 1 August 2003].

Jagadeesan, P. *Marriage and Social Legislations in Tamil Nadu*. Madras: Elatchiappen Publications, 1990.

James, William. *The Varieties of Religious Experience*. 1902; New York: Penguin Books, 1985.

Jayawardena, Kumari. *The White Woman's Other Burden: Western Women and South Asia During British Rule.* New York: Routledge, 1995.

Jayawardena, Kumari, and Malathi de Alwis, eds. *Embodied Violence: Communalising Women's Sexuality in South Asia.* London: Zed, 1996.

Jeffrey, Robin. *The Decline of Nayar Dominance: Society and Politics in Travancore, 1847–1908.* New Delhi: Vikas, 1994.

Jenkins, Paul. "The CMS and the Basel Mission." In *The Church Mission Society and World Christianity, 1799–1999,* ed. Kevin Ward and Brian Stanley, 43–65. Grand Rapids, MI: Eerdman's; Studies in the History of Christian Missions, 2000.

Jeyaraj, Daniel. "Missionary Research of Tamil Bhakti Religions of the Eighteenth Century." In *Mission Today: Challenges and Concerns,* ed. Abraham P. Athyal and Dorothy Yoder Nyce. Chennai, India: Gurukul Lutheran Theological College and Research Institute, 1998.

———. "Halle-Danish (Tranquebar) Mission and Western Protestant Missionary Tradition." *Zeitschrift für Missionswissenschaft und Religionswissenschaft* 84 no. 1 (2000): 3–28.

———. ed., *Ordination of the First Protestant Indian Pastor Aaron.* Chennai, India: Lutheran Heritage Archives, 1998.

Jones, Kenneth W. *Arya Dharm: Hindu Consciousness in 19th Century Punjab.* Berkeley: University of California Press, 1976.

———. *Socio-Religious Reform Movements in British India.* Cambridge, UK: Cambridge University Press, New Cambridge History of India III.1, 1989.

Joshi, Rama, and Joanna Liddle. "Gender and Imperialism in British India." *Economic and Political Weekly* 20 (26 October 1985): WS72–78.

Kapadia, Karin. *Siva and Her Sisters: Gender, Caste, and Class in Rural South India.* Boulder, CO.: Westview, 1995.

Kelly, John. *A Politics of Virtue: Hinduism, Sexuality, and Countercolonial Discourse in Fiji.* Chicago: University of Chicago Press, 1991.

Kent, Eliza F. "Tamil Bible Women and the Zenana Missions of Colonial South India." *History of Religion* 39, no. 2 (1999): 117–149.

Kerber, Linda K. "Separate Spheres, Female Worlds, Woman's Place: The Rhetoric of Women's History." *Journal of American History* 75, no. 1 (1988): 9–39.

Kersenboom-Story, Saskia C. *Nityasumangali: Devadasi Tradition in South India.* Delhi: Motilal Benarsidass, 1987.

Ali Mumtaz Khan, *Mass-conversions of Meenakshipuram: A Sociological Inquiry.* Madras: Christian Literature Society, 1983.

King, Anthony. *Colonial Urban Development: Culture, Social Power and Environment.* London: Routledge and Kegan Paul, 1976.

Kolenda, Pauline. "Widowhood among 'Untouchable' Chuhras." In *Concepts of Person: Kinship, Caste and Marriage in India,* ed. Lina Fruzetti and Steve Barnett, 172–220. Dehli: Oxford University Press, 1983.

Kooiman, Dick. "Change of Religion as a Way to Survival." In *Religion and Development: Towards an Integrated Approach,* ed. Quarles van Ufford, 167–185. Amsterdam: Free University Press, 1988.

———. "Mass Movement, Famine and Epidemic." *Indian Church History Review* 22, no. 2 (1988): 109–31.

———. *Conversion and Social Equality in India: The London Missionary Society in South Travancore in the 19th Century.* New Delhi: Manohar, 1989.

Kopf, David. *British Orientalism and the Bengal Renaissance 1773–1835.* Berkeley: University of California Press, 1969.

_____. *The Brahmo Samaj and the Shaping of the Modern Indian Mind.* Princeton: Princeton University Press, 1979.

Kosambi, Meera. "Gender Reform and Competing State Controls over Women: The Rakhmabai Case (1884–1888)." In *Social Reform, Sexuality and the State,* ed. Patricia Uberoi, 265–90. New Delhi: Sage, Contributions to Indian Sociology Occasional Studies No. 7, 1996.

Kranidis, Rita S. *The Victorian Spinster and Colonial Emigration.* New York: St. Martin's, 1999.

Krishnamurty, J., ed. *Women in Colonial India: Essays on Survival, Work and the State.* Delhi: Oxford University Press, 1989.

Kumar, Dharma. *Land and Caste in South India: Agricultural Labour in the Madras Presidency During the Nineteenth Century.* Cambridge, UK: Cambridge University Press, 1965.

Kumar, Radha. *The History of Doing: An Illustrated Account of Movements for Women's Rights and Feminism in India, 1800–1990.* Delhi: Kali for Women, 1993.

Kumaradoss, Vincent. "Negotiating Colonial Christianity: The Hindu Christian Church of Late Nineteenth Century Tirunelveli." *South Indian Studies* 1, no. 1 (1996): 35–53.

Kusuman, K. K. *Slavery in Travancore.* Trivandrum: Kerala Historical Society, 1973.

Lal, Maneesha. "The Politics of Gender and Medicine in Colonial India: The Countess of Dufferin's Fund, 1885–1888." *Bulletin of the History of Medicine* 1 (1994): 29–60.

Lalitha, K., and Susie Tharu, eds., *600 B.C. to the Early 20th Century.* Vol. 1 of *Women Writing in India.* New York: Feminist Press, 1991.

Larson, Gerald. *India's Agony over Religion.* Albany: State University of New York Press, 1995.

Lehmann, E. Arno. *It Began at Tranquebar.* Trans. and ed. M. J. Lutz. Madras: The Christian Literature Society, 1956.

Leslie, Julia. *The Perfect Wife: The Orthodox Hindu Woman According to the Stridharmapaddhati of Tryambakajivan.* New Delhi: Oxford University Press, 1989.

_____. ed. *Roles and Rituals for Hindu Women.* London: Pinter, 1991.

Lincoln, Bruce. *Discourse and the Construction of Society: Comparative Studies of Myth, Ritual and Classification.* New York: Oxford University Press, 1989.

_____. *Authority: Construction and Corrosion.* Chicago: University of Chicago Press, 1994.

Lind, Mary Ann. *The Compassionate Memsahibs: Welfare Activities of British Women in India, 1900–1947.* New York: Greenwood Press, 1988.

Lokugé, Chandani, ed. *Saguna: The First Autobiographical Novel in English by an Indian Woman.* Delhi: Oxford University Press, 1998.

Long, J. Bruce. "Mahasivaratri: The Saiva Festival of Repentance." In *Religious Festivals in South India and Sri Lanka,* ed. Glenn Yocum and Guy Welbon. New Delhi: Manohar, 1982.

Ludden, David. *Peasant History in South India.* Delhi: Oxford University Press, 1989.

_____, ed. *Contesting the Nation: Religion, Community and the Politics of Democracy in India.* Philadelphia: University of Pennsylvania Press, 1996.

Luria, Keith P. "The Politics of Protestant Conversion to Catholicism in Seventeenth-Century France." In *Conversion to Modernities: The Globalization of Christianity,* ed. Peter van der Veer, 23–46. New York: Routledge, 1996.

Mallampalli, Chandra. "Contending with Marginality: Christians and the Public

Sphere in Colonial South India." Ph.D. diss., University of Wisconsin-Madison, 2000.

Mani, Lata. "Contentious Traditions: The Debate on *Sati* in Colonial India." In *Recasting Women,* ed. Kumkum Sangari and Sudesh Vaid, 88–126. New Delhi: Kali for Women, 1989.

Manickam, Sundararaj. *The Social Setting of Christian Conversion in South India: The Impact of the Wesleyan Methodist Missionaries on the Trichy-Tanjore Diocese with Special Reference to the Harijan Communities of the Mass Movement Area, 1820–1957.* Wiesbaden, Germany: Steiner, 1977.

Marriott, McKim. "Stratification: Review of Homo Hierarchicus." *American Anthropologist* 71 (1971): 1166–75.

McClintock, Anne. *Imperial Leather: Race, Gender and Sexuality in the Colonial Context.* New York: Routledge, 1995.

Meduri, Avanthi. *Nation, Woman, Representation: The Sutured History of the Devadasi and Her Dance.* New York: New York University Press, 1996.

Metcalf, Barbara Daly, ed. *Moral Conduct and Authority: The Place of Adab in South Asian Islam.* Berkeley: University of California Press, 1984.

Metcalf, Thomas R. *The Aftermath of Revolt: India, 1857–1870.* Princeton: Princeton University Press, 1964.

Midgely, Clare, ed. *Gender and Imperialism.* Manchester, UK: Manchester University Press, 1998.

Minturn, Leigh. *Sita's Daughters: Coming Out of Purdah.* New York: Oxford University Press, 1993.

Moffatt, Michael. *An Untouchable Community in South India: Consensus and Replication.* Chicago: University of Chicago Press, 1979.

Mukherjee, S. N. *Calcutta: Essays in Urban History.* Calcutta: Subarnarekha, 1993.

Murray, Jocelyn. "The Role of Women in the Church Missionary Society, 1799–1917." In *The Church Mission Society and World Christianity, 1799–1999,* ed. Kevin Ward and Brian Stanley, 66–90. Grand Rapids, MI: Eerdman, Studies in the History of Christian Missions, 2000.

Murshid, Ghulam. *Reluctant Debutante: Response of Bengali Women to Modernization, 1849–1905.* Rajshahi: Sahitya Samsad, 1983.

Nageswari, A. "A Study of Social Change among the Nadars of Tamil Nadu (with Special Reference to Women)." Ph.D. diss., Bangalore University, 1994.

Nair, Janaki. "Uncovering the Zenana: Visions of Indian Womanhood in English-women's Writings, 1813–1940." *Journal of Women's History* 2 (1990): 8–34.

———. "The Devadasi, Dharma and the State." *Economic and Political Weekly* (10 December 1994): 3157–67.

———. *Women and Law in Colonial India: A Social History.* Delhi: Kali for Women, 1996.

Nandakumar, R. "The Missing Male: The Female Figures of Ravi Varma and Concepts of Family, Marriage and Fatherhood in Nineteenth Century Kerala." *South Indian Studies,* 1 no. 1 (1996): 54–82.

Nandy, Ashis. *The Intimate Enemy: Loss and Recovery of the Self under Colonialism.* Delhi: Oxford University Press, 1983.

Neill, Stephen. *A History of Christian Missions.* Harmondsworth, UK: Penguin, 1964.

———. *A History of Christianity in India: The Beginnings to AD 1707.* Cambridge, UK: Cambridge University Press, 1984.

———. *A History of Christianity in India, 1707–1858.* Cambridge, UK: Cambridge University Press, 1985.

Newbigin, Leslie. *A South Indian Diary*. London: S.C.M. Press, 1960.

Niranjana, Tejaswini. *Siting Translation: History, Post-Structuralism, and the Colonial Context*. Berkeley: University of California Press, 1992.

Nock, A.D. *Conversion: The Old and the New in Religion from Alexander the Great to Augustine of Hippo*. Oxford: Oxford University Press, 1933.

Oddie, Geoffrey A. "Christian Conversion in the Telegu Country, 1860–1900: A Case Study of One Protestant Movement in the Godavery-Krishna Delta." *Indian Economic and Social History Review* 12, no. 1 (January–March 1975): 61–79.

_____. *Social Protest in India: British Protestant Missionaries and Social Reforms*. Delhi: Oxford University Press, 1979.

_____. *Hindu and Christian in South-East India: Aspects of Religious Continuity and Change, 1800–1900*. London: Curzon, 1981.

_____. "Old Wine in New Bottles? Kartabhaja (Vaishnava) Converts to Christianity in Bengal, 1835–1845." *Indian Economic and Social History Review* 32, no. 3 (1995): 189–224.

O'Hanlon, Rosalind. "Issues of Widowhood: Gender and Resistance in Colonial Western India." In *Contesting Power: Resistance and Everyday Social Relations in South Asia*, ed. Douglas Haynes and Gyan Prakash. Delhi: Oxford University Press, 1991.

Oldenburg, Veena Talwar. "Lifestyle as Resistance: The Case of the Courtesans of Lucknow." *Feminist Studies* 16, no. 2 (1990): 259–87.

Orr, Leslie C. *Donors, Devotees, and Daughters of God: Temple Women in Medieval Tamilnadu*. New York: Oxford University Press, 2000.

Packiamutthu, David. "Royal Clarinda." Unpublished manuscript, Bishop Stephen Neill Archives, Tirunelveli.

Pandian, M. S. S. "Meanings of 'Colonialism' and 'Nationalism': An Essay on Vaikunda Swamy Cult." *Studies in History*, n.s. 8, no. 2 (1992): 167–85.

Papmek, Hanna, and Gail Minault, eds. *Separate Worlds: Studies of Purdah in South Asia*. Delhi: Chakanya Publications.

Parker, Rozcika. *The Subversive Stitch: Embroidery and the Making of the Feminine*. London: The Women's Press, 1984.

Patmury, Joseph, ed. *Doing Theology with the Poetic Traditions of India: Focus on Dalit and Tribal Poems*. Bangalore: PTCA/SATHRI, 1996.

Pearson, M. N. *The Portuguese in India*. Cambridge, UK: Cambridge University Press, 1987.

Peel, J. D. Y. "For Who Hath Despised the Day of Small Things? Missionary Narratives and Historical Anthropology," *Comparative Studies in Society and History* 37, no. 3 (1995): 581–607.

Philips, C. H. *The East India Company, 1784–1834*. Manchester, UK: Manchester University Press, 1961.

Pollock, J. C. *The Keswick Story*. London: Hodder and Stoughton, 1964.

Poovey, Mary. *The Proper Lady and the Woman Writer*. Chicago: University of Chicago Press, 1984.

Presler, Franklin A. *Religion under Bureaucracy: Policy and Administration for Hindu Temples in South India*. Cambridge, UK: Cambridge University Press, 1987.

Price, Pamela G. *Kingship and Political Practice in Colonial India* Vol. 51 of *University of Cambridge Oriental Publications*. Cambridge, UK: Cambridge University Press, 1996.

Prochaska, F. K. *Women and Philanthropy in Nineteenth-Century England*. Oxford: Clarendon, 1980.

Rafael, Vicente L. *Contracting Colonialism: Translation and Christian Conversion in Tagalog Society under Early Spanish Rule.* Ithaca, NY: Cornell University Press, 1988.
———. "Mimetic Subjects: Engendering Race at the Edge of Empire." *Differences* 7, no. 2 (1995): 127–49.

Raheja, Gloria Goodwin, and Ann Grodzins Gold. *Listen to the Heron's Words: Reimagining Gender and Kinship in North India.* Delhi: Oxford University Press, 1996.

Rajan, Rajeswari Sunder. "Women between Community and State: Some Implications of the Uniform Civil Code Debates in India" *Social Text* 18, no. 4 (2000): 55–82.

Ram, Kalpana. *Mukkuvar Women: Gender, Hegemony and Capitalist Transformation in a South Indian Fishing Community.* London: Zed, 1991.

Ramanujan, A. K. *The Interior Landscape: Love Poems from a Classical Tamil Anthology.* Bloomington: Indiana University Press, 1975.
———. *Hymns for the Drowning: Poems for Vishnu by Nammalvar.* Princeton: Princeton University Press, 1980.
———. "Where Mirrors Are Windows: Toward an Anthology of Reflections." *History of Religions* 28, no.3 (1989): 187–216.

Rambo, Lewis R. *Understanding Religious Conversion.* New Haven: Yale University Press, 1993.

Ramusack, Barbara. "Cultural Missionaries, Maternal Imperialists, Feminist Allies: British Women Activists in India, 1865–1945." In *Western Women and Imperialism: Complicity and Resistance,* ed. Margaret Strobel and Nupur Chaudhuri, 119–36. Bloomington: Indiana University Press, 1992.

Ravindran, V. "The Unanticipated Legacy of Robert Caldwell and the Dravidian Movement." *South Indian Studies* 1, no.1 (1996): 83–110.
———. "Discourses of Empowerment: Missionary Orientalism in the Development of Dravidian Nationalism." In *Nation Work: Asian Elites and National Identities,* ed. Timothy Brook and Andre Schmidt. Ann Arbor: University of Michigan Press, 1999.

Ray, Bharati, ed. *From the Seams of History.* Delhi: Oxford University Press, 1995.

Rege, Sharmila. "Caste and Gender: The Violence against Women in India." In *Dalit Women,* ed. P. G. Jogdand. New Delhi: Gyan Publishing House, 1995.

Reiniche, Marie-Louise. *Les Dieux et Les Hommes: Étude des cultes d'un village du Tirunelveli Inde du Sud.* Paris: Mouton éditeur, Cahiers de L'Homme: Ethnologie, Geographie, Linguistique, 1979.

Riley, Denise. *"Am I That Name?" Feminism and the Category of "Women" in History.* Minneapolis: University of Minnesota Press, 1988.

Robbins, Nancy E. *Not Forgetting to Sing.* London: Hodder and Stoughton, 1967.

Robert, Dana L. *American Women in Mission: A Social History of Their Thought and Practice.* Macon, GA: Mercer University Press, 1996.

Rooden, Peter van. "Nineteenth-Century Representations of Missionary Conversion and the Transformation of Western Christianity." In *Conversion to Modernities: The Globalization of Christianity,* ed. Peter van der Veer, 65–88. New York: Routledge, 1996.

Rudolph, Lloyd I. and Susanne Hoeber Rudolph. *The Modernity of Tradition: Political Development in India.* Chicago: University of Chicago Press, 1967.

Ryan, Mary P. *The Empire of the Mother: American Writing about Domesticity, 1830–1860.* New York: Haworth, 1982.

Sahlins, Marshall. *Islands of History.* Chicago: University of Chicago Press, 1987.

Said, Edward W. *Orientalism.* New York: Vintage, 1979.

Sangari, Kumkum, and Sudesh Vaid, eds. *Recasting Women: Essays in Colonial History.* Delhi: Kali for Women, 1989.

Sarkar, Sumit. *Modern India, 1885–1947.* Delhi: Macmillan India, 1983.

——. "Conversions and the Sangh Parivar." *The Hindu* (9 November 1999).

Sastri, K. A. Nilakanta. *A History of South India: From Prehistoric Times to the Fall of Vijayanagar.* New Delhi: Oxford University Press, 1955.

Scott, David. *Formations of Ritual: Colonial and Anthropological Discourses on the Sinhala Yaktovil.* Minneapolis: University of Minnesota Press, 1994.

Scott, James. *Weapons of the Weak: Everyday Forms of Peasant Resistance.* New Haven: Yale University Press, 1985.

——. *Domination and the Arts of Resistance: The Hidden Transcripts.* New Haven: Yale University Press, 1990.

Scott, Joan W. *Gender and the Politics of History.* New York: Columbia University Press, 1988.

——. "Gender: A Useful Category of Historical Analysis." In *Feminism and History,* ed. Joan W. Scott, 152–82. Oxford: Oxford University Press, 1996.

Seal, Anil. *The Emergence of Indian Nationalism.* Cambridge, UK: Cambridge University Press, 1968.

Sengupta, Padmini. *Portrait of an Indian Woman.* Calcutta: YMCA Publishing House, 1956.

Shah, Nayan. "Cleansing Motherhood: Hygeine and the Culture of Domesticity in San Francisco's Chinatown, 1875–1900." In *Gender, Sexuality and Colonial Modernities,* ed. Antoinette Burton, 19–34. London: Routledge, 1999.

Sherinian, Zoe. "The Indigenization of Tamil Christian Music: Folk Music as a Liberative Transmission System." Ph.D. diss., Wesleyan University, 1998.

Shobanan, B. *The Temple Entry Movement and the Sivakasi Riots.* Madurai: Raj, 1985.

Singer, Milton. *When a Great Tradition Modernizes.* Chicago: University of Chicago Press, 1972.

Singh, Maina Chawla. *Gender, Religion, and the "Heathen Lands": American Missionary Women in South Asia, 1860s–1940s.* New York: Garland, 2000.

Sinha, Mrinalini. " 'Chatams, Pitts, and Gladstones in Petticoats': The Politics of Gender and Race in the Ilbert Bill Controversy, 1883–1888." In *Western Women and Imperialism: Complicity and Resistance,* ed. Nupur Chaudhuri and Margaret Strobel. Bloomington: Indiana University Press, 1992.

——. *Colonial Masculinity: The "Manly Englishman" and the "Effeminate Bengali" in the Late Nineteeth Century.* Manchester, UK: Manchester University Press, 1995.

Sklar, Kathryn Kish. "Hull House in the 1890s: A Community of Women Reformers." *Signs* 10 (Summer 1985): 658–77.

Smith, Solveig. *By Love Compelled: The Story of 100 Years of the Salvation Army in India and Adjacent Countries.* St Albans, UK: Salvation Army, 1981.

Smith, Wilfred Cantwell. *The Meaning and End of Religion: A Revolutionary Approach to the Great Religious Traditions.* San Francisco: Harper and Row, 1978.

Smith-Rosenberg, Carroll. "The Female World of Love and Ritual: Relations between Women in Nineteenth-Century America." In *Feminism and History,* ed. Joan W. Scott. Oxford: Oxford University Press, 1996.

Spear, Percival. *The Nabobs: A Study of the Social Life of the British in Eighteenth Century India.* London: Oxford University Press, 1963.

Spivak, Gayatri Chakravorty. "Three Women's Texts and a Critique of Imperialism." In *"Race," Writing and Difference,* ed. Henry Louis Gates Jr., 262–280. Chicago: University of Chicago Press, 1986.

Spivak, Gayatri Chakravorty, and Ranajit Guha, eds. *Selected Subaltern Studies*. New York: Oxford University Press, 1988.

Srinivas, M. N. *Religion and Society among the Coorgs*. Oxford: Oxford University Press, 1952.

_____. *The Cohesive Role of Sanskritization and Other Essays*. New Delhi: Oxford University Press, 1984.

_____. *The Dominant Caste and Other Essays*. New Delhi: Oxford University Press, 1987.

Srinivasan, Amrit. "Reform and Revival: The Devadasi and Her Dance." *Economic and Political Weekly* 20, no. 44 (1985): 1869–76.

Stanton, Elizabeth Cady. *The Woman's Bible*. 1898; Salem, NH: Ayer, 1988.

Stein, Burton. *Peasant State and Society in Medieval South India*. Delhi: Oxford University Press, 1994.

Stoler, Ann Laura. "Carnal Knowledge and Imperial Power: Gender, Race and Morality in Colonial Asia." In *Gender at the Crossroads of Knowledge: Feminist Anthropology in the Postmodern Era*, ed. Miceala di Leonardo, 51–101. Berkeley: University of California Press, 1991.

Strobel, Margaret. "Gender and Race in the Nineteenth- and Twentieth-century British Empire." In *Becoming Visible: Women in European History*, ed. Claudia Koonz et al. Boston: Houghton Mifflin, 1987.

_____. *European Women and the Second British Empire*. Bloomington: Indiana University Press, 1991.

Swaisland, Cecillie. "Nineteenth Century Recruitment of Single Women to Protestant Missions." In *Women and Missions: Past and Present*, ed. Fiona Bowie, Deborah Kirkwood and Shirley Ardener, 70–84. Oxford: Berg, 1993.

Tapper, Bruce Elliot. "Widows and Goddesses: Female Roles in Deity Symbolism in a South Indian Village." *Contributions to Indian Sociology* 13, no. 1 (1979): 1–31.

Tarlo, Emma. *Clothing Matters: Dress and Identity in India*. Chicago: University of Chicago Press, 1996.

Tawney, R. H. *Religion and the Rise of Capitalism*. Gloucester, MA: Peter Smith, 1962.

Templeman, Dennis. *The Northern Nadars of Tamil Nadu: An Indian Caste in the Process of Change*. Delhi: Oxford University Press, 1996.

Thangaraj, M. Thomas. "The History and Teachings of the Hindu-Christian Community Commonly Called Nattu Sabai in Tirunelveli." *Indian Church History Review* 5, no. 1 (1971).

_____. *The Crucified Guru: An Experiment in Cross-Cultural Christology*. Nashville, TN: Abingdon Press, 1994.

Thapar, Romila. "Syndicated Hinduism." In *Hinduism Reconsidered*, ed. Gunter-Dietz Southeimer and Hermann Kulke. New Delhi: Manohar, 1997.

Thompson, E. P. *The Making of the English Working Class*. New York: Vintage, 1966.

Trautmann, Thomas R. *Aryans and British India*. New Delhi: Vistaar, 1997.

Trawick, Margaret. *Notes on Love in a Tamil Family*. Berkeley: University of California Press, 1990.

Tyrrell, Ian. *Woman's World/Woman's Empire: The Woman's Christian Temperance Union in International Perspective, 1800–1930*. Chapel Hill: University of North Carolina Press, 1991.

Uberoi, Patricia, ed. *Social Reform, Sexuality and the State*. Delhi: Sage, 1996.

Urban, Hugh B. *The Economics of Ecstasy: Tantra, Secrecy and Power in Colonial Bengal*. New York: Oxford University Press, 2001.

Vaid, Sudesh. "Ideologies on Women in 19th Century Britain, 1850s–1870s." *Economic and Political Weekly* 20 no. 43 (1985): WS63–67.

Van der Veer, Peter. *Religious Nationalism: Hindus and Muslims in India.* Berkeley: University of California Press, 1994.

_____. *Imperial Encounters: Religion and Modernity in India and Britain.* Princeton: Princeton University Press, 2001.

_____. ed. *Conversion to Modernities: The Globalization of Christianity.* New York: Routledge, 1996.

Viswanathan, Gauri. *Masks of Conquest: Literary Study and British Rule in India.* New York: Columbia University Press, 1989.

_____. "Religious Conversion and the Politics of Dissent." In *Conversion to Modernities: The Globalization of Christianity,* ed. Peter van der Veer. New York: Routledge, 1996.

_____. *Outside the Fold: Conversion, Modernity, and Belief.* Princeton: Princeton University Press, 1998.

_____. "Literacy in the Eye of the Conversion Storm." *Polygraph* 12 (2000): 13–26.

Wadley, Susan S., ed. *The Powers of Tamil Women.* Syracuse, NY: Maxwell School of Citizenship and Public Affairs, Syracuse University, 1991.

Waghorne, Joanne Punzo. "From Robber Baron to Royal Servant of God? Gaining a Divine Body in South India." In *Criminal Gods and Demon Devotees: Essays on the Guardians of Popular Hinduism,* ed. Alf Hiltebeitel, 405–426. Albany: State University of New York Press, 1989.

_____. *The Raja's Magic Clothes: Re-Visioning Kingship and Divinity in England's India.* University Park: Pennsylvania State University Press, 1994.

Waghorne, Joanne, and Norman Cutler, eds. *Gods of Flesh, Gods of Stone: The Embodiment of Divinity in India.* New York: Columbia University Press, 1996.

Walker, Pamela J. *Pulling the Devil's Kingdom Down: The Salvation Army in Victorian Britain.* Berkeley: University of California Press, 2001.

Ward, W. R. *The Protestant Evangelical Awakening.* Cambridge, UK: Cambridge University Press, 1992.

_____. "The Evangelical Revival in Eighteenth-Century Britain." In *A History of Religion in Britain,* ed. Sheridan Gilley and W. J. Shiels. Oxford: Oxford University Press, 1994.

Webster, John C. B. "Christians and the Depressed Castes in the 1930s." In *Economy, Society and Politics in Modern India,* ed. D. N. Panigrahi. New Delhi: Vikas, 1989.

_____. *The Dalit Christians: A History.* Delhi: ISPCK, 1992.

Wellman, Sam. *Amy Carmichael: A Life Abandoned to God.* Uhrichville, Ohio: Barbour, 1998.

Williams, C. Peter. *The Ideal of the Self-Governing Church: A Study in Victorian Missionary Strategy.* Leiden: E.J. Brill, 1990.

_____. "The Missing Link: The Recruitment of Women Missionaries in Some English Evangelical Missionary Societies in the Nineteenth Century." In *Women and Missions: Past and Present Anthropological and Historical Perceptions,* ed. Fiona Bowie, Deborah Kirkwood, and Shirley Ardener. Oxford: Berg, 1993.

Wolpert, Stanley. *A New History of India.* 4th ed. New York: Oxford University Press, 1993.

Yalman, Nur. "On the Purity of Women in the Castes of Ceylon and Malabar." *Journal of the Royal Anthropological Institute of Great Britain and Ireland* 93 no. 1 (1963): 25–58.

Yesudas, R. N. *A People's Revolt in Travancore: A Backward Class Movement for Social Freedom*. Trivandrum: Kerala Historical Society, 1975.

Young, Richard Fox. *Resistant Hinduism: Sanskrit Sources on Anti-Christian Apologetics in Early Nineteenth-century India*. Vienna: E. J. Brill, 1991.

Zelliot, Eleanor. *From Untouchable to Dalit: Essays on the Ambedkar Movement*. Delhi: Manohar, 1992.

Zupanov, Ines G. *Disputed Mission: Jesuit Experiments and Brahmanical Knowledge in Seventeenth-Century India*. New York: Oxford University Press, 1999.

Index

Abbott, John, 145, 148
Abeel, Mr., 91
Abraham v. Abraham, 172–173,
 270 n.15
adultery, 169
agriculture, 62–65
Agur, C. M., 29–30
Aiyannar, 57
akam, 136
All-India Women's Conference,
 84
A.L.O.E. *See* Tucker, Charlotte
Alwis, Malathi de, 143
American Board of Commissioners
 for Foreign Missions, 16, 43,
 82, 114, 122, 168
American College, 16–18
American Madurai Mission, 70, 82,
 102, 114–116, 118, 151, 153, 158–
 159, 168–169, 200
Amman goddesses, 57–58
Anderson, Rufus, 122, 263 n.112
Anglicization
 seen as "moral progress," 190
 resistance to, 193
antarmahal, 128, 136, 138
Anti-Nose-Jewel Society, 223
Apollos, Catechist, 217–218, 221
Appadurai, Arjun, 19–21, 67,
 252 n.1, 255 n.39
Appasamy, Paul, 93

architecture
 and Christian towns, 190
 and Christianization, 129, 160–
 162, 184–185, 188
 hybrid style of, 108, 184–185
 and immurement of women, 136,
 138–139
 and organization of social
 structure, 24–36
Arden, Rev. C. W., 229
Arminianism, 98
Arnold, David, 105
Arumaināyakam. *See* Sattampillai,
 Arumai Nayakam
Aryans, 195, 229–230, 253 n.12
Asad, Talal, 5
astrology, 28, 30
Atonement, doctrine of the, 99, 101–
 102

Baierlain, Rev. E. H., 227–228
Ballhatchet, Kenneth, 87
Banerjee, Babu Kali Charan, 86–
 87
Banerjee, Sumanta, 153
Baylis, Rev. F., 211
belief, 5, 94
Besant, Annie, 84
bhadralok, 141, 153–154
Bible, the
 translated as *Veda*, 24